Educating for Shalom

xiv - global development, anti-AFE Day// xvii - perspectival, Chr scholarship not distinctive, just
faithful/ xvii - what's wrong w/ "integration"// xvii - what's wrong w/ worldview thinking/
xix - purpose of education / 4)- God Sum of Descartes + functionalism / 59-beliefs & dispositions/
156 - God Sum of the ways Chris intervile faithd learning / "Particularist

Perspectives" - good on RM + Chr in Academy / "Un Learning..." Good
defense of Chr-learning

23-Shalom

Educating for Shalom

ESSAYS ON CHRISTIAN HIGHER EDUCATION

by

Nicholas Wolterstorff

Edited by

Clarence W. Joldersma *&* Gloria Goris Stronks

William B. Eerdmans Publishing Company
Grand Rapids, Michigan / Cambridge, U.K.

Wm. B. Eerdmans Publishing Co.
255 Jefferson Ave. S.E., Grand Rapids, Michigan 49503 /
P.O. Box 163, Cambridge CB3 9PU U.K.

Printed in the United States of America

09 08 07 06 05 04   7 6 5 4 3 2 1

Library of Congress Cataloging-in-Publication Data

Wolterstorff, Nicholas.
    Educating for shalom: essays on Christian higher education /
  by Nicholas Wolterstorff; edited by Clarence W. Joldersma & Gloria Goris Stronks.
        p.   cm.
    Includes bibliographical references and index.
    ISBN 0-8028-2753-5 (alk. paper)
    1. Christian education — Philosophy. 2. Reformed Church — Education.
  3. Church colleges. I. Joldersma, Clarence W. II. Stronks, Gloria Goris. III. Title.

BV1464.W66   2004
378′.071 — dc22

                                2004040354

www.eerdmans.com

Contents

CONTENTS

Preface

Over the course of his many years of teaching at Calvin College and Yale University, Nicholas Wolterstorff has delivered a wealth of academic papers and speeches in the area of higher education. Although each is valuable separately, collected together their value increases for three reasons. First of all, they collectively show a coherent framework that combines a Reformed confessional Christianity with an increasingly radical social conscience and progressivist pedagogy. Second, the essays show how Wolterstorff's own thinking developed away from a more intellectualist, liberal-arts approach toward one framed by concerns for social justice in the context of educating more than just the mind. And third, the essays show Wolterstorff's wide-ranging interaction with a variety of thinkers, including not only Reformed thinkers such as Calvin, Kuyper, Jellema, and Plantinga, and traditional philosophers such as Augustine, Aquinas, Locke, Reid, and Kant, but also theorists from a variety of disciplines, including Oakeshott, Weber, Taylor, Popper, Kuhn, Freire, Habermas, Hesse, Adorno, Laudan, MacIntyre, and Parsons.

The first three essays in this volume are an early indication of Wolterstorff's developing thought. His focus in these essays is on the purpose and mission of Christian educational institutions. "Rethinking Christian Higher Education" is an early call for Christian colleges to become agents of renewal as their contribution to the calling of the Christian community in the world. Similarly, in "Teaching for Shalom: On the Goal of Christian Collegiate Education," Wolterstorff rejects the maturation, socialization, and humanization models for education, calling instead to teach for justice and shalom. Here his social-practice emphasis is beginning to emerge. "The Mission of the Christian College at the End of the Twentieth Century" sets this in terms of stages of development. Here Wolterstorff calls for a move beyond "Stage I," with its focus on evangelism and flight from the world, and "Stage II," with its focus on culture (liberal arts, high culture), to "Stage III," with its focus on society.

This means becoming, as institutions, agents of healing and justice in a globalizing, international community.

The next three essays shift the focus to the nature of Christian scholarship or learning. Using the science of psychology as a case study, Wolterstorff argues in "The Integration of Faith and Learning — The Very Idea" that the collapse of the Cartesian view of science means that a Christian perspective for academic psychologists involves developing new (or revising old) psychological models rather than settling for the "compatibilism" that marks much current integration talk. He develops this further in his essay "On the Idea of a Psychological Model of the Person That Is Biblically Faithful," where he argues for going beyond the "delimitation" strategy of compatibilism and outlines a non-deterministic psychological model of being human guided by his Christian control beliefs, a model that highlights responsibility or responsive agency. The next essay, "The Point of Connection between Faith and Learning," develops his view of Christian learning by tracing neo-Calvinism's pluralistic alternative to Descartes's consensual view of science back to Kuyper's "two-science" perspectivalism, and by correcting Kuyper in calling for a conception of Christian scholarship as an interactive, social practice. This is a view of Christian learning that emphasizes faithfulness rather than distinctiveness.

The next five essays form an interesting group if taken together. In "The World for Which We Educate," Wolterstorff focuses on the social context for his vision of shalom. He does so by understanding the call for shalom as meeting the challenges put up by the world-systems phenomena of global interaction, the dynamics of capitalism, a prevalent individualist expressivism, and society's religious pluralism. One might be forgiven for thinking that traditional scholarship has no place within an educational and scholarly program animated by the call for shalom. However, in "A Case for Disinterested Learning," Wolterstorff suggests that the call to shalom must also include "disinterested" Christian scholarship that is faithful to a biblical vision and to the accepted social practice of scholarship. This is not so much because of such scholarship's power or freedom, but because humans are hermeneutic creatures who disagree on meaning in the world. Disinterested learning, however, does not require denying one's Christian perspective. In "The Project of a Christian University in a Postmodern Culture," Wolterstorff argues for scholarship guided by a vision of shalom. He does so by finding Locke's foundationalism of reason-governed belief-formation problematic and by using Reid, Kuyper, and Lyotard to defend the Christian's participation in scholarship as a social practice. But the vision of shalom also has implications for teaching. In "Teaching for Justice: On Shaping How Students Are

Disposed to Act," Wolterstorff criticizes Kant's view of human moral formation and calls for teachers to develop in their students dispositions to act
justly. This requires developing a cognitive framework of critical consciousness, social justice, and world-systems awareness; and it requires a more interactive pedagogy of giving reasons, modeling, and developing empathy
with students. Together, these four essays radicalize the ideas about scholarship, society, and teaching introduced earlier. Collectively they show the
power of the idea of shalom for Wolterstorff's thought development. The last
essay in this group, "Autobiography: The Story of Two Decades of Thinking
about Christian Higher Education," is Wolterstorff's self-reflection on his increasing discomfort with liberal-arts "mind" formation, summarizing the
development of his thought toward emphases on character formation,
world-systems models of society, perspectivalism, science as social practice,
and society (not just culture).

The next three essays focus again on the idea of Christian scholarship,
or "learning," as Wolterstorff often calls it. In "Can Scholarship and Christian
Conviction Mix? Another Look at the Integration of Faith and Learning," he
argues against Weber's differentiation model of theoretical or academic
knowledge by using Kuhn's perspectivalist understanding of science as social
practice. In this essay Wolterstorff develops the idea of faithful scholarship
by means of an equilibrium model, where Christian scholarship means developing a responsible and critical balance among the empirical data, the discipline's theories, and one's Christian control-beliefs. In "Abraham Kuyper
on Christian Learning," he develops this further through an in-depth analysis
of Kuyper's postmodern, perspectivalist model of learning. Here he argues
that Kuyper's model gives us a notion that Christian scholarship can contribute to academia a particular point of cognitive access to reality.

The next three essays focus more directly on Christian academics in the
context of society. "Particularist Perspectives: Bias or Access?" continues
Wolterstorff's focus on cognitive access points. But here he sets his Kuyperian idea of particular cognitive access in the context of postmodernism's critique of the "Grand Project's" ideas of objective knowledge and foundationalism. In "Academic Freedom in Religiously Based Colleges and Universities,"
Wolterstorff takes the idea of particular cognitive access to make a case for
academic freedom for Christian scholarship. He does so by contrasting infringing on scholarship with qualifying it perspectivally, arguing that academic freedom in an academic climate that embraces religious pluralism and
perspectivalism must make room for appropriate religiously-qualified scholarship. The focus on the relation to society continues in "Christian Learning
In and For a Pluralist Society," where he suggests that what Christian aca-

demics might contribute to the larger academic community is a public voice for justice, one inspired by a vision of shalom. Together these three essays make us more cognizant of the fact that Christian scholarship has important contributions to make to society and the general academic world, not merely to the Christian community.

The next two essays seem to take us full circle, back to Wolterstorff's earliest preoccupations with Christian higher education. In "Should the Work of Our Hands Have Standing in the Christian College?" he argues "in house" with those Christian institutions wishing to preserve "pure liberal arts" that teaching students critical discernment for society's formation is equally important. And in "What Is the Reformed Perspective on Christian Higher Education?" he gives a fresh summary of "the" Reformed themes that have shaped his thinking over the decades he has written about Christian higher education. But to end the collection with that essay would not do justice to Wolterstorff's outward-looking thought and his restlessness. Thus the last essay, "Call to Boldness: A Response to *Fides et Ratio*," highlights not only Wolterstorff's ecumenism but also his continuing, restless search for access to and contact points with other traditions and with adequate expressions of Christian voice in the world.

Books such as these do not, of course, appear without a team of people to produce them. We would like to thank James Bratt and the Calvin Center for Christian Scholarship at Calvin College for its generous grant to finance the book's production. We would also like to thank Carrie Pierson for her most competent and tireless work with the many technical aspects of the manuscript, including scanning, proofreading, and indexing; without her efforts this book would not have been possible. Finally, we would like to thank Nick Wolterstorff for his enthusiasm and close guidance on the project, including writing the concluding reflection in the collection.

CLARENCE W. JOLDERSMA
GLORIA GORIS STRONKS

Introduction

We seem to be living in a time of multiple crises. The robust American economy of the 1990s has nose-dived over the last several years, becoming anemic if not moribund. The gap between rich and poor is increasing at an alarming rate. Urban decay seems to be an intractable and permanent feature of American society. Health care costs are skyrocketing out of reach, even for the vanishing middle class. The threat of terrorism is creating a feeling of siege within the United States and the Western world, one that seems to require pre-emptive strikes of massive proportions to contain it. Together these might suggest that we are not living in the best of times.

In this setting, institutions of Christian higher education in North America — Catholic, Lutheran, Wesleyan, Calvinist, Methodist, evangelical, fundamentalist — all struggle to understand their purpose and identity. Who are we? What are we here for? What ought to be our relationship to an increasingly fragmented and seemingly post-Christian society? What contribution might we make to alleviating society's multiple problems?

Issues facing Christian higher education are also more directly internal. How do we maintain historical identities and missions while seeking to embrace increasing diversity for our very survival? How do we address the looming double threat by on-line degree mills that promise credentials for a song and by escalating costs for students who increasingly seem to want credentials rather than an education? How are our students going to successfully face increasingly high education debts with diminishing job prospects? How do Christian scholars contend with the felt pressure to produce "safe" scholarship that will not hinder recruitment of students and money? Chrisian higher education is not without its questions.

What resources might Christian higher education draw on as it thinks its way into the twenty-first century?

Nicholas Wolterstorff's collection of essays is one such powerful resource. Although they have been written over the course of the last twenty-five years, and although they are not a prognosis of — let alone a blueprint for — education's future, these essays do develop a powerful philosophical framework for thinking about scholarship and institutional purpose. The vision Wolterstorff has developed over time for Christian higher education is in many ways more important today than when he first began shaping it. His vision is a valuable resource for such institutions precisely because his philosophical framework naturally links challenging ideas on Christian scholarship with a broad vision of the mission of Christian colleges and universities. Wolterstorff's central message is one increasingly concerned with social justice, something he attempts to capture with the term *shalom*.

These essays show a certain restlessness of ideas. Wolterstorff often articulates dissatisfaction with his previous renditions of the nature of Christian scholarship or the mission of Christian higher education. In the Afterword to this collection, Wolterstorff admits that there must have been "some burr under my saddle prompting me to depart from the familiar." His self-analysis is that his developing and changing thought points to an emerging set of ideas slowly developing over time. That may be. But the restlessness evident in the essays also seems to embody the very thing that Wolterstorff sometimes calls for — a "holy dissatisfaction" with present conditions and structures. On this reading, Wolterstorff's restlessness comes not so much from changes in thought as it does from an ethical call. It seems to come from a call from the suffering in the world, from those in pain and poverty, from the oppressed and marginalized voices in our society and around the world. It is as if Wolterstorff increasingly has felt an ethical call — one that surely includes doing Christian scholarship in the context of quality Christian higher education — a call that comes precisely *through* the plight of these neighbors and strangers. As if this ethical call awakens a restless longing for the human flourishing promised in the coming Kingdom, with Messiah's second coming. It is as if this messianic call quietly but constantly disturbs his comfortable articulations that favor quality liberal arts education or Christian scholarship confined to developing Christian perspectives on disciplinary knowledge. As if the suffering in society disrupts the possibility of a pure focus on culture. As if entanglements in concrete social practice disturb the serenity of the disengaged stance of contemplating reality theoretically. In short, it is as if the burr under his saddle is fundamentally an ethical one, one mediated by neighbor and stranger, one of seeking *shalom*.

Shalom as Vision and Call

I'd like to unpack this idea of shalom in Wolterstorff's thought. It is a vision of human flourishing. Shalom means people living in right relationships with God, themselves, each other, and nature — and in taking delight in such relationships. Shalom involves finding meaning in our experiences and celebrating the actualizing of creation's potentials. Shalom involves recognizing in ourselves that place where God's goodness finds its answer in our gratitude. Shalom is an ethical community where all the members have a full and secure place in the community. As such, it embraces a "non-abandonment" view of the creation that involves redeeming it.

But shalom is more than a vision for Wolterstorff; it is a command to humans living here and now, in a fallen world, in a society that is filled with pain, suffering, and woundedness. Shalom commands us to pray and struggle not only for developing the potentials of creation but also for the "release of the captives." It is especially the latter that becomes Wolterstorff's focus. Shalom as a command asks us to respond — now — to the cries and tears of human suffering: to the pangs of the hungry, to the frustration of those with no jobs despite long searches, to the anguish of those abandoned to refugee camps for generations, to the squalor of inner cities, to the pollution of modern industrial society, to the fear and danger facing those not accepted by the community, to the domination of the poor by the rich, to the places of war around the globe.... The list goes on and on. Shalom as a command is a call for us to struggle to bring about human flourishing in our community, our society, our world, precisely because so much of humanity cries out, suffers, is wounded. The messianic light pulls us forward to take action in the world, to help bring about human flourishing, suggesting that we cannot remain indifferent to the plight of those around us. We see the tears of God behind the wounds of the world, meet a wounded God behind the injustices that exist around the globe. Shalom is a call to address these injustices, to take action here and now — it cannot wait.

As such, it is a call to be heralds and agents of Christ's Kingdom. The church exists not for itself but for the sake of humanity. And although we cannot bring about the Kingdom's fulfillment by ourselves, our efforts do make a difference; Wolterstorff suggests that the "Kingdom will not come about without our efforts." This means that our work as Christians is here, in the world, and now, at this time; we are not meant to withdraw from the world around us and wait for some future time. The Christian narrative calls us to share in God's work, including particularly a "hope for humanity." We are to "act redemptively" and bring a "healing word" of the Christian gospel in the world and for the world.

Thus our work as agents and heralds of Christ is to bring justice and peace, joy and delight — especially justice. For Wolterstorff, justice is the ground of shalom, and responsible action is its vehicle. The voice of justice is not the shrill call of Christian self-interest but an inclusive call to help the "widows, orphans, aliens" — that is, those who suffer and who have no voice of their own, now, here, in our cities, our country, our world. Bringing justice means honoring everyone's rights, developing an ethical community where no one needs to hide in fear of judgment and oppression. Justice arrives when the marginal ones are no longer discriminated against, whether that be because of race, social class, ethnicity, gender, language, religion, or sexual orientation.

The call of shalom animating Wolterstorff's writings adds a distinctive voice to the issues currently facing Christian higher education. The vision of shalom not only forms a framework for his thought but also penetrates deeply into the details of it — into his analyses of the social context of Christian higher education, the idea of Christian learning, the purpose of education, the curriculum, and the nature of teaching. By addressing each of these briefly, I'd like to show how Wolterstorff's ideas are a valuable if challenging resource for Christian higher education as it thinks through current issues and problems.

Economic and political globalization is becoming an increasingly obvious context for understanding society, including the educational institutions within it. How does globalization shape the identity and purpose of Christian higher education? Can we safely ignore it, focusing on liberal-arts education or on preparing our students for careers in North America? Is adding a nod to Third World development and missions abroad sufficient?

Wolterstorff's notion of shalom propels us toward a world-systems analysis of global development. He suggests that at least some of the pain and suffering around the world occurs precisely because we in the West form the center or core of the economic system, and developing countries form the periphery. Our capitalist ecomony doesn't just "accidentally" exploit these countries: domination and exploitation of other world regions is built into capitalism's very structure. This suggests that Christian higher education in North America ought to pay attention to the world system of which we are a part. In this context, striving for justice would include deliberately developing an international, global consciousness for those of us involved in Christian higher education. The "center" and "periphery" structure of global development means that we are already involved in the divide between rich and poor, both within our own society and between nations. Our students need to develop an "international consciousness" to discern this oppressive structure that dominates global relations.

Concretely in this context, educating for shalom in a globalizing world might imply resisting the drumbeats of war calling to protect a nation's self-interests in the name of global security but aimed at maintaining lifestyles that need cheap labor, oil, and resources from abroad. Or, more positively, it might suggest developing relationships with institutions of higher education in impoverished countries — and being responsive to their needs rather than paternalistically exporting Western education without question. Wolterstorff's shalom-inspired world-systems analysis asks those in Christian higher education to think within a global context, challenging the options of isolation and indifference. We must educate our students to work *for* the betterment of the world in which we live, not merely to survive *in* it.

Furthermore, Wolterstorff's shalom framework moves him to focus on what he calls society, not just culture (fine arts, pure academics, theoretical knowledge, disciplines). Society is composed of persons in relationships and thus includes social roles, social institutions, social structures, and social forces. Wolterstorff suggests that capitalism is a major force in shaping social relationships and social structures. In particular, it has an invasive force that "colonizes" traditionally non-economic relationships and social roles. This results in an increasingly contractual understanding of human relationships. A vision of shalom might suggest that human living is impoverished when relationships are contractualized, whether they be spousal or parent-child relationships, work, leisure, or civic relationships. This touches Christian higher education directly if only because our students are themselves informed by this social dynamic. Thus part of their education would involve helping them to become aware of this framework as a force present in their lives that works against struggling for shalom.

Moreover, Wolterstorff's analysis might call us to take issue with language in promotional literature that calls students "customers," education "a sales product," and degrees "best bargains." It might argue against importing ideas from business administration into higher education, such as "being on the bus" to bring recalcitrant faculty into line. It might mean rethinking education in terms other than a contract for credentialing — that is, for providing a select group of students a communally subsidized opportunity to pursue the private self-interest of getting ahead of the others in the classroom, the community, and society. Or it might ask us to rethink the ethics of establishing "elite" departments with mid-career scholars by paying them salaries far out of proportion with those of the rest of the institution. And it might help give pause to the perennial pressure on institutions to acquiesce to the possible demands of successful entrepreneurs in exchange for financial stability.

Wolterstorff's shalom-inspired social analysis of capitalism's incursions might be considered a prophetic call for critical discernment that is especially important in today's economic and political climate.

Christian Scholarship

Wolterstorff's understanding of *Christian learning* is significant for today's institutions of Christian higher education. He frames this also in the context of shalom, calling for both "disinterested" and "praxis-oriented" Christian scholarship. The former is important because humans are created as hermeneutical beings who hunger for meaning; thus interpretation is a basic need. But Wolterstorff also suggests that there is no such thing as generic understanding; it is always perspectival — hence the need for Christian disinterested learning. Furthermore, the prejudgments and beliefs with which we as academics inevitably approach our scholarship also can act as a privileged access point to reality, thus making Christian scholarship a positive contribution to disciplinary conversations. As such it contributes to human flourishing by answering our questions and making explicit the details of a Christian vision of "the good."

However, "praxis-oriented" Christian learning is also important. Because society and not just culture is crucial in understanding our struggle for shalom, much Christian scholarship must be aimed at changing the world, not merely understanding it. This includes developing penetrating critiques of injustice in society, shaped by hope and framed by the biblical narrative of shalom. Wolterstorff suggests that this Christian voice in the public square of academia brings a healing word about social structures and their dynamics, about our idolization of wealth, and about our indifference or hostility to the rest of the world. It is scholarship that struggles directly to do justice.

For Wolterstorff, scholarship is never generically human, carried out by a cognitive being above the fray of history and culture. Instead, scholarship is a social practice, an activity (a set of skills and knowledge) that must be learned. It is a practice that is both explained and modeled to us, one that we are inducted into socially. Such social practices are embedded historically as traditions. Thus, when we are inducted into the social practice of a discipline, we are to embrace its standards of excellence and observe its rules of procedure. But the historicity and plurality of traditions means that there is never "the" standard of excellence or "the" method — these are always plural, contestable, changeable, malleable. In particular, then, as Christian scholars we are always to face in two directions, one inward and intra-perspectivally toward the Christian community, and one outward and inter-perspectivally toward the others in the academic discipline. This allows us to both learn and give insight.

In particular, Wolterstorff suggests that since scholarship is a perspectival practice and a social practice, it involves the equilibrium of three things: data, theory, and control beliefs. Christian scholarship also involves holding these three "components" in dynamic balance. The point of such scholarship is to work internally in a discipline — whether it be physics, history, theology, education, or sociology — in order to develop its theories, knowledge, and methods. But in doing so, we always approach the task as perspectival beings inducted into a social practice. Thus our weighing of theories is informed by our prejudgments, including our religious ones. But the reverse occurs too, where the theories of our discipline inform our religious beliefs. Similarly for data: they are theory-laden, but they also shape theory and control beliefs. There is no unidirectionality in adjudicating potential (or actual) conflicts between these three, and there are no algorithms for doing so. As a result, sometimes Christians will find themselves in the (perhaps odd) situation of agreeing with non-Christian colleagues and disagreeing with Christian ones. The fault lines of disagreement can flow in several directions. Wolterstorff's conclusion is this: Christian scholarship ought to be faithful, not distinctive per se (although he thinks it will very often be distinctive).

Wolterstorff's idea of Christian scholarship adds an important voice in current discussions. First of all, his language itself conceptually challenges ideas that are becoming increasingly prevalent. His use of the phrase "Christian learning" rather than the currently favored "integration of faith and learning" involves not merely a preference of taste but a conceptual dispute. The current talk of "integration" often seems to equate Christian scholarship with adding pious "faith talk" to the presentation of the existing theories and knowledge of a particular discipline. But this does not challenge the conceptualizations, theories, models, or methodologies within a discipline, something Wolterstorff means to indicate in his notion of Christian learning. Sometimes "integration" language seems to take the form of denouncing a discipline's "secular humanism" and then substituting theology for the content of the discipline. Christian learning, by contrast, means to engage the discipline internally, developing theories, models, and so forth that address problems and issues within the discipline's academic conversation — a pluralist notion of academic learning. Often "integration" talk is translated as the project of finding a particular "religious" niche within a discipline, such as studying the voting patterns of Christians, describing the history of evangelicalism, or preserving the sacred music of the Christian tradition. Wolterstorff's idea of Christian learning suggests that this research, although no doubt important, is based on an inadequate understanding of the task of the Christian academic, which he sees as developing an equilibrium between data, theory, and control beliefs. Finally, sometimes "integration" talk signals settling for a mediocre, in-house conversation with other Christian academics. Wolterstorff's notions of "privileged cognitive access" and the "double direction" imply that Christian learning involves participating in the conversations of one's discipline with others of differing perspectives, offering a unique access point shaped by a passion for the suffering and wounded in the world. Generally, "Christian learning" means to signal a critical engagement with the theories and methodology of the discipline itself, one that shapes and is shaped by one's particular Christian vision of human flourishing and social justice. This is what gives Christian scholarship its particular point of cognitive access in a plurality of viewpoints within an academic discipline.

Wolterstorff also challenges those who see Christian scholarship as merely working within the confines of one's worldview. He suggests that Christian learning is risky business, involving the *interaction* of data, theory, and belief. This is a challenge to those scholars and administrators who know beforehand what conclusions one might come to, which positions are to be taken and which to be avoided. Wolterstorff's notion of religiously qualified academic freedom still means allowing for the freedom of having the theories or data of one's discipline reshape one's "control beliefs," one's deep convictions. This is what makes scholarship a social practice, in Wolterstorff's estimation, rather than merely a set of deductions drawn from one's fundamental beliefs. Such a view of Christian scholarship challenges Christian higher education to leave room for the risky business of going against some of the cherished articulations of its worldview.

Teaching for Shalom

These essays will also challenge institutions of Christian higher education to rethink their particular vision of their purpose and task. This is especially true of those many colleges and universities whose tradition and distinction is liberal arts. They might have a tendency to stress the twin qualities of academic excellence and developing Christian minds, sometimes adding a list of "virtues" as a way to address the moral dimension of students. Or they may remain framed within an "evangelism" understanding of their educational mandate, where students are prepared for Christian service narrowly defined. Wolterstorff's "shalom" model of education is a refreshing, expansive, challenging alternative to these narrowed views of the purpose of Christian higher education.

For Wolterstorff, the goal of Christian higher education is to energize students for a certain way of being in the world here and now — to encourage them to struggle for shalom. As institutions, we are to witness to the coming of shalom, to serve all people (not just Christians) in relieving misery and pain and in responding to the wounds of humanity. The goal of Christian higher education is to change the world by making it a place of human flourishing. It means nourishing forms of community in which openness and acceptance are fostered. It means maintaining cultural inheritances discriminately. It means keeping before us the faces and voices of those who suffer. The goal is to prepare students for the life and work of the Kingdom, for struggling for human flourishing where justice is the ground and responsible action is the vehicle, where delight and joy are intrinsic features of right human relationships with God, the natural world, the self, and others. Although the focus of a school is disciplined study, the framing goal should be promoting shalom.

This has implications that might challenge some of the prevalent curriculum structures that currently exist at institutions of Christian higher education. Many Christian colleges and universities remain wedded to the structure of the German research university, in which the institution's curriculum is divided rigidly along disciplinary lines. Wolterstorff's shalom model challenges the walls that separate curriculum into tidy compartments. His focus on society and not just culture suggests more interdisciplinary or thematic majors and minors, including studies that focus on poverty, war and peace, ecology, gender, race, urban squalor, globalization, crime and punishment, and the environment. Thus he calls for "bridging elements" between culture and society. That would mean building into the curriculum an international emphasis which would allow students to see the interlocking structure of the world and the impact the core has on the periphery, both within our particular society as well as globally. And it would mean bringing students face to face with the wounds and the suffering of society and the world.

This might also mean creatively rethinking departmental administrative structures to more easily include cross-departmental appointments. Or it might mean rethinking the course content, sequence, and focus of traditional majors if they are to meet the challenge to include not just culture but also society, to embrace the call of being a healing presence in society. Wolterstorff's vision of a curriculum for shalom clearly implies that it needs to include the pressing social issues and problems of the day, with an eye toward bringing about human flourishing in the world.

Alongside much traditional curriculum is often a mode of instruction that operates primarily as a transfer mechanism, transferring a discipline's body of theoretical knowledge to the novice learner. Well-organized lectures, information-filled textbooks, and comprehensive testing on the material are the stock-in-trade of such pedagogy in Christian higher education. Then students' repeating the information and thoughts of their professors is often taken for developing personal thinking.

Wolterstorff's ideas quarrel with such a narrow, unidirectional conception of teaching. Treating students as passive recipients of "perspectivalized" knowledge simply will not do. He wishes to broaden our conception of pedagogy, making it more interactive. Although not in favor of the idea that all thoughts are equal, he challenges professors to make teaching an interaction with their students. His vision of teaching for shalom views students as responsible agents. Thus he suggests that our role as teachers is to develop dispositions in our students, something that is done through giving reasons, developing discipline, modeling, and encouraging empathy. In particular, he suggests, we need to cultivate in them a critical consciousness and empathy for those suffering in the world. Students need to understand and distance themselves from the social forces that might pull them away from struggling for shalom. They need to understand society's dynamic interaction of forces such as capitalism, contractualism, nationalism, and individualism; we might consider energizing them toward alternative ways of living, away from the typical American dream. We need to teach them how to cope with intransigent and unjust social structures, showing them how to sustain hope, how to pray "your Kingdom come," how to keep the struggle against injustice alive even when it seems futile. And they need to learn how to delight in the traces of shalom already present in the world. They need to experience communities that are safe and inclusive, that have an ethos of compassion. We need to cultivate dispositions in them to act for justice, to view society from the messianic light, to have a passion for shalom. We need to help our students acquire an adequate cognitive framework about issues of social justice through group dialogue, discussion, and challenging assignments.

In general, Wolterstorff's vision of shalom as a guide for Christian higher education adds a challenging voice to current discussions and practices. It is a voice that asks us to engage not only in culture but also in society, not only by preserving our Christian heritage but also by going beyond it. It challenges Christian academics to not be satisfied with talking to other Christian academics but to include participating in more diverse conversations in their academic disciplines, both to learn and to contribute. Wolterstorff has a pluralist view of education contextualized by a critique of capitalism from a "world-systems" viewpoint and a postmodern perspectivalist understanding of knowledge. It is a view of students as responsible agents and of academic scholarship as a social practice. The call of shalom precludes withdrawal from the world and society into the safety of a homogeneous Christian community, instead asking Christian institutions of higher education to become voices for social justice and human flourishing. Engaging in Christian higher education is educating for shalom.

CLARENCE W. JOLDERSMA

Educating for Shalom

Rethinking Christian Higher Education

The number of church-related colleges that are today engaged in fundamental rethinking of their mission or have done such rethinking within the past decade is quite astounding. What that means, surely, is that the traditional ways of understanding our mission are breaking down, becoming obscure, or being questioned. If the traditions were vital, understood, and accepted, we would be dealing with details, not with fundamental rethinking.

Why is this fundamental rethinking taking place? Why is there the shared sense of losing our grip on a tradition? History provides some clues.

Historical Background

The great period for the formation of church-related colleges in the United States — and the United States is peculiar in regard to its abundance of church-related institutions of higher education — was of course the nineteenth century, as the Christian church spread westward — past the Appalachians, across the prairies, up to the Rockies. The church, in all its branches, was persuaded of the importance of education; wherever it went, it founded colleges. Although the need for an educated clergy was usually uppermost in the minds of the founders, customarily there was also the conviction that higher education was needed for training the leaders of our democratic society.

At the very time that the churches were engaged in this quite astounding project of founding colleges across the land, the American system of public elementary and secondary schools was taking shape. I would guess that

This speech, originally titled "The Mission of the Church-Related College," was delivered at Goshen College in 1977.

the fundamental reason for the difference in governance of higher and lower education — church-governed colleges and state-governed elementary and secondary schools — was the importance of clergy training in the colleges. The education provided by the state was to be for all comers; "nonsectarian," it was often called. Those who wanted sectarian education, of whatever sort and for whatever purpose, had to provide it themselves. Given the divisions of the church, the education of clergy was necessarily "sectarian."

As for those who went on to college but were not training for the clergy, probably for the most part they did not sense any big difference between the education they had received in the public lower schools and the education they were getting in their church-sponsored college; the continuity was more striking than the discontinuity — at least for Protestants. A rather generic Protestantism reigned in the public schools; unless one was training for the clergy, that same generic Protestantism shaped most collegiate education.

It should be added that already in the nineteenth century there were colleges free of church relationship; in particular, there were colleges and universities that were state-supported and state-operated. But throughout the nineteenth century, these had but a minor place in the big scheme of American higher education.

A massive change took place after World War II. The state universities ballooned in size, becoming, with the exception of a few of the old private universities, the most powerful and wealthy components in the system. All the church-related colleges in the country began to feel threatened and beleaguered. Their reactions, in retrospect, were predictable. The state universities were massive; the church-related colleges took to praising the educational benefits of smallness. The liberal arts were but a small component within the total curriculum of the state universities; the church-related colleges took to praising the liberal arts. And so forth.

Social Context: Public Piety, Commonality, Accommodation

The rethinking that the church-related colleges are currently engaged in seems to me motivated, in good measure, by this massive alteration in the system represented and caused by the growth of the state universities. I am inclined to think, however, that it is not the major motivation, since much of the rethinking induced by this alteration took place a decade or two in the past; it does not explain the rethinking that has been taking place recently.

What does explain it? Let me make a suggestion. Fundamental to

American life, molding us into one people and distinguishing us from other peoples, is what may be called (following Richard Neuhaus) our *public piety*. By that I mean our complex of national rituals and symbols; our venerated leaders, places, events, and artifacts; our goals as a people; and our beliefs concerning the significance of the American people. This cluster of beliefs, goals, rituals, symbols, and objects of veneration together give expression to the American people's shared sense of the transcendent, the sacred. In recent years this totality has often been referred to as *the American civil religion* — though for reasons that I will not go into now, I judge that to think of it as a distinct religion is to distort the situation.

This public piety is distinct from every true religion in American society — as can be seen at a glance by noticing that Washington and Lincoln are venerated figures in the public piety, whereas they are not "saints" in any of the religions in our society. What is equally true, though, is that the public piety interacts with the various distinct religions; the two by no means merely co-exist.

As I see it, the relation between the public piety and the various distinct religions is one in which two fundamental dynamics are at work. Within the public piety there is what I shall call the *dynamic of creative commonality*. By this I mean that there is constant change and development in the public piety in response to the emergence of new patterns of thought in American culture, including new patterns of religious thought. These revisions in the public piety are creative revisions, in that new lines of thought are not merely added to what was already there, nor is a new common denominator found; rather, a new amalgam emerges. I call it a dynamic of commonality because the goal is that almost everyone be able to embrace the public piety, no matter what his or her religion or ideology.

The counterpart, on the side of the diverse religions, is what may be called the *dynamic of accommodation*. The particular religions are constantly accommodating themselves to changes in the public piety. They harmonize their views and practices with the public piety, so that, with minor exceptions, they all become recognizably *American* religions. I do not want to suggest that the church has never played a prophetic role in America; certainly it has. But I do think the reason many people think there is no significant tension, let alone contradiction, between the Christian religion and the American public piety is that, on the one hand, the public piety has been shaped (in part) by the churches, and on the other hand, the churches have at the same time accommodated themselves to the public piety. It is because of this bi-directional dynamic interaction between the public piety and the diverse religions that people fail to see any gap between being a good Christian and being a good American, instead viewing the various particular religions as optional sectarian versions of the public piety.

It is my impression that recent developments are causing a tension between these two beyond what any mutual accommodation can ease. More and more, the churches are seeing themselves not as specific versions of the public piety but as in conflict with that piety; a sense of "overagainstness" is arising.

In our culture today there is a powerful current of anti-religious, libertarian, self-centered sensualism; the public piety is gradually being revised to accommodate this current. The churches are accommodating themselves to some of this by, here and there, urging us to get in touch with our bodies, encouraging transactional analysis, and the like; but they are finding it difficult to swallow the whole lump. I have to concede that at the beginning of the nineteenth century one could scarcely have believed that the church would come around to believing that the goal of human beings on earth is to accumulate personal wealth by competing with each other; yet in good measure it did. Just possibly the same sort of accommodation may happen again; but I doubt it.

Be that as it may, it has not happened yet. Instead, in many of our churches there has emerged a much deeper sense of overagainstness with respect to American culture than was ever present before, including, in particular, overagainstness with respect to the public piety. The implication for the church-related colleges is that the cozy notion that we could base our teaching on what everybody in our society holds in common, adding to that our own sectarian peculiarities, seems less and less plausible. My speculation is that this is the major cause of the rethinking going on in all directions.

If I am right about this, then the need of the day is for a new vision of the mission of the church-related college; we can no longer think of it as a college in which sectarian peculiarities are added on to what all Americans share in common. I should add that some church-related colleges have responded by no longer even trying to add on sectarian peculiarities. When asked to justify their existence in the shadow of the state universities, they plead no more than smallness and concentration on the liberal arts.

A New Vision: Religiously Alternative Education

What might a new vision of the mission of the church-related college look like?

We will have to dig down to religious and theological fundamentals. In the beginning, God created humans out of dust; we human beings are one with our fellow creatures in terms of our physical constitution. Nevertheless, we are unique among them. We alone have a calling, a calling issued by God; we alone are answerable. That calling is to tend and cherish the earth, to love our neighbors as we also rightly love ourselves, and to acknowledge God in all God's ways.

We defected from that calling. We rebelled. We fell into sin, with all its attendant miseries. But God, so the Christian confesses, was not content to let us wallow in the misery of our sin. God has been working for renewal, for restoration, for redemption. In large part God has done so by creating and calling a people to be God's agents on earth — first, a distinct race, Israel; then, at Pentecost, the church, a new nation, no longer a race but a transnational people consisting of those committed to following Christ in carrying out God's work.

We can summarize the calling of that people, the church, in the world today with three words. The church is called to *witness* — to be a witness to the coming of God's Kingdom, God's work of renewal, urging all people everywhere to repent and join the band of Christ's followers. The church is called to *serve* — to serve all people everywhere by relieving their misery and their lack of joy, both attacking the structures that victimize and alleviating the misery of the victims. And the church is called, in its own life and community, to *give evidence* of the new life — not just to wait around in the promise that someday there will be a new heaven and a new earth, but to exhibit the fact that in Christ there is a new Power and that the Kingdom has broken in.

It must be said forthrightly, with pained regret, that, as Christ warned his disciples, to the end of the age there will be alienation and even hostility between the church thus understood and the surrounding society. For that surrounding society lives by other values; it has other goals, and it worships other gods. Our American attempt to treat and see the various Christian denominations, indeed, the various religions, as nothing more than specific versions of the public piety that unites us all — that is a deep illusion.

I can now state what I see as the nature and mission of the church-related college — or, as I prefer to call it, the Christian college. The Christian college is a project of and for the Christian community. An implication of what I said above is that the Christian community exists not for its own sake but for the sake of all people. Nonetheless, the mission of the Christian college is determined, at bottom, by the fact that it is a project of and for the Christian community. It is obvious that in the modern world, if the Christian community is to share in God's work of renewal by being witness, servant, and evidence, its young members will need an education pointed toward equipping them to contribute to that calling.

This means, as I see it, that we will have to commit ourselves to alternative education — that is, *religiously* alternative education. Whether our education also comes in small units, and whether it focuses almost all of its attention on the liberal arts, are, to my mind, negotiable matters.

Educational Implications

If I am right about this, then, as I see it, there are six large areas in which together we must begin to explore what the alternative should look like.

First, we shall have to work out a pedagogy appropriate to the Christian college. By pedagogy I mean how we teach what we teach. It is my impression — possibly I am betraying my ignorance — that none of us has done much of anything in this area. No doubt we have all moved *away from* the rather authoritarian pedagogical techniques used in the past; but I doubt that any of us has fully thought through what we should be moving *toward*. In recent years some teachers at some of our schools have begun to use behaviorist or quasi-behaviorist techniques — without, however, first engaging in a thorough Christian assessment of the foundations of behaviorism. Others have begun using self-realization techniques, again without any thorough Christian assessment of the self-realization ideology now sweeping our country.

Second, we must work out a curriculum appropriate to the Christian college — by which I mean a structure of required and optional courses. We all do have a curriculum, of course. Nonetheless, it is my impression that we have not put much deep and sustained thought into the curriculum required by our goals.

Third, we must work out a community structure appropriate to the Christian college. A college is perforce a community of a certain sort, or at least a society. Students are there primarily to receive the educational services offered; and faculty are there primarily to offer the services for which students have come. There is a large support staff in addition to the faculty, and an administration that keeps — or tries to keep — the whole enterprise working harmoniously and effectively. Within this structure, authority and responsibility for various tasks are distributed around the community; and there are rules for the comportment and functioning of the various components of the community. I am impressed — astounded, actually — at the paucity of thought that most of us have given to the question about the sort of authority and responsibility structure appropriate to the Christian college.

Fourth — and this is so obvious that it scarcely needs saying — we must work at making the content of what we teach responsive to the Christian gospel.

Fifth, we must think seriously about the place and role of worship within that community which is a Christian college.

And last, we must work out the rationale for the education we offer, asking what such learning has to do with life. Naturally our answer will have an impact, or should have an impact, on what we do in the other five areas. Is our goal to pass on and help create an intellectual culture? Is our goal to make ministers and missionaries of all our students? In short: What is our image of the successful graduate? The answer to that question determines a great deal.

All six of these topics press hard for consideration on our part if we view the challenge presently facing the Christian college along the lines I have suggested.

Teaching for Shalom: On the Goal of Christian Collegiate Education

Over the past decade and a half, teachers in Christian colleges have spoken a great deal about the need to integrate Christian faith with learning. Here and there, now and then, they have gone beyond talk to produce such learning. In thus urging and practicing integration, they have moved decisively beyond the nineteenth-century paradigm according to which Christianity was to be added onto neutral secular learning.

Integration of faith and learning speaks to the content of Christian higher education, not the goal. Teaching is an engagement between teachers and students; and its goal is always to bring about some change in students — such as an increase in knowledge, understanding, sensitivity, imagination, or commitment. Integrating Christian faith with learning is just a different thing from that sort of personal engagement; to say that Christian *scholars* must seek to integrate faith with learning is not to specify a goal for Christian *teachers*.

When it comes to goals, it appears to me that we have pretty much been content to accept the educational goals handed on to us by our predecessors. I think it is time to change that. As a counterpart to our thinking anew about the relation of faith to learning, we must think anew about the *goal* of Christian collegiate education. In this talk I wish to propose such a goal. To prepare the way, let me identify the most common of the extant goals.

This lecture, originally titled "Making Higher Education Christian: Teaching for Justice," was delivered in the 1980s.

Four Models of Collegiate Education

Many of those who work in the Christian colleges operate with what may be called the *Christian service* model. The idea is that the goal of Christian collegiate education is to train students to enter Christian service, understanding this to be a certain range of "Christian" occupations or "Kingdom work" — evangelism, church education, church ministry, mission-field medicine, Christian communications, and the like. Probably in most Christian colleges there are some educators who think in terms of this model; probably there are some colleges in which *most* educators do their thinking in these terms.

The popularity of the model, if nothing else, makes it imperative that it be taken seriously and be engaged. I will refrain from doing that on this occasion, however. It regularly happens that even in colleges that begin with this as their dominant model, various dynamics sooner or later set in which cause people to find it too restrictive. As a result, such training colleges regularly transform themselves into liberal arts colleges. Why this shift so often takes place would be interesting to explore; but I think it best on this occasion to spend our time engaging the models that people tend to move on to once they have left behind the Christian service model.

Among the most prominent of these alternatives is what may be called the *Christian humanist* model; let me spend more time on this alternative than any of the others.

Oakeshott's Education for Freedom

A theme that sounds like a sustained pedal tone in the thought of Christian humanists is *freedom:* education is for freedom. Many of those who hold this view simply identify liberal arts education with the humanist model of education, and then play on the etymology of the word "liberal" — liberal education is education that liberates or frees us.

Frees us *from* what and *for* what? No more eloquent answer to that question has ever been composed than that of the Cambridge political theorist Michael Oakeshott in his long essay entitled "Education: The Engagement and Its Frustration."[1] Indeed, I judge this to be one of the most profound and

---

1. Oakeshott, "Education: The Engagement and Its Frustration," in *Education and the Development of Reason,* edited by R. F. Dearden, P. H. Hirst, and R. S. Peters (London: Routledge & Kegan Paul, 1972), pp. 19-59. Subsequent references to this essay will be made parenthetically in the text, and appear here with permission from the publisher.

articulate essays on education published in the twentieth century — and I say this in spite of deep disagreements with its perspective. Oakeshott's theory is not a theory of *Christian* education. But I propose beginning with him just because he develops more profoundly than anyone else in the contemporary world the theme fundamental in the vision of the Christian humanist — namely, that education liberates us by initiating us into the great cultural heritage of humanity.

Oakeshott explicitly grounds his theory of education in a vision of what it is to be human. This, for me, is one of its attractive features. Every theory of education is grounded in a vision of what it is to be human, but usually that foundation is concealed or left unexposed. Not so in Oakeshott's case.

To be human, says Oakeshott, is to *understand* the world and oneself, to *construe* the world and oneself in one way or another. Or to put the point in yet another way: to be human is to *invest* the world and oneself with *meaning*. That is only the beginning, however. To be human is also to *respond* to reality thus invested with meaning: to respond in the human way, which is different from the animal way of merely "behaving." Human beings, says Oakeshott, "are creatures of want"; but their "wants are not biological impulses or genetic urges; they are imagined satisfactions, and are eligible to be wished-for, chosen, pursued, procured, approved or disapproved." To be human is to imagine possibilities in response to one's understanding, to desire some of the possibilities imagined, and then to act on some of those desires. It is to choose "to say or to do *this* rather than *that* in relation to imagined and wished-for outcomes," each such performance being a "disclosure of a man's beliefs about himself and the world and an exploit in self-enactment" (20).

This adventure in understanding, imagining, desiring, and enacting that constitutes us as human is not conducted in solitude. Being human is "recognizing oneself to be related to others, not as the parts of an organism are related, nor as members of a single, all-inclusive society, but in virtue of participation in multiple understood relationships and in the enjoyment of understood historic languages of feelings, sentiments, imaginings, fancies, desires, recognitions, moral and religious beliefs, intellectual and practical enterprises, customs, conventions, procedures and practices; canons, maxims, and principles of conduct, rules which denote obligations and offices which specify duties" (20-21). In sum,

> a human being is the inhabitant of a world composed not of "things" but of meanings; that is, of occurrences in some manner recognized, identified, understood, and responded to in terms of this understanding. It is a

world of sentiments and beliefs, and it includes also human artifacts (such as books, pictures, musical compositions, tools, and utensils), for these, also, are "expressions" which have meanings and which require to be understood in order to be used or enjoyed. To be without this understanding is to be not a human being, but a stranger to the human condition. (21)

Entering this human heritage of understandings, imaginings, desirings, and enactings requires learning; there is no other way. The "educational engagement is necessary because nobody is born a human being, and because the quality of being human is not a latency which becomes an actuality in a process of 'growth'" (21-22). It is by way of learning, and only by way of learning, that "a postulant to the human condition comes to recognize himself as a human being in the only way that is possible; namely, by seeing himself in the mirror of an inheritance of human understandings and activities" (22). Thus Oakeshott sees education as that "transaction between human beings and postulants to the human condition in which newcomers are initiated" into the heritage of human consciousness, thus becoming human.

Oakeshott recognizes that much of such learning takes place casually, informally, and episodically; but education in the full sense, as he sees it, begins with "the deliberate initiation of a newcomer into a human inheritance of sentiments, beliefs, imaginings, understandings, and activities. It begins when the transaction becomes 'schooling'" (23).

Oakeshott cites five characteristics of schooling, among them the one at which I have been aiming. Let's have all of them before us. The project of a school is, for one thing, "that of a serious and orderly initiation into an intellectual, imaginative, moral, and emotional inheritance" (23-24). Secondly, school represents "an engagement to learn by study," a difficult undertaking calling for effort and discipline. Another element in the concept of a school is

> [that] of a personal transaction between a "teacher" and a "learner." The only indispensable equipment of "School" is teachers: the current emphasis on apparatus of all sorts . . . is almost wholly destructive of "School." A teacher is one in whom some part or aspect or passage of this inheritance is alive. He has something of which he is a master to impart . . . and he has deliberated its worth and the manner in which he is to impart it to a learner whom he knows. He is himself the custodian of that "practice" in which an inheritance of human understanding survives and is perpetually renewed in being imparted to newcomers. To teach is to

13

bring it about that, somehow, something of worth intended by a teacher is learned, understood, and remembered by a learner. (25)

A fourth mark of a school is that it is "an historic community of teachers and learners, neither large nor small, with traditions of its own, evoking loyalties, pieties, and affections, devoted to initiating successive generations of newcomers to the human scene into the *grandeurs* and servitudes of being human; an Alma Mater who remembers with pride or indulgence and is remembered with gratitude" (26).

In my summary of Oakeshott's marks of a school I have skipped over the one that is of principal interest to me here, the third in his list of five. So let's go back to that one. A mark of a school

is that of detachment from the immediate, local world of the learner, its current concerns and the directions it gives to his attention. . . . "School" is a place apart in which the heir may encounter his moral and intellectual inheritance, not in the terms in which it is being used in the current engagements and occupations of the world outside (where much of it is forgotten, neglected, obscured, vulgarized, or abridged, and where it appears only in scraps and as investments in immediate enterprises) but as an estate, entire, unqualified, and unencumbered. "School" is an emancipation achieved in a continuous redirection of attention. Here the learner is animated not by the inclinations he brings with him, but by intimations of excellences and aspirations he has never yet dreamed of; here he may encounter not answers to the "loaded" questions of "life," but questions which have never before occurred to him; here he may acquire new "interests" and pursue them uncorrupted by the need for immediate results; here he may learn to seek satisfactions he had never yet imagined or wished for. (24-25)

In short, education in the full sense — that is, school education — is education for freedom. Authentic education is for liberation and emancipation from the closed-in particularities of one's specific historical and social situation into the wide-open possibilities of humanity's understandings, imaginings, and desirings as a whole. The minimal accomplishment of education is that it brings about the humanity of students by initiating them into the realm of meanings that they will inhabit. Its wide, overarching goal is to deliver them from the particularity of their concrete situations into the universality of the human condition. A truly "educational engagement," according to Oakeshott, is thus both "a discipline and a release; and it is the one by virtue of being the other. . . . Its reward is an emancipation from the mere 'fact of living,' from the immediate contingencies of place and time of birth, from the tyranny of the moment and from the servitude of a merely current condition" (47-48).

Jellema's Christian Humanism

It is this theme of liberation that is central in the Christian humanist model of education. The great benefit of liberal arts education — so it is said over and over — is that it liberates and frees us. Most if not all of those involved in Christian education would dissent from the repudiation of human nature that underlies Oakeshott's thought, as they would from his suggestion that all meaning is invested by us in the world rather than some being discovered. But Oakeshott's notion of education is aimed at liberating us from the contingent factual particularities of our situation into the wide world of humanity's understandings, imaginings, desirings, and enactings. This has been a prominent theme in the Western world ever since the time of the Renaissance, and Christian educators have sounded the theme as often and as loudly as any. It should be added, for the sake of historical accuracy, that it was not the goal of Renaissance educators to engage *all* the different ways in which humanity has understood, imagined, desired, and enacted; it was their goal to engage the student primarily with classical antiquity. Only when romantic nationalism came into the picture did educators begin to say that *all* humanity has something of worth to teach us.

Recall Oakeshott's insistence that to become human, our cultural inheritance of understandings, imaginings, desirings, and enactings must *itself* be understood. The "states of mind in which the human condition is to be discerned as recognitions of and responses to the ordeal of consciousness . . . can be entered into only by being themselves understood" (47). To be human is to understand not only our world but also our heritage of consciousness. Not only do we invest our world with meaning; we also invest our cultural heritage with meaning. It is at this point that we can move beyond humanism in general to speak about Christian humanism.

The goal of Christian education, as seen by the Christian humanist, is indeed to free students from their particularity by initiating them into a more universal human consciousness; but it is not *just* that. The Christian humanist holds that it is impossible to interpret our cultural heritage in some generically human way; we can only do so as *religious* beings — and then as beings of *diverse* religions. Believers come to understand the world and their heritage

15

and to invest those with meaning in particular, nongeneric ways. Christians do so in one way; Muslims do so in another; and so forth for all other religious believers.

This particular element of the Christian humanist vision has never been developed more profoundly than it was by one of my teachers, the esteemed Christian philosopher William Harry Jellema.[2] When Jellema surveyed that vast cultural inheritance into which he, along with Oakeshott, ardently believed the student should be initiated, he did not see just episodic ebb-and-flow of understandings, imaginings, desirings, and enactings. He saw a grand, sweeping pattern. He saw the rise and fall of *kingdoms,* or *cities,* as he liked to call them — *faith communities,* if you will. It was Jellema's view that if we want to understand the fundamental pattern and dynamic of history and culture, then what is most important to attend to is not individuals, or even social institutions, but the spiritual kingdoms of which individuals are members and institutions are expressions. In thus interpreting history, Jellema saw himself as standing in the lineage of Augustine, who viewed human life in time as the interaction between the City of God and the City of the World — *civitas dei* and *civitas mundi.*

Jellema saw these spiritual kingdoms as objective realities. The City of God is not the totality of individual Christians at some particular time, or even at all times; it is an objective spiritual reality of which individual Christians are members. Neither is a particular kingdom a certain totality of individual cultural products; it is that of which the cultural products are an expression. "A *civitas* cannot be identified with cultural products, nor with the will to culture, nor with cultural activity." Rather,

> The *civitas* lives and is realized therein. It is realized in and by eating and drinking, cobbling and carpentry, work and play, science and education, law and government, love and worship; nothing human but enters into the city. The *civitas* is not one, or some, nor even all the objects tangible and intangible, which man produces or assimilates, but is the city that is objectified in the producing and assimilating of the cultural objects.[3]

Not only is the pattern of history the coming to expression of humanity's kingdoms and the struggle among them. Every kingdom, in turn, has an internal structure. Determinative of every *civitas* is a worldview, or *mind,* as

2. See especially Jellema's "Calvinism and Higher Education" in *God-Centered Living* (Grand Rapids: Baker, 1951).

3. Jellema, "Calvinism and Higher Education," p. 120.

Jellema was fond of calling it. He spoke especially of the mind of pagan antiquity, of the Christian mind, and of the mind of modernity. He did not claim
that every citizen of a kingdom has its formative mind as a whole clearly before him or her. His claim was rather that, if we inquire into what it is that
makes sense of the way of life of the members of a *civitas*, we discover that its
members operate with certain fundamental assumptions about reality and
life. Thus, just as a kingdom comes to expression in the cultural activities of
its members, so in turn a kingdom is itself the expression of a mind.

In turn — and here we get to the heart of the matter — the objective
mind or worldview of a *civitas* also has its own internal structure. It too is not
just an assemblage; it too has a determinative center. Every human being, according to Jellema, is forced to give some answer to the question of who God
is. Some answer in such a way that they misidentify or misdescribe God; others may be so far mistaken that they identify something other than God *as*
God. Nonetheless, everyone must give an answer, mistaken or not. The answer one gives shapes the mind with which one thinks; and this mind in turn
determines one's particular way of being-in-the-world. Or to state the point
better, since this is to put it too individualistically: the mind of a *civitas* is
shaped by its answer to the question of who God is, and this in turn shapes its
way of being-in-the-world; and an individual adopts the mind of a *civitas*,
thereby becoming its member, by accepting its idea of God. Thus Jellema remarks that "the essence of all choices, the essence of moral choice, is religious
decision. The *civitas* chosen is the continuous living expression of a man's religious faith; it is his answer, writ in large letters, to the question who God is."[4]

Education for Jellema was ultimately then always both a manifestation
of the life of some religious kingdom and an initiation into that life. "Formal
education in the schools," he wrote, "articulates the meaning and structure
of a chosen *civitas*, also when it professes neutrality; and inseparably in the
same process forms, molds, and educates the citizen in the meaning and
structure of (whichever) *civitas*. . . . Education is by a kingdom and for citizen-
ship in that kingdom."[5] Education is always religious in its import. The situation is not that the Christian educator practices committed education while
everyone else practices neutral education; ultimately everyone practices
committed education. "All formal education," says Jellema,

> even such as professes to be neutral, reflects some *civitas*. That it cannot
> escape doing so is but a phase of the fact that humankind cannot escape

4. Jellema, "Calvinism and Higher Education," p. 121.
5. Jellema, "Calvinism and Higher Education," p. 122.

answering the question who God is, and articulating the answer in life; that is to say, cannot escape religious decision and allegiance to some kingdom. . . . The difference between Christian and non-Christian education is, therefore, not that religious faith is present in the one and not in the other; the difference is between the Christian definition of God and a non-Christian definition; and is thus a difference and opposition between kingdoms.[6]

The goal of Christian education for Jellema was to initiate the student into the Christian mind. He was fond of saying that the important thing is not so much *what* one thinks as the mind *with which* one thinks. Students must be freed from the bondage of thinking with the mind of modernity and led to think with the Christian mind. To accomplish this, the educator must lead students to converse with those across the ages who have thought with the Christian mind. It is important to realize, however, that those who have thought with the Christian mind have not had a monopoly on truth. Accordingly, students in Christian colleges must also be engaged in conversation with historical representatives of alternative minds, from which they can learn and against which they must struggle.

I judge that the Christian humanist model of curriculum is one of the perennially attractive models for Christian educators when they move beyond the Christian service model. No one else has developed it with Jellema's profundity. But always the core idea will be there: the curricular goal of Christian collegiate education is to initiate students into the cultural heritage of humanity from a Christian perspective, thus freeing them from their parochialism and partiality.

Educating for Maturation or Socialization

On this occasion I can give only brief descriptions of the other models of education to be found in our colleges and in society more generally. Oakeshott discusses some of these other models under the rubric of *attacks* on education. Since he has presented the humanist model as *the proper* understanding of education, those who embrace alternatives are automatically put into the position of being opposed to education. I think this is a mistaken way of looking at the situation. Education is a social practice; and like social practices generally — painting, farming, diplomacy, and so on — the practice en-

6. Jellema, "Calvinism and Higher Education," p. 125.

dures amid considerable disputes concerning goals and considerable alteration of them. Nonetheless, what Oakeshott says is insightful.

One of the alternatives Oakeshott cites enjoys great currency in our society generally but very little in the Christian colleges. It may be called the
maturation model — my term, not Oakeshott's. Oakeshott's description is so
mischievously marvelous that I cannot refrain from quoting part of it:

> The maturationist holds that for schooling should be substituted an
> arena of childish self-indulgence from which all that might contain im-
> pulse and inclination and turn them into deliberate and knowledgeable
> choice has been purposely removed: a place where a child may be as rude
> as his impulses prompt and as busy or as idle as his inclinations suggest.
> There is to be no curriculum of study, no orderly progression in learning.
> Impulse is to be let loose upon an undifferentiated confusion called, al-
> ternatively, "the seamless robe of learning" or "life in all its manifesta-
> tions." What may be learned is totally unforeseen and a matter of com-
> plete indifference.
>
> Each child is expected to engage in such individual projects of so-
> called "experimental" activity as he feels inclined, to pursue them in his
> own way and for so long as his inclination to do it lasts. Learning is to be
> a personal "finding out" and consequently it becomes the incidental, ex-
> iguous, and imperfectly understood by-product of "discovery." To "dis-
> cover" nothing is to be preferred to being told anything. The child is to be
> shielded from the humiliation (as it is thought) of his own ignorance and
> of intellectual surprise, and sheltered in the unfrustrating womb of his
> own inclinations. Teaching is to be confined to hesitant (preferably word-
> less) suggestion; mechanical devices are to be preferred to teachers, who
> are recognized not as custodians of a deliberate procedure of initiation
> but as mute presences, as interior decorators who arrange the furnish-
> ings of an environment and as mechanics to attend to the audiovisual ap-
> paratus.
>
> "Discoveries" may become the subjects of "free" group discussions; or
> they may be written about in compositions to be esteemed, not on ac-
> count of their intelligibility, but for their "freedom" of expression. It does
> not matter how they are written so long as they are "creative": to stutter
> independently is a superior accomplishment to that of acquiring the self-
> discipline of a mother tongue.... Seeing and doing are preferred to think-
> ing and understanding: pictorial representation is preferred to speech or
> writing. Remembering, the nursing mother of learning, is despised as a
> relic of servility. (28)

Oakeshott adds that "it may be doubted whether anything exactly like this exists, even in America"!

Another model that Oakeshott discusses is what he calls, appropriately, the *socialization* model. He interprets this as coming to the fore with the emergence of nationalism, and as originally intended to make the lower classes well-functioning contributors to the welfare of the nation. Here is some of his description of it:

> After a brief but not wholly ineffective attempt to extend the opportunity of education to more of those who had not hitherto enjoyed it, this has become the most notable feature of the recent history of European "education": the enterprise of *substituting* "socialization" for education.
>
> By "socialization" . . . I mean here an apprenticeship to adult life-teaching, training, instructing, imparting knowledge, learning, etc. governed by an extrinsic purpose. The most common version of this alternative to education has been that which emerged from the efforts of rulers and others to equip the poor to make a more effective contribution to the well-being of "the nation," and which has since been elaborated into more-or-less systematic arrangements for imparting to successive generations the knowledge and the skills required to sustain the enterprises and provide the satisfactions characteristic of a modern industrial and commercial society. . . .
>
> The alternative to education, invented for the poor as something instead of virtually nothing, was designed (for the most part by politicians) as an apprenticeship to adult life which, far from offering a release from the immediacies, the partialities, and the abridgements of the local and contemporary world of the learner, reproduced this world in its already familiar terms and provided the learner with more information about what was already within his reach and with skills in which he was reckoned to be "interested" because he was already aware of them in use or in his own talents. The engagement was not to initiate him into a difficult and unfamiliar inheritance of human understandings and sentiments but to give him a somewhat firmer grasp of what he recognized to be "relevant" to himself as he was and to the "facts of life." He was not to be put in the way of understanding himself in a new context or of undergoing a palingenesis in which he acquired a more ample identity; he was merely to be provoked to see himself more clearly in the mirror of his current world. Those who promoted this alternative to education believed that its products would be "more useful members of society." (39-41)

I think there can be little doubt that this socialization model has gained a good deal of currency in the Christian colleges, no doubt especially among those who teach in professional and pre-professional programs. Indeed, the *Christian service* model, of which I spoke first, is really a version of this model, a version that focuses on a rather narrow set of occupations for which students are to be trained.

Educating for Academic Discipline

I judge that we are still missing one of the most prominent models of Christian education to be found in our colleges. In addition to the Christian humanist model and the socialization model, of which the Christian service model is a species, there is what may be called the *academic-discipline* model. On this model the goal of education is to introduce students to the academic disciplines, thereby putting them in touch with reality to the extent and in the way that theory does that — doing so, let it be immediately added, in Christian perspective. While those who favor the Christian humanist model characteristically defend their choice by stressing the importance of developing in the student a Christian mind able to engage in discourse with other minds, those who favor the Christian academic-discipline model tend to defend their preference by appealing to the cultural mandate given to humanity at creation.

Oakeshott briefly mentions the academic-discipline model of education and treats it as beginning roughly with Francis Bacon. He says, "In the doctrine of Bacon and his near contemporaries, Comenius, Hartlib, Milton, *et al.*, 'education' stands not for a transaction between the generations of human beings in which the newcomer [is] initiated into an inheritance of human understandings, sentiments, imaginings, etc., but for a release from all this in which [the student] acquires 'objective' knowledge of the workings of a 'natural' world" (31). Elsewhere Oakeshott explains that "knowledge, so the doctrine ran, derives solely from the experience of observation of 'things'; and it represents 'the empire of man over things'" (30).

This depiction of the origins of the academic-discipline model seems to me incomplete and misleading. The idea that the goal of the university is to introduce students to the sciences — *scientiae, Wissenschaften* — is much older than Bacon. It was the dominant model in the medieval European universities, and as such it is the most venerable post-antiquity model of education that we have in the West, more venerable even than the humanist model.

We now have before us the dominant curricular models to be found today in those colleges that present themselves as Christian colleges. No doubt the Christian humanist model appeals especially to those teaching in the humanities, the academic-discipline model to those teaching in the natural and social sciences, and the socialization model to those engaged in professional and pre-professional education. But each model has an appeal that goes well beyond its home base.

A Shalom Model for Collegiate Education

I have come to think that each of these models is deficient. Let me forego an analysis of what I find lacking in each of them separately in order to concentrate on what seems to me especially deficient in all of them together.

None of these models responds adequately to the *wounds* of humanity — in particular, the *moral* wounds; none gives adequate answer to our cries and tears. The academic-discipline model reminds us that the cultural mandate requires us to develop the potentials of creation by bringing forth science and art. But what about our liberation mandate to free the captives? The Christian humanist model stresses that we must be freed from our cultural particularities in order to participate as Christians in the great cultural conversation of humanity. But what about those who lack the strength to converse because they have no food in their stomachs? The Christian socialization model emphasizes that we must train our students to work as Christians within their occupational callings. But what about all those people who after searching long and hard find no occupation? Our traditional models speak scarcely at all of injustice in the world, scarcely at all of our calling to mercy and justice. I submit that the curriculum of the Christian college must open itself up to humanity's wounds.

Let me say immediately that this is not a call to abolish the teaching of the humanities, or of the natural and social sciences, or of professional education. It is not a call for a curricular model that is different from those canvassed in that it is constricted in yet a different direction from those. It is a call for a more comprehensive model — a model that incorporates the arts, the sciences, the professions, and yes, the worship and piety of humanity, along with humanity's wounds, and brings them together into one coherent whole rather than setting them at loggerheads with each other.

What might such a model be? What should be the overall goal of Christian collegiate education?

There is in the Bible a vision of what it is that God wants for God's human creatures — a vision of what constitutes human flourishing and of our appointed destiny. The vision is not that of disembodied individual contemplation of God; thus it is not the vision of heaven, if that is what one takes heaven to be. It is the vision of *shalom* — a vision first articulated in the poetic and prophetic literature of the Old Testament, but prominent in the New Testament as well under the rubric of *eirene*, peace.

There can be no shalom without justice. Justice is the ground floor of shalom. In shalom each person enjoys justice, enjoys his or her rights. If persons do not enjoy and possess what is due them, if their rightful claims on others are not acknowledged by those others, then shalom is absent.

Shalom goes beyond justice, however. Shalom incorporates right relationships in general, whether or not those are required by justice: right relationships to God, to one's fellow human beings, to nature, and to oneself. The shalom community is not merely the *just* community but is the *responsible* community, in which God's laws for our multifaceted existence are obeyed.

It is more even than that. We may all have acted justly and responsibly, and yet shalom may be missing; for the community may be lacking *delight*. A nation may be living in justice and peace with all its neighbors while its members are still miserable in their poverty. Shalom is the antithesis of this; shalom incorporates *delight* in one's relationships. To dwell in shalom is to find delight in living rightly before God, to find delight in living rightly in one's physical surroundings, to find delight in living rightly with one's fellow human beings, to find delight even in living rightly with oneself.

What is your and my relation to this appointed human destiny of shalom? What is our relation to the vision of the just and responsible community of delight? The biblical witness is clear. The vision of shalom comes to us, for one thing, as a two-part command: We are to pray and struggle for the release of the captives, and we are to pray and struggle for the release of the enriching potentials of God's creation. We live under both a liberation mandate and a cultural mandate. And the vision comes to us as a two-part invitation: We are invited to celebrate such manifestations of shalom as appear in our world, and invited to mourn shalom's shortfall.

Now for the last link: Can the Christian college do anything else than guide its endeavors by this vision of shalom? If God's call to all humanity is to be liberators and developers, celebrators and mourners; and if to that call of God the church of Jesus Christ replies with a resonant yes, then will not the Christian college have to find its place within this great commission? Of course a college is not a political action organization, or an architectural firm, or a mission board. It is a school; and it is *as a school* that the lure of shalom will direct and energize it. But given that understanding, the curricular model that I propose for Christian collegiate education is what I shall call the *shalom* model. The goal for which Christian educators are to teach is that our students be agents and celebrators of shalom, petitioners and mourners.

Curricular Implications of Shalom

Will a curriculum aimed at shalom teach the sciences? That depends on whether the knowledge of reality achieved by the sciences contributes to that mode of flourishing which the Bible calls *shalom*. No doubt it does. We are created to find fulfillment in knowledge of God and of God's world.

Will a curriculum aimed at shalom teach the arts? That depends on whether knowledge and practice of the arts contributes to that mode of flourishing which is shalom. Assuredly it does. Without art, life limps.

Will a curriculum aimed at shalom teach history? Will it teach about Periclean Athens and thirteenth-century Paris? That depends on whether historical knowledge contributes to that mode of human flourishing which is shalom. I cannot escape the conviction that it does. Where our knowledge of what it was to be human in other times and places is diminished, there our own humanity is diminished.

Will a curriculum aimed at shalom cultivate piety and teach liturgy? That depends on whether such cultivation and such learning contribute to that mode of human flourishing which is shalom. Without a doubt they do; shalom is incomplete without participation in the disciplines of piety and the liturgy of the church.

Will a curriculum aimed at shalom teach for justice? Will it present to its students the injustice and the deprivation of the world? Will it teach them to recognize those? Will it ask what if anything can be done about those wounds? Will it ask what *should* be done about them? Will it teach for liberation? I cannot escape the conviction that it will.

So I do not propose the abolition of the teaching of humanity's history; I do not propose the abolition of the teaching of humanity's art; I do not propose the abolition of the teaching of humanity's sciences; I do not propose the abolition of teaching for various occupational practices. I propose that the moral wounds of the world also find a place in our curricula, and that we ask how we ought to respond to such wounds. I propose that we adopt a shalom model for our curricula.

When I say that the moral wounds of the world must find a place in our curricula, what I mean is not just that we must teach *about* justice — though we must; I mean that we must teach *for* justice. The graduate whom we seek to produce must be one who *practices* justice. How we do that is a thick and complex matter that I cannot get into here; it will have to be the topic for some other occasion. Instead I want to address, in conclusion, one of the many objections to my proposal.

One objection to teaching for justice is that it will politicize the college, alienating it from its community and introducing conflict into the faculty. Given my own advocacy for justice for the Palestinians, I have sometimes pointedly been asked whether I think we should try to turn all our students into advocates of the right of the Palestinians to their own state. The thinly veiled point of the question, of course, is that anyone can foresee the calamitous consequences of doing that!

Note how curious this anxious question appears when seen in the context of what Christian educators do generally. Nobody thinks it is illicit for a professor of philosophy to indicate to students his conviction that Thomas Reid's philosophy is superior to David Hume's. Nobody thinks it is illicit for a professor of music to indicate to her students her conviction that Beethoven's music is superior to Boccherini's. But if someone defends the rights of the Palestinians in some course, then suddenly a plaintive plea for objectivity breaks out.

It is important to distinguish college policy from the practice of individual faculty members. No college should adopt as institutional policy that Beethoven is to be taught as superior to Boccherini as a composer, or Reid as superior to Hume as a philosopher. But we cannot leave the matter at the point of distinguishing college policy from individual practice, comfortable as that would be. For though Scripture does not present God as preferring Beethoven to Boccherini, or Reid to Hume, it does say that the cries of the poor, of the oppressed, and of the victimized touch God's heart, and it does indicate that the groans of God's created but now polluted earth bring tears to God's eyes. We are touching here not on issues of taste or judgment but on issues of right teaching, of orthodoxy. We are touching on our understanding of the nature of God. If a college is to commit itself to serving the God of the Bible, it must commit itself, as an academic institution, to serve the cause of justice in the world. I find no detour around this conclusion. The God who asks Christians to go into all the world to preach the gospel of Jesus Christ is the very same God who loves justice.

So we can and should discuss among each other effective and sensitive ways of teaching for justice. We can and should discuss among each other effective ways of opening up our students to the wounds of the world. We can and should discuss among each other effective and sensitive ways of handling the controversies that will arise when we teach for justice. But the God whom believers acknowledge in their lives and celebrate in their worship asks that we teach for justice-in-shalom. For that God is the God revealed in Jesus Christ, the Prince of Shalom. The graduate who prays and struggles for the incursion of justice and shalom into our glorious but fallen world, celebrating its presence and mourning its absence — that is the graduate the Christian college must seek to produce.

The Mission of the Christian College
at the End of the Twentieth Century

The nineteenth century was the heyday of the founding of colleges across the American Midwest and on toward the far West. Almost all of those beginnings were Christian; and of those, almost all were what you and I would recognize as either evangelical Christian or mainline confessional. What I want to do on this occasion is pick up the story at the end of the nineteenth and the beginning of the twentieth century.

Christian scholars in nineteenth-century America typically had a simple and pleasant view of the relation of scholarship to the Christian faith. They thought that scholarship, no matter who conducted it, would nicely harmonize with the Christian faith just so long as it was competent. The two fit neatly together into one harmonious whole. More than that: the nineteenth-century scholar believed that competent scholarship, in at least some of its branches, provides evidences for the truth of Christianity. Nature and history, when studied with care, provide arguments for the existence of a wise Creator and a benevolent Redeemer.

Twin Dangers: Evolution and Higher Criticism

Then two mighty hammer blows caused that reassuring edifice to totter and sway. Darwin proposed his theory of evolution, a theory that, in its claim to be able to account for biological design without a designer, seemed to many incompatible with the Christian gospel. Christians initially responded according to the established pattern. They tried to show that Darwinism was

---

This essay originally appeared in the *Reformed Journal* 33, no. 6 (June 1983): 14-18. It is reprinted here with permission.

incompetent science. Or rather, they ridiculed it with hundreds and thousands of jokes and cartoons; for they could not really show that Darwinism was incompetent, and in their hearts they knew that. By all the standards of the age, the theory of evolution was thoroughly competent science. Yet it could not be smoothly integrated with the gospel as most nineteenth-century Christians understood that.

That was trouble enough. But at the same time there arose in Germany a development that was, if anything, even more threatening. I refer to the higher criticism of the Bible. For eighteen hundred years Christians had regarded the Bible as the very speech of God. It was a word addressed to us from outside our existence. But then in the nineteenth century a body of scholars, once again, *competent* scholars, said, "Not so." The Bible is not a message from One who dwells beyond the horizon of our existence. It is the finest flowering of the human religious imagination. These scholars buttressed this vision by rubbing the noses of their readers and listeners in the humanity of the Bible. The Bible, they said, was not composed in bursts of ecstatic inspiration but stitched together from previously existing documents and traditions. It is possible to discern the stitches. Furthermore, these stitched-together documents and traditions do not fully harmonize. And in any case, they contain a number of claims that are false judged by the results of science and offensive to the enlightened moral conscience.

Design without a designer; revelation without a revealer. American evangelical Christianity went into a tailspin. It became deeply defensive. In many places it became anti-intellectual. And where it did not, its scholarship became strange, eccentric, out-of-touch. It could not cope confidently with the threats facing it. So evangelicals acted as frightened people generally act. The famous Scopes trial seemed the final blow before the darkness of bewildered consciousness descended. William Jennings Bryan, that great gladiator and three-time candidate for the presidency of the United States, entered the trial to show what fools these evolutionists be. But he was cleverly maneuvered into the witness stand and there subjected by Clarence Darrow to merciless, withering, scornful cross-examination. In the end it was he who was made to appear the fool. Five days after the trial ended, he died of exhaustion; with his death, the darkness descended.

Stages of Response: Evangelism and Culture

Though evangelical colleges did not go out of existence, they did, in effect, go underground. Probably they did not at the time have the resources to do much else. They emphasized personal piety. They stressed evangelism, especially foreign. And from the cultural heritage of the past and the cultural accomplishments of the present they carefully picked and chose, lifting out what was judged safe and placing the rest under lock and key. They sought to quarantine and inoculate their students against the cultural developments of the day. And toward society they acted ambivalently. They thought and talked of America as a Christian nation; yet they made clear that a vast number of roles in American society were unfit for their students. Education in the evangelical Christian colleges became culturally and socially disengaged.

Let me call this pattern of response, prominent in the American evangelical colleges from the beginning of the century up through the Second World War, *Stage I.* I daresay that some of you are wondering whether in describing Stage I have not drawn a caricature. At many points it sounds strange and unfamiliar to you, not to mention unattractive. Of course there were always teachers in the colleges who did not fit this pattern, teachers who opposed it, who argued against it. But these were lonely figures. The fact that you and I now find this pattern of response odd and unfamiliar is a sign not of the inaccuracy of my description but of the fact that evangelical colleges today are in a different stage, call it *Stage II.* Stage II is now in full flower. The flower opened sometime after World War II, though exactly when, is not altogether clear. Let me explain what I see as the essence of this new stage.

Think for a moment of the works of high culture that human beings have produced down through the ages: works of natural science, of philosophy, of theology, of music, of painting, of poetry, of architecture. The image that immediately comes to my mind is that of a mighty stream, ever widening as it approaches us, flowing down from the distant past. I suggest that the best way to think of liberal arts education is to think of it as education designed to enable the student to interact fruitfully with that stream of high culture. A liberal arts education enables you to appropriate some of that poetry and some of that music for your own; it enables you to understand some of that philosophy; it enables you to attain some of the comprehension offered by that science.

In my view we should not argue that the worth of this lies in making us better persons; often it does not. Neither should we argue that it is indispensable for becoming critical thinkers; there are other ways. Nor need we argue that it is indispensable for certain professions, though it is. All that need be said is that science and art enrich our lives. When science opens our eyes to the astonishing pattern of creation, and when music moves us to the depths of our being, then we experience some of the shalom that God intends for us.

Art and theory are a gift of God in fulfillment of our humanity. A life devoid of the knowledge that theorizing brings us, and of the images that art sets before us, is a poor and paltry thing, short of what God meant our lives to be.

What characterizes Stage II in the history of American evangelical colleges is that, with defensiveness largely overcome, these colleges have resolutely insisted on introducing their students to the full breadth of that stream of high culture. Quarantines have been lifted. But beyond this, they have also resolutely insisted that our appropriation of that stream be integrated with Christian faith. Faith and culture are to be united. Indeed, "integration" has become so much a buzzword that I am sometimes tempted to propose a ten-year moratorium on its use in any Christian college.

Not only has there been an insistence on the integration of faith and learning; people have come to see that scholarship itself is conducted out of differing perspectives, and that the integration of faith and learning beckoning us does not consist in tying together two things independently acquired but of practicing scholarship in Christian perspective. No longer is the guiding image the nineteenth-century image of simply adding the Christian faith to competent scholarship; competent scholarship is seen to be a pluralistic enterprise. A piece of scholarship may well be competent and yet yield results incompatible with the Christian gospel, for it may be the articulation of a perspective alien to Christianity. Accordingly, the calling of the Christian scholar is to practice scholarship in Christian perspective and to penetrate to the roots of that scholarship with which she finds herself in disagreement, along the way appropriating whatever she finds of use.

In short, what I find fascinating is that a new consensus has emerged as to the nature of scholarship and its relation to the Christian faith. That consensus is profoundly different from the consensus of our nineteenth-century forebears and has enabled us to come to grips in a non-defensive way with high culture. We are able now to see that scholarship is not merely competent or incompetent. In scholarship, as in art, we are confronted with the articulation of divergent religious perspectives. At the same time, we have learned to acknowledge that even from scholarship with which we disagree, and from art whose animating vision is foreign to us, we may receive benefit and delight.

One of the remarkable and gratifying benefits of this new stage in the history of the evangelical colleges is that alliances have been forged between evangelical colleges and confessional colleges. The confessional colleges always felt uncomfortable with the defensiveness of Stage I and with its near exclusive emphasis on personal piety and evangelism. By contrast, in Stage II we have found that we can work together, one of the results of this being that almost seventy evangelical and confessional colleges are now united in the Coalition of Christian Colleges.[1]

Furthermore, within the past ten or fifteen years Christian psychologists, historians, literary scholars, philosophers, and visual artists have all founded their own organizations and established their own journals. The members of these organizations are not dubious scholars on the fringe. Among them are some of the most prominent names in their fields. In my own field of philosophy, three of the last four presidents of the Western division of the American Philosophical Association are members of the Society of Christian Philosophers. All of this would have been inconceivable before the Second World War. To my mind it is clear evidence that we are now in a different stage.

The Next Stage: Reforming Society

Is this the final stage? Is it now the mission of the Christian college simply to do more of the same but do it even better — with more penetration, more imagination, more creativity, more courage, more self-confidence, more fidelity to the gospel of Jesus Christ? Or could it be that we are called to enter a third stage? Could it be that our mission at this point in our own history and at this point in the world's history requires us to take a large step and enter the uncertain future of a Stage III?

I think it does. What I have to say may well prove unsettling to some. Decisively to enter Stage III would be to move beyond the patterns of thought and action with which we have grown familiar without knowing exactly what we are moving toward. I cannot tell you in detail what a college in Stage III would look like; I do not have a blueprint. But I am persuaded that the issues I wish now to raise must become matters of serious and sustained discussion among us all.

One preliminary remark. Our entrance into Stage III must not be a repudiation of our concern with the cultural heritage of human beings. That concern must be incorporated into a yet richer perspective. Let us not discard what we have gained but carry it along forward.

In describing Stage II, I have spoken repetitively of *culture*. Reflect now for a moment on the fact that culture is something different from *society*. Cul-

1. This organization is now the Council of Christian Colleges and Universities (CCCU). As of 2003, there are 103 colleges in North America and 58 affiliates in 21 different countries around the world that are part of the CCCU.

ture, as I understand it, consists of *works* of culture. Society, by contrast, consists of *persons* who interact in various ways. From that interaction arise social roles, social practices, and social institutions. And though students in college may learn how to appropriate various offerings of the stream of culture, when they leave college they cannot simply appropriate culture. They have to fill certain social roles, engage with their fellows in certain social practices, participate with them in certain social institutions. My question is this: can we in the Christian colleges allow that just to take care of itself? Can we all but ignore society and concentrate on culture? Can we assume that students will somehow find out for themselves how to live as Christians in society and that they will act on what they have learned?

If all was as it should be with society, then the college could teach its students how to appropriate the stream of culture, perhaps supplementing that with some instruction relevant to some vocation, and then send them forth, confident that whatever else they needed to know would be taught them by the ambient society itself. But all is not well with society. Have you heard of the Palestinians whose hearts are aching to the point of bursting for a place they can call home and whose hearts are now filled with rage at the American-made planes and bombs that rain destruction upon them? Have you heard of the Jews who are fearful to the point of paranoia that another holocaust awaits them somewhere on the horizon? Have you heard of the more than ten million Americans who lack the fundamental dignity of work, and of the nearly thirty million people in the Western world who lack that dignity? Have you heard Charles Colson and others calling our attention to the utterly degrading conditions of life in many of our prisons? Have you heard of the sickly self-indulgence and the unbounded toleration that now characterize our Western society? Have you heard of the 17,000 nuclear warheads our country has poised to be fired, and have you heard some judging even this to be woefully inadequate? Have you also heard of the nuclear warheads poised to be fired at you and at me by the Soviet Union? Have you heard of the Poles struggling bravely to throw off the oppressive shackles of communism? Have you seen the shuddering squalor of our inner cities in which bearers of the image of God are forced to live? Have you seen and smelled the smog of Los Angeles? Have you heard that the Parthenon in Athens has decayed more in the last twenty-five years than in the preceding twenty-five hundred?

I tell you nothing new. The social world in which we find ourselves is desperately in need of re-formation. Our ears cannot be stopped, our eyes cannot be closed. Particularly not your ears and eyes, nor mine. For you and I represent the body of Jesus Christ. We are his feet and hands in the world, his heart, his mind, his voice, his eyes, his ears. We are the bearers of his word of comfort, heralds of the coming of his kingdom of peace.

We are more than heralds. We are also agents. We do the work of him who in turn did the work of his Father. We heal and we liberate. We struggle for shalom in all dimensions of human existence, realizing indeed that our efforts will not bring about the kingdom in its fullness, but knowing also that the kingdom will not come about without our efforts. We cannot let society go its own way when the way it is going is so far from the Way of the Lord.

What does this have to do with the Christian college? A great deal. The most fundamental thing to say about the Christian college is that it is an arm of the body of Christ in the world. It is of and by and for the church. It exists to equip members of the people of God for their lives as members of that people — a people that exists not for its own sake but for the sake of all humanity and thereby to the glory of God. So I am led by iron chains of argument to conclude that the Christian college cannot neglect the suffering of humanity. It cannot neglect the suffering produced by alienation from God, and it cannot neglect the suffering produced by the natural world. But neither can it neglect the suffering produced by the social world. It cannot burrow into culture while neglecting society.

You protest that the liberal arts college has no competence in this area. Is that true? To act responsibly in reforming one's society one must know the structure and dynamics of that society. Can the Christian college not provide such knowledge? To act responsibly in reforming one's society one must know the likely effects of various strategies. Can the Christian college not provide such knowledge?

So once again: we are challenged to enter a new stage. If the focus of Stage I was on piety and evangelism, and the focus of Stage II was on culture, without losing the concern for piety and evangelism, then the focus of this new stage, without losing the contribution of those earlier stages, must be on society — on *the Christian in society.*

Educational Implications

I have already said that I cannot foresee in detail what a Christian college that has entered fully into Stage III would look like. But I do have a dim picture in my mind's eye, and in that picture I think I can discern three characteristics.

Such a college will, I believe, be much more international in its concerns and consciousness than any of our colleges is at present. We do indeed live today in what McLuhan called a global village. You and I are citizens of the United States. But American influence spreads throughout the world — sometimes for good, sometimes for ill; and in turn, our society here is profoundly influenced by what happens across the globe. It is for that reason that the Christian college which enters Stage III will have to become internationalized. That it is an arm of the church is here a tremendous advantage. The church, and the church alone, is "one o'er all the earth."

Second, such a college will have to explore new ways of packaging the learning it presents to students. When our concern is simply to appropriate the stream of culture, then the relevant packages are available and familiar: physics, literary criticism, music theory, economics, and so on. But when our concern is to equip our students to reform society, then we walk in uncharted territory. Perhaps we shall need programs in peace and war, nationalism, poverty, urban ugliness, ecology, crime and punishment.

Third, such a college will have to be far more concerned than ever before with building bridges from theory to practice. Throwing some abstract political science at the student along with some abstract economics and sociology will not do the trick. The goal is not just to understand the world but to change it. The goal is not just to impart to students a Christian world-and-life-view but to equip and motivate them for a Christian way of being and acting in the world. There is not a shred of evidence that simply putting abstract theory in front of them will alter their actions.

Such talk makes us nervous. Should the Christian college really aim at shaping the social actions of its students? Is that not indoctrination? Should we not rather put the various options in front of students and let them choose? My answer is that we have never acted this way in the past. Does the Christian college not *cultivate* understanding? Does it not *cultivate* authentic piety? Can it now responsibly do anything else than cultivate peace, cultivate the dignity of the prisoner, cultivate the care of the earth, cultivate a home for Palestinians?

Internationalization, new ways of packaging, fresh strategies for bridging theory and practice, those are some of the consequences I foresee if we do indeed enter Stage III. Beyond that, I do not know. This I do know, that the church of Jesus Christ is called to be an agent of shalom in the world, and that we in the colleges must no longer be content with evasive answers when we are asked why we act so hesitantly in promoting that dimension of our mission.

Evangelicals are finally beginning to get it through their heads that we in America do not live in a Christian society. We live in a mixed, pluralistic society in which the body of those committed to Jesus Christ is just one of the components in the pluralism. At the same time — thank the Lord — we are beginning to get it through our heads that it is unworthy and disobedient for the church in this mixed society to cower in timid silence. We are beginning to recognize that the church has a liberating word to speak to that society and a healing hand to extend to it. It may not withhold that word and that hand. We are ready for Stage III.

One final matter. I have said that the task of the Christian college must never be isolated from the mission of the church. It often strikes me, however, that evangelicals do not much care for the church. They like to think of *Christians,* not of the church. And if they do think of the church, they tend to think of it as born yesterday, and of Christians around the world as waiting for what we in the Western church have to teach them. That those Christians might have something to teach us is never thought. But the church was not born yesterday. Neither was it born in the Wesleyan revival. It was not even born in the Reformation. Trace back your ancestors in Christ and you will find yourself going back beyond Wesley, back beyond the Reformation, to the Catholic church of Western Europe. And then you will find that you must go back farther yet, back to where the western Catholic Church had not parted from the Eastern Orthodox Church, back to the apostles themselves. Those long lines stretching to the very origins of the church constitute your spiritual ancestry and mine. We receive what has been handed on to us. And perhaps we have been handed more than we have been willing to receive. It may just be that not all wisdom and fidelity is ours. The Eastern Orthodox Church, as no other, has kept alive the practice of prayer and contemplation. The Catholic Church has never let go of the role of the sacraments in Christian life. The Reformers, with startling force, taught all Christendom to listen for the Word of God. And yes, the evangelical tradition, as no other, has perceived the importance of repentance and second birth.

The anxiety and defensiveness of evangelicals have begun to quiet down. As they do, I think I witness stirrings of an awareness that the church is vastly larger than evangelicals ever admitted. Perhaps, then, Stage III will prove to be not only the stage of the Christian in society but the stage of the Christian *in the church* in society.

So let us move on into the uncertainties of that most certain future of working for the coming of our Lord's kingdom of justice, peace, and love.

The Integration of Faith and Learning —
The Very Idea

Why suddenly all this talk among psychologists about the integration of faith and learning? A decade ago you would have heard little about it; two decades ago, almost nothing. Psychologists are not alone in this; Christians in all the academic disciplines have expressed the same concern. We are participants in a remarkable movement.

I submit that the fundamental reason Christians in academic scientific psychology begin to talk about the integration of faith and psychology is that, when they work in contemporary psychology, they bump up against developments that make them feel uneasy; their faith appears to them in tension with those developments. So they begin to ask: How can we get these two things together? They are not about to give up their faith; but neither are they about to give up psychology. So they ask how the tension can be released.

My thesis, in short, is that this spreading concern for integration is not the result of the writings of theorists in ivory towers. Neither is it the result of a calm concern to bring integration where previously there was peaceful but segregated coexistence. It is the result of an existential sense of tension between two things that we care about, and the desire to relieve the tension in some acceptable fashion.

Disturbing Determinism

What is it that characteristically bothers Christians about contemporary academic psychology? What is it that prompts attempts at integration? No

This essay previously appeared as "The Integration of Faith and Science — The Very Idea" in the *Journal of Psychology and Christianity* 3, no. 2 (Summer 1984). It is reprinted here with permission.

doubt a lot of different things. But speaking now as someone who surveys psychology from the outside, whose profession is that of philosopher rather than psychologist, it appears to me that if we dig beneath the surface, we usually find one or the other of two roots of tension.

Often what disturbs us about psychology is its deterministic assumptions. The model of the person that is tacitly or explicitly at work is one according to which the life of human beings is totally determined by their external environment and their internal drives. The reason this disturbs us is that it seems incompatible with both the biblical emphasis on responsibility and the biblical assumption of human creativity.

The other source of tension is that in much contemporary psychology it is assumed that if only the individual can be freed from external influence and from internal inhibitions, then that individual will blossom out into a loving, caring, healthy individual. What disturbs us about this assumption of the inherent goodness of human beings is that it seems incompatible with the biblical emphasis on sin.

These two sources of tension can seem themselves to be in tension with each other; one would guess that they are at work in different streams of contemporary psychology. Yet in such developmental theorists as Piaget and Kohlberg one finds a curious and fascinating blend of the two assumptions: we are both determined and inherently good.

If I am right in my identification of these two sources of tension, then what disturbs Christians about contemporary psychology is not little things here and there. What bothers them is that there are fundamental models of the person at work that seem alien to a Christian model of the person. In the one case, the model of the person is that of something wholly determined and hence not free and responsible in any authentic sense; in the other case, the model of the person is that of someone who would be good if he or she could be free, but who in fact finds constant impositions and constraints.

What have we typically done to ease the tension? What have we characteristically done to calm the disturbance? What have been our typical strategies of integration?

Ways of Integration: Harmonizers, Compatibilists, Delimiters

Sometimes we are persuaded on reflection that *something has to give*, that the tension we feel is caused by real conflict, and that to release it we must accordingly give something up. Often what we decide to give up so as to release the tension is some facet of our understanding of the Christian faith. We engage in what, in some of my writings, I have called *harmonizing*: we revise our understanding of the faith so as to harmonize it with our scientific convictions. I well remember the Christian philosopher who introduced a talk on these matters by remarking that since determinism was a standard assumption of the human sciences, and since Christians should not allow themselves to be forced into beating a hasty retreat as they have so often done in the past, he would explore ways of construing the Christian faith along deterministic lines. That was a flamboyant example of harmonizing. In the same way, someone would be engaged in harmonizing if, after observing that a standard assumption of contemporary human science is that the individual is potentially good, and would in fact be good if freed from baleful influence, he or she undertook to reinterpret the Christian faith so that it taught nothing in conflict with this. In all such cases it is assumed that there really is conflict, that something must give, and that it is the understanding of the faith that must give. Harmonizing is one familiar strategy of integration.

An obvious alternative is to assume that nothing has to give in either science or faith, that the tension proves, upon close analysis, not to be based on real conflict. We do not have to revise our faith in any significant way, nor do we have to revise our psychology. What has to be revised is the belief that there is a genuine conflict. An illusion must be eliminated.

This strategy comes in various versions. One version is what Stephen Evans has called *compatibilism*.[1] The compatibilist says there is no problem. Human behavior is entirely determined; but we are also responsible and free. These are both true, two truths, if you will; a bit of mystery here perhaps, but no real contradiction. Or if the other assumption is in the forefront of attention, the compatibilist says that the root of evil is that the innocent individual is in one way or another "put upon"; if she were not, she would blossom forth in love and charity. On the other hand, it is also true that there are within us dark impulses of hostility. Two truths, mysterious that they should both be true; but so it is. When doing science we speak as scientists; when engaged in religious activities we speak as religious people. These are simply two languages, each with its own vocabulary, speaking about one complex reality; difficulty arises only if we try to mingle the languages.

Most of us do not rest easy with compatibilism. We do not relish mysteries very much, at least not those we suspect to be mysteries of our own making. Accordingly, most of those who are convinced that the felt tension has no solid basis in fact seek to release it in a different way, namely, by insisting that the *scope* of psychology and the *scope* of faith both be limited so as to

1. See Evans, *Preserving the Person* (Downers Grove, Ill.: InterVarsity Press, 1977).

prevent them from getting into each other's hair. They follow the strategy of *delimitation*. Psychologists, they say, do indeed discover that we are creatures of stimulus and response; they do indeed discover that our actions are determined by our environment and by our inner drives. We need not suppose, however, that this is true for *all* our actions; nothing in psychology proper shows that. Any psychologist who generalizes in that fashion is going beyond the proper scope of psychology. In addition to the realm of determination there is a realm of freedom: nothing that psychologists have discovered should lead us to think otherwise. So too, psychology does indeed show us that if we free people from the bondage of internal inhibition and external influence, allowing them to grow and mature naturally, love will flow forth; but we need not suppose that this is true across the board. If psychologists claim that it is, they are going beyond their competence as psychologists and speaking as philosophers. There is more to human existence than what psychology informs us of. It is in this "more" that we come up against the dark fact of sin.

These are the strategies of the *delimiters*. They delimit the scope both of psychology and of Christian faith. They suggest that when we discern the proper scope of psychology and the proper scope of faith, our feelings of tension are released. Nothing in science or faith has to be given up so as to release the tension; only something in our *understanding* of them, specifically, in our understanding of the proper scope of their claims.

These are the three main strategies that Christian scholars have followed for the practice of integration: that of the *harmonizers,* who insist that something has to give in our understanding of the faith, and those of the *compatibilists* and *delimiters,* both of whom insist that nothing has to give except our conviction that there is real conflict. I judge that it is the delimiters who are today in the majority. I could not count the number of times Christian psychologists have said to me that there is no problem in accepting radical behaviorism provided we do not follow Skinner in thinking that it applies to everything. When Skinner goes off into making universal claims, he is no longer speaking as a psychologist but as a philosopher!

To my mind, this response of the delimiter is mindless. It may be true that some of our actions are conditioned in exactly the manner that Skinner understands operant conditioning to work and that others of our actions are not. It may be true that sometimes when we remove inhibitions and domination from some aspect of a person's life, that aspect of her life begins to flower without this being true across the board. However, if you as a psychologist say that operant conditioning as Skinner understands it holds for some human behavior but not for all, *and do not then go on to give a more comprehensive theory which explains that remainder, which points out the borderline between the two, and which shows how this remainder fits with that area where conditioning works,* then this response of delimitation is empty of theoretical content. Until you provide that more comprehensive theory, people will try to make use of Skinnerian theory across the board; for you have given them nothing else either for thought or research.

Albert Bandura has earned the theoretician's right to say that Skinner's operant conditioning theory applies only to a certain area of human life because he has proposed a more comprehensive theory that both provides a limited place for operant conditioning, as Skinner understands it, and offers a theoretical account of very much of the rest of human behavior as well. Furthermore, Bandura's alternative theory has suggested to him a host of fruitful and suggestive research projects. By contrast, the Christian delimiter who says that the Christian cannot accept Skinner's claim that his theory applies to all human behavior, but that otherwise there is no conflict, gives no suggestions whatsoever as to alternative research programs. We know what sort of research will be undertaken by this individual; it will be Skinnerian operant conditioning research.

What I mean to suggest is that the delimitation strategy for integration comes to nothing unless it is backed up by an alternative *psychological model* of the person that is more comprehensive than either the determinist model or the self-realizationist model. I am suggesting, in turn, that that model will come to nothing, will not even be a *psychological* model, unless it actually suggests theories to us and is supported and implemented by a research program. The model must at the same time be faithful to the biblical vision; for if it is not, then, though we may have a psychological model, we do not have a *Christian* psychological model.

My own profession, as I mentioned, is that of philosopher. With respect to psychology, I have done nothing more than dip into it. The deepest dip I took occurred when I was writing my book, *Educating for Responsible Action*. The question addressed in the book was how we can effectively and responsibly shape how students and others act. In order to answer the question I pored through whatever psychological literature I could find that was relevant to the topic. In pursuing this literature, I found several different psychological models of the person at work. I found none that I could embrace as a Christian; all seemed to me deficient in that regard. So I felt I had no choice but to use a theological-philosophical model of the person and pick and choose, in terms of that model, among the results reported in the psychological literature, hoping to arrive at a coherent picture. What I needed, but did not have, was a psychological model that was faithful to the theological model but went beyond it by actually giving a comprehensive theory of psychological dynamics, founded on and suggestive of a program of research. I am not aware that anything of that sort has yet emerged.

Integration through Psychological Revisionism: Responsible Agency

I have suggested that in much of psychology there is a deterministic model of the person at work, and that in a good deal of the rest of psychology there is a self-realization model at work. I have further suggested that the Christian must struggle toward the formulation of an alternative model that is both biblically faithful and is genuinely a psychological model, in that it comprises theories which are supported by and suggestive of research projects. Let me now bring out the assumption that lies beneath this recommendation. Our Christian faith should function as guide and critic in our practice of psychology and other disciplines. Sometimes when there is a felt tension between psychology and Christian faith, the tension is genuine, and what should give way is not our understanding of the Christian faith but our psychological convictions. Sometimes the struggle toward integration should take the form of *psychological revisionism*. Sometimes the Christian is right to be bothered in a deep way by developments in psychology. Sometimes what he or she should do in response is struggle to reconstruct psychology, allowing Christian conviction to function as what I called, in my book *Reason within the Bounds of Religion*, "control beliefs."

Consider again that Christian philosopher who pointed to the felt tension between the determinism of the contemporary psychologist's model of persons and the traditional Christian understanding of persons. My response to this felt tension was the opposite of his. I agreed that something has to give; but what should give is not the faith but the psychology. For as a Christian, I am persuaded that we are free and responsible agents before God and our fellows. What is there in contemporary psychology that forces me to buckle under at this point? Has it proved its deterministic claims? Where are the proofs? What are the deterministic laws? It is psychology, not my faith, which must be reformed at the point of tension.

Many Christian scholars are reluctant to follow this advice. They are reluctant to *practice* psychology in Christian perspective, preferring instead to *look* at psychology, as customarily practiced, in Christian perspective, thus to construct what might be called *a theology of psychology*. Why the reluctance to make our faith rather than our psychology determinative?

One reason is that many of us in the twentieth century who are Christians do not see the world through biblical eyes. In some abstract way we hold to the tenets of the Christian faith; but our faith is non-operative when we actually think about, and deal with, human beings. Other frameworks of conviction shape our vision and our practice. Our faith, whatever it may be, is not for us a way of seeing human reality.

There is also the longing for professional prestige and the sense of intimidation that often accompanies that. Christian scholars feel intimidated by the members of their profession. If you want to gain professional prestige, you have to go along with the academic consensus and make your peace with that. This psychological factor of intimidation must not be discounted in explaining why many Christian psychologists feel nervous and reluctant in the face of my advice.

There is a third reason for uneasy feelings when I talk about the gospel functioning as critic and guide, a third reason for feeling uneasy when I say that one's Christian convictions should function as control beliefs in one's practice of psychology. Following this advice sounds like inserting faith where it does not belong. We work with a certain vision of science and of the proper business of the scientist according to which one's faith is simply irrelevant to the proper conduct of a science. Let me explore briefly this particular understanding of a true science by going back to the French Renaissance philosopher Descartes, who formed our modern understanding of knowledge, rationality, and science.

Cartesian Science

Descartes was impressed with the diversity of human opinion. Reflecting on his education in one of the best schools of France, he highlighted the fact that his teachers disagreed with each other. A twentieth-century student would have reveled in this diversity. Descartes, by contrast, was persuaded that it was the indication of something amiss in his education. What was amiss was that the sciences had not yet been set on their proper foundation.

Do you see what a fateful assumption this was? Descartes was assuming that a true science will gain the consensus of all rational persons, and that it will gain that consensus not in some eschatological future but right here and now and every step of the way. True science is consensus science. Descartes's vision was that in the midst of this enormous diversity of human opinion it is possible to erect a great tower — that's the image that comes to my mind — on the foundation of rational consensus, a tower to which each of us can add our own small brick, a tower that from generation to generation will show progress, a tower from which all personal idiosyncrasy has been eliminated and which is objective, impartial, and consensual.

Let me go on to list five other assumptions that Descartes made, as-sumptions equally as influential as the first. Descartes assumed, second, that there are within us common shared capacities for the acquisition of knowl-edge; and that if we use these in the right way we will achieve the consensus needed for science. Method is of prime importance. Third, in mathematics and mathematical physics, scientists are already using the right method; in these sciences there is already, for the most part, the desired consensus. These sciences thus are paradigms of rationality. Fourth, to find out the proper method for using our knowledge-acquiring capacities, we should ex-tract from mathematics and physics the method there in use and employ this method across the board. Fifth, the proper method is axiomatic, starting with certitude. Others, later, would relax Descartes's rigorism and allow in-ductive reasoning; but all would share Descartes's lust for grounding our sci-entific beliefs in certitude. And sixth, science properly conducted will never conflict with the Christian faith. As a corollary, to insert one's faith into the process of building up a science is to pollute that process with the very diver-sity and lack of consensus that we are struggling to eliminate. We must prac-tice methodological atheism.

This cluster of Cartesian assumptions has been profoundly formative of our way of thinking about theorizing. Why has psychology been so much in the grip of the model of the physical sciences? Because we have adopted Descartes's conviction that in those sciences we are in the presence of the fin-est flowering of human rationality. Is there not consensus in these sciences? It must be, then, that here the right method has been found. Why have we thought that in the practice of the sciences we have to keep faith out? Because we have adopted Descartes's conviction that the project of science is a con-sensus project — a here-and-now consensus, not an eschatological consen-sus. In the sciences one confines oneself to what any rational person would accept. The Christian faith most emphatically does not satisfy that condition.

Beyond the Cartesian Picture: Popper, Kuhn, Marx

When we confront contemporary academic psychology with this Cartesian picture of a true science, we feel dissonance between the picture and the ac-tuality. The picture tells us that between science responsibly conducted and faith properly understood, there will never be conflict. Yet we feel tension. The thing to notice, however, is that most of us resolve the felt tension without giving up the Cartesian picture. If we are harmonizers, we revise our understanding of the Christian faith; we conclude that we must have understood it incorrectly at some point. If we are compatibilists, we say that everything is in order as it is. If we are delimiters, we say that we must have drawn mistaken conclusions about the scope of extant theories or about the scope of faith. Our image of science remains that of a consensus enterprise. Faith does not gain so much as a handhold within it.

This whole Cartesian picture of genuine science has come under powerful attack in the last twenty-five years. Let me quickly sketch some of the developments. Karl Popper has argued that science proceeds neither in deductive nor inductive fashion. It matters not at all, says Popper, how you get your theories, whether by induction or whatever; what matters is only whether or not your theories have been falsified. If they have not been falsified, you are entitled to hold on to them whether or not other scientists happen to agree with you. Consensus, as Popper sees it, is at best an eschatological hope rather than an initiating insistence. Various followers of Popper, such as Imre Lakatos, have gone beyond their master to point out how slithery even is the notion of falsification. Strictly speaking, theories are rarely falsified. What rather happens is that anomalies turn up which force one into making increasingly ad hoc qualifications if one is to hang onto the theory, but rarely force one to give it up. The full picture that emerges from the Popper school is that the rationality at work in science is very different from what the Cartesian tradition thought it was; Lakatos has gone so far in repudiating the consensus vision as to say that science advances by way of a plurality of tenaciously held-to theories.

Another line of thought comes from such as Kuhn and Feyerabend, who argue that what often happens, even in such paradigm sciences as mathematics and physics, is not rational by anyone's understanding of rationality. Non-rational shifts in paradigm occur; and worse yet, just plain old-fashioned stubbornness, jealousy and rhetorical persuasiveness. Whatever may have yielded consensus in these sciences, one cannot simplistically say that it was rationality working at its highest pitch.

And all the while that these new theories and analyses of science have been emerging, physics and mathematics have themselves been on the move into dark and bewildering terrain. New and profoundly perplexing developments have taken place right within them.

The Marxists have also had their say, arguing that our faculties for the acquisition of belief and knowledge are not the common property of humanity, neutral and impartial, but are corrupted and polluted by our social situations. Psychologists of all sorts have argued that even perception is polluted by beliefs and expectations, not to mention indigenously human distortions of our sensory mechanisms. Continental thinkers have insisted that the physical sciences must not be taken as the paradigm for all science since, while their goal is nomological explanation, the goal of the human sciences is something quite different, namely, interpretation resulting in understanding (*Verstehen*). And lastly, philosophers have argued that Cartesian foundationalism is untenable either as a theory of knowledge or of rationality.

Positive Pluralism

For all these and yet more reasons, the Cartesian picture of science has collapsed in the last quarter century. We live and work in the midst of the wreckage. No comprehensive picture has yet emerged to take its place. I too am not able to offer a comprehensive picture, though I think I do see what has to be said of a number of issues. Let me mention just one of those.

I think that as we struggle to form a new image of science, we shall have to give up the vision of science as a consensus enterprise other than in some ultimate eschatological sense. We shall have to give up the notion that one must limit oneself to saying what every rational person would agree on. We must instead see science as the articulation of a person's view of life, in interaction, of course, with the world and with one's fellows. Did Skinner win consensus on his deterministic model of the person before he set about doing his research in that framework? Did Carl Rogers win consensus on his self-realization model before he began his work? Of course not. We have to start taking seriously the actual pluralism of the academy and stop overlooking or excusing it. The traditional assumption was that pluralism in the academy is proof that things were going wrong, that at least one of us was not acting in fully rational fashion — not rightly using the right methods. We shall have to discard this picture. The responsible pursuit of science does not yield consensus but pluralism; we human beings *see* things differently, without that fact itself being the sign of irrationality on anyone's part. The central beliefs with which we each unavoidably operate do not enjoy consensus.

My plea is that in this pluralism of the academy the Christian psychologist occupy his or her rightful place. Occupy it as a Christian who sees the world in the light of the gospel; but occupy it also as a psychologist, not as one who surveys the scene from outside and now and then makes some clucking noises. Occupy it as one who participates in the nitty-gritty of actual psychological explorations. Do not just be a critic. Be a creative initiator, faithful in both your thinking and your doing to the gospel of Jesus Christ.

On the Idea of a Psychological Model
of the Person That Is Biblically Faithful

Sometimes when Christians study contemporary psychology their experience is that of illumination. They have the sense of genuinely noticing things about the psychic dimension of human beings that they had not noticed before. Sometimes their experience is that of confirmation. Psychology gives support to what they already believed. But sometimes they experience tension. What the psychologist says appears to conflict with what they hold as Christian believers. Sometimes this felt tension occurs at a relatively superficial level. Perhaps the psychologist makes some claim about the dynamics operating in some group of believers that does not ring true to the ears of the Christian; nothing much within psychology hangs on whether the claim is true or false. Sometimes, by contrast, the felt tension occurs at a deep level: one of the items yielding tension is deep in the scheme of Christian belief and the other is deep in the scheme of psychology.

It is important for Christians to acknowledge the first of these points, that sometimes psychology provides illumination, and to do so ungrudgingly. Christians all too often talk as if this does not happen; they construct theological schemes according to which it could not happen, or give the clear impression that they much prefer that it not happen. Such behavior is unworthy, failing to acknowledge with gratitude the work of the Spirit where in fact it occurs. Yet I think that if we want clarity on the relationship of Christianity to psychology, it is all in all more important to meditate on the points of felt tension than on the points of felt illumination. These, especially, illumine the *structure* of the relationship.

This essay previously appeared in *Christian Approaches to Learning Theory,* volume 2: *The Nature of the Learner,* edited by Norman de Jong (Lanham, Md.: University Press of America, 1985), pp. 1-19. It is reprinted here with permission.

Resolving Conflict between Psychology and Christian Belief

How should Christians respond when tension is felt between their Christian belief and what some reputable psychologist claims? The first thing they ought to do is try to determine whether the felt tension is based on real conflict. Sometimes it is not; the conflict is only apparent. On first blush it appears that my Christian belief is in conflict with what some reputable psychologist is claiming; but once I get clear on what I believe and on what he or she is claiming, I see that there is no conflict. The felt tension disappears. Of course it may take a very long time before one is satisfied that one has gotten firm enough hold of what, on the one hand, one believes, and of what, on the other hand, the psychologist is claiming, to determine whether there is or is not real conflict.

Compatibilism and Harmonization

Though sometimes the clarification process yields the conclusion that the apparent conflict is not real, sometimes it yields the conclusion that the conflict is very real indeed. What do Christians do when they find themselves in that situation? Well, some take the path of saying that nothing has to give, a position which has come to be known as *compatibilism*; others claim that something does indeed have to give on one side or the other.

To be frank, I do not understand compatibilism. Or to put my point more precisely: there is no view which I grasp such that it might appropriately be called compatibilism and also sensible people might hold it. I know, of course, how those who hold this view talk. Nowadays they regularly appeal to Wittgenstein's notion of language-games. In the situation envisaged we are presented with two different language games, the language game of Christian belief and the language game of contemporary psychology. Each of these games has its own integrity and its own utility; it would be inappropriate to silence either. But the two games cannot be mingled, nor can they be transcended. So when in Jerusalem, you talk as the Jerusalemites do; and when in Athens as the Athenians do. There may be jarring differences between these two dialects. The Jerusalemites may regularly speak of human beings as free and responsible while the Athenians regularly talk about laws of nature holding for human beings that fully account for what they do. But it would be inappropriate to try to get either party to cease talking as it does. These are two different ways of speaking of the one reality which confronts us, and both have their utility. If in *one single* game one said both that human beings are free and that causal laws fully explain their actions, that would spell trouble. But so long as these two modes of speech occur in two different language games — no problem.

This, I say, is how those talk who hold that neither side has to give so as to relieve the tension; what has to give is only the *view* that something has to give. But suppose you come down, where I do, and think that something on one side or the other does have to give. What then are the options available?

One option is to revise your Christian belief so as to eliminate the conflict. On various occasions I have called this strategy *harmonizing:* you can bring your Christian convictions into harmony with psychology by revising your Christian convictions so as to eliminate the conflict. Sometimes Christians have executed the harmonizing strategy in so radical a fashion that no conflict could ever possibly arise. They have revised their Christian beliefs so thoroughly that belief-content is entirely sucked out and all that remains are certain attitudes toward the world and certain values. I myself think that so radical a harmonization is no longer a revision of Christian belief but a departure from it.

Delimitation

The alternative to harmonizing is, of course, to move in the other direction and give up one or another of one's scientific convictions. One version of this — all in all the most conservative in that it requires fewest revisions — is worth singling out for special attention simply because it is so popular among Christian psychologists. The version I have in mind is the strategy of *delimiting.* One tries to resolve the conflict by giving the scientific theory a narrower scope than was originally assigned to it, narrow enough to avoid all conflict — or so one hopes. One *delimits* the scope of the theory. Perhaps one feels that the behaviorist claims made by B. F. Skinner in *Beyond Freedom and Dignity* conflict with certain claims of Christianity. One resolves the conflict by saying that though conditioning, as understood by Skinner, does indeed apply to some of human life, it does not apply to all; and in particular, it does not apply to those areas where the Christian wants to say that freedom is present. Skinner was illicitly extrapolating from some to all. Perhaps at the point of extrapolation he was no longer even speaking as a competent psychologist but had allowed himself to slip out of psychology into the speculative musings characteristic of philosophers!

I think that delimitation is sometimes exactly the strategy that ought to be followed in the face of conflict, as, indeed, harmonizing is sometimes the strategy that ought to be followed. Just as sometimes our actual Christian belief diverges from authentic Christian commitment, with the result that harmonizing is appropriate, so too, in the excitement of new ideas, people sometimes illicitly extrapolate the scope of scientific theories. Nonetheless, delimitation *all by itself* seems to me a mindless strategy. It may be true that some of our actions are conditioned in exactly the manner that Skinner understands operant conditioning to work, and that others of our actions are not thus conditioned, or not conditioned at all. But if you as a psychologist say that operant conditioning, as Skinner understands it, holds for some human behavior though not for all, and do not then go on to develop a more comprehensive theory that theoretically accounts for the remainder, that points out the borderline between the two, and that explains how the conditioned fits together with the unconditioned into one human being, this response of delimitation is empty of theoretical content. Until you provide such a more comprehensive theory people will try to make use of Skinnerian theory across the board; for you have given them nothing else.

What I mean to suggest is that the delimitation strategy comes to nothing unless it is backed up by an alternative psychological model of the person along with an accompanying body of theories. And I mean to suggest, in turn, that that model will come to nothing in the field of psychology, will not even truly be a *psychological* model, unless it actually suggests theories and is actually supported and implemented by a research program. Lastly, I assume that the Christian is bound to struggle to make the model he or she composes faithful to what God teaches us in the Scriptures.

Called to construct a psychological model and body of theories faithful to what God teaches us in the Scriptures: some of you will have smelled out that that was the point at which I wished to arrive. Sometimes, when confronted with conflict between one's Christian beliefs and the claims and assumptions of psychology, one ought to stick with one's Christian beliefs and give up those claims and assumptions of psychology. One ought to give them up because they conflict with what, so far as one can tell, God teaches us in the Scriptures, and because — not unrelated — there is no decisive evidence in favor of them. Sometimes this giving up of psychological claims and assumptions occurs at a relatively superficial level. Perhaps all one has to give up is a proposed application of a certain psychological theory. But sometimes what has to be given up is fundamental. One has to give up one of the basic theories; or one has to give up large elements of that psychological model of the person which the theory presupposes.

Suppose that such surrendering puts one in the position of being without a theory concerning some dimension of human existence, perhaps even in the position of being without an adequate psychological model of the person. What then does one do? Well, if one is a psychologist, one tries to develop an alternative model of the person and an alternative theory — this time, a model and theory faithful to the biblical witness. One uses one's acceptance of the contents of the biblical witness as control over one's construction of an alternative psychological model and theory. It is my own view that the most urgent challenge facing Christian psychologists today is the construction of a psychological model that is biblically faithful, a model which is in that sense a *Christian* psychological model; and of developing a body of theories that describe and explain the various processes and dynamics of the person as understood on that model. I say this because it seems to me that the conflict is very deep indeed between standard psychological models and theories, on the one hand, and what God teaches us, on the other.

Psychological Models

Some of you are ready to ask what I mean by a *psychological model*. I cannnot on this occasion identify and delineate for you the psychological dimension of reality. Not only would doing so distract me from my main purpose here; I do not in fact know how to identify and delineate with rigor this dimension of reality. However, most of us do come with some intuitive feeling for what belongs to this dimension of reality; for our present purposes, that will be quite sufficient.

As to what I mean by a *model,* I can and should offer some explanation. A *model* of something is a *way of conceptualizing* that thing. A model of the atom is a way of conceptualizing the atom; a model of the person is a way of conceptualizing the person. And a *psychological* model of the person is a way of conceptualizing the psychological dynamics, processes, and mechanisms of the person. Given such a model, psychologists try to *describe* in detail how those processes work, and at some points, to *explain* how they work. They try, in short, to discover a body of theories which detail and perhaps explain the psychological processes of the person when conceived on that model. If the model and the theories are truly psychological, they will interact with competing models and theories in the field of psychology, illuminating for us just where those models and theories are mistaken and why. The theologian also tries to construct a model of the person. But a theological model of the person, though intimately connected with a Christian *psychological* model, is yet something different. The concepts it uses are different; and it does not interact directly with alternative psychological models. If one has only a theological model of the human person, one does not yet know just where the radical behaviorist model of the person holds and where it does not, nor *why* it holds where it does and *why* it does not hold where it does not. A Christian psychological model, when paired with accompanying theories, *would* answer such questions.

Unless I have been looking in all the wrong places, I find that even those psychologists who want to take the biblical witness with full seriousness have not done much by way of what I am calling for. They have done other things, often worthwhile; but not this. I find them, for example, taking parts of extant psychological models and theories and using them to do research in the psychology of religion. But Christian psychologists, while not neglecting the psychology of religion, will not make it the center of their attention. Rather they will seek to illuminate *the whole person* for us. Again, I find Christian psychologists lodging theological objections against extant psychological models and theories. There is nothing wrong with this; it is, in fact, an important preliminary to what I am calling for. But this does not yet give us an alternative model and body of theories. Again, Christian psychologists construct theological models of the person. No doubt this helps us in the task of allowing the biblical witness to exercise a controlling function over our formation of psychological models and theories. But as I have already indicated, a theological model is not yet a psychological model. It does not detail for us the workings of psychological processes. Again, there are Christian psychologists who elaborate for us the *biblical* model of the person — or perhaps I should say, a biblical model, for we should not assume that we find just one model of the person in the Bible. In recent years the favorite way of doing this has been by conducting biblical word studies. About this project of describing biblical models of the person, one thing worth noting is that it is different from, and in some ways less important than, the formulation of a theological model. For I take it that the authority of Scripture pertains to what God *teaches* us therein, not to everything assumed therein; and it seems to me clear that not all the details of the ancient Semitic models of the person which are assumed in the Bible are taught us by God. What we need is a sorting out of the authoritative from the non-authoritative; and this, as I see it, is exactly what we try to do in constructing a theological model. Thus the description of biblical models is, as it were, two steps removed from what I am calling for when I call for a Christian psychological model.

Again, I am not calling for the integration of theology and psychology, as that is customarily understood. Those who call for integration usually want to know how the discipline of psychology relates to theology. But I am not now calling for a discussion on what these two disciplines have to do with each other. I am calling for the practice of psychology in Christian perspective. I am calling for the study of the psychological dimension of human existence as seen through the eyes of the Christian. That will leave us with the two distinct disciplines of psychology and theology, whose relation to each other we can then discuss; but it will not leave us with a person's Christian belief and his practice of psychology as two things that need integrating. They will be wound together more tightly than any integration can achieve.

There is one side of me which says loudly and insistently that I ought to stop right here and say no more. What I as a Christian philosopher can do is set before you the concept of practicing psychology in Christian perspective, with the goal of constructing a psychological model and body of theories faithful to the biblical witness. I can set before you the challenge that this, above all, is what needs doing in your field. But I cannot do it. For I am not a psychologist, only a philosopher; and only a person who is both a psychologist widely versed in the field of contemporary and historical psychology and a committed Christian can do what I am calling for. Since I am not the former of these, I should stop and let you carry on from here.

Perhaps, though, there is something more that I as a philosopher can do. A Christian psychological model of the person will overlap with, though also go beyond, a Christian *philosophical* model. Perhaps then I can call your attention to some elements in that overlap that will be helpful and suggestive for you. Let me say, though, that even when it comes to this overlap, I do not think that the thing needed is philosophers giving hortatory speeches to psychologists. What is needed is back-and-forth conversation. For example, I will be speaking of *desires*; that is part of my model of the person, part of my way of conceptualizing the person when I am dealing with philosophical matters — as indeed it is one of the concepts we all use in everyday conversation. But it may well be that one of the things you have to say to me is that the category of desires, for the psychologist, is well nigh useless. Perhaps it simply will not bear the weight that you, as a theorist in psychology, would have to place on it. If so, then I as a philosopher have to engage in some reassessment. It may be that I will eventually decide that for philosophical purposes I cannot do without the concept. But whether or not I come to that conclusion, at least I shall want to rethink my model, and if at all possible, bring our two models into full harmony on this point.

An Alternative Psychological Model of the Human Person

Let me not skirt the edges of our topic but head straight to the center, to one of the points where I and a good many other reflective Christians feel the tension between Christianity and contemporary psychology most acutely. Christianity teaches that we are responsible agents before God. It teaches that this is intrinsic to our very status as human persons. We are made of dust; but at the same time we, these dusty creatures, are graced by God with responsibilities. We are given an office, a mandate, with respect to the world, with respect to each other, and with respect to God. This is definitive of our uniqueness amidst our fellow earthlings.

Now so far as I can see, if one is responsible for what one has done, then one's action is not fully to be explained in terms of causal laws. One acted, or could have acted, "under the aspect of the good," as the medievals described it. Or as most contemporaries would say, one acted, or could have acted, for a reason. And acting for a reason, or under the aspect of the good, is just a different thing from one's actions being causally determined. Furthermore, it is my view — though the matter is controversial — that if we are capable of acting for a reason, or under the aspect of the good, then sometimes at least we could have acted otherwise than we did. In specific situations there may be factors that make it impossible to have acted otherwise, even though we did act under the aspect of the good; but that will not be true in general.

Determinism Rejected

To get to the other pole of the tension to which I wish to call attention, we must note that a great deal of contemporary psychology is committed to what I shall call *comprehensive determinism*: committed, so far as I can see, not in the weak sense that comprehensive determinism is a philosophical interpretation laid on the data after the research has been conducted, but committed in the strong sense that comprehensive determinism enters at a fundamental point into that model of the person which guides the thought and research of psychologists. A full treatment of the topic would explore whether I am right about this, whether comprehensive determinism does indeed enter in this intimate and essential way into contemporary psychology. Here I shall have to forgo such an exploration. It will be important, though, for me to explain what I have in mind by *comprehensive determinism*.

Determinism is a thesis about the future for any given moment. At any given moment there are many different ways the world *could* go henceforth, in the sense of *ontologically* could. The determinist holds that only one of those ontological possibilities is a physical and psychological possibility. All the others are physical or psychological impossibilities, violating laws of nature. The laws of nature coupled with the actual past of our world fully determine the future. Given the actual past of our world plus the laws of nature, all but one future is physically and psychologically impossible. That is the thesis of determinism. And *comprehensive* determinism says that those laws of nature fully expain human action; there is nothing more to be said about human action that would count as an explanation.

It's easy now to see where the trouble lies. The comprehensive determinist holds that there are causal laws that fully account for human action, and that there is nothing else to be said about them that would also count as an account. The Christian holds that we are responsible creatures, and that this implies that we are capable of acting under the aspect of the good — that is, capable of doing something *because* one judges it is the right thing to do. It is my view that this in turn implies — though let me say once again that the matter is controversial — that sometimes at least one could have acted otherwise, that it was physically and psychologically possible not to have done what one did. That is to say, one could have acted otherwise without some law of nature being violated. And that obviously implies, in turn, that the laws of nature plus the actual past do *not* fully determine the future. Not everything falls under the sway of laws of nature — in particular, certain human actions do not.

Now suppose we agree that God teaches us that we are responsible agents; then the proper solution of this conflict does not lie in giving up the conviction that we are responsible agents. Suppose we also agree that responsibility implies that one had it in one's power to act under the aspect of the good. Then what must be given up is comprehensive determinism; for then an explanation can be given for one's action that is not a causal explanation. And if acting under the aspect of the good implies that it was possible sometimes to have acted otherwise, then determinism as such must be given up.

What ripple-effect in psychology will our surrender of comprehensive determinism have? What revisions will be required? So far as I can tell, most Christians who have reflected on the matter tacitly or explicitly assume that very little revision is required. They hold that psychologists have misconstrued their actual enterprise. Their actual results do not support the philosophical tenet that comprehensive determinism is true, nor does their practice require the *assumption* that it is true. Consider, for example, this passage from a recent essay by Stephen Evans:

... it is erroneous that psychologists must assume the truth of universal determinism to carry on their business. Psychologists do not have to assume there are determining causes for all behavior in order to look for what determining causes there are. One does not need and cannot get a guarantee of success in order to try to do something. The rejection of *determinism* still leaves psychology free to investigate human behavior in any manner it wishes, to discover the actual degree to which human behavior is constrained. Moreover, the regularities which psychologists discover are invariably probabilistic and statistical in character. The existence of such regularities neither presupposes nor implies determinism. If human agents are some times rational in their behavior, their behavior might be regular and predictable to a high degree without being mechanistically determined. Such behavior may also be explainable in terms of the agent's beliefs and desires, even if we are not able to formulate any regularities.[1]

Evans's conclusion from these eminently correct points is that it is purely gratuitous for the psychologist to be a (comprehensive) determinist. His argument is that one does not have to assume (comprehensive) determinism in order to practice psychology; one can look for what *is* causally determined in human action without assuming that everything is causally determined or that causal explanation is the only acceptable mode of explanation. And conversely, the existence of such regularities as the psychologist discovers is fully compatible with indeterminism. Hence nothing interior to psychology needs to change if we give up the assumption of (comprehensive) determinism.

My response is that though the points Evans' makes do indeed show that comprehensive determinism is a gratuitous assumption on the part of psychologists, unnecessary for the practice of their discipline, it does not follow that nothing has to change other than giving up the gratuitous assumption. For when one looks at the *model* that psychologists have of the human being, their way of conceptualizing the human person, a huge gap of incompleteness is left if one removes the assumption of comprehensive determinism, and a huge gap of inexplicability is left if one removes the assumption of determinism per se. That is why such observations as Evans makes have relatively little impact on most psychologists. It is true that regularities do not establish determinism, and it is true that one can look for such determinations as there are without assuming that everything is determined. Yet remove the

---

1. Evans, "Must Psychoanalysis Embrace Determinism?" *Psychoanalysis and Contemporary Thought* 7 (1984): 339-75.

determinism and Skinner's model of the person no longer makes sense — nor do the models of most other psychologists.

Let me say again that Evans is correct in his claim that such regularities as the psychologist discovers do not provide evidence for the truth of determinism; determinism is not even *probable* with respect to such facts as psychologists have discovered. Since the point is of prime importance, let me take a moment to elaborate it, since so many people go wrong right here.

If psychologists had discovered a good many laws of nature pertaining to human psychology, that would indeed be some evidence for the conclusion that *all* human behavior is governed by laws of nature. To decide whether in fact to accept that conclusion, we would then have to weigh up that affirmative evidence against such negative evidence as there may be. And we would have to decide whether, amongst the negative evidence, we should count those cases in which researchers looked long and hard and failed to discover any laws of nature.

But the situation is in fact very different from this. Psychologists have in fact discovered no laws of nature — or at least, precious few. What psychologists have discovered are, in Evans's words, "invariably probabilistic and statistical in character." But the phenomenon of A-like events being followed by B-like events more often than not is not a law of nature. We can go farther: even invariant regularities — and psychologists seem to have discovered few even of those — are not necessarily laws of nature. Perhaps the regularity is only coincidental. An old example of Bertrand Russell's makes the point vividly. It seems that whenever the siren blew in a certain factory in Manchester, five minutes later workers in a certain factory in Birmingham walked out with lunch buckets in hand. No one supposes this to be a law of nature. Some philosophers, attempting to get at the difference, have said that for a generalization to be a law of nature it must support what in philosophy are called its correlative *subjunctive conditionals*. For example, in the case before us it would have to be true that, for any time, if the siren *would* blow in factory A at that time, men *would* walk out of factory B five minutes later with lunch buckets in hand. The regularity of which Russell took note does not support that subjunctive conditional. And I submit that likewise very few of the sequences discovered by psychologists support their correlative subjunctive conditionals.[2] In short, very few of the regularities discovered by psychology are laws of nature; at best perhaps a few physiological regularities are that. We should

2. Perhaps even supporting its correlative subjunctive conditionals is not enough to turn a generalization into a law of nature. See Peter van Inwagen, *An Essay on Free Will* (New York: Oxford University Press, 1983), pp. 6-7.

see determinism for what it is in those who hold it: a highly speculative item of faith.

Dimensions of Responsibility

This is the point at which the discussion is usually dropped — or perhaps it is dropped after the determinist has been allowed to make some derogatory remarks about the arbitrary and aleatory quality of the indeterminist's universe. But I wish to suggest that the truly interesting issues lie yet before us. What we need is not just an attack on the determinist model of the person but a replacement of that model with an alternative. Let's see how far we can get.

Virtually everybody who participates in the modern discussion assumes that there is only one form of causation: event-causation. Virtually everybody assumes, that is, that the cause of an event is always another event. That is why it seems to almost everybody that we have to choose between a determinist universe and a universe which is, in part, chance or aleatory. But suppose we question the assumption. *Must* the cause of an event be another event?

You ask, what else might it be? How about a *person?* Perhaps in addition to event-causation there is agent-causation. I think the Christian will resonate to this suggestion at once. How else, after all, is the creative activity of God to be understood? The creation of the universe was not caused by some event, was it? Or if you say that it was caused by the event of God's decision to *create,* that decision was not in turn caused by some event. God as agent brought about that decision; God as agent took that decision. May it not be that we, created as we are in the image of God, are also causally effective agents?

How can we understand this? Perhaps in part along the following lines. All of us form intentions. And often we act on those intentions. Indeed, if it is truly an intention, the only reason for its not being acted on is that one's intention was to do something when and if some condition was satisfied, and that condition has not yet, in one's judgment, *been* satisfied. Let us, for convenience, say that an acted-on intention is an *undertaking.*

But does this not imply that certain events, specifically, those undertakings, just pop up uncaused? Not at all. *I* am the cause of my undertakings. *I* bring them about. Well OK, says the objector; but at least your view implies that our universe at pivotal junctures is an aleatory, chance universe with arbitrary happenings. Not at all. Though a person's free undertakings are not event-causally determined, it does not follow that they are arbitrary. Why operate with this disjunction? Perhaps whenever persons undertake something they do so for a motive. Perhaps there are no unmotivated undertakings. *If* so — and it seems to me likely that this is indeed so — our undertakings are not at all arbitrary. To act on a motive is surely not to act arbitrarily.

And what is a motive? There are different understandings of motives. For our purposes here it will be satisfactory to think of a motive as a desire that such-and-such will occur which, when coupled with the belief that one's undertaking may well bring about that which one desires, constitutes the reason for one's undertaking.

Aha, says the objector: then the desire coupled with the belief *determines* the undertaking, and we are back in our old familiar cozy deterministic universe. Not at all. Perhaps when I undertake to leave this room I do so out of the motive of wanting to drink some coffee; that is the good which I desire. But it does not follow from this that I *had* to undertake to leave, that I could not have acted otherwise. Motives, as the medievals put it, incline without necessitating. Even when I undertake to leave the room out of the motive of wanting to drink some coffee, it is in my power *not* to undertake that action on that motive.

If I am right in supposing that all our undertakings have motives, then it is easy to see how we can influence what a person does even though the person acts freely — whereas so often it is supposed that influence proves determinism. We can influence what people do by altering their motives, and of course, their beliefs. If you succeed in persuading me that caffeine in coffee is highly destructive of brain cells, that may well diminish my desire to drink coffee and thus influence my undertakings. Or if you succeed in persuading me that I do not have to go to the coffee shop to get coffee, that there's some right here in this room, that too will influence my undertakings.

Understanding what a person does or what transpires within a person is, in my judgment, a multi-faceted thing. Too often we have thought that there was only one kind of understanding. In fact there are many. Surely in one sense of "understand" we understand what persons have done when we grasp their undertakings and their motives for those undertakings. Hermeneutic psychology, as I understand it, focuses especially on this mode or type of understanding. It tries to discern patterns in our undertakings and their motives. Surely that is a legitimate and important enterprise.

But once we see that a person's free undertakings are nonetheless motivated, we naturally wonder about the origin of those motives. What are the processes that bring about our beliefs and our desires? Clearly few of them are present in us because we have undertaken to have them. Accordingly, for all my stress on the importance of undertakings, undertakings are not everything. The point is obvious, yet it must be emphasized. For whereas I find it characteristic of all too many American psychologists that they ignore our undertakings, I find it characteristic of certain strands of European psychology that they ignore everything *but* our undertakings — talking as if we were imperial angelic creatures floating lightly over the earth. The truth is that we are both creatures of habit and disposition, and creatures of free undertakings. The challenge of the psychologist is to show how those facets of ourselves are interwoven.

Reid's Idea of Belief Dispositions

An important component in my own philosophical model of the person is this concept of a disposition to which I just alluded — the concept of a tendency, or causal power, or capacity. As I see it, we all have an enormous array of dispositions, the activation of which accounts for a great deal of what transpires in us. Each of us is disposed, for a vast array of specific cases, to respond in such-and-such a way upon such-and-such stimulation in such-and-such circumstances. My choice of the word "respond" and "stimulation" will clue you in to the fact that not only does the concept of a disposition enter into philosophical models of the person; it enters into psychological models as well. Indeed, it seems to me that far and away the most fundamental concept in contemporary psychological models of the person is the concept of a disposition. It is at the very foundation of all behaviorist theories, with behaviorists focusing their attention on how dispositions can be induced, on how they can be extinguished, and on how they can be altered. Likewise it is at the foundation of maturational theories of all sorts. In spite of all the opposition between Piaget and Skinner, both can be seen as using the concept of a disposition as their fundamental category. It is, of course, because of the fact that so much of what transpires in us is due to the activation of dispositions that people are inclined to think of the person as (comprehensively) determined.

I judge that there is very much indeed about dispositions that we do not yet understand. Yet I suspect that it is mistaken to think of them as working deterministically. Perhaps it is best to think of them as varying in strength from those in which the tendency is quite weak to those in which it is very strong, perhaps so strong as to be invariant and irresistible.

Some of you will have been longing for some time now for a bit less generality and a bit more specificity. Let me see if I can go some way toward satisfying that longing. My own interest in epistemology has led me especially to reflect on those dispositions which may be called *belief dispositions* —

dispositions whose outcome is that the person now believes, or accepts, or assents to, some proposition. Since reflection on such dispositions is also directly germane to the topic here, let me become more specific by saying something about these. I have learned a great deal here from the eighteenth-century Scotch philosopher Thomas Reid; so let me cast what I have to say mainly as a report of his observations.

At the very foundation of the cognitive psychology that undergirded Reid's epistemology was his claim that at any point in our lives we each have a variety of dispositions (propensities, causal powers) for believing things — belief dispositions. What accounts for our beliefs, in the vast majority of cases anyway, is the triggering of one and another such disposition. For example, we are all disposed, upon having certain sensations in certain situations, to have certain beliefs about the external physical world. Upon having certain other sensations in certain situations, we are all disposed to have certain beliefs about other persons. Likewise we are all so constituted as to be disposed in certain circumstances to believe what we apprehend people as telling us — the *credulity* disposition, as Reid rather fetchingly called it. And to cite one last example, we are all so constituted that upon judging some proposition that we already believe as good evidence for another proposition not yet believed, we are disposed to believe that other proposition as well. This is the *reasoning* disposition.

In typical eighteenth-century fashion Reid focused his attention entirely on our good and noble belief-dispositions. But once one conceptualizes the person along these lines, then shortly it occurs to one that we must also include those ignoble belief-dispositions of which Marx and Freud made so much: our disposition to believe what gives us a sense of security, our disposition to believe what serves to perpetuate our position of economic privilege, our disposition to adopt clusters of beliefs which function as ideologies and rationalizations concealing from our conscious awareness the ignobility of those dispositions, and so forth. Some of you will recall that at the time of the Reformation there was a dispute over whether our fall has resulted in a "darkening of the mind," with the Calvinists insisting that it has and the Thomists insisting that only the will has been corrupted. Perhaps in noticing these ignoble belief-dispositions we are seeing that Calvin was right: the mind has indeed been darkened.

But back to Reid. Not only does Reid call to our attention the various belief-dispositions that we actually do possess at a given moment in our lives; he also speaks about the origin of these dispositions. It was his conviction, in the first place, that somewhere in the history of each of us are to be found certain belief-dispositions with which we were simply "endowed by our Creator." They belong to our human nature. We come with them. Their existence is not the result of conditioning. It must not be supposed, however, that all such non-conditioned dispositions are present in us at birth. Some, possibly most, emerge as we mature. We have the disposition to acquire them upon reaching one and another level of maturation.

In addition to these indigenous non-conditioned belief-dispositions, we adults all have a number of belief-dispositions which we have acquired by way of conditioning. Reid calls attention to a certain range of these as being belief-dispositions induced in us by the working of the *inductive principle*. The inductive principle is not itself a belief-disposition; it is an indigenous non-conditioned disposition for the acquisition of belief-dispositions. Reid says, "It is undeniable, and indeed is acknowledged by all, that when we have found two things to have been constantly conjoined in the course of nature, the appearance of one of them is immediately followed by the conception and belief of the other."[3] He adds that it is a "natural, original and unaccountable propensity to believe, that the connections which we have observed in times past, will continue in time to come."[4] It seems clear that Reid's thought concerning the workings of the inductive principle can readily be stated in the language of contemporary psychology. What accounts for some of our beliefs is that a process of classical conditioning has taken place whereby we have acquired a new belief-disposition, which then has been activated so as to produce the belief in question.

Vast numbers of our non-indigenous belief-dispositions are not acquired in this way, however, but rather by way of what we would nowadays call *operant* conditioning, working on our native belief-dispositions. In Reid's own thought this comes out most clearly in what he says about the credulity principle. It was his view that the working of this principle "is unlimited in children"[5] in the sense that whatever children apprehend someone as asserting, they believe. But shortly the principle begins to be "restrained and modified," as Reid puts it. What induces the restraint and modification is the discovery that sometimes the principle produces false beliefs in us. We believe what people tell us but what they told us proves false. Notice: a person's conviction that some of the beliefs produced in her by testimony are false does not *destroy* her disposition to give credence to testimony; rather it results in that disposition's becoming restrained and modified. It seems clear that we

3. Reid, *Inquiry into the Human Mind on the Principles of Common Sense*, edited by D. R. Brookes (Edinburgh: Edinburgh University Press, 1997), VI, 24.

4. Reid, *Inquiry into the Human Mind on the Principles of Common Sense*, II, 9.

5. Reid, *Inquiry into the Human Mind on the Principles of Common Sense*, VI, 24.

can think of this, too, in terms of modern conditioning theory. The original, unqualified credulity principle is altered by way of operant conditioning. One's discovery, or conviction, that certain of one's beliefs thus produced are false, functions as an aversive consequence, diminishing to the point of extinguishing the workings of the disposition in such cases. That new, slightly altered, disposition is then in turn submitted to the same sort of testing.

All I have wanted to do is illustrate my claim that the concept of a disposition or causal power is basic in understanding how persons come to know and believe. Let me add that it also seems to me basic in the phenomenon known as modeling — a phenomenon to which I have paid some attention in certain of my writings. It would appear that what is operative in modeling is the disposition of a person, under certain circumstances, to *imitate* the behavior of another.

Let me say a brief word, lastly, about conditioning. It appears to me that Albert Bandura is correct in his claim that in human beings, conditioning for the most part works by evoking expectations in us concerning desirable and undesirable consequences of action, and should in fact be seen as a special case of the more general phenomenon of the alteration of behavior by the production or alteration of beliefs. For example, if I have been driving on ice at a speed suitable for normal conditions, I will probably slow down if I see the car ahead of me spin out of control, just as I will probably do so if my own car begins to swerve a bit. The latter would by many psychologists be understood as a case of operant conditioning. But then it should be noticed that the expectations which have been aroused in me do not serve to alter my disposition but to influence my undertakings: I now undertake to drive more slowly. By contrast, an alteration in behavior produced by the triggering of some disposition is precisely the sort of thing which is *not* undertaken. For example, my belief that I am now sitting on a chair was not produced in me by my undertaking to believe it but by the activation of one of my sensory belief-dispositions. The contemporary psychological category of *conditioning* thus proves to be a very mixed bag indeed — perhaps too mixed to be of much real use without substantial revision. It straddles and confuses the very distinction I have wanted to make between actions freely undertaken and changes produced by the activation of some disposition.

Being Biblically Faithful

What I have set before you is the skeletal outline of a model of the person. In spite of its generality, it seems to me to be a genuinely *psychological* model, though of course very incomplete. It interacts with alternative models in the field of psychology; to some extent I have come to my conclusions by trying to put my finger on just where the alternative psychological models seemed to me unsatisfactory. Furthermore, it opens up wide fields for empirical enquiry in many different directions. On the other hand, I see it as also a model that is biblically faithful. The model attempts to respect the human responsibility that is so fundamental in the biblical vision. It does not, however, go to the extreme of treating us as angels whose only relation to the material world is that we act upon it. The world also acts upon us — not for the most part in deterministic ways, but nonetheless it acts upon us. The model is thus an *interactive* model. Of course there are a good many other features of the biblical vision than just these which ought also to function as control on our models and theories; I have not had time here to call attention to those other features. Also I have not had time to show how the model applies to the activities of teaching and learning. But I dare say you can see that the applications are readily at hand.

I think that there is much to be said for the model, as far as it goes; it has helped me in my own thinking. But I do not set it before you as something for you just to accept and flesh out. I set it before you as something for you to consider, and even more, as an illustration of what I mean when I speak of a psychological model that is biblically faithful. The challenge to develop such models and the theories to accompany them is what, above all, I want to leave with you. For that, so I believe, is the core of developing psychology in Christian perspective.

The Point of Connection between
Faith and Learning

One of the most insistent and provocative claims of the neo-Calvinist movement[1] in our century and at the end of the last is that scholarship as a whole is not religiously neutral. What the members of the movement had in mind was of course *non-theological* scholarship; no one would claim that *theology* is religiously neutral. And it was *competent* scholarship on which they had their eye. Their point was that scholarship *may satisfy all the criteria for competence* and yet not be religiously neutral. They meant, furthermore, that this situation is no accident. Until all God's children are religiously united in the Kingdom of Peace, there is no possibility of unified science. Pluralism in the academy, running along the fault-lines of religious divergence, cannot be eliminated.

The Leibnizian Ideal of Learning

This view has provoked controversy; for it stands in opposition to the view of science held almost universally in the West for some six centuries. As a prominent American philosopher of science, Larry Laudan, puts it,

> For a very long time, philosophers generally have been inclined to accept what I shall call the Leibnizian ideal. In brief, the Leibnizian ideal holds

1. A line of thought originating with the Dutch thinker Abraham Kuyper is often called neo-Calvinism. A branch of this line, developed by philosophers such as Herman Dooyeweerd whose ideas influenced thinkers in places such as the Free University in Amsterdam and the Institute for Christian Studies in Toronto, is sometimes called "Reformationalism."

This essay was first published as a book chapter entitled "On Christian Learning," in *Stained Glass: Worldviews and Social Science*, edited by Paul Marshall, Sander Griffioen, and Richard Mouw (Lanham, Md.: University Press of America, 1989). It is reprinted here with permission.

that all disputes about matters of fact (including disputes over theories) can be impartially resolved by invoking appropriate rules of evidence. At least since Bacon, most philosophers have believed there to be an algorithm or set of algorithms which would permit any impartial observer to judge the degree to which a certain body of data rendered different explanations of those data true or false, probable or improbable. Philosophers have expressed varying degrees of optimism about whether we now know precisely what those evidential rules are.[2]

There is complexity concealed behind that bland phrase, "any impartial observer." Most scholars have acknowledged that we each bring to our practice of science various psychological quirks that make it impossible for us to be fully impartial. Nevertheless, since science is a communal enterprise, these private quirks, so it is assumed, will be corrected by the discourse of the community. How exactly this is supposed to happen has usually not been spelled out in detail. Be that as it may, however, the thought was that *enduring* disagreement on any theoretical issue must be due to the fact that the appropriate rules of evidence — the appropriate rules of method — had not yet been discovered or put into effect. Moreover, no one supposed that divergent religious commitments might make it impossible to agree on appropriate rules of method. On this matter, too, impartial judgment was assumed to be an attainable ideal within the academic community.

It was *the Leibnizian ideal,* as Laudan calls it — in my own writings I have attributed the ideal to Descartes rather than Leibniz — that the neo-Calvinists repudiated. There is no hope, they said, of consensus in science. Science is ineluctably pluralistic. The ideal of rational consensus on methods whose application would yield rational consensus throughout the disciplines is unattainable. The fundamental reason for the unattainability of that ideal is the permanence of religious divergence. There is Christian learning and there is non-Christian learning; only religious conversion will change that.

It must be conceded that the neo-Calvinists were not wholly without antecedents on this point. Augustine had already insisted that love of God is a condition of knowledge. *Credo ut intelligam,* he said: "I believe in order that I may know." Faith is the condition of knowledge and knowledge, conversely, is the *telos* of faith, But the knowledge Augustine had in mind was knowledge of God — or more generally, knowledge of the eternal. We cannot know God, he said, until we love God in faith. Hostility to God makes knowledge of

2. Laudan, *Science and Values: The Aims of Science and Their Role in Scientific Debate* (Berkeley and Los Angeles: University of California Press, 1984), p. 5.

God impossible. Augustine never extended this suggestive claim concerning the entwinement of love and knowledge, hostility and ignorance, to the disciplines in general.

Abraham Kuyper's View of Learning

The acknowledged leader of the first generation of the neo-Calvinist movement in Holland was Abraham Kuyper. Let us see how he articulated the point that religious pluralism makes consensus in *scientia* unattainable — that it makes dissensus not only normal but inevitable. What we want to look at is Kuyper's famous (or infamous) chapter entitled "The Twofold Development of Science" in his *Principles of Sacred Theology.*[3]

Two Humanities

Kuyper launches his argument not from an analysis of the sciences but from theological considerations. Among all the differences in conviction and commitment among human beings, there is one that does not have its root in psychological dynamics — one that "does not find its origin within the circle of our human consciousness, but *outside* of it" (152). Or so the Christian religion claims:

> For it speaks of a regeneration *(palingenesis)*, of a "being begotten anew" *(anagenesis)*, followed by an enlightening *(photismos)*, which changes man in his very being; and that indeed by a change or transformation which is effected by a supernatural cause.... This "regeneration" breaks humanity in two, and repeals the unity of the human consciousness. If this fact of "being begotten anew," coming in from without, establishes a radical change in *the being* of man, be it only potentially, and if this change exercises at the same time an influence upon his *consciousness*, then as far as it has or has not undergone this transformation, there is an abyss in the universal human consciousness across which no bridge can be laid. (152)

Concerning those differences among us which have their root in psychological dynamics, we can hold out the hope of emergent consensus through

3. Kuyper, "The Twofold Development of Science," in *Principles of Sacred Theology,* translated by J. Hendrik De Vries (Grand Rapids: Eerdmans, 1954), pp. 150-82. Subsequent references to this volume will be made parenthetically in the text.

communal interaction (150-51). But concerning the difference whose cause lies outside ourselves, whose cause is God, there is no hope of consensus, or even convergence.

The fact that there are two kinds of people results inevitably in two kinds of science, says Kuyper. Of course both kinds of people are human,

> ... but one is inwardly different from the other, and consequently feels a different content rising from his consciousness; thus they face the cosmos from different points of view, and are impelled by different impulses. And the fact that there are two kinds of *people* occasions of necessity the fact of two kinds of human *life* and *consciousness* of life, and of two kinds of *science*. ... (154)

Conversely: "The idea of the *unity of science,* taken in its absolute sense, implies the denial of the fact of palingenesis, and therefore from principle leads to the rejection of the Christian religion" (154).

Nothing could make Kuyper's basic line of thought more clear than those last words. His understanding of the relation of religion and science was not derived from a slow, careful, cautious, detailed "scientific" analysis of the history of the disciplines; it was derived by straightforward inference from the claims of the Christian gospel, as he understood them.

Common Ground

Having said that there must be two kinds of science, given the difference between Christian and non-Christian, Kuyper went on at once to make clear that he is not to be taken as holding that there is no commonality between these two kinds of people in their practice of science. At the bottom of Kuyper's way of thinking about the academic disciplines was his insistence on the importance of acknowledging the contribution of the subject to the practice of science. Theorists are not blank tablets, *tabula rasa,* on which the facts of the world are inscribed; they are dynamic, structured selves, the dynamics and structure of the self unavoidably coming to expression in the scientific results at which they arrive. What the subject brings to the practice of science includes, as we have seen, whether he or she is regenerated or not. But regeneration, though radically comprehensive in scope, does not touch everything in the human self. In Kuyper's view it "works no change in the senses" (157). "The entire empiric investigation of the things that are perceptible to our senses ... has nothing to do with the radical difference which separates the two groups." Accordingly, "Any one who in the realm of visible things has observed and formulated something with entire accuracy, whatever it be, has rendered service to *both* groups" (157).

It's true that sensory observations constitute only the bottom rung of the empirical sciences. Nonetheless, "it should be gratefully acknowledged that in the elementary parts of these studies there is a *common* realm, in which the difference between view and starting point does not enforce itself" (158). We say without reluctance "but with gladness, that in almost every department there is some task that is common to all . . ." (161). Kuyper recognized that the workings of our senses are influenced by what earlier I called psychological quirks; he devoted an extraordinarily perceptive section to developing the point. But he shared the general conviction that the influence of these subjective quirks would be corrected by the discourse of the community of scholars.

Another element in the human subject unaffected by regeneration is what Kuyper called "the formal process of thought" (159) — in other words, our apprehension of entailments. Here, too, "a certain mutual contact between the two kinds of science" (160) is possible. For example, "the accuracy of one another's demonstrations can be critically examined and verified, in so far at least as the result strictly depends upon the deduction made" (160).

Two Sciences

So two things remain untouched by regeneration: the workings of the senses and the workings of our capacity for apprehending entailment. These are the extent, however, of what remains untouched. And because the workings of these two capacities fall far short of what is necessary for the construction of the sciences, Kuyper concludes that there are two distinct sciences in every discipline. Admittedly the difference is not dramatic in mathematics and natural science; but even there, he seems to have thought, it is not negligible.

> This would not be true if the deepest foundations of our knowledge lay outside of us and not in us, or if the palingenesis operated outside of these principles of knowledge in the subject. Since, however, this is not the case, because, like sin, whose result it potentially destroys, palingenesis causes the subject to be different in his innermost self from what he was before; and because this disposition of the subject exercises an immediate influence upon scientific investigation and on scientific con-

viction; these two unlike magnitudes can have no like result and from this difference between the two circles of subjects there follows of necessity difference between their science.

This bifurcation must extend as far as the influence of those subjective factors which palingenesis causes to be different in one than in the other. Hence all scientific research which has things *seen* only as object, or which is prosecuted simply by those subjective factors which have undergone *no* change, remains the same for both. Near the ground, the tree of science is one for all. But no sooner has it reached a certain height, than two branches separate. . . . (168)

As partisans of the different branches, "we encounter one another in open conflict, and a universally compulsory science, that shall be compulsory upon all men, is inconceivable" (182).

What this view implies, Kuyper maintained, is that from the point where the sciences begin to use more than our capacities of sense and reason, and hence to separate, there is no hope of any rational adjudication of disagreements. From that point on "it will be impossible to settle the difference of insight. No polemics between these two kinds of science, on details [which do not involve simply the workings of those two unaffected faculties of sense and reason] can ever serve any purpose" (160). All each party can do is explain to the other why, at the point of branching, it follows the branch it does.

The importance of offering such explanations must not be underrated (160-61). Yet they must be seen clearly for what they are: "the confession of the reason why one refuses to follow the tendency of the other . . ." (160). As each party offers to the other its account of why it proceeds as it does, it finds itself saying things with which the other party disagrees; and it discovers that often it is unable, at these points of disagreement, to argue for its beliefs in such a way that it succeeds in persuading the other party, or even in making the other party no longer epistemically justified in withholding its assent. But this stand-off in persuasion and justification does not mean, for Kuyper, that Christians are rationally obligated to surrender their convictions — nor that *non*-Christians are obligated to surrender theirs. Both parties are justified in believing as they do. What Kuyper sees when surveying science is a pluralism of contradictory but nevertheless justifiedly held positions. Obviously, there is an understanding of rationality at work here very different from that of classic foundationalism.

In saying that there are two kinds of science, non-Christian and Christian, Kuyper is employing a formal criterion for calling some body of inquiry a *science.* He thinks that as a totality non-Christian science is not true — and he is fully aware that the non-Christian theorist will return the favor. Thus if a condition of calling something "science" were that one regarded it as *true,* each party will hold that there is only *one* science, namely, its own. What Kuyper means by science can be seen from the following description:

> . . . both parts of humanity . . . feel the impulse to investigate the object, and, by doing this in a scientific way, to obtain a scientific systemization of that which exists. The effort and activity of both bear the same character; they are both impelled by the same purpose; both devote their strength to the same kind of labor; and this kind of labor is in each case called the prosecution of science. But however much they may be doing the same thing formally, their activities run in different directions, because they have different starting points. . . . Formally both groups perform scientific labor, and . . . they recognize each other's scientific character, in the same way in which two armies facing each other are mutually able to appreciate military worth. But when they have arrived at their result they cannot conceal the fact that in many respects these results are contrary to each other, and are entirely different; and as far as this is the case, each group naturally contradicts whatever the other group asserts. (155-56)

The Gap in Kuyper's Analysis

Thus far I have avoided mentioning the point in Kuyper's theory where I, at least, am most eager to have illumination. There are many points we might like to question. Is science really so nicely structured into a lower level of sensory reports on which there is consensus and an upper level on which there is not? Is it true that the distorting effects of our subjective quirks of sense and reason are always winnowed out by the discourse of the community? But these questions and others, though important, are not central. What we most want from Kuyper is clarity on how the religious divergence to which he persistently calls our attention works itself out in science so that, as he sees it, "scientific investigation can be *brought to a close* in no single department by all scientists together, yea, cannot be *continued* in concert, as soon as palingenesis makes a division between the investigators" (161).

Unfortunately it is right here — at its very core, not somewhere out in the periphery of details — that Kuyper's theory is most unsatisfactory. In dividing up humanity as he does, Kuyper is of course standing in the tradition of Augustine who saw history as the struggle between the *civitas dei* and the *civitas mundi*. Given his theological convictions on the significance of rebirth, and given his convictions on the centrality of the role of the subject in science, Kuyper thought the struggle between the *civitas dei* and *civitas mundi* must find expression in a struggle between Christian learning and non-Christian learning. But when it comes to showing exactly how the connection works, Kuyper abandons us. He says such things as these: ". . . their activities run in opposite directions, because they have different starting points" (155); ". . . because of the difference in their nature they apply themselves differently to this work, and view things in a different way" (155); ". . . because they themselves are differently constituted, they see a corresponding difference in the constitution of all things" (155); ". . . there are two points of departure" (167); ". . . palingenesis causes the subject to be different in his inner-most self from what he was before; and . . . this disposition of the subject exercises an immediate influence upon scientific investigation and our scientific conviction" (168); "[Christian learning is] that which the student of 'the wisdom of God' derives from his premises" (176); "[The effort to develop a science] is ever bound to the premises in our nature from which this effort starts out" (180); "[Christian learning is] governed by the fact of palingenesis" (181); ". . . the fact of palingenesis governs the whole subject in all investigations" (181).

What Kuyper gives us here is a multiplicity of metaphors: Christians have different *starting points*, different *points of departure*, different *premises* (in another passage, different *presuppositions*). Christians *view* things differently. The fact of rebirth *governs* the investigations of Christians; it *influences* them. But what do these metaphors really tell us? I submit that this brandishing of metaphors neither illuminates the way religion influences scholarship nor does it support the contention that this influence must result in two kinds of science.

The weakness of Kuyper's analysis at this point (more accurately, the non-existence of analysis) did not go unnoticed by his followers in the neo-Calvinist movement. What is striking to me, surveying these developments from a distance of fifty to a hundred years, is the number of people who responded to their awareness of this central lacuna in Kuyper not by questioning the thesis itself of "two kinds of people, hence two kinds of science," but rather by working industriously to show where the differences were and how exactly they came about. Especially in the so-called "Reformational" movement, many were convinced that the thesis *must be* true, and that all that was required was to point out the differences convincingly and to offer a general account of how they came about.

Kuyper's followers acknowledged (as did Kuyper himself) that for various reasons the two kinds of people might not be faithful to their "starting points," with the result that differences between the sciences actually produced by Christians and non-Christians might not be great. Unlike Kuyper, however, his followers were usually inclined to lay the principal blame for this upon Christians; they were inclined to impute a single-mindedness to non-Christian scholars in their labors that they did not impute to Christian scholars. Hence, their analysis of the actual differences was regularly mingled with exhortations to their fellow Christians to be more single-mindedly devoted in purging the elements of "apostate" thinking from their minds. The suggestion was repeatedly made that if such devotion were forthcoming, the difference between the two kinds of science would be evident to all in every discipline.

Neo-Calvinism's Religious Totalism

Why were so many *a priori* convinced that the thesis, "two kinds of people, hence two kinds of science," must be true? Evidently we are here touching upon elements deep in the overall neo-Calvinist vision. We have seen how Kuyper himself justified the thesis; but I think that in those passages Kuyper was not as he might have been concerning the deep motivation. I suggest that the answer is something along the following line. Characteristic of the Calvinist tradition in general has been an impulse toward religious totalism — toward the conviction that one's whole life must be lived in obedience to God-in-Christ, that faith must penetrate all. This is the element in the Calvinist character of which Max Weber caught sight and which he called "this-worldly asceticism." Anyone who says, "Lo, here faith makes a difference but not there," can expect from the Calvinist an intuitive aversion. Upon reflection the Calvinist may concede the point in certain cases; recall that Kuyper himself said that faith makes no difference to the working of our senses and reason. But the intuitive response of the Calvinist will be to resist every claim of "here but not there."

The gospel says that we are to obey all the commands of God; there is a deep impulse in the Calvinist to understand this as meaning all of life is to consist of obeying the commands of God. The gospel says that we are to serve nothing but God, or perhaps, nothing which in any way conflicts with our service of God; there is a deep impulse in the Calvinist to understand this as meaning that all of life is to consist in service of God. I think it is accurate to say that in the neo-Calvinist movement, and especially in its "Reformational" branch, this impulse toward religious totalism, indigenous to the Calvinist tradition generally, was as powerful as it has ever been.

Beneath this impulse in neo-Calvinism, and again most decisively in its "Reformational" branch, has been the tendency, when reflecting on whether we have an indigenous human nature that is a well-spring of thought and action, either to deny any such nature or to see it as very narrow and constricted. Repeatedly the pejorative charge of dualism has been fired by "Reformational" thinkers at any position which divides the human self into those capacities and dynamics that belong to our indigenous human nature and those rooted in faith. Kuyper himself has been accused by some of his followers of having fallen into dualism — or perhaps more accurately, of having marched boldly into it.

The impulse toward construing the life of the authentic Christian as rooted entirely in faith and not at all in human nature will have, as its counterpart, the impulse toward construing the life of the non-Christian as rooted entirely in idolatry and not at all in human nature. The life of the non-Christian is seen as penetrated through and through by idolatry in a way formally similar to the way the life of the authentic Christian is seen as penetrated through and through by faith. All of life, it is said, is religion — that is, all of *everybody's* life is religion. So there *must be* two kinds of science, on pain of dualism. And if that appears not to be the case, the reality is concealed from us by a lack of perceptiveness on the part of those who survey the sciences, along with a lack of single-minded devotion on the part of those Christians who practice science.

Kuyper's Legacy for Faith and Learning

I suggest it has been for reasons like these that various followers of Kuyper have *a priori* accepted his thesis, "two kinds of people, hence two kinds of science." A fair number, however, have gone beyond this *a priori* conviction and sought to display the differences between the two sciences and to give a general account of how those differences actually come about. Those attempts have mainly gone in one or the other of two directions.

Worldviews Shape Learning

Some have argued that the link between religion and scientific inquiry lies in *worldviews* — what my former teacher, William Harry Jellema, called *minds*.

Every human being has a worldview or mind, so it is said; and to be a Christian is to adhere to a certain worldview. The worldview with which a scholar engages in a discipline shape his practice of it.[4]

My own judgment is that this line of thought, at least as developed so far, constitutes little if any advance on Kuyper. The claim is that it is the worldview inherent in Christianity that shapes the practice and results of science; worldview is the link. But to claim that worldview is the link is only marginally different from setting before us the phenomenon that we hoped Kuyper would illuminate in the first place. The question now is: how exactly do worldviews do this? In addition, the person who adopts this approach assumes the obligation of explaining and refining the concept of a *worldview*; that has proved to be no easy task.

To be a human being is to be a creature of knowledge and belief — a creature of assent. It is to take reality a certain way, to "represent" reality a certain way. To be human is also to be a creature with aims, desires, values, and wants. These two dimensions of the human self — call them the *assentive* and the *affective* — are profoundly connected. We are deeply attached to some of our beliefs; some of our beliefs are even formed (in part) by our attachments. And all of us, in acting intentionally, act *on* beliefs and *out of* motives.

Worldview theorists propose to select, from a person's entire corpus of assent, those of his beliefs which constitute his *worldview*. Then they ask such questions as whether this person has the same worldview as that person, whether this person has changed his or her worldview, and so forth. All this, to repeat, has proved to be no easy task. There is no problem in placing a person's beliefs on various continua: some beliefs are more general, others more specific; some are more firmly held, others less firmly; some are more central, others more peripheral; and so forth. There is likewise no problem in comparing the beliefs of different persons in these various respects. I myself doubt, however, that any benefit is to be gained from refining the vague notion of worldview so that we can pick out that segment of a person's beliefs which constitute his worldview, thereby enabling us to answer all these questions about similarities and differences between the worldviews of different persons.

4. "A worldview is a matter of the shared everyday experience of humankind, an inescapable component of all human knowing, and as such it is nonscientific, or rather (since scientific knowing is always dependent on the intuitive knowing of our everyday experience), *prescientific* in nature. It belongs to an order of cognition more basic than that of science or theory. Just as aesthetics presupposes some innate sense of the beautiful and legal theory presupposes a fundamental notion of justice, so theology and philosophy presuppose a pretheoretical perspective on the world. They give a scientific elaboration of a worldview." Albert Wolters, *Creation Regained* (Grand Rapids: Eerdmans, 1985), p. 9.

Herman Dooyeweerd's explication and use of the concept of *ground-motive* is probably best placed within the context of the worldview approach. A particular ground-motive is the most fundamental dimension of a certain shared worldview and, at the same time, a basic determinant of action. It is both motif and motive.[5]

Idolatry and Reductionism Distort Learning

The second main strategy for displaying the differences between the two kinds of science, and for giving an account of how those differences come about, makes central use of the concepts of *faith* and *idolatry* rather than that of worldview. This line of thought begins with the anthropological claim that an ineradicable feature of human beings is the irresistible impulse to bring unity to life by taking something as absolute, by giving ultimate allegiance to something or other — be it the transcendent God or something immanent in the created order. The former manifestation of this impulse is faith; the latter, idolatry. The argument goes on to claim that idolatry manifests itself in the academic disciplines in (futile) reductionist attempts to treat some dimension of created reality as the clue to the whole. The argument concludes by claiming that only if one takes the transcendent God as absolute is such reductionism avoidable.

Unlike the worldview approach, this approach has the virtue that it tells us what to look for in order to discover that there are indeed two kinds of science. It says: look for reductionism. And reductionism is indeed a phenomenon in the sciences, albeit tantalizingly elusive when one tries to give a general account of what it is.

Yet this approach also has its debilitating deficiencies. For one thing, it is curiously constricted: is the connection of religion to the practice and results of science channeled entirely through this phenomenon of reductionism? Does the practice of Christian learning amount to nothing more than avoiding (illicit) reductionism? The other side of the coin in this approach is its almost reckless boldness. To hold that reductionism is the clue

5. Cf. the explanation of "ground-motive" offered by John Kraay: "the dynamic in unity establishing expressions of ultimate meaning in terms of which Western civilization has been, and still is being, shaped." See Kraay's translator's preface to *Roots of Western Culture* by Herman Dooyeweerd, edited by Mark Vander Vennen and Bernard Zylstra (Toronto: Wedge Publishing Foundation, 1979), p. ix. All this is remarkably similar to what Jellema said, for example, in "Calvinism and Higher Education" in *God-Centered Living* (Grand Rapids: Baker, 1951), and in his pamphlet entitled *The Curriculum in a Liberal-Arts College*.

to the plausibility of the thesis of "two kinds of people, hence two kinds of science," and to hold that reductionism can legitimately be seen as a manifestation of religious idolatry, one must show that *whenever* scholars fail to take God as absolute, their scholarship will display the telltale structure of being illicitly reductionist. It is right here, at this central point, that the approach breaks down. For while there is indeed a good deal of reductionism in the academy, much if not most of it rooted in idolatry or quasi-idolatry, it would appear that there are also many examples of the practice of science by non-Christians that neither display nor imply reductionism. Neither Dooyeweerd, who especially embraced and elaborated this approach, nor anyone else, has succeeded in showing otherwise.

Christian Learning: Not Different but Faithful

Up to this point I have spoken of the neo-Calvinist movement as though it were "out there" — as though I were not myself a part of it. That is not the case. I myself was reared intellectually within this movement. It was the context within which my own intellectual life began. Its denial of the neutrality and autonomy of scholarship with respect to religion was something I embraced early on and which I continue to embrace. Nonetheless, I have come to feel acutely that the first- and second-generation founders of the movement did not succeed in pinpointing the connection between religion, on the one hand, and the practice and results of scholarship, on the other. It was for this reason that I developed the notion of "control beliefs" in my book *Reason within the Bounds of Religion*.[6]

Faithful Learning

What impelled my own reflections was not only the sense that illumination was in short supply concerning the point of connection between religion and scholarship. I also found myself disagreeing on various substantive matters. I came to be skeptical about the basic thesis of "two kinds of science." Not that I came to doubt that there is such a thing as Christian learning, nor that Christians who are scholars are called to practice such learning. I myself have frequently made as powerful an appeal as I could for that very thing. In making my appeal, what I meant by Christian learning was *faithful* learning:

6. Wolterstorff, *Reason within the Bounds of Religion* (Grand Rapids: Eerdmans, 1976).

Christian learning is learning practiced in fidelity to the gospel. That is also what Kuyper meant by Christian learning. But in Kuyper and many of his followers the notion of Christian learning as faithful learning has been paired off with, and often overshadowed by, another understanding. Christian learning, it is said, is different learning. There *must* be two kinds of science in all the disciplines.

We have seen what this claim came to in Kuyper. With respect to the deliverances of the senses and of reason, the Christian and the non-Christian can talk to each other. Usually they will find themselves in agreement on such matters; where they do not, the disagreement is not due to religious divergence but to subjective psychological quirks whose effects can be corrected by the discourse of the academic community. Beyond the deliverances of the senses and of reason, however, there is no agreement, nor even any hope of rational adjudication of disagreement. All we can do is state our positions and agree to disagree. It is in that sense that there are two kinds of science.

Surely this is false to the experience of all of us who work in the academy. All of us who are Christian scholars find ourselves agreeing with our non-Christian colleagues on vastly more than the deliverances of the senses and reason. And where we disagree on matters other than such deliverances, it is our experience that often there exist rational methods of adjudication. It is not true that all each party can do is declare, "Here I stand." Kuyper's mistake was to suppose that if some dynamic in a person is fallen but susceptible to healing by regeneration, then all the results of that dynamic in a person not touched by regeneration will be unacceptable to the Christian. Surely that is not the case.

The point can be put like this: even if we set aside the deliverances of the senses and of reason, consensus and dissension in the sciences are not to be found neatly along the fault lines of the break between Christian and non-Christian. Kuyper's model fails to account adequately for the areas of consensus and controversy that actually exist within the sciences.

I know how some convinced neo-Calvinists will reply. They will grant that I have correctly described how things *appear* to be, but then go on to insist that either I misperceive where the differences actually are, or the infidelity of Christian scholars results in differences failing to develop where they ought to. I concede that we do often misperceive where the differences actually lie between Christian and non-Christian scholarship, and that Christians have often been less than fully faithful in their scholarship. But here is the question I want to raise: Why take for granted that consensus (beyond the senses and reason) is always *merely* apparent? Why *must* this be so? Why assume that the scholarship of Christians and non-Christians *must* always and everywhere be different except for those thin points of commonality? Why not instead let the differences fall where they may? Why should the Christian's project be defined primarily in terms of its *difference* from that of others? Why is fidelity not enough? Why is it not enough to urge that Christians be *faithful* in their scholarship? Why not be thankful for genuine agreement, rather than ever suspicious and querulous? Must we not balance suspicion with gratitude?

Faithful scholarship as a whole will be *distinctive* scholarship; I have no doubt of that. But difference is to be a consequence, not an aim. And if at some point the difference is scarcely large enough to justify calling this segment of scholarship a "different kind of science" — Christian science in contrast with *non*-Christian — why should that, as such, bother us? Again, is not *faithful* scholarship enough? Difference is not a condition of fidelity — though to say it yet once more, it will often be a *consequence*.

Furthermore, it is a profound and even insulting mistake to lump all non-Christian scholars into one large group, labeling them all naturalists or humanists. The faithful Jewish scholar is not a naturalist or humanist. Neither is the faithful Muslim scholar. If it is difference that defines Christian learning, then it must be noted that Christian scholars differ from their Jewish colleagues on some matters, from their Muslim colleagues on others, from their naturalist colleagues on yet others, and so on. Nothing is served by lumping those all together. The differences are different. There are *many* "kinds" of *scientia*, not just two. Furthermore, we must seriously consider the possibility that, at least in the case of Jews and Muslims, the non-Christian is *not* worshipping an idol but worshipping differently the same god, the one and only God. Worshipping God deficiently — so I as a Christian believe — but nonetheless worshipping *God*.

Life Beyond Affect and Volition

I have suggested that Christian scholarship is faithful scholarship. By this I mean that is to be defined not by its difference but by its fidelity. I mean something else as well. I observed earlier that there is a powerful impulse in the neo-Calvinist movement to think of every human life as being in service to something or other, to God or idol. Two things are striking about this. For one thing, to think of human life in this way is to think of it as fundamentally affective in nature, with our affections often functioning as motives for intentional action. Second, it is to think of our affections as having a hierarchical structure, oriented as a totality around God or idol. Though Kuyper does not make his thought fully explicit, my surmise is that he believed that this model holds for all that transpires in the sciences except for coming to believe something through the senses or reason. Perhaps he saw these latter as grounded in dispositions rather than affections and decisions. And though he would surely think that at least some of the dispositional structure of the human self is also altered and healed by regeneration, perhaps his thought was that these *belief*-dispositions are not so affected.

I contend that there is a large area of human life to which this affective/volitional model does not apply. Many of our actions, and many of the changes in our consciousness, are due not to affects and intentions but to created *dispositions* and acquired *habits*. We are all disposed to believe certain things about the past when we have what may be called memory experiences; we are all disposed to model our actions on the actions of those we admire; and so forth. In short, many human actions are not performed in the service of anything at all, and many changes in consciousness do not come about because of our service to something. They come about because of our dispositional and habitual natures.

We must tread carefully here. I do not mean that habits and dispositions — and the actions and changes that emerge from their workings — are isolated from and impervious to our new life in Christ. We are all capable of *monitoring* our habits and dispositions; and where we find them out of accord with that new life, we are to undertake the discipline of seeking to alter them. For habits and dispositions are also fallen. But the fact that I have altered some habit or disposition of mine so that it now works in accord with my ends and principles does not mean that that habit or disposition has disappeared *in favor of decisions* to act on those principles or ends. Though I can work on altering my disposition to believe what people tell me, to alter it is not to eliminate it.

So when I say that *fidelity* is the basic *desideratum* for the Christian in his or her practice of scholarship, I mean to avoid that radical obliteration of our habitual and dispositional nature to which the neo-Calvinist is so regularly tempted. What the gospel asks of us is that we obey all the commands of God in our life, not that we attempt the impossible task of making all of life consist of acting out of obedience to the commands of God.

An Interactive View of the Relation of Faith and Learning

This leads me to a final point of disagreement with prominent representatives of the neo-Calvinist movement. A crucial failing in Kuyper and many of his followers is that they overlook the fact — or resist acknowledging the fact

— that developments in scholarship sometimes lead persons to alter their re-ligious convictions, and that sometimes this is fully justified, even obligatory. The notion that scholarship may at times yield religious illumination is ab-horrent to many neo-Calvinists. Their picture of the relation between Chris-tian conviction, on the one hand, and scientific practice and result, on the other, is entirely uni-directional, from faith to science. Kuyper's emphasis, you will recall, is entirely on the way palingenesis influences science. (It may be observed that Karl Marx also held a uni-directional view concerning the place of religion in life. For him, however, the direction was just the opposite: religion is never cause but always effect.)

Neo-Calvinism's Expressivism

What lies behind this uni-directional, non-interactionist view of the relation between religion and the practice of scholarship, so it seems to me, is what Charles Taylor in his fine books, *Hegel* and *Hegel and Modern Society,* calls the *expressivist* vision of life. In this vision, human activity and life are regarded as expressions of the self. According to Taylor, the expressivist vision was char-acteristic of the Romantics.[7] Yet we find it in Kuyper as well.

7. Here is, in part, Taylor's description of the expressivist vision:

[As a] protest against the mainstream Enlightenment view of man as both subject and ob-ject of an objectifying scientific analysis . . . Herder and others developed an alternative no-tion of humanity whose dominant image was rather that of an expressive object. Human life was seen as having a unity rather analogous to that of a work of art, where every part or aspect only found its proper meaning in relation to all the others. Human life unfolded from some central core — a guiding theme or inspiration — or should do so, if it were not so often blocked and distorted. . . .

[The] image of expression was central to this view not just in that it provided the model for the unity of human life, but also in that men reached their highest fulfillment in expres-sive activity. It is in this period that art came to be considered for the first time the highest human activity and fulfillment, a conception which has had a large part in the making of contemporary civilization. These two references to the expressive model were linked: it is just because men were seen as reaching their highest realization in expressive activity that their lives could themselves be seen as expressive unities. . . .

But men are expressive beings in virtue of belonging to a culture; and a culture is sus-tained, nourished, and handed down in a community. The community has itself on its own level an expressive unity. It is once more a travesty and a distortion to see it as simply an in-strument which individuals set up (or ought ideally to set up) to fulfill their individual goals, as it was for the atomist and utilitarian strand of the Enlightenment.

Expressivism also sharply broke with the earlier Enlightenment on its notion of man's relation to nature. Humanity is not body and mind compounded but an expressive unity

Of course Kuyper and his followers believed in an objective, structured reality. Often they used the language of sight: the Christian gospel enables us to "see" aright. Thus neo-Calvinism, when it comes to interpretation, is most nearly akin to that vision of the medievals in which the universe is treated as a text whose meaning we are to interpret, and in which meaning for the self is found by conforming to reality. Yet the overwhelming emphasis in Kuyper's discussion of science is that science is an expression of the self; and since there are two kinds of selves, there must be two kinds of science. This understanding of science was just part of Kuyper's yet larger vision: he understood culture and society in general as, at bottom, expression, specifically, as expression of religion. Not surprisingly, then, he scarcely noted any influence in the opposite direction: the influence of culture and society on the religion of the self.

Science is not solely an expression of the self. It is also the outcome of the impact of the world on us, coupled with the impact on us of the social practice of science. Self, world, social practice: it is from the interaction of these three that science emerges. It is true, indeed, that out of the heart are the issues of life; but issues also go *into* the heart.

The Social Practice of Science

In my book entitled *Reason within the Bounds of Religion*, I approached these matters not by way of a discourse on the relation between the abstract phenomena of religion and science, nor, as does Kuyper, by way of a discourse on the contribution of the subject to science; instead I reflected on the actions involved in an individual's engagement in the practice of science, and then, specifically, a *Christian* individual. Action — *doing* scholarship — was put on center stage. The basic issue I discussed was "the role of one's Christian commitment in one's practice of scholarship."[8]

A variety of interconnected actions go into the practice of scholarship. I suggested in my book, however, that it might prove especially illuminating to focus on the action of *weighing* some claim or proposal of scholarship —

---

englobing both. But since humanity as a bodily being is in interchange with the whole universe, this interchange must itself be seen in expressive terms. Hence to see nature just as a set of objects of potential humanity use is to blind ourselves and close ourselves to the greater current of life which flows through us and of which we are a part.

Hegel and Modern Society (Cambridge: Cambridge University Press, 1979), pp. 1-3.

8. Wolterstorff, *Reason within the Bounds of Religion*, p. 21.

that is, of deciding whether to accept or reject it. This action of weighing, though far from constituting the whole of the practice of scholarship, is absolutely central to it.

If I were writing the book today I would, in turn, set a person's weighing of some proposal or claim of scholarship within the context of his or her participation in the *social practice* of scholarship. The social practice should be taken as the basic context for our reflections; the actions are an exercise of the practice. There are also scientific *results*, scientific *equipment,* and all of that, but these emerge from, and gain their significance from, the social practice of science.

Though the notion of a social practice enters deep into contemporary thought on a multitude of topics, it has never, to the best of my knowledge, been given a sustained and penetrating analysis. The best analysis of which I am aware is the brief analysis offered by Alasdair MacIntyre in his book, *After Virtue.* Let me briefly mention some of the salient features of social practices to which MacIntyre calls our attention.

A social practice, such as farming or figure skating, is a complex activity that the practitioner *learns* to do. It requires knowledge and skills that do not emerge simply through maturation, nor are we born with them. We have to learn them. The requisite learning occurs in part without explicit teaching, by way of modeling in apprentice situations. Almost invariably, however, explicit teaching also has an important place. Furthermore, as practices become increasingly complex, experts arise who are not themselves practitioners but whose business it is to induct newcomers into the practice by instruction: coaches, advisers, teachers, etc. I use the word "induct" advisedly. Practices have histories, traditions — novices are inducted into an ongoing activity and tradition that existed before they entered it.

To be inducted into a practice is to assimilate goals for one's engagement in the practice and standards of excellence for one's performance in it. It is to learn what are the various goals of farming, what constitutes excellence in figure skating, and the like. It is of prime importance to recognize that these goals and standards are not, for the most part, definitive of the practice. Among contemporary participants in a practice there will often be considerable disagreement as to the appropriate goals and standards. Likewise across the history of the practice there will usually be considerable change in the dominant goals and standards. Sometimes these changes result from the implementation of new ideas coming in from the surrounding society. Sometimes they are responses to technological innovations. Sometimes they result from the influence of a practitioner who has a new and creative vision of possibilities within the practice. The malleability of practices with respect to goals and standards means that they are open to new modes of human endeavour and excellence.

An implication of this openness is that it is a mistake to ask for *the* goals and *the* standards and *the* methods of a social practice such as art or science — as though art and science were static Platonic essences descending into history in the fullness of time. Today the hypothetico-deductive method is prominent in the natural sciences; in the eighteenth century it was almost universally frowned upon and the method of induction was favored. A high medieval like Aquinas would have thought both were alarming and lamentable fallings away from the true method of starting from what one sees to be true and proceeding exclusively by deduction.

Much more could be said about the notion of a social practice; but enough has been said for my purposes on this occasion. As I now see it, the fundamental issue to be posed here is how the convictions, goals, and practices of the Christian intersect with the social practice of science (*Wissenschaft*, academic learning).

Control Beliefs

Let me return to what I put on center stage: a person of Christian commitment engaged in the act of weighing some claim or proposal of scholarship. We are to visualize this person as having been inducted into the relevant part of the practice of scholarship. I stress in my book that such a person, both by virtue of being a Christian and by virtue of being inducted into the practice of scholarship, will always approach such an episode cloaked in beliefs — as indeed in motivations and dispositions. Invariably some of those beliefs, some of those *praejudicia*, will function as "control beliefs" for the weighing of theory or interpretation.

What do I mean? Well, among the propositions one believes will typically be some that one regards as evidence for or against the claim or proposal one is weighing. This is not always the case. Sometimes one finds oneself without any evidence for or against the proposal; then one simply has to wait. And sometimes evidence may be irrelevant: one either "sees" the proposal to be true or one "sees" it to be false and that is the end of the matter. Usually, though, one will have what I called, in my book, "data-beliefs," these consisting of one's body of evidence for and against the proposal.

What I especially wanted to call attention to, however, was that in addition to data-beliefs one has beliefs that *control* one's weighing of the theory, that is, beliefs as to the *type* of theory acceptable on the matter in question. If we approach these matters from the side of the results of science, we may never notice the presence and relevance of such beliefs. But if we approach them from the angle of engagement in the practice of science, then we see at once that discussions and disputes in the sciences are by no means confined to "factual" claims, that is, to disputes about theories, interpretations, and evidence. There are also disputes over the cognitive standards and goals of science, and — so closely connected with these as to make it difficult sometimes to draw the line — disputes over the proper methodology for attaining these standards and for achieving these aims.[9]

Examples are abundant. The intuitionist in mathematics says we should avoid committing ourselves to entities for which no "construction" is at hand, the nominalist, that we should avoid committing ourselves to abstract entities. Some in the social sciences insist that the proper goal is the construction of a nomological science, others, that it is the construction of a hermeneutic science. Some practitioners of seventeenth-century physics thought hypotheses about non-perceptible entities were an appropriate part of their science; others thought good physics would consist entirely of inductive generalizations from and to the perceptible. Throughout the modern period some have thought that the goal of science is certitude, while others have argued that we must embrace fallibilism. So it goes, on and on. In none of these cases was the topic of dispute the acceptability of a particular theory or interpretation; it was, rather, the acceptability of certain cognitive goals or standards, or of the methods appropriate for achieving those. The dispute, in short, was over what *sorts* of theories are acceptable. Such disputes open our eyes to the presence of control beliefs among the *praejudicia* that we carry with us to the action of weighing a theory or interpretation.

In my book I suggested that if we want to understand the connection between a person's Christian convictions and his or her weighing of some claim or proposal of scholarship, it will very often be illuminating to focus on this phenomenon of control beliefs — of *praejudicia* concerning aims, standards, and methodology. For among that person's *praejudicia*, functioning as control beliefs, will be various of his or her religious convictions. Not only will this actually be so; I argue in my book that it will appropriately be so, provided, of course, that the person is epistemically justified in holding those convictions.

I am presupposing that between Christian conviction, on the one hand, and particular scholarly claims or proposals, on the other, there can be genuine conflicts or affinities. There are those who deny this, who hold that

---

9. Laudan offers an especially good discussion of the interconnection of such disputes.

though we may feel tension now and then, there are no real points of conflict. The point has been developed in various ways, sometimes by giving a non-realist construction of science, sometimes by giving a non-realist construction of religion. I cannot argue the case here but must content myself with affirming that, as I see it, the Christian gospel speaks not only about God but also about this world, and that scholars speak not only about this world but also about God. Hence an ever-shifting blend of conflict and affinity is what the Christian must expect when he or she engages in the social practice of *scientia*.

It is at this point that my rejection of the expressivist vision, in its neo-Calvinist version, becomes especially relevant. I firmly insist that in the case of conflict between one's Christian convictions, on the one hand, and something presented for one's acceptance in the pursuit of science, on the other, often it is science that ought to give way. In my book I launch an attack on the foundationalist claim that that kind of retreat in science would be appropriate only if one had grounded one's Christian conviction in what is self-evidently or incorrigibly certain. On the other hand, I also insist that in cases of conflict between religion and science, people should sometimes alter not their scientific but their religious convictions. Though at times the acceptable and even obligatory thing to do is to maintain one's religious convictions and make one's science conform, at other times the acceptable and even obligatory thing to do is resolve the tension by revising one's religious convictions. At a certain point Christians were no longer justified in believing that the geocentric theory is an essential component of Christian conviction.

God's Word to Fallen Creatures

I am well aware that to say these things is to evoke anxiety in a good many Christians. Some will be made uneasy by the fact that there is no criterion telling us when to resolve conflicts by changing our science and when to resolve them by changing our religious convictions. Others will fear that if we surrender uni-directionality, either as causal fact or epistemic duty, then we can no longer acknowledge that there is a Word from outside our existence commanding acceptance and obedience — a Word from God. Earlier I said that Christian learning is fundamentally faithful learning. The worry is that the acids of history will eat away at fidelity until there is nothing left.

This worry deserves full discussion. Here I must content myself with stating the main point that I would make if I were to compose a full discussion. The Christian conviction that there is a Word from outside our existence, calling us to acceptance and obedience, is fully compatible with acknowledging that we as Christians, along with the rest of humanity, are often mistaken in our religious convictions. It is even compatible with the claim that we sometimes find ourselves in the presence of evidence so compelling against some element of our religious convictions that we *ought* to give up that element. The Word of God comes to fallen creatures, creatures fallen in their religion as well as in the rest of their lives. It comes to creatures not lifted out of the fallenness of their existence by having bowed their hearts and minds before the voice of the Lord their God — not even out of the fallenness of their *religious* existence. That is the essence of what I would say.

The World for Which We Educate

Education in general, and school education in particular, is a goal-directed enterprise; it's an intervention in the lives of people with the aim of effecting some alteration in their lives. If we as educators are to answer the fundamental questions concerning the education we offer, we must be clear on which alterations we are, and which ones we should be, aiming at. We also need clarity on, for example, the strategies most likely to achieve the goals we set for ourselves. But without clarity on goals, discussions on education get nowhere.

Let me add that sometimes we do not want our discussions to get anywhere. Our talk is not for the sake of clarifying what we are doing and steering us toward what we should be doing; it's to conceal from ourselves what we are doing, or to make us feel good about what we are doing, or to develop resistance to changing what we are doing.

Models of Education

It is my impression that if those who teach in the Christian colleges today were asked to state what they regard as the proper goal of Christian collegiate education, their answers, with few exceptions, would fall into one of four types. Some would espouse what may be called *the Christian service model;* the goal is to train students to enter one and another line of so-called "Kingdom work" such as evangelism, ministry, church education, mission-field medicine, and the like. Others would espouse *the Christian humanist model;* the goal

---

This lecture, part of a series of lectures called "The Christian University as an Agent of Shalom," was delivered at Seattle Pacific University in the mid-1980s.

is, from a Christian perspective, to induct the student into the great cultural heritage of humanity — its art, its science, its literature, its philosophy, its music, its theory. Yet others would espouse *the Christian academic-discipline model*; the goal is, from a Christian perspective, to introduce students to the academic disciplines, thereby putting them in touch with reality in the way in which theory does that. Most of the remainder would espouse *the Christian vocation model*; the goal is to train students for whatever roles they will be entering, especially occupational or professional roles, and to teach them to conduct themselves as Christians within those roles. It will be noticed that the first model I mentioned, the Christian service model, is really a version of this last. On the Christian service model, the college confines itself to training for that narrow range of occupations which constitute so-called Kingdom work; on the Christian vocation model, the college trains for Christian life and action in a wide range of occupational callings.

My own view has come to be different from all of these. Originally I embraced the Christian humanist model. That was the dominant model in my own collegiate education; I embraced what I was taught. I moved from there to a blend of the Christian academic-discipline model and the Christian vocation model. In retrospect it is clear to me that the effect of my graduate school education was the main cause of my moving away from the Christian humanist model; whereas my graduate school education trained me to "do philosophy," as we called it in those days, the Christian humanist model seemed to be oriented entirely toward the past.

It was the slow and halting recognition that none of these models responds adequately to the *wounds* of humanity that led me to move beyond all of them. I continued to believe in the importance of being inducted into our cultural heritage, I continued to believe in the importance of engaging in the academic disciplines, and I continued to believe in the importance of training for the knowledge-intensive professions; but I also came to believe that we must energize our students to pursue justice and struggle against injustice.

The question that then confronted me was how to acknowledge the worth and relevance of all these goals without having just a grab bag of good things on my hands. The answer I arrived at was that the biblical concept of *shalom* holds them all together. Justice requires shalom; one cannot read the poetic and prophetic literature of the Old Testament and miss that. But when I looked carefully at how shalom was described, it seemed evident to me that culture and theory also enhance shalom; they enhance our flourishing. On this occasion I will assume that all of you, from your own reading of the psalms and the Old Testament prophets, have a fairly clear idea of what constitutes that mode of human flourishing which the Bible calls shalom.

If we are going to teach for justice — justice being the ground floor of shalom — we will have to understand, and enable our students to understand, the society in which we educate. That is only marginally true for the Christian humanist and the Christian academic-discipline models of Christian collegiate education; for the shalom model, social analysis is indispensable. So what I want to do on this occasion is present to you an interpretation of our modern world, and then make some comments on how we teach for justice if that is indeed the world in which our students will be living, and we along with them.

Our Enlightenment Legacy

In the heady atmosphere of the European Enlightenment there arose the conviction that humanity was finally emerging from its long-drawn-out adolescence and coming of age. There were thought to be many signs of this coming of age, including progress in science and technology, the rapid destruction of inhibiting traditions, and recognition of the "rights of man." But always one sign was prominent in the minds of the great Enlightenment thinkers: the decline of religion, or at least of so-called revealed religion. Humanity was growing out of religion and becoming secularized. The grip of wicked and obscurantist priests was being broken, and enlightenment, along with its inevitable corollary, emancipation, was being spread abroad. Ever since those heady days, sociologists and historians have used the category of *secularization* as one of their basic tools for trying to understand how a modern society differs from its ancestors.

It is clear by now that the Enlightenment deluded itself. It's true of the Western world today that religious institutions and officials have fewer sanctioned privileges, and enjoy less by way of legally grounded voice, than they did in medieval times. And it's true that there are now many spheres or sectors in society in which people typically make their decisions independently of their religions. Furthermore — to move from the level of society to that of culture — it's true that so-called secular humanism has a much larger voice in the West today than anything of the sort had in medieval times. But it's obvious that modernization as such does not destroy religion — not even particularistic revealed religion. In Western Europe today there is a marked decline of traditional institutional religion. But it's preposterous to suggest that in the United States, in Latin America, in Africa, in the Middle East, in Poland, even in Russia, the process of modernization has caused a decrease in religiosity. Perhaps there was for some time some plausibility to the thesis that modernization has caused the privatization of religion; that was Max Weber's variant on the Enlightenment thesis of the disappearance of religion. But recent developments make even that thesis seem implausible.

Yet our present-day social world is different, profoundly different, from the social world from which it emerged. So what are some of its hallmarks? I myself do not believe that the desire on the part of secular humanists to implement their ideas accounts for very much in our present-day social world — in spite of the relative prominence of secular humanism, at least recently, in elite culture of the West. But what then does? What are the dynamics of modernity?

A drama is a set of interlocking roles that persons can repeatedly perform. It proves illuminating to think of a society as structured like a drama. Every society creates an interlocking set of roles, coherent and typical ways of acting, which members of the society then learn to perform.

Loss of Ethically Infused Social Roles

In most of the world's societies a high proportion of the social roles that people played or were expected to play were simply *ascribed* to them rather than allotted on the basis of choice. The eldest son of the king was born to be king; it was his "nature" to be king. The son of a serf was born to be a serf; it was his "nature" to be a serf. Such ascriptivism has increasingly disappeared in modern society. It's true that a person's choice of social role in our society is often made under considerable duress, and that the availability to a given person of certain social roles is often conditioned on that person's possession of various native abilities. Nonetheless, role assignment in modern society is determined by *will* to an extent never before known.

Not only is the proportion of social roles allotted by ascription much lower in our society than it was in earlier ones; the roles themselves are typically both different and understood differently among us. Traditionally, to play a certain social role was not just to act in a certain typical and coherent way but to see oneself and to be seen as subject to a specific cluster of *requirements,* the fulfillment of these being enforced and reinforced by social expectations. To have the role of serf required one to spend a high proportion of one's time laboring for the lord on the manor; to have the role of lord required one to provide protection and security for one's serfs. These requirements were for the most part not legal requirements. But neither were they merely instrumental requirements — that is, causal conditions for achieving one's goals. They were *moral* requirements, matters of duty and right. And in good measure they were not just *general* moral requirements pertaining to all persons in all roles; rather, a particular role comprised a specific ethic. To occupy a certain station in life was to be subject to a specific set of duties and to enjoy a specific set of rights. There was an ethic of the knight, an ethic of the physician, an ethic of the lawyer, and so forth. The recognition of all these moral requirements, specific and general, was customarily caught up in a picture of the universe according to which all of us not only have duties with respect to human beings and social institutions but also have duties with respect to the sacred, the divine. Indeed, the duties and rights comprised in one's social roles were understood as grounded, in one way or another, in one's duties to the divine.

Of such ascribed and ethically infused social roles there are only traces left in the lives and consciousness of contemporary Europeans and Americans. Perhaps the clearest trace is to be seen in the role of son and daughter. Not only do we not choose to occupy the role of child of parents; probably most of us still understand this role as incorporating a specific complex of rights and responsibilities. To one's parents one has duties that one has to no one else, just by virtue of being their child; and they, correspondingly, have duties to their child.

The Rise and Spread of Capitalism

It seems to me indubitable that the principal cause of the decline of ascriptivism, and of the near disappearance in reality and consciousness of ethically infused social roles, has been the rise and spread of capitalism. A prominent feature of the spread of capitalism into new sectors of society is that more and more things are put on the market, with the result that the presence of contractual relations among human beings is increased enormously, and the loyalty, and expectations of loyalty, to persons and institutions characteristic of traditional societies is destroyed. Under capitalism, workers put their labor on the market and make contracts with owners of capital whereby for such-and-such quality and quantity of labor the workers will receive such-and-such pay; in most societies there was no such thing as a labor market. Under capitalism, land is put on the market and contracts are signed whereby title is transferred for such-and-such payment; in most societies it was impossible to transfer title to land by contract. Thus under capitalism the generalized ethic of contract becomes more and more the pervasive ethic of society. The range of that for which one *must* contract is expanded, and the limits on that for which one *may* contract are removed;

what is morally required increasingly becomes just that one keep the contracts one has made.

The corollary of this increase of contractual relations under capitalism is that one's occupation of social roles is increasingly determined by decision rather than ascription. And a natural if not inevitable consequence is that choosing a social role is understood less and less as taking onto oneself a specific range of duties and disciplines and more and more as choosing a way of acting that promises to satisfy one's private goals. Even such a social bond as marriage is increasingly understood not as a complex of rights and duties into which one enters by commitment or ascription, but as a contractual arrangement to provide benefits for benefits received.

One more feature of a capitalist economy is worth noting: namely, the increasing differentiation, or sectoring, of social roles and of the institutions in which those roles are played out. In particular, people's occupations, their "work," is increasingly differentiated from their other social roles. And given the other features of the system, one is invited to choose and practice one's occupation not by reference to its intrinsic satisfactions or social benefits, and certainly not by reference to whether it is one's calling, but solely by reference to whether or not it serves some private goal: a large paycheck, a conspicuous career, or whatever.

What then shapes life outside of work? Well, it turns out that the regimented, bureaucratized, differentiated, competitive character of work in a capitalist economy leaves fundamental sides of a person's nature unsatisfied and unfulfilled. And that, combined with the decrease of ethically infused social roles, yields the phenomenon to which many sociologists have called our attention: namely, that in the core areas of our world economy, people tend to look for love, intimacy, pleasure, and self-expression outside the workplace, in family, in sports, in art, in sex. And let me add: in religion. A pervasive privatism, heavily colored with hedonism, begins to characterize the lives of people outside of work. And it is to our lives outside of work that religion is increasingly consigned.

I have been speaking of the dynamics of capitalism; and I have suggested, as some of the micro-structural features of the social world that capitalism has helped to produce, the diminishing of ascriptivism, the contractualizing of human relations, and the differentiation of roles and institutions. I might have added the feature to which Max Weber so insistently called attention and which he regarded as basic: the rationalization of action — that is, the demise of tradition as a determinant of action and the governance of action instead by calculation as to what will most effectively achieve one's goals.

Religious Diversity and Nationalism

I do not regard capitalism as the sole fundamental dynamic determining the shape of modern Western society. Let me mention two others that I regard as fundamental, discussing them, however, much more briefly. One is the rise of religious diversity in modern Western societies. Typical of traditional societies was the presence of just one religion within a given society; to be a member of the society was to be a participant in that religion. Such religious monolithicism was ruptured in Greco-Roman society of middle and late antiquity; it was, however, in good measure recovered by the "Constantinianism" of medieval Western society. Then it was again ruptured and, as we now know, destroyed for good in the West by the Protestant Reformation. Since the Reformation, the various states of the West have all had to cope with an ever-increasing diversity of religions among their citizenry. They have experimented with a variety of strategies for coping with such diversity. It is clear, in retrospect, that there has been a powerful dynamic toward giving equal legal standing to an increasingly large range of religious groups and religious convictions — and indeed, to an increasingly large range of anti-religious groups and irreligious convictions.

I see a good many features of modern Western society, and especially of the role of religion in this society, as due to this phenomenon of increasing religious diversity. It has meant that religious groups see themselves as working in a marketplace, competing for clients. It has meant that religious persons, confronted with alternatives to their own religious convictions, feel it necessary to explain and justify themselves, or turn in the direction of subjectivism. It has meant that since our life together can less and less be grounded on shared religious convictions, we have to adopt other strategies for achieving social consensus and appeal to other dynamics for securing social loyalty. For many it has meant that what they care about most deeply is increasingly removed from public discussion as irrelevant to the goals of the discussion. It has meant that religion is increasingly removed from public life to private life after work — a result, as we have seen, also provoked by the dynamics of capitalism. And it has meant, as already noted, that ecclesiastical and other religious bodies enjoy less and less by way of legally sanctioned privilege and voice.

One of the questions these comments raise is whether something other than religion plays the traditional role of securing social cohesion in modern societies, or whether modern societies manage without anything of that sort. To some extent they do; our societies legitimate themselves by reference to what is supposedly necessary to maintain a capitalist economy and to achieve our ever-increasing mastery over nature and enjoy the benefits thereof. But that is not the whole of the matter; and it is here that I see the third of what I regard as the great formative forces of our modern world coming into view: the dynamics of nationalism, patriotism, and statism. Loyalty to one's people, one's civil society, or one's state — these have proved to be powerful dynamics in the modern world, leading nations (peoples) to ride roughshod over other nations, leading nations to make the state their own, leading states to flout international law, leading states to ride roughshod over other states, leading nations and states to make religion serve their own purposes, leading nations and states to trample the dignity and violate the rights of those who do not bend to their will or who find themselves in their way. In a world where capitalism increasingly makes the ethic of contract into the fundamental ethic of human relationships, in a world where religious diversity increasingly makes one's religion a matter of one's privacy — in such a world, nationalism, patriotism, and statism stand ready to fill the hollowed-out void within our social existence.

No doubt some of you are already finding this much too heavy — though I trust you can see glimmerings of its relevance to our educational goals. But before concluding I must turn our thoughts in a different direction. I have been talking about some of the salient characteristics of modern Western society. I am profoundly convinced that if we leave the matter there, distortion enters our thought and vision. We must speak of the global world.

A World-Systems Interpretation of Global Society

There are, as I and others see it, two main schools of interpretation of the structure of our modern global social world, one older and vastly more prominent in the First World, having its roots especially in Max Weber, the other newer, finding great popularity in the Third World.

We may call the former of these interpretations the *modernization* interpretation. Modernization theorists see our world as containing a large number of distinct societies, each at a certain point in the process of modernization. If one attends to the examples of societies that modernizationists cite, one sees that their maps of the distinct societies of the world come close to coinciding with the political map of the world. The United States constitutes a society, so does Australia, and so forth. Modernization theorists realize, of course, that these distinct societies interact; but they see this interaction as the interaction of distinct societies — rather like the interaction of distinct persons.

By comparing societies that they consider to be at different stages in the process of modernization, modernization theorists try to isolate the essential features of modernization and its crucial dynamics. We have already looked at some of these. But apart from claims concerning the defining features of the process of modernization and its deep dynamic, two theses lie at the very core of the modernization theorist's way of thinking. First, it is in principle possible for all societies simultaneously to reach a high point of modernization without any fundamental structural alteration in the already established, highly modernized societies; and second, the causes of a given society's low level of modernization are mainly to be found within that society itself and not, to any significant degree, in the impact of the highly modernized societies upon that one. Something is amiss within the non-modernized society: a lack of money for investment, the wrong kind of character formation, the wrong kind of religion, or whatever. Depending on what is thought to be amiss, the highly modernized societies can perhaps help with the cure; perhaps they can supply the money needed for investment, or the missionaries necessary for a better religion. But in any case, they are not the *cause*, not even *a* cause, of what is amiss.

The main alternative to modernization theory is *world-system* theory. Where modernization theorists see the world as containing a number of distinct societies at various stages in the process of modernization, world-system theorists see the world today as containing just one society — or social system, as they prefer to call it. This one social system displays the historically unique feature of having a single integrated economy combined with a multiplicity of distinct states, a multiplicity of distinct peoples or nations, and a multiplicity of distinct religions. It seems obvious that in the world today there is a division of labor that straddles states and peoples. TV sets sold in the United States are made in China; cell phones made in Finland are sold in Italy.

This combination of social entities is historically extraordinary; usually economies, states, and peoples coincide — or in the case of empires that comprise many peoples, economies and states coincide. Our world today is different. Furthermore, our unique structure of one economy straddling diverse states and diverse peoples is by now pretty much worldwide; almost every area of the world has been integrated into one economy, though of course to widely differing degrees.

World-system theorists emphasize that the world economy is capitalist in its structure. There are socialist states — and even some communist states — that participate in the structure. But socialist and communist states, when they enter the world market, prove just as capitalist in their behavior as the most capitalist of individual entrepreneurs.

World-system theorists also emphasize that the capitalist economy of our world-system has a horizontal structure of core and periphery. Even a cursory glance at our world-system reveals the fact that wealth is not evenly distributed throughout the geographical areas of the system — and more importantly, that *capital* wealth is not evenly distributed. Today its heaviest concentrations are to be found in North America, northwest Europe, and Japan. Those areas of heaviest capital accumulation constitute the core of the system; those of least capital accumulation, the periphery. Today the core of the system is heavily engaged in capital-intensive, high-technology, high-wage production, whereas the periphery is dominantly engaged in labor-intensive, low-technology, low-wage production.

However, the idea behind calling certain areas "core" is not so much that they are the richest in capital, but that they have the preponderance of economic voice and power in the system, this being both result and cause of their concentration of capital wealth. The core dominates the periphery; or, to put it from the other side, the periphery is subordinated to the core. A consequence of this domination is that the core exploits the periphery; in the interaction between the two, the core almost always gets the better of the deal because it has more power. It has modes of power at its disposal that the periphery lacks.

It is characteristic of world-system theorists to argue that this domination of a periphery by a core is a necessary dynamic of the system, not an accident. The vision of the modernization theorist that we can all advance simultaneously into the glorious future of high modernization is a cruel illusion. There are deep and profound reasons why TV manufacturers have moved their production from the United States to China: what they find there are low wages and no strikes. If that ceases to be true, they will find some other place to produce TVs.

World-system theorists argue that this system has been in operation for roughly four centuries. Accordingly, there has been, in their view, a development of underdevelopment. Two centuries ago, Bangladesh was a relatively prosperous part of the world; today it is impoverished. What contributed to the change was the interaction of England with the Bengalis.

Obviously there are issues of tremendous importance here that we cannot possibly discuss on this occasion. My own view is that the world-system interpretation is definitely correct in its general guidelines. A world in which a core dominates and exploits a periphery — that, it seems to me, is the world in which we find ourselves. I discover that a good many Christians are inclined to shy away from any theorist who discerns domination and exploitation in society. They immediately interpret that as Marxist and reject it out of hand. My own feeling is that Christians should be the last to be surprised by the presence of domination and exploitation in society and the last to be annoyed at the one who bears news of this. They above all should expect that; and their response should be the opposite of rejecting such claims out of hand. "Exactly what we would have expected," they should say. "Tell us the details of how it works."

This is the society in which we and our students live. It is for life in this society that we teach.

Implications for Christian Higher Education

Suppose now that you agree with me that the goal of Christian education is to equip and energize our students for a certain way of being in the world, not just for a way of thinking, though certainly also that, but for a certain way of being — a *Christian* way, not one of your standard American ways of being. Suppose further that you agree with me that this way of being can be described thus: to pray and struggle for shalom, celebrating its presence and mourning its absence. How do we do that? What is the pedagogy — and indeed, the curriculum — for an education with that goal?

If my analysis of the structure of our modern social world is correct, then I think at least the following three things will have to be central in our program. First, our students do not come unformed by the dynamics of capitalism, nationalism, and religious pluralism; they do not come oblivious to the ideologies of progress, of individualism, and of our modern turn to the world. They come formed by these. So one thing we must do is teach them to hold up these practices and these ideologies to the scrutiny of the Bible. That means loosening the grip of these things on them. It means bringing them to the point of *critical involvement* — not bringing them to the point of non-involvement, not leaving them at the point of uncritical involvement, but bringing them to the point of biblically critical involvement.

Second, having done that, we must offer them alternative ways of thinking and guide them into, and energize them toward, alternative ways of living. We must combat and counteract the "oblivion of the normative" which, so I argued, is becoming characteristic of our society. There is, of course, a good deal of discussion nowadays about the "ethic" of this and of that: business ethics, medical ethics, and so forth. What I am proposing is something quite different from what is customarily discussed under these headings. Such discussions typically take for granted the structure of law, of business, of engineering, and so forth to be found in modern society, and then consider how the quandaries that arise are to be handled. I suggest that what we in the Christian colleges and universities need to do before we become immersed in the quandaries of some profession or occupation is stand back and ask: In modern society, what should be the goals of medicine, and of law, and of business, and of farming, and of education, and of recreation? What are the norms appropriate to each of these sectors of modern human life?

The appropriate response to the sectoring of modern society is not, in my judgment, to adopt a regressive romanticism and try to return to what once was. Not only is that impossible; this sectoring or differentiation is a corollary of the unfolding of the potentials of creation that God offers to us and asks of us as God's human children. Rather than trying to recover a less differentiated society, we must struggle to see to it that no one of these sectors dominates our life as a whole — that our life together does not become economized or politicized or whatever; and that each sector pursues goals leading to health rather than illness.

And third, we have to teach for justice — not only on our local scene but on a global scale. Justice, in the biblical sense, occurs when the little ones are not only protected against oppression but also have a voice in the community. Our common humanity would call for us to care about justice in distant societies; the fact that we live in a world-system, with our own area at its core, makes that imperative.

Let me adopt a word from Paulo Freire to pull together what I have been saying; I think it is exactly the right word. Our challenge is to "conscientize" our students. The people Freire was concerned to conscientize were "the little people," the ones at the bottom of history; our students are in the core. But the challenge is the same: how to conscientize them?

As far back as I began to think independently about these matters, it has been my conviction that Christian education is for life, not just for thought. For quite some time I thought individualistically, however; social analysis was not my cup of tea. And for a long time I assumed what my teachers assumed — namely, that to shape life one shapes thought.

Slowly and somewhat reluctantly I was led to take seriously this question: How does one responsibly and effectively shape how a person tends to act? I read all I could find on the topic, mulled it over, and wrote up my conclusions in my book entitled *Educating for Responsible Action*. My major conclusion was that the assumption I had imbibed from my teachers, that one shapes life by shaping thought, represented an exceedingly naive view on how tendencies are formed. By introducing students to high culture, we inculcate in them habits and tendencies relevant to engaging high culture;

there is no evidence that we also, coincidentally, shape what they tend to do in life and society. What we all say to ourselves is that one has to know these things in order reflectively to engage the social issues facing us. I also said that; and I believe it, believe it still. But the point is that such learning does very little to energize action, other than the actions relevant to participating in culture and theory. Indeed, the study of theory is often *counter*productive; it makes us comfortable with things the way they are. For often it is ideologically based, consciously or not.

What I concluded from my studies was that there are three great shapers of action: discipline, modeling, and reasoning. That last, when fully developed, becomes praxis-oriented theory. If I were writing the book today, I would add two considerations and make three corrections. I would add radical conversion; radical conversion profoundly shapes what people tend to do. I suppose the reason I overlooked radical conversion was that I was looking for strategies, and there is no strategy for inducing radical conversion. And I would add empathy. Empathy with those who suffer, whether they appear before one face-to-face or in film or in literature, profoundly shapes what one tends to do.

The corrections I would make are these. Ethical theory, certainly since Kant, has focused on individual actions; recently philosophers have been arguing that the fundamental ethical issue is not which individual actions one ought to perform but how one ought to live one's life. I fell into the modern trap; the Protestant notion of a calling would have been a healthy corrective. Second, I neglected the dimension of delight; the book, I fear, comes across as sober, even grim. Delight is an indispensable component of shalom. And third, we must all reflect much more than any of us has on *coping* — that is, on what to do when there is nothing to do.

A Case for Disinterested Learning

On various occasions in recent years I have argued that we in the Christian colleges should teach for justice. Usually I have also made some comments how we can do that, arguing that, among other things, it requires praxis-oriented scholarship. By that I mean scholarship whose *governing interest* is an analysis of the structure and dynamics of our social world, a critical appraisal of that structure and those dynamics, and an uncovering of the strategies that have some chance of preserving what ought to be preserved and changing what ought to be changed.

It is by no means my view, however, that all scholarship that is taught and practiced in the Christian college should be praxis-oriented scholarship. So what I want to do in this talk is state briefly why I think the Christian college, if it is to fulfill its calling, must also be a center of disinterested Christian scholarship.

Culture and Society

It is indispensable for what follows that we keep in mind the distinction between culture and society. When speaking of teaching for justice, I had my eye on society; on this occasion it is culture that I have in view. Culture, for us in the modern West, is a vast river originating from a wide variety of sources. The cultural property of most societies is minute compared to ours; and what they do have is, for the most part, produced within that society itself or in its near past. For us, the art of ancient China, the dramas of ancient Greece,

---

This essay appeared previously as "The Christian College and Christian Learning" in the *Seattle Pacific University Review* 6, no. 1 (Autumn 1987). It is reprinted here with permission.

the philosophy of the medieval Europeans, the bronze castings of the medieval Benin tribe, the music of the baroque Europeans, all belong to our cultural patrimony. A consequence is that much of our cultural heritage is relatively disengaged from our ordinary social interactions. It is stored in museums, housed in libraries, remembered only by specialists.

Two features of our modern Western culture are especially worth keeping in mind for our subsequent discussion. Theory has an unusually prominent place within our culture. And our culture represents vast ideological diversity. The culture of the Zuni people is unified, homogeneous, consensual; ours is diverse, heterogeneous, conflictual.

Disinterested learning is *a component within culture* that, in good measure, *engages* culture as its object. My thesis is twofold: the Christian community ignores that component of culture at its peril. And the participation of the Christian community in that form of culture is one way in which it can contribute to that mode of human flourishing which is *shalom*.

Let me set the stage for my comments by calling attention to certain of the attitudes toward learning that are to be found outside the academy. It has been a deep impulse in American Christianity of the nineteenth and twentieth centuries to see piety and disinterested learning in opposition to each other. Nathan Hatch, in a fine essay, quotes Bela Bates Edwards as remarking in 1853 that "there is an impression somewhat general . . . that a vigorous and cultivated intellect is not consistent with distinguished holiness, and those who would live in the clearest sunshine of Communion with God must withdraw from the bleak atmosphere of human science."[1] The attitude of one hundred and fifty years ago described by Edwards has endured in significant segments of American Christianity, especially of American evangelicalism. The controversies over theological liberalism early in our century, and the shattering outcome of the Scopes trial, contributed to the suspicion of twentieth-century evangelicals toward much, if not most, learning. But that suspicion did not begin then, nor has it been confined to evangelicals. Hatch argues that the competitive democratic spirit of religion in America and its intensely practical orientation have combined to make disinterested learning suspect for a long time now and by many religious people. My guess is that all of us who teach in American Christian colleges have experienced this suspicion in personal ways. We have all had students, young or old, tell us that for years they were convinced that if they really wanted to *think*, they had to leave the Church.

1. Quoted by Hatch in "Evangelical Colleges and the Challenge of Christian Thinking," in *Making Higher Education Christian: The History and Mission of Evangelical Colleges in America*, edited by Joel A. Carpenter and Kenneth W. Shipps (Grand Rapids: Eerdmans, 1987), p. 155.

It is also important to have before us the attitude of American society generally toward learning, not just the attitude of Christians. An economy like ours of post-industrial capitalism tends to make two fundamental demands on learning. For one thing, various kinds of scholarship are indispensable to the maintenance and advance of such an economy; such an economy cannot operate without rather widespread technological and administrative knowledge and skills. Accordingly, it asks of its schools that they provide this. But second, such an economy creates, for many of its members, a rather sharp division between life at work and life after work; and it is the experience of many that immersion in culture provides delight and refreshment in one's life after work. Some people devote their private lives to muscle-building, to team sports, to fishing, to sexual escapades, to going to religious meetings, and so forth; for these activities, not much learning is required. But other people like to read books, listen to music, study painting, and talk philosophy.

Prominent educators in recent years have taken to bemoaning the fact that our public schools are oriented almost entirely toward teaching the skills necessary to hold down jobs, rather than the skills necessary for informed and judicious participation in the polity of our society. I think that the implied description of our public schools in this lament is not entirely accurate. Our public schools not only train students to hold down jobs but also offer courses designed to make life after work interesting and pleasurable. It is exactly this dual-focus sort of education that one would expect a society such as ours, of post-industrial capitalism, to offer its young members. It may be added that the lament of educators will do little or nothing, by itself, to change this. By and large, societies get the education they want.

But is this combination of an instrumental and hedonic attitude toward learning adequate? I do not deny that learning *can* serve our goals of mastery, nor do I deny that it *can* serve our goals of providing some delight in our existence. Neither do I wish to denigrate these goals; mastery of the right sort, and enjoyment of the right sort, have their place in shalom. But is that all? Is the significance of humanity's theorizing just that it serves our desire to alter our physical and social circumstances, and that it enables us to find delight?

Learning for Meaning in Community

Down through the ages there have been those who claimed that disinterested learning changes one for the better — that somehow it ennobles us ethically. This conviction was especially prominent among the Renaissance humanists, and it remains a common element in the outlook of those who advocate what might be called a humanist approach to education. I think it is difficult in the face of the evidence to maintain this view. The Nazis, remember, were not cultural illiterates.

Another view as to the worth of disinterested learning is that it liberates us, frees us from the parochialisms of our own situation by opening up to us the diversity of ways in which human beings have expressed their humanity. Some there are who, playing on the etymology of the word "liberal," argue that this is of the essence of liberal education. I think there can be no doubt that learning does in this way liberate us. However, we must interpret this "liberation" in such a way as to acknowledge that learned people may be closed-minded. Knowing something of the diversity of ways in which human beings have expressed their humanity by no means invariably results in empathy for those ways; not uncommonly it results instead in a judgmental attitude.

Let me pursue a somewhat different line of thought from either of those above. I do not regard this as the only line worth pursuing; I make no pretensions here at an exhaustive treatment of our topic. I present it just as one approach to the significance of disinterested learning.

We human beings are unavoidably *hermeneutic creatures*. It belongs to our very nature to interpret our experience, to find meaning in it; and then, on the basis of our interpretation, to desire, feel, and act. No doubt some of our patterns of interpretation are common to all human beings, and the consequence neither of volition nor reflection. All of us immediately interpret our experience as involving enduring physical objects of which we have various modes of awareness. But that is not true for the totality of anyone's interpretation. In everyone's interpretation of experience there is a contribution of reflection and volition.

The fact that we human beings struggle to interpret our experience is not a mark of our fallenness; rather, it is one of those things that God had his eye on when, contemplating his creatures, he said that what had been made was very good. In all of us there is a longing to understand, to have insight, to see how things hang together, to discern what it all means. God is not only behind answers to our longing for insight: God is behind the questions as well.

I suggest that the arts and sciences — using "science" in the broad sense of *Wissenschaft* — represent humanity's most profound and sustained attempts to find meaning in existence, to critique the meaning purportedly found by others, and to give expression to the meaning it does find. Is this not what our philosophy and poetry, our social theory and theology, are ultimately about? Are they not about the sense, the meaning, of our human existence? Art and theory are not some odd and dispensable luxury. They are the expression of our nature as hermeneutic creatures.

But as we all know and as I have mentioned, we human beings *disagree* as to the meaning we find in our existence. We do not disagree on everything: let's not forget that. But we disagree on very much indeed. In scholarship, fundamental issues of meaning are fought out. Not *only* there, but *certainly* there. What choice then does the Christian have but to engage in that complex dialectic of cooperating with one's fellow scholars in the *human* task of pursuing meaning while yet working out a *Christian* interpretation of experience and of meaning? This, if pursued persistently and systematically, will result in something that is recognizably *Christian* learning.

Someone might object: do not the Scriptures interpret reality for us? Do they not give us a system of meaning? We do not have to *devise* some system of meaning; certainly we do not have to do so in the sustained and systematic way that results in theory, *scientia*. All we have to do is accept and hand on the framework of meaning to be found in Scripture.

To this objection a twofold answer is appropriate. The Scriptures do indeed provide us with an interpretation of reality and experience. But, in the first place, everyone's interpretation goes beyond that, unavoidably so. We must all interpret dimensions of reality and experience about which Scripture says nothing, except in the most general and schematic way. And second, it is the fulfillment of our created nature to follow our longing for insight beyond the merely indispensable toward the development of the arts and sciences — to pursue the insight science can give us into the physical dimension of reality, the biological, the psychological, and so on. It is our calling in our interpretation to be *faithful* to the biblical interpretation; it is not our calling to refuse to go beyond that — if that were even possible. Even Christian theology is more than mere repetition of Scripture. I am here assuming the falsehood of that medieval tradition of contemplative Christianity which said that only insight into the nature and ways of God is of intrinsic worth. I am assuming the validity of the "turn toward the world" that the Reformation represents.

One more factor must be brought into the picture. We do not each work out our own interpretation of experience and culture in solitary confinement. Our interpretations are influenced by the expressions of those of others. So too the Christian community does not work out its interpretation in solitary confinement. It is influenced in its interpretation by the expressions of those of others — sometimes for good, sometimes for ill. Sometimes what shapes the interpretation of the Christian community is interpretations which are, at root, alien to the Scriptures. What is needed, accordingly, is a discerning engagement of Christians with the culture surrounding them — and in particular, a discerning engagement of Christian scholars with the "scientific" culture surrounding them.

I trust you now see why I say that the Christian community neglects engagement with the world of scholarship at its own peril. To neglect scholarship is to neglect one of the fundamental shapers of meaning in our society, and thereby one of the fundamental shapers of life. And to neglect that is to run the risk that the community's own interpretation of meaning and its own way of life will unwittingly be shaped by systems of meaning alien to its faith and subversive of its witness.

The Social Practice of Faithful Learning

In recent years the evangelical community in America has begun, in a certain way, to realize these truths. It has begun to talk about the influence of that particular system of meaning called *secular humanism* on the thought and action of society in general and on the thought and action of the Christian community. And it has discerned the central role played by scholars in the articulation and spread of this system of meaning.

I think it important not to credit secular humanism with more influence than it actually has. It is typical of people unhappy with social trends to project their dissatisfaction onto some cultural movement. Not liking where our economy of post-industrial capitalism has led us, along with our legal structure of *no establishment,* people say the trouble lies in the spread of the philosophy of secular humanism. I submit that it is not secular humanism that has led to the disappearance of required Christian prayers from our public schools. Their disappearance is due to the application by the courts, in our society of increasing religious diversity, of the legal injunction that there shall be no establishment of religion. The point remains, however, that systems of meaning, expressed in theory and art, do shape our general society and our particular communities.

The call for disinterested Christian learning that I have issued does not go without challenge. Let me cite three objections from among those commonly raised. First, it is said that to go down the road of developing Christian learning is to run the serious threat of breaking fellowship with the academic community generally. For some, this prospect is a matter of painful poignancy. They have only recently, with great effort and even trauma, achieved such fellowship. Are they now to toss away what has been earned at such great price?

Secondly, there are those who are convinced that scholarship, if properly pursued, is not the expression of our different interpretations of reality and of our differing narratives and scenarios concerning the course of history, but is instead the expression of our shared human nature: of our common perceptual capacities, of our common rationality, of our common capacity for self-awareness. Those who think thus would be inclined to challenge the entire perspective within which I have cast the enterprise of theorizing. Theorizing is not, they would say, the attempt to find and to express meaning; it is the attempt to discover and report facts.

And thirdly, it is said that the results seen thus far are too paltry to warrant pursuing the project further. Where is the distinctively Christian mathematics, the distinctively Christian physics, the distinctively Christian chemistry, the distinctively Christian psychology? Even the supposedly distinctive Christian philosophy: is that anything more than a blend of Christian theology with a philosophy that is not distinctively Christian but one that could perfectly well be accepted by non-Christians?

This is not the place to respond to these objections with a full-blown discussion of the nature of Christian learning. In my *Reason within the Bounds of Religion* I have spoken far more amply on the topic than I am able to do here. Let me content myself with making two comments which, though they do not directly address the objections, may at least contribute to clearing the air and thus to seeing the situation with more clarity.

In the first place, the aim of Christian learning is *not to* be different or distinctive but to be *faithful*. Let the differences fall out as they may. It is my own conviction that fidelity in the field of scholarship will yield plenty of difference. But difference is not the goal; indeed, Christian scholars should be delighted when others accept their views. I find a great deal of confusion on this score, both by proponents of Christian learning and by opponents. It may be the case that in some areas faithful Christian learning will not yield results different from those at present established in the academy; perhaps this is true for large parts of mathematics. But that does not endanger the project of Christian learning. One hardly shows that there is no such thing as Marxist learning by showing that other people agree with Marxists on some matters. Why then should it be thought that one shows that there is no such thing as Christian learning by showing that Marxists agree with Christians on some matters — or that behaviorists do, or functionalists, or intuitionists, or Jews, or Muslims, or whoever?

Second, I think it is helpful, in reflecting on how commitments and values shape science, to focus more on the social practice of the academic disciplines than on the results. The results often conceal such shaping; the practice exhibits them. The social practice of science is filled with disputes over proper methods, proper goals, proper standards for appraisal of theories, proper ontologies, and the like. It is in this contentious social practice that

Christians participate. They do not start over, counter to what some advocates of Christian learning seem sometimes to suggest; they enter the ongoing practice. But they enter the practice as persons who have their own goals,
beliefs, interpretations, and values, rooted in their Christian faith; they are
entitled and even obligated to participate in the practice in accord with those.
Of course I am here assuming the falsehood of the compartmentalization
thesis, according to which science and religion pertain to separate, water-
tight compartments of life and reality.

Once again, then: for the integrity of the Christian community and the
vitality of its healing work in the world, the Christian colleges of this land
must be places where sustained and serious disinterested Christian learning
takes place. For it is in the realm of scholarship that many of the fundamental
issues of how we interpret our world are fought out. The resolution of those
issues shapes our thought and shapes our life — both the thought and life of
our society generally, and the thought and life of the Christian community.

It is my view that if we take seriously this contention that in the realm
of scholarship fundamental issues of meaning are at stake, we will, in the first
place, be especially concerned to nourish and promote theology, history, and
philosophy. For it is these disciplines, or at least these disciplines when properly conducted, that provide the context for the others. Secondly, I think that
if we take seriously what I have argued, we in the humanities must reflect
much more seriously than we have on the *canon* of texts and works that we
present to our students. A canon is not some objectively determined hierarchy of worth — though canons do of course express judgments of worth;
canons are shaped by ideologies. We must ask seriously whether the canon
of English literature, of world literature, of philosophy, of social theory, of visual art, as found in secular institutions, is satisfactory for us as we engage in
Christian learning. And thirdly, I think that if we take seriously what I have
argued, we will do less by way of just handing over information to our students which they are then free to use when and where and as they wish —
what Paulo Freire calls the "banking" concept of education — and will instead do more by way of introducing students to the *practice* of that discipline,
even enabling them on their own level to engage in that practice.

I know very well that there are obstacles to the Christian colleges of this
land becoming centers of creative Christian scholarship. For one thing, all
too often the administrators of these colleges are inclined to give low priority
to scholarship. Usually that is not whimsical and arbitrary on their part;
there are pressures on them which push them in that direction. I do not say
that the promotion of scholarship is the only thing that counts. I want passionately to insist, however, that it is one thing, and that this should be put in

the balance when administrators make their decisions. To act otherwise is to act with great shortsightedness.

Too often our supporting constituencies have no sense of the importance, or the difficulty, of Christian scholarship. As I have already mentioned, often they think of scholarship, even that done by members of their own community, with suspicion. I view it as an obligation on the part of our administrators and on the part of us, the faculty, to do what we can to lead and teach our constituencies on the importance of committed scholarship. Why should we insultingly treat them as a mass to be pacified so that the money will keep pouring in rather than seeing ourselves as having an obligation to instruct them? But also I want to say to us, the faculty, that it is an obligation on our part to be both pastoral and courageous in our dealing with constituents. Why, I often ask myself, do scholars endemically think that life ought to be so arranged that, though courage may rightly be expected of others, it should never be expected of scholars?

Administrators and constituencies must give faculty room for trying out new ideas; but we the faculty must then do this responsibly. When our investigations prove to have gone in mistaken directions, we must cultivate in ourselves the inner serenity to say that we were wrong. And we must get over the arrogant tendency to think that when we have published some new idea, others ought to bow down and exclaim that this is just exactly the insight that they have been waiting for all these years. Even when things go as well as they can, we must expect that there will be tensions. Ours should not be the unattainable goal of eliminating all tensions, but the elusive though yet attainable goal of making those tensions healthy and instructive.

The Project of a Christian University
in a Postmodern Culture

There is a dispute raging today between those who see the Enlightenment project of governing our existence by Reason as an unfinished project, promising liberation, on which we should all continue to work; and those who see in that project little but the tyranny of Reason. The first party says that if we do not continue the struggle to govern our lives by Reason we can only expect more of the terrors of irrationalism. The second party says that if we do continue to govern our lives by Reason we can only expect more of the terrors of rationalism. That, in brief, is the dispute between the defenders of modernism and the defenders of postmodernism — intense and confused.[1]

I wish to begin today by entering that dispute; but from a side door, as it were. I think the discussion as a whole can only be advanced if we unravel the issues and then discuss them with care. Reason enters into our lives in various ways. We act on reasons so as to achieve goals. That has been called *instrumental rationality*. We offer reasons to each other as we converse. That has been called, especially by Jürgen Habermas, *communicative rationality*. But also we believe things for reasons. Some have borrowed a word from the Greek and called this latter, *epistemic rationality*.[2] It is mainly about epistemic rationality that I will be speaking.

In the early months of 1671, the English philosopher John Locke had a discussion with some five or six friends on matters of morality and revealed

1. As just two examples, see Jürgen Habermas, *The Philosophical Discourse of Modernity*, translated by F. G. Lawrence (Cambridge: Polity Press, 1987), and Willem van Reijen, *De Onvoltooide Rede* (Kampen, The Netherlands: Kok, 1987).

2. See, for example, Richard Foley, *The Theory of Epistemic Rationality* (Cambridge: Harvard University Press, 1987).

This is Wolterstorff's inaugural address delivered at the Free University of Amsterdam, published by VU Boekhandel/Uitgeverij in 1988. It is reprinted here with permission.

religion. The discussants, says Locke, "found themselves quickly at a stand by the difficulties that arose on every side. After we had awhile puzzled ourselves, without coming any nearer a resolution of those doubts which perplexed us, it came into my thought that we took a wrong course, and that before we set ourselves upon enquiries of that nature it was necessary to examine our own abilities, and see what objects our understandings were or were not fitted to deal with."[3] What eventually emerged from that resolution was Locke's *Essay Concerning Human Understanding*. The culmination of the *Essay* was Locke's proposal as to the proper role of Reason in the governance of our beliefs.

Locke's proposal, so I contend, became classic for the mentality of the modern West — in its central features of course, not in all its details. And for centuries natural science was held up as the prime exhibit of the worth of following the proposal. Today it is agreed by virtually all who have participated in the discussions of recent years that reputable natural science simply does not fit the Lockean proposal, nor anything remotely similar to it. Previously, when it was observed that *religion* did not fit the proposal, many concluded: so much the worse for religion. Now that it is starkly clear that reputable science does not fit the Lockean proposal, most have concluded: so much the worse for the proposal. The Lockean picture of the proper place of Reason in our lives has been rejected at so deep a level that, in this respect, our mentality can appropriately be called postmodern.

Modernity and Locke's Place for Reason

We must be guided by Reason in all our believings, said Locke. What he meant by that and why he said it are what we must try to understand.

There are, said Locke, facts of certain sorts which we as human beings directly perceive, with varying degrees of luminosity. Or, to put it from the other side: certain of the facts of reality are directly present to the eye of the mind. In that situation, we have full certitude. How could anything yield higher (epistemic) warrant than direct perception? And certitude is knowledge.

3. "Epistle to the Reader," in John Locke, *An Essay Concerning Human Understanding*, edited by Peter H. Nidditch (Oxford: Clarendon Press, 1975), p. 7.

Locke's Positive Role for Belief

The scope of such insight is severely limited, however. Not much of reality is directly present to the eye of the mind: mainly facts consisting of relations among one's ideas and of one's having such-and-such an idea, a few facts to the effect that this and that idea is caused by something outside of one, and the fact of one's own existence. Beyond that, so far as insight is concerned, everything is darkness. The fundamental cause of the darkness is our inability to know the real essences of things outside ourselves. Not knowing the real essence of gold, for example, we cannot just *see* that all gold is malleable.

Contrast this picture with that of a high medieval such as Aquinas. Aquinas also called attention to the phenomenon of directly perceiving certain facts. He placed this phenomenon at the basis of what he called *scientia*, science; and he thought of science itself as the conclusions of demonstrative inferences from necessary truths that we have directly and immediately perceived. But in part because he thought we were capable of grasping the essences of very many things indeed, Aquinas was confident that science was in principle of wide scope. The darkness Locke so often lamented finds no acknowledgement in Aquinas. Of course Aquinas recognized the obvious fact that not all our assent has the status of knowledge; much of it has only the status of *opinion*. In our opinions we ought to follow those authorities who have probity. And coming in between knowledge and opinion there is *faith* — which consists of believing something on God's say-so. Yet even faith is deficient when compared to knowledge. For knowledge consists of seeing or proving something to be true. And who does not agree that seeing or proving something to be true is better than taking it to be true on someone's say-so — even if that someone be God?[4] Thus Aquinas would feel profoundly claustrophobic in Locke's framework. For though Locke likewise claimed that we directly perceive certain facts, the facts we directly perceive are almost all interior facts pertaining to the relations among our own ideas. What we know is mostly the contents of our own minds.

Locke's innovative genius lies in what he went on from here to say. We must be grateful, says Locke, that God has given us more than a faculty for insight. Life would be impossible if we were limited to that. The darkness of unconquerable ignorance is too vast. God has also given us a faculty for *belief* —

---

4. In defense of the interpretation of Aquinas that I offer here and in later points in this essay, see my essay entitled "The Migration of the Theistic Arguments: From Natural Theology to Evidentialist Apologetics," in *Rationality, Religious Belief, and Moral Commitment*, edited by R. Audi and W. J. Wainwright (Ithaca, N.Y.: Cornell University Press, 1986), pp. 38-81.

for believing something to be a fact even when we do not perceive it. For example, for believing that it is now four o'clock even though no one sees that it is four o'clock; what one actually sees is, at most, that one's watch shows four o'clock.

Reason's Governing Role over Beliefs

But belief, says Locke, needs governing; for beliefs ungoverned are often false. How should they be governed? Should we look around for authorities of probity, as Aquinas and all the medievals said, and believe those authorities? Certainly not, said Locke. Authority, and her sister, tradition, are the worst of guides. There is scarcely any opinion, no matter how crazy, which is not somewhere propounded by some so-called authority and passed down by some tradition. Authority and tradition must be put to the test, forced to display their credentials, if they have any. It is to Reason that we must appeal. Only thus can we get beyond the unreliable parochialism and contingency of tradition and authority, down to what is universal and solid. (It is important to recall here that Locke was writing in the context of the religious and political turmoil of England in the century following the Reformation; he explicitly saw his proposals as a way of dealing with that.)

What is Reason? Reason is a faculty. It is, for one thing, that faculty whereby we see that such-and-such a conclusion follows from such-and-such premises. Notice the metaphor "see": Reason is a faculty of direct perception. But Reason does more than enable us to perceive entailment relations among propositions. Reason also enables us to perceive probability relations among propositions. It is by Reason that we perceive the degree of probability that a proposition has on some evidence. In saying this, Locke was making use of our modern, then newly-born, concept of probability.[5] And the essence of his innovation was to say that belief is not to be governed by authorities of probity; it is to be governed by what one's Reason tells one is the probability of the proposition on the evidence of the facts. "To the facts themselves" was the motto: authorities and traditions, even language, must be set off to the side so as to get at the facts.

How are we to make use of Reason's deliverances? There are, after all, options. In this way: First — unless one's other obligations take precedence — we are to collect adequate satisfactory evidence for the proposition in

5. See Ian Hacking, *The Emergence of Probability* (Cambridge: Cambridge University Press, 1975).

question and reflect carefully on the logical strength of that evidence; then we are to proportion the firmness of assent we give the proposition to the degree of probability that our Reason tells us it has on our evidence. These are the fundamental principles in the Lockean ethic of belief. And part of Locke's innovation was to insist that this ethic holds for everyone on all matters of fundamental importance — not just for scientists when doing science. Max Weber argued that Calvinists took asceticism out of the monasteries and placed it in the world. Locke proposed taking the replacement of authority and tradition by insight out of the halls of science and into public life.

Locke's Idea of Responsible Beliefs

In recent years it has often been said of principles such as Locke's that they are *foundationalist*, specifically, *classical* foundationalist; I have said so myself. And indeed they are. But I have come to think that it is important to dig deeper and ask *why* Locke chose the foundation he did, and why the mode of support of superstructure by foundation.

Because of the lure of certitude: he wanted our beliefs to be grounded in and governed by what is certain. Yes, but deeper yet. It was his conviction that here and there we directly perceive reality. Our beliefs, to be responsibly held, must be grounded on the certitude of direct insight and held with a firmness proportioned to what the equally certain direct insight of Reason tells us is their probability on the evidence of the foundation. If we do not thus appeal to insight, we can only wander aimlessly in the darkness of ignorance, forever the victim of those two tempters, tradition and authority.

What emerges within this comprehensive vision is a new project of natural science, and indeed of social science as well, though Locke recognizes that the project is so different from what the medievals called *scientia* that he himself does not call it science but "natural philosophy." We can never have direct insight into whether *all* gold is malleable, neither immediately, nor mediately by way of demonstration. Real essences are not directly present to us. We must be content with mere belief; knowledge is here beyond us. But our belief must be responsible. The task of the scientist is to go out and collect adequate evidence of the right sort, calculate the probability on the evidence accumulated, and regulate assent accordingly. Notice, once more, that insight is still fundamental to this project: we look for our evidence in what we directly perceive, and then we directly perceive the probability of the proposition on that evidence. But the result is never insight into the reality outside us. The benefit of natural science for Locke is no longer the benefit of that insight into reality for which the ancients and the medievals hoped, but the new, eminently modern, benefit of improving the conditions of our existence. Science is for power, as Bacon also said — and Yes, for admiring the artistry of nature's Maker.

Locke was a Christian, reared in Puritan circles; and he did not neglect to discuss how Christian faith is to be fitted into this comprehensive picture of knowledge and responsible belief. Faith is not knowledge but a form of belief; it ought then to be governed, like all belief, by Reason. What God reveals is certainly true; we can "see" that. But whether the Scriptures report revelations from God, whether they do so accurately, and whether we are interpreting those reports correctly, are matters to be determined by weighing up the probabilities and then believing accordingly. (It is easy to see why modern higher biblical criticism emerged from Locke's circle.) It was Locke's own conviction that the evidence is sufficient for the conclusion that the Scriptures do reliably report revelations from God.

And what, finally, about norms — in particular, ethical norms? Locke's project was initiated, remember, by a discussion on religious and *moral* matters coming to a standstill. It was here that Locke ran into his greatest difficulties, difficulties which have proved to be a foretaste of three centuries of difficulties for Enlightenment thought! Initially Locke hoped that a true *scientia* of ethics could be developed consisting of necessary moral facts which we human beings just perceive. Eventually he concluded, with reluctance, that we have no choice but to accept our ethical principles on God's say-so as reported in Scripture — once we have rationally confirmed that God did indeed reveal those principles.

Locke has drawn for us an elegant and winsome picture, constructed out of a complex and innovative interweaving of notions of knowledge, insight, responsible belief, degrees of firmness of assent, epistemic warrant, Reason, science, religion, and probability.[6] It became the classical picture, seldom accepted in each and every detail, yet always exerting its influence. At the heart of the picture is a project — the project of becoming a responsible believer by following the voice of Reason and the deliverances of insight. We must set off to the side the parochial contingencies of authority and tradition and guide our assent — in science, in religion, everywhere — by insight into reality.

6. I by no means wish to suggest that Locke had no significant antecedents. See especially Henry G. van Leeuwen, *The Problem of Certainty in English Thought: 1630-1690* (The Hague, The Netherlands: Martinus Nijhoff, 1963); and Barbara J. Shapiro, *Probability and Certainty in Seventeenth-Century England* (Princeton: Princeton University Press, 1983).

Cracks in Locke's Picture

Over the centuries, the point at which the Lockean project was thought to be most invulnerable was its theory of reputable science. It is that very point which has come under powerful and sustained attack over the past quarter century.[7]

For the most part, the attacks have come in the form of someone's taking a reputable specimen of science, comparing it to the Lockean model, and showing that the specimen does not fit the model. It has been argued that theories are typically under-determined by their empirical and logical evidence, several different theories usually being compatible with the same evidence. It has been argued that the evidence for theories is itself theory-laden. It has been argued that the relation of evidence to theories is seldom that of inductive support. It has been argued that values other than truth-likelihood enter into our appraisal of theories, for example, simplicity and elegance; and that sometimes these values are given priority over truth-likelihood. It has been argued that the nature of probability is not that of some quasi-logical relation among propositions. It has been argued that the atomism of Locke's picture is mistaken; theories confront data as wholes, not in bits and pieces; and difficulties that arise can always be handled by a variety of different adjustments in the theory. It has been argued that we must think of theories as historical entities, specifically, as research programs; and that a research program is not given up, nor should it be given up, the moment it encounters some difficulty. It has been argued that metaphors and picture-thinking enter crucially into science. It has been argued that we cannot escape from tradition, and that both tradition and authority are intrinsic to the practice of science. It has been argued that we cannot set our language off to the side so as to gaze at the facts unencumbered by our linguistic categories. It has been argued that much of science is hermeneutic rather than nomological. It has been argued that the appeal to rules and the use of reasons in science is less like the unambiguous application of an algorithm and more like a judge's decision in a complicated legal case. It has been argued that our desire to conceal from ourselves unpleasant truths about ourselves influences our formation and choice of theories. It has been argued that in good measure we do not so much believe theories as merely *accept* them, to see where they lead and what they can do. And so forth, on and on.

The effect of all this is to destroy the plausibility of any classical

---

7. A very helpful entrance to the discussion is Richard Bernstein, *Beyond Objectivism and Relativism* (Philadelphia: University of Pennsylvania Press, 1983).

foundationalist picture of science. But more fundamentally, its effect is to destroy the conviction that reputable science is constructed simply by appealing to insight. Locke already discarded the ancient and medieval picture of science as *yielding* insight into reality, replacing it with the more modest picture of a science *grounded on* and *governed by* insight. Today even that more modest picture has been rejected.

Reid's Alternative to Locke

But are the ruins perhaps less devastating than at first sight they appear to be? Locke's deep concern, remember, was to set the parochialism, the contingency, the "positivity," of tradition and authority off to the side; then to make reliable judgments about reality based on those points at which we have direct access to reality; and finally to go back and critique traditions and authorities. I think we must grant that reputable science, counter to Locke's hope, is not simply grounded on and governed by insight. But may it be that necessity and universality can be achieved in another way? The eighteenth-century Scotch philosopher Thomas Reid argued against Locke that perceptual beliefs, memory beliefs, and so on, are not the products of inference from insight. My perceptual belief that there are persons in this room is not, said Reid, the result of my *inferring* that there are probably persons here, on the basis of my direct awareness of certain person-images. I have certain sensations and the belief just emerges. Perceptual beliefs are the outcome of how we human beings process reality's input. We are structured beings who interact in structured ways with a structured reality, this by virtue of how we were created. That was Reid's picture. What arises from this perspective is the hope that science can be built entirely out of what our shared nature constrains us to believe as we interact with reality.

Something of great importance is given up here; namely, the hope that life and science can be grounded on and governed by insight. Yet it is also true that something immensely important to Locke and to the entire Enlightenment is salvaged: if science can indeed be grounded on and governed by what our shared structured nature constrains us to believe as we interact with a structured reality, then the hope of eliminating the parochialism and contingency, the "positivity," of tradition and authority remains alive.

It is my own conviction that Reid's perspective is tremendously important and promising in our present situation. We are indeed created with a structured nature whereby we interact in structured ways with a structured reality. Those who draw from recent discussions the antirealist conclusion that reality's structure depends entirely on us, that reality is a social construction,[8] or the conclusion that our convictions and commitments are entirely the artifacts of society coupled with individual will, have gone far beyond what the discussion justifies.

Nonetheless, I think we have to grant that a Reidian picture of science will also not do. Reputable science is not some generically human phenomenon, the product solely of our shared nature, bearing no traces of the parochial and the contingent. Science is not lifted above our particularity. Science *displays* our particularities — and let me add, it displays our fallenness, along with our devious attempts to conceal that fallenness. Science is always a modern Western, or a medieval Arabic, or an ancient Oriental, phenomenon, or whatever. Science is the outcome of a complex interplay of insight, of the constraints of our nature as it interacts with reality, and of the positivity of our social circumstances and individual decisions. It is itself a project of science to discover, in so far as we can, where one of these leaves off and another begins. We do not first complete that project before we do science. We engage in it as part of the practice of science.

Kuyper and Science as a Social Practice

I think it is appropriate to add that what I have been saying here was already said in its essentials one hundred years ago by Abraham Kuyper. Kuyper argued that science is not and can never be simply the product of the constraints of our shared human nature as we interact with reality. Kuyper was a postmodern in the heyday of modernism.[9]

Often the picture of science now proposed is that of a conversation: science does not at bottom consist of individuals directly perceiving reality and then governing their beliefs accordingly, but of individuals participating in a certain kind of conversation. This metaphor of a conversation is deficient in an important respect, however. Often we break off the conversation to reflect, to calculate, to weigh, to look, to make a piece of technology — in short, to find out what reality is like at a certain point. Science is one of the modes whereby we human beings interact not only with each other but with reality. Better then to think of science as a *social practice*. Social practices have

8. See my essay entitled "Are Concept-Users World-Makers?" in *Philosophical Perspectives*, volume I: *Metaphysics*, edited by James E. Tomberlin (Atascadero, Calif.: Ridgeview Publishing, 1987), pp. 233-68.

9. For a defense of my interpretation of Kuyper, see "The Point of Connection between Faith and Learning" in this volume.

histories and traditions: to be inducted into a social practice is to be inducted into a tradition. Likewise social practices embody norms and have authorities who display or teach or enforce those norms: to be inducted into a social practice is to be confronted with the norms embodied in the practice. But these embodied norms change, and almost always at any given time some are contested. Connected with such change and such contention is the fact that new goals for the ancient practice regularly emerge, sometimes under the impact of a powerful and imaginative personality, sometimes because of possibilities opened up by a new piece of technology, sometimes as the result of the emergence of a new religion. Science is not an eternal form slowly manifested in history; science is a social historical practice, essentially involving tradition and authority, ever changing and ever controverted in its goals and norms. If Locke had succeeded in expelling tradition and authority from science, he would have succeeded in killing off science.

In this practice, reason is at work. We believe things for reasons as well as doing things for reasons and offering reasons to each other. And all the practitioners make discriminations between good and bad reasons. But we change our minds and we disagree on our discriminations. The great hope of modernity, that somehow we could attach all our reasons either to direct perceptions of reality or to what human nature constrains us to believe, *knowing* that we had thus attached them; and the corresponding great hope, that we would all simply be able to 'see' the correct universally applicable norm for discriminating good reasons from bad ones — those hopes have proved illusory.

Postmodernity and Lyotard's Critique of Legitimation

I shall return to some of these matters when I ask, shortly, what bearing these developments have on the project of a Christian university. But first I want briefly to discuss another related change that has been taking place in our Western mentality.

You may have asked yourself, in the course of my brief discussion of the medieval notion that science yields insight into necessity, why the medievals thought such insight important? The answer is that they saw such insight as constituting the deepest happiness available to us human beings — especially since they believed it culminated with insight into the divine. Insight yields happiness. Perhaps we make the same point if we speak of *meaning* rather than happiness: The fundamental meaning of human existence consists of insight into the objective realm of immutable necessity.

One of the deep consequences of the emergence of the modern Lockean view of science is that the medieval view had to be given up. Neither science nor anything else in this present life of ours yields direct insight into reality external to the mind and its contents. Thus at the beginning of the modern world two fundamental questions were posed: What does constitute meaning? And how, if at all, is the pursuit of science related to that? What legitimates science?

Lyotard's Diagnosis of the Postmodern Condition

Let me introduce what I wish to say here by considering some of Jean François Lyotard's central theses in his book *The Postmodern Condition*.[10] Lyotard argues that we in the modern West, when called upon to legitimate the practice of science, have traditionally offered one or the other of two grand narratives — narratives of human destiny, I shall call them, to emphasize the universality of their supposed scope. The one he considers first, the "more political" one, was developed in all its power and attractiveness in France of the Enlightenment. It sees meaning and happiness as consisting of, or at least requiring, freedom; it sees modernity as the growth of freedom; and it sees the fundamental validity of science as lying in its contribution to the expansion and exercise of freedom. The second, "more philosophical," narrative was first told in nineteenth-century Germany. Here the development of science was not treated as a component in the self-realization of civil society, contributing to its struggle for "emancipation from everything that prevents it from governing itself" (35), but as a moment "in the becoming of Spirit" (35). Without science, Spirit is not realized. And in Spirit's realization through the life of humanity is to be found the fundamental meaning of human existence.[11]

10. Lyotard, *The Postmodern Condition: A Report on Knowledge*, translated by G. Bennington and B. Massumi (Minneapolis: University of Minnesota Press, 1984). Subsequent references to this volume will be made parenthetically in the text.

11. If Spirit is truly to be realized, however, science must not be in the service of some concrete local human entity, such as society or state, but must follow its own inner dynamics. Further, science as a whole must incorporate a speculative philosophical dimension in which all the elements of positive learning are united into a philosophical narration of the story of Spirit that utilizes and displays the contribution of those merely positive elements in the story. Philosophy constructs the encyclopedia of the sciences. And this is "the great function to be fulfilled by the university," says Lyotard: "to lay open the whole body of learning and expound both the principles and the foundation of all knowledge. 'For there is no creative scientific capacity without the speculative spirit'" (Lyotard, *The Postmodern Condition*, p. 331). According to

It is then one of Lyotard's central theses that "The grand narrative" of science "has lost its credibility, regardless of what mode of unification it uses, regardless of whether it is a speculative narrative or a narrative of emancipation" (37). And for Lyotard, the dying of the grand narratives of science is what makes our age *postmodern*.

Let me first qualify and then generalize Lyotard's thesis concerning the dying of narratives. The modern world has known at least one important, science-legitimating narrative in addition to those that Lyotard discusses; namely, the one to which Locke already alluded: Science is legitimated by showing its contribution to the story of our increasing mastery of the world. This narrative, the narrative of technological mastery, has certainly not died. We still believe that our human mastery of nature will continue to increase. However, an important traditional corollary of the mastery narrative has died. Until not long ago we believed that humanity was on the march into a future of simultaneous high development. The proper seeds just had to be planted in the underdeveloped areas of the world and they too would flower. Most of us no longer believe this. We no longer see increasing mastery as providing ecumenical happiness. At most it promises happiness for the lucky ones who happen to live wherever the core of the world system happens to be located at a certain time. And even there, new pleasures exact the price of new sorrows.

Utilitarian and Expressivist Legitimation of Science

Now for the generalization. Most of us have believed that the modern world represents something unique in humanity's history. We have seen that uniqueness as lying in some historical process or other, set going in the 1500s. We have seen that process as continuing. So we have constructed narratives and scenarios pointing to that process. Many of these have been optimistic. And most of the optimistic ones have seen science as playing a key role in the story. Marx, whose narrative was also optimistic, placed his faith instead in the tension-laden dynamics of capitalist production. But no matter: One and all of the optimistic narratives and scenarios concerning the sig-

---

the narrative of emancipation, science can make its contribution to a society's freedom without the story of that contribution ever being narrated. By contrast, the realization of Spirit requires the narration of the story of the realization of Spirit. And items of positive learning are validated not by their utility but by their finding a place in the philosophical narration of Spirit's realization — a narration which in turn finds its validation in being itself a moment in Spirit's realization.

nificance of modernization are dying. We no longer believe that the proletariat is the suffering servant destined to bring salvation to the world. We no longer believe that mastery of nature is destined eventually to bring high simultaneous development. We no longer believe that history is the story of liberty with America in the vanguard. The book of our mood is *Ecclesiastes*. It is indicative that even Jürgen Habermas, one of the great present-day defenders of the Enlightenment, sees the significance of modernity in a *project*, that is, in commitment to a struggle. He does not claim an ongoing process; he offers no scenario. Or if we do still believe some narrative concerning the past and ongoing significance of modernization, it is one of the pessimistic narratives. Perhaps the one that underlies so much of our sociology; namely, that modernization is the instrument of our fall from a happy world of *Gemeinschaft* into this present evil world of fragmentation and anomie. Or perhaps the narrative of increasing mastery, shorn now of its promise of ecumenical happiness. Or perhaps the narrative told by Weber, that modernization is the progressive disenchantment of the world, the spread of secularization. (But now a good many scholars are concluding that even the secularization thesis is not universally valid. Though it may hold for Europe, it does not hold for the rest of the world. Religion is more resilient than was thought.)

Yet science continues among us. It must be that we see something else as validating this durable, malleable, social practice — something other than one of those grand optimistic narratives and scenarios of destiny. Here again I find Lyotard's discussion perceptive. Increasingly the worth of science is seen, on the macro level, as consisting in its contribution to the maintenance and economic advancement of some particular part of the world system; and on the micro level, as consisting in its contribution to a given person's functioning effectively within the system. Naturally this has a profound impact on education. Let me quote Lyotard:

> If the performativity of the supposed social system is taken as the criterion of relevance . . . higher education becomes a subsystem of the social system, and the same performativity criterion is applied to each of these problems.
>
> The desired goal becomes the optimal contribution of higher education to the best performativity of the social system. Accordingly, it will have to create the skills that are indispensable to that system. These are of two kinds. The first kind are more specifically designed to tackle world competition. They vary according to which "specialities" the nation-states or major educational institutions can sell on the world market. . . .

Secondly.... higher learning will have to continue to supply the social system with the skills fulfilling society's own needs, which center on maintaining its internal cohesion. Previously, this task entailed the formation and dissemination of a general model of life, most often legitimated by the emancipation narrative. In the context of delegitimation, universities and the institutions of higher learning are called upon to create skills, and no longer ideals — so many doctors, so many teachers in a given discipline, so many engineers, so many administrators, etc. The transmission of knowledge is no longer designed to train an elite capable of guiding the nation toward its emancipation, but to supply the system with players capable of acceptably fulfilling their roles at the pragmatic posts required by its institution. (48)

Lyotard adds that one can expect this new model to place great emphasis on teamwork, for "teamwork is related to the predominance of the performativity criterion in knowledge. When it comes to speaking the truth or prescribing justice, numbers are meaningless. They only make a difference if justice and truth are thought of in terms of probability of success" (48).

It would be superfluous to cite evidence that Lyotard's description increasingly fits research and higher education in the Netherlands and in the United States. In the United States, the old motto of learning and education for a free society begins to sound whimsical and nostalgic. I would make just one qualification in Lyotard's thesis. Ever since the Romantic questioning of the legitimacy of modernity, the expressivism celebrated by the Romantics has been seen as mortally opposed to the instrumentalism celebrated by the mastery narrative. I think we can see Western society beginning to work out an unstable compromise between these: We will be functionalists at work and expressivists after work. Functionalist considerations will guide us in our operation of the productive/bureaucratic mechanisms. Expressivist considerations will guide us in our enjoyment of the benefits of these mechanisms in our privacy after work. It turns out, however, that science and education are also relevant to the latter. So I think we can expect that educational institutions, in addition to offering programs satisfying the demands of performativity, will increasingly offer courses enabling us to satisfy our expressive interests: in religion, poetry, painting, sex, sports, whatever one happens to have a taste for.[12]

12. My main concern here has been with the cultural system of modernity, not the social system. To forestall confusion, I should perhaps remark here that I see no reason to think that

Christian Participation in the Social Practice of Science

When I was describing social practices as historical norm-bearing entities with traditions and authorities, and suggesting that science — *wetenschap, Wissenschaft* — is best thought of as a social practice, I dare say some of you were struck by the similarities to Christianity. For though Christianity is not a social practice but a religion embodied in a community, that community perpetuates itself in the form of tradition, and that community has authority functioning at many different points in many different ways on many different issues. Central in the whole network of authority which characterizes the community are the scriptures of the Old and New Testaments — texts that are passed down with interpretations which themselves function authoritatively within the community in one way or another. Many other texts also play important roles within the community, sometimes even authoritative roles — texts of canon law, books of common prayer, encyclicals. But the authority of the texts that constitute the Bible are unusually central and unusually decisive for the life of the community. That remains true in spite of the most astounding range of disputes concerning the details of the authority of these texts — not to mention disputes over the details of what these texts actually say. Indeed, I think it can be said that the very identity of the Christian community across time and space is determined by the authoritative role of these texts within it, along with the fact that the community preserves and celebrates the liturgy, which in turn gives central place to these texts. When someone on the outside observes Christians, often he or she will not see much difference in their ordinary behavior from that of others. What he or she will see, though, is that that text plays a role among them different from what it plays in any other community, an authoritative role; what he or she will see further is that they all interpret that text as speaking very centrally about Jesus of Nazareth; and he or she will see that they all celebrate a liturgy in which that text plays a central role.

The question I want now to consider is this: What can be said about the way in which such people, Christians, should participate in the practice of

---

the *social* system of modernity is changing in any fundamental respect. I myself think that the deep innovations of modernity with respect to social structure were, in the first place, capitalism (under "capitalism" I include both state capitalism and "free market" capitalism); secondly, an arrangement whereby economies are substantially integrated across distinct states and nations — these latter two, in turn, usually not coinciding in their boundaries; and thirdly, the pervasive introduction of bureaucracy into the state. The endurance of this modern social system is proving (so far) to be compatible with deep alterations in our modern cultural system. (A full description of our modern social system would also have to give ample attention to the phenomenon of religious diversity within single states.)

science in our postmodern situation? Of course not all of them will participate. But by way of those who do, the community vicariously participates.

Notice that I do not ask *whether* the community should participate in
the practice of science; I ask *how* it should participate. The day is long past
when it was relevant to ask *whether*. Learning has been shaping Christianity
and Christianity has been shaping learning for almost two millennia now.
We could no longer untangle the two even if we wanted to. In my judgment
we should not want to. I shall organize what I have to say under five heads.

A Christian Theory of Responsible Belief

In the first place, the developments I have traced, and others within epistemology that I have not had time to mention, mean liberation for religion in general
and for Christianity in particular. They constitute the overthrow of a tyranny.
Not indeed the tyranny of reason, for reason as such is not tyrannical, but the
tyranny of a certain view as to how reason ought to function in our lives.

The actual practice of science has not been much influenced by general
a priori prescriptions delivered by philosophers telling scientists how they
ought to do their work — whether the prescription be Locke's generalized
ethic of belief or some alternative. Scientists have gone about their business
and ignored philosophers — except perhaps when they stood back and tried
to give a general description of what they were doing. Then they have often
claimed *to be* doing what philosophers said they *should be* doing. The fact that
scientists have ignored Locke's ethic of belief is, of course, what brings it
about that we can take reputable segments of science, compare them to the
Lockean ethic, and see that the two do not fit.

By contrast, indifference to the Lockean ethic has not been characteristic of *Christians* — or more precisely, not characteristic of the intelligentsia in
the Western Christian community. Many of them have instead been intimidated by the Lockean ethic. Confronted with conflict between Christianity
and the Lockean ethic, they have tried to strip down Christian faith to the
point where finally it seems to meet the Lockean demands. Sometimes that
point has been the point of its no longer being Christian faith. It may be observed that already Locke himself used his ethic of belief as a weapon for trying to intimidate religious believers; specifically, those who in his day were
known as "enthusiasts." However, the enthusiasts, having no esteem for the
esteem of England's intelligentsia, simply ignored what Locke said.

Perhaps one clue as to why Christianity sometimes thrives in the presence of modernization and sometimes does not is to be found in whether the

churches have allowed themselves to be intimidated by the Enlightenment demands. Liberation theology has arisen from situations where Christianity is thriving. One of the many things striking about it is that its books do not begin with prolegomena asking whether theology is a science. Of course on that account liberation theologians have had to suffer the charge that their theology is not "truly scientific." My own guess is that one hundred years from now it is liberation theology that will still be read.

In saying that the Enlightenment intimidation of religion should be seen as discredited, am I making a case for irrationalism in religion? Of course not. I have already said that it is not the tyranny of *Reason* that has been overthrown but the tyranny of a certain view as to how reason should function in our lives. Reason itself is a gentle useful servant. Christians have always offered reasons for their beliefs. They will continue to do so. And in my view this should not be a purely internal affair. They should offer reasons to those who are not Christians and should listen to the reasons those offer in turn. It would be remarkable indeed if Christianity were nothing but surrogate wish-fulfillment, much more remarkable than if the theories which yield the conclusion that it is that were themselves nothing but surrogate wish-fulfillment, or the outcome of some similarly pitiful psychological dynamic. But if those who make this claim offer reasons, Christians should listen to those reasons.

Am I then saying that in religion, anything goes by way of belief? That though there are reasons, it makes no difference what those reasons are? Of course not. Christians discriminate between good and bad reasons. They will continue to do so. Christian discourse is at least as normative as scientific discourse. Notice, though, that responsible belief cannot be equated with beliefs being held for good reasons. For though we often have reasons for our reasons, somewhere that must end. Not even Locke, extreme rationalist that he was, thought that rationality was everything. He saw that reasoning has to start somewhere. He thought it should always start with immediate insight. The collapse of that view means that we are going to have to think anew about what the reasons of Christians appropriately start from; which is to say, we are going to have to think anew about the relation of the beliefs of Christians to the experience of Christians. May it be, for example, that people sometimes have experiences that they appropriately interpret as God's presence, or even as God speaking to them? I do not mean, experiences from which they *infer* a belief to this effect, but *such experiences?*[13] May it be that

13. See William P. Alston, "Christian Experience and Christian Belief," in *Faith and Rationality,* edited by Alvin Plantinga and Nicholas Wolterstorff (Notre Dame, Ind.: University of Notre Dame Press, 1983), pp. 103-39.

some of our experience is sacramental experience? I think that we, in our theology, our biblical criticism, and our philosophy of religion, must take that possibility seriously. In my judgment, what ultimately makes the Christian see the practice of treating Scripture authoritatively as more than mere social tradition is the conviction that at the basis of Scripture and of our reception of it is sacramental experience. That, plus the conviction that there is no other path than this to that mode of flourishing which the biblical writers call *shalom*.

I can imagine objectors speaking up once more. I grant you, they say, that Christians have and give reasons. And I grant you that they make discriminations between good and bad reasons, and between responsibly held beliefs and those not responsibly held, be these reason-based or not. But do they make the *right* discriminations? I do not hear you offering any criterion. Without that, it is in fact true that anything goes, whatever the participants may think.

I answer by pointing to another implication of the recent discussions about science. How is a criterion of responsible belief to be arrived at?[14] One can arrive at it as did the great Enlightenment philosophers: *a priori*, in advance, from above. But in fact science proceeds by its participants operating with intuitions concerning particular cases (or rather small sets of cases), making their judgments on the basis of those intuitions. They do not have some general criterion in mind which they just apply. And the history of science tells us that when our intuitions about cases conflict with some philosopher's general prescription, over and over we trust our intuitions rather than trusting the philosopher. I suggest that it is the same in religion. Christians make normative judgments about beliefs; and they do so on the basis of their intuitions about the cases, not by applying some general rule.

In part these intuitions are learned. Some of them change over time. And many of them are contested, even within the community. Sometimes the contest ends in consensus, sometimes not. Philosophers can try to discern some pattern in these intuitions. If there were consensus on the intuitions, their discerning of the pattern of the consensus would amount to arriving at a criterion of responsible belief. But since often there is no consensus, philosophers, if they are to arrive at a criterion of responsible belief, will have to do something more than just describe the pattern of the consensus. After careful reflection they will have to make up their own minds on the contested issues. They will have to appeal to their own reflective intu-

14. See Alvin Plantinga, "Reason and Belief in God," in Plantinga and Wolterstorff, *Faith and Rationality*, pp. 74-78.

itions — without assuming that these are all the result of insight or of the constraints of universal human nature. (They remember that data are often theory-laden.) That done, then finally they can formulate a criterion to fit the intuitions. Obviously someone with different reflective intuitions will have to formulate a different criterion. It may even turn out, on some matters, that a significant disagreement of intuitions arises between Christians and certain non-Christians. Perhaps the intuitions of Christians on what constitutes responsible belief are in part shaped by their acceptance of the Scriptures as authoritative. If so, then something like a *Christian* theory of responsible belief may emerge.

You see the point: A theory of responsible belief must *emerge* from careful reflection on the practice of religion and science, rather than being laid down in advance. And it itself is a result of the practice of science, rather than something one has to have in hand before one does science.

Interactions in the Conversations of Science

A second implication of our postmodern situation is that Christians are entitled to enter the conversation of science *as Christians.* They do not first have to undertake the (anyway impossible) task of becoming the Human Being Itself or the Scientist Itself, entering only if they succeed at that. They are those for whom the Scriptures are authoritative in life and who participate in the liturgy. They are entitled to enter as just that kind of people. For we have learned that the practice of science is not some purely and generically human enterprise, nor some autonomous self-governing and self-sustaining enterprise; but an eminently concrete social-historical enterprise incorporating goals and standards and intuitions and values that people bring to it and that emerge from their interaction with each other after their induction into the practice. We enter the conversation of science as concrete beings of diverse convictions and commitments. We do not shed all our ordinary convictions and commitments at the door of the conversation room of science and enter nakedly human; nor do we shed them all to put on some pure white cloak of science. We enter as who we are; and we begin conversing on whatever is the topic in hand. When some disagreement turns up, we deal with that. We do not make sure that we have forestalled it in advance. Often we learn from our disagreements.

An implication is that we shall have to work out quite a different model of the relation between faith and learning from those that have been handed down to us. Aquinas, as we saw, believed that in science we start from insight and proceed by insight to wind up with new insight. He saw faith as having several relationships to this project, but especially two. We try to transmute as much as possible of the content of faith, altering it from things taken on God's say-so into things seen or proved to be true, thereby also constructing a defense of those truths against objections. And in theology we start from the content of faith and proceed to deduce things from that, on the assumption that the content of faith has been seen to be true by God and the blessed.

Locke's model was different. By practicing science in accord with the Lockean ethic of belief we accumulate evidences for the existence of God and for the reliability of Scripture as God's revelation. Then, tempering the firmness of our assent to Scripture's content to the strength of the probabilistic evidence for its being revealed, we make use of those contents wherever relevant — in particular, to ethical matters.

Abraham Kuyper's view was again different. Kuyper argued exactly what I have been arguing; namely, that Christians are entitled to practice science *as Christians*. He saw clearly that science is not an autonomous enterprise but one shaped by a wide range of our human aspirations and convictions. Yet Kuyper did not think of science as ongoing conversation and practice in which the Christian participates. He thought of it along expressionist lines: Christians give scientific expression to their basic principles — *beginselen* — the outcome being "Christian science." Thus in Kuyper there was always the temptation to use metaphors which suggest that the Christian reforms science from the ground up — from the *beginselen*.

You may have noticed that the model I have myself been using is an interactionist model. The Christian as Christian enters the ongoing practice of science and there interacts with the other participants, sometimes in agreement, sometimes in disagreement; but either way, interacting. Down through the ages thinkers have tried to assign faith and science to separate areas. They have tried to build fences between them — or let me say, dig ditches and build dikes. Christianity, so it is said, deals with matters on this side of the ditch or dike; science, with matters on that side. I think all such attempts at ditch-digging and dike-building have failed and will continue to fail.

So what actually happens when the Christian enters the conversation room of science and begins conversing? A great many different things happen; we should honor the diversity. Sometimes Christians find that they agree with everyone in the room on the topic of conversation. At other times, they find they disagree on some matters. Sometimes the root of the disagreement seems to them to lie in their adherence to Christianity; sometimes it does not seem to lie in that. Either way, they will argue their case and try to bring the others around to their view. They try to offer reasons that attach to what the others already believe, or to provide experiences which alter their beliefs. They may find they have some allies in this. These allies may be other Christians. Then again, they may not be. They may in fact find that they have other Christians in opposition. And sometimes, though they do not much disagree with what is said in the conversation, they do not think the topic is very important; so they try to change the topic. Or they think the discussants are giving much too much importance to the practice of science. So they argue against that; if things get bad enough, they may even use the category of "idol."

Sometimes the disagreement in the group goes so deep that the conversation breaks down and the group divides into subgroups, different subgroups for different topics. On some topics, the big group may divide up along the lines Christian/non-Christian; on many topics, it does not divide up along those lines. Sometimes a Christian may deliberately seek out fellow Christians with whom to talk over certain things. Sometimes these will be theological matters; other times, they will not be. Sometimes the outcome from this latter sort of discussion can appropriately be called "distinctively Christian learning." One hardly ever knows in advance when that will happen. But often the outcome is not like that — though sometimes when it is not, there may nonetheless be distinctively Christian motivations behind it. The general goal of the Christian in the conversation of science will not be difference but fidelity; not scholarship different from that of all non-Christians but scholarship faithful to Scripture and to God in Jesus Christ. And lastly, sometimes the conversation of science leads the Christian to change her mind on something she had earlier thought essential to her fidelity.

You see my point: We must honor the diversity. Learning pursued by Christians does and should take many different forms. Let us be open to them all. Let us not impose a strait-jacket.[15]

Developing Ethical Critique Framed by Hope

A third implication. My topic is the project of a Christian university in a postmodern culture. Yet thus far I have spoken only of Christian scholars and their way of participating in the conversation of science, not of the

---

15. Some of the points I have made in this section have been developed more amply in "The Point of Connection between Faith and Learning" in this volume, and in my book entitled *Reason within the Bounds of Religion*, 2d edition (Grand Rapids: Eerdmans, 1984). See also the last chapter of my book entitled *Until Justice and Peace Embrace* (Grand Rapids: Eerdmans, 1983).

Christian university. Of course it belongs to the project of a Christian university, such as the Free University of Amsterdam, to nourish those modes of participating in the conversation of science of which I have been speaking. But let me move on to some points pertaining more directly to the university.

It will have occurred to many of you, as I was speaking of the death of the great narratives of modernity, that Christianity is deeply invested in this dying of narratives. For the Christian scriptures also present to us a narrative, a competing narrative, a narrative that bursts apart our secular visions by speaking of the interaction of *God* with humanity, a narrative in which *God* is our savior and not we ourselves, a narrative that calls humanity to share in *God's* work. It is a narrative that, like all the great narratives, both calls forth hope and launches critique. When narratives have died, can hope for humanity endure and fundamental critique of our practices remain plausible? I myself doubt it. But in any case, the Christian Scriptures do evoke hope for humanity and they do launch fundamental critique against the practices of all our societies. And they do so by presenting to us a narrative. They speak of shalom, where everything exists in right relationship with everything else — God, humanity, nature. And those right relationships, they insist, include justice. Without justice, without all the marginal and voiceless persons of the world being brought back into community and given voice, there is no shalom. Shalom goes beyond what is *right*, however. Shalom includes delight, joy — that very thing we are almost always embarrassed to talk about, maybe because to all but children true joy seems so far beyond reach that we feel childishly silly in speaking about it, not to mention expressing our suspicion that God might some day bring it about. And intertwined with their depiction of shalom, the Scriptures preserve for us the memory of the denunciations by the prophets and Jesus of the practices that violated shalom in their day, and of their unmasking of the sly and devious ways in which the members of their societies tried to conceal from themselves the evil of those practices. The relevance to our own society of these denunciations and unmaskings is obvious, as is the utopian depiction of what it is for humanity to flourish.

I submit that one of the enduring projects of the Christian university is to nourish critique that is shaped by the hopes and memories of the biblical narrative, including then, ethical critique of the practices of society generally. To a society mired in parochial concerns of performativity and expressivity, forgetful of what binds us all together as human beings, oblivious to the call of authentic human flourishing, there will be much to criticize — though let us remember that the art of true critique is knowing when to say Yes as well as when to say No.

When Christian critics speak to society generally, to what do they appeal, when so many in their society do not take the biblical texts as authoritative? They attach themselves to whatever ethical convictions they find in the members of their society. If there is almost no connection between the others' convictions and their own message, then perhaps they must adopt something like Jonah's strategy. Jonah preached doom. One can imagine, however, another prophet in Jonah's circumstance trying the opposite strategy of painting in attractive colors a picture of an alternative way of living — or even of inviting people to experience such a way if somewhere on earth it is to be found. If the gap is less great between one's message and the ethical convictions of the people in one's society, one can speak as Amos is recorded as having spoken to the surrounding nations in the opening chapters of his book. In condemning their violence, Amos appeals to the shared international conviction that such violence is wrong. It is when Amos turns to his own society that his full and rich denunciations, especially of oppression, break loose; for with these people he has much in common — in ethical *conviction,* of course, not in practice.[16]

Thus Christian critics do not just say to their society, "This is what the Bible says" and let it go at that. Ethical critics are not missionaries, nor even Barthian preachers. Their ethical perceptions and convictions are formed and informed by the Scriptures. But they proceed by interpreting the practices, desires, motivations, and convictions of the members of their society, searching for acknowledgment of the principles they believe correct. Very often they succeed. They discover that their fellow citizens have condemned themselves out of their own mouths. My own U.S. government, Congress and administration alike, have regularly charged that the Soviet Union breaks its treaties with the U.S. Nonetheless Congress, in clear violation of an undertaking signed in 1947, voted recently to close the PLO offices attached to the United Nations; and the administration, in delivering the closure orders, announced that it would not feel bound by any negative verdict rendered on this action by the World Court in the Hague. Thus does one condemn oneself out of one's own mouth. Of course, showing people that they have condemned themselves out of their own mouths does not always get them to change their ways. Sometimes people prefer hypocrisy.

And what if the members of one's society, when it comes to issues of social, personal, and ecological ethics, do not even think in normative terms anymore? What if they suffer from oblivion to the normative? What if their

---

16. What I say in this paragraph has been greatly influenced by Michael Walzer, *Interpretation and Social Criticism* (Cambridge: Harvard University Press, 1987).

reflections never rise above those that are internal to the social practices that they just happen to have selected? Could that have been Nineveh's situation? It seems to me that our present social structure, especially the capitalist dimension of it, is in fact destructive of fundamental ethical thought. Wherever capitalism spreads, it replaces the fine texture of substantive ethical relations found in traditional societies with the generalized ethic of contract. And then, in turn, it does nothing to counteract our tendency to think of the keeping of contracts in prudential rather than ethical terms; on the contrary, capitalism has a destructive impact on the very communities in which fundamental ethical thought and practice is learned. I do not find it surprising, then, that many in the West are saying that the only relevant question to raise about issues of social, personal, and ecological behavior is this: What would I feel comfortable doing? I find it difficult to believe that there could ever be a human society whose members thought only in prudential terms, not at all in authentically ethical terms — especially if prudential considerations are reduced to hedonistic considerations. But in so far as our own Western societies are drifting in that direction, the Christian university is called to reflect on how to nourish those forms of community life in which openness to the ethical is developed. It must itself try to be such a community.[17]

Maintaining Cultural Inheritance Discriminately

A fourth implication is this. I have been saying, in effect, that the Christian university must resist the enormous tragedy taking place, in our times, of reducing the rich enduring social practices of science and education to what serves our parochial performative and expressive concerns. It must do this, I have been saying, by nourishing *critique*. But it must also do so, I am persuaded, by continuing to introduce its students to the *cultural* inheritance of humanity. For the Christian narrative which serves to guide and inspire it sees human beings as something quite other than merely producers and pursuers of pleasure. It sees them, among other things, as interpreting beings, as hermeneutic beings, as creatures who unavoidably interpret experience in order to find meaning. To be human is to hunger for meaning. And in the arts

17. On some of the points made in this paragraph, see Robert Bellah et al., *Habits of the Heart* (Berkeley and Los Angeles: University of California Press, 1985); and Alasdair MacIntyre, *After Virtue* (Notre Dame, Ind.: University of Notre Dame Press, 1981). MacIntyre focuses quite exclusively on changes in the cultural system of the modern world that have led to "oblivion to the ethical." I do not deny the relevance of those changes. But I am inclined to think, as will be clear from the text above, that changes in the social system are even more important.

and sciences and religions of humanity, that fundamental dimension of our existence comes to its most glorious, and also its most agonized, expression. Let me add that John Calvin, one of the great initiators of that tradition of Christendom from which this university — the Free University, the *Vrije Universiteit* — sprang forth, stressed, in a famous passage of his *Institutes* (II.ii.15), that what is good and enduring in humanity's culture should not be seen as purely human but as the consequence of the work of God's Spirit. The Spirit of God broods over humanity's cultural endeavors.

We in our university must, in my judgment, struggle to preserve this part of our tradition. If we are to be delivered from our parochialisms, it is not by the strategy that Locke recommended but by interacting with humanity beyond our own narrow horizons. Of course, like everything else, humanity's culture must in each age be appropriated anew; in every age again we must sift through it, uttering a discriminating Yes and No. What we must not do is ignore it and allow ourselves to sink into the vulgarity of Nietzsche's "last men," who concern themselves with nothing more than production and pleasure.

Developing Empathetic Ears for the Voices of Suffering

Fifth, and last, there are certain realities immensely important to the Christian which the Christian university, so I suggest, should do what it can to keep before its staff and students. I cite just two.

It must keep before them the faces and voices of suffering from around our world. Critical ethical discussions conducted in the academies of the well-to-do in the West lose touch with human reality. To compensate, a Christian university must do what it can to confront its members with the suffering of the world — partly to let us learn from the wisdom so often present in the voices of suffering, partly to evoke in us the empathy which is the deepest spring of ethical action, partly to remind us that an ethic that does not echo humanity's lament does not merit humanity's attention.

I think I can best point you to the second reality, and also close my address, with a parable. A visitor came one day to the Free University of Amsterdam and stopped at the information desk. "Where can I change some money?" he asked. "Right here behind me, to your right." "And where can I get something to eat?" "Down this hall and then take a left. You'll see the cafeteria almost right away." "And do you have a chapel somewhere?" asked the visitor. "A chapel?" said the officer. "Oh yes, I think we do; let me ask a minute." "Yes, I'm told it's on the sixteenth floor. Take the elevator over there, all the way up to the fifteenth floor; you will then see a small stairway going up to the chapel."

The visitor stood in line to change his money. He pushed his way through the crowd to get some lunch — a bowl of soup, and two currant buns. Then he took the long ride up to the fifteenth floor, got out, and climbed the stairway to the chapel. He turned the handle; but the door was locked. After looking around and seeing no one, he descended to the madding crowd.

Teaching for Justice: On Shaping
How Students Are Disposed to Act

My topic is the ethical formation of students, particularly their formation with respect to doing justice and struggling against injustice. I have two texts for my talk. The first is from the twentieth-century German philosopher, Theodor Adorno, who, though ethnically Jewish, never explicitly departed from the standpoint of secularism. It consists of the opening sentences of the very last section of his book *Minima Moralia:*

> The only philosophy which can be responsibly practiced in face of despair is the attempt to contemplate all things as they would present themselves from the standpoint of redemption. Knowledge has no light but that shed on the world by redemption; all else is reconstruction, mere technique. Perspectives must be fashioned that displace and estrange the world, reveal it to be, with its rifts and crevices, as indigent and distorted as it will appear one day in the messianic light.[1]

My second text comes from the last section of Karl Barth's *Church Dogmatics*, a section translated and published after his death under the title, *The Christian Life:*

> Christians are summoned by God's command not only to zeal for God's honor but also to a simultaneous and related revolt, and therefore to entry into a conflict.... Revolt or rebellion is more than the rejection of a partic-

1. Adorno, *Minima Moralia: Reflections from Damaged Life,* translated by E. F. N. Jephcott (London: Verso, 1978), §153.

This essay appeared first as a book chapter in *Making Higher Education Christian: The History and Mission of Evangelical Colleges in America,* edited by Joel A. Carpenter and Kenneth W. Shipps (Grand Rapids: Eerdmans, 1987), pp. 201-16. It is reprinted here with permission.

ular possibility. Rejection can undoubtedly mean non-participation in actualizing the possibility. But it does not have to do so. One can obviously reject a possibility, that is, judge it negatively, and then for various reasons take part in its actualization. Furthermore, even the sharpest rejection does not in itself induce within it one [further] thing namely, entry into the struggle for the actualization of a very different possibility opposed to the first one. In the thought, speech, and action demanded of Christians, the issue is not just that of rejecting what they see to be a bad possibility but that of rising up and revolting against its actualization: a revolt that has positive meaning and inner necessity because another possibility stands with such splendor before the eyes of the rebels that they cannot refrain from affirming and grasping it and entering into battle for its actualization.... Christians thus exist under a binding requirement to engage in a specific uprising.[2]

My aim is to lead us in reflecting together on how students can be led into rejecting all those actualities of our society, and all those possibilities it pursues, which oppress people and deprive them of their rights, which violate justice. And beyond being led into rejecting those actualities and possibilities, how they can be led to engage in that specific uprising to which Jesus Christ — along with the prophets and song-writers of old — calls us. Eventually it will become clear that, in my judgment, it is indispensable for success in this task that we see things from the standpoint of redemption. It is indispensable that we view them in the messianic light.

Of course one hopes and even expects that by guiding, leading, and shaping their students, schools will help move social instutions in general to reject the justice-destroying actualities and possibilities of this present age and to engage in the specific uprising. But I will not have anything to say, directly, on how that hope and expectation can be enhanced. I will confine myself to speaking of the ethical formation of students themselves with respect to social justice.

Developing Dispositions for Justice

Engaging in the "specific uprising" of which Barth spoke requires knowledge and skills of various sorts. But when I ask how we can cultivate the doing of

2. Barth, *The Christian Life*, translated by G. W. Bromiley (Grand Rapids: Eerdmans, 1981), pp. 206-7.

justice and the struggle for it in students, I have in mind more than the knowledge and skills necessary for acting justly and for promoting justice. I have in mind the *disposition* to act thus. How can we cultivate *that* in them? How can we form their character in this regard? It will be important to remember that the "them" of whom we speak here will mainly be ones who, in the political economy of the present world live in one of the most powerful and well-to-do segments of the world. How can we cultivate *in these* the disposition to respect and struggle for the rights of the little ones on earth?

The contemporary branch of learning that comes closest to dealing with our concerns is that body of thought pertaining to what is called "moral education." Yet there are various peculiarities of that 'discipline' which considerably diminish its helpfulness. One of those is the regular assumption that the issues here are all issues of strategy, technique, how-to. Surely that is not true. Of course there are important issues concerning strategy. But deeper than those are issues concerning goals. What sort of person is it that we want to educate? What sort of person is an ethical person? What goal are the strategies concerning moral education meant to serve? Perhaps if we all already agreed on the goal we could safely leave it to philosophers in their leisure to make the concept of an ethical person into an object of self-conscious reflection. But that is emphatically not the case. We disagree on the goal; and many of our disagreements on means are to be traced to disagreements on the goal. We cannot avoid beginning our reflections on ethical formation with reflections on what sort of person it is that we want to form.

Kant's Idea of Moral Education

To show you that this is true, rather than just asserting that it is, let me briefly describe the views on moral education of Immanuel Kant. For not only did Kant think deeply about what constitutes an ethical (or as he would say, *moral* agent). He also worked out, with acuity and self-consciousness, views on moral education that fit what he saw as the goal of such education.

Kant's moral theory is customarily exegeted as having at its center a theory as to the ground and structure of moral rules. I think there is good reason, instead, to see it as having at its center a certain account of the wellsprings of moral action. Kant placed himself in opposition to that long and virtually unbroken tradition of Western thought which said that ultimately it is our desire for happiness that leads us to act as we do.

How can we understand that tradition? Perhaps by reflecting along the following lines. Most of our experience is not received by us with neutral affect but rather with pro or con affect. We like the experience or we do not. Let me say, for want of any other available expression, that most of our experience is *valorized*. The experience of buying a new car and then, a week later, having it side-swiped, is for most of us a negatively valorized experience — decisively so! We do not like it at all; we strongly prefer that it not happen. By contrast, the experience of a sunny day in spring is for most of us a positively valorized experience. I cannot spend the time here talking further about this dimension of human experience; indeed, the vocabulary *for* talking about it is woefully limited and underdeveloped. Nevertheless, it is one of the deepest and most pervasive dimensions of our human existence. What is truly surprising, I think, yet obviously true, is that not only phenomena like physical pain and sensations and sexual experience and emotions are valorized for us; so too are beliefs — i.e., believings. Most of our deepest suffering is caused by our believing (or knowing) something to be the case.

My suggestion is that when the long tradition of the West spoke of happiness *(eudaimonia, beatitudo, felicitas)*, what it had in mind, to put it cumbersomely, was *positively valorized experience*. They did not have in mind pleasure. Pleasure is, for most of us most of the time, positively valorized; just as pain is negatively valorized. But brief reflection will make clear that that is not invariably true. There have been ascetics who disliked pleasure, just as there have been masochists who liked pain. The state of complete happiness, on the traditional understanding, is that state in which one has no negatively valorized experience but considerable positively valorized experience.

Kant then raised this question: consider someone who recognizes that doing so-and-so is her duty; and suppose that she does not expect the effect of doing that to be a positively valorized experience; she does not expect that it will, other things being equal, make her happy. On the traditional view, she lacks the requisite motivation for doing what she recognizes to be her duty; since, to say it again, that motivation consists ultimately in the desire for happiness. Yet, says Kant, surely we do not conclude from the fact that one's desire for happiness does not motivate some action that one was mistaken in thinking it was one's duty. If it really *is* one's duty, one must be *able* to perform it; ought implies can. Yet duty does not depend on whether we just happen to be so constituted that we expect doing the right thing to make us happy. Hence it is not true that the desire for positively valorized experience is the only thing that gets us to act in a certain way, when combined with beliefs as to what will yield such experience. The fact of duty implies that we all can, and sometimes should, rise above how we happen to be constituted with respect to what gives us happiness. We can act out of duty, not only out of the desire for happiness. It may be that some of us find in ourselves a certain feeling of respect for the moral law. But we must not slide into thinking of *that* now as the moral motive. For that would once again make our being subject to duty contingent on happenstance. We must acknowledge that there is a transcendent self; and that our ultimate dignity consists in letting that transcendent self act out of its own nature — that is, its own *rational* nature. Dignity consists in letting that transcendent self act autonomously. To act thus is to act out of duty rather than out of the desire for happiness.

What would moral education be like on such a view? Kant sees the issues with great clarity. For one thing, punishment does not produce moral character. Says Kant, "If you punish a child for being naughty, and reward him for being good, he will do right merely for the sake of the reward; and when he goes out into the world and finds that goodness is not always rewarded, nor wickedness always punished, he will grow into a man who only thinks about how he may get on in the world, and does right or wrong according as he finds either of advantage to himself."[3] Neither does it help to cultivate sympathy. "'Sympathy' is a matter of temperament. . . . 'Sympathy' is really sensitiveness, and belongs only to characters of delicate feeling" (97). "We must arouse the sympathies of children, not so much to feel for the sorrows of others as to a sense of their duty to help them. Children ought not to be full of feeling, but they should be full of the idea of duty" (104).

But can the appeal to the desire for happiness, to the valorized dimensions of human experience, play no role whatsoever in moral education? That would be too negative a claim, says Kant. By appealing to the desire for happiness we can develop in a child the *form*, as it were, of morality. "Morality is a matter of character" (96). Of course not every character is a *moral* character. Nonetheless, morality is indeed a matter of character; and we can enhance character formation by suitable rewards and punishments.

What is meant here by "character"? Character in general, says Kant, "consists in the firm purpose to accomplish something, and then also in the actual accomplishing of it" (98-99). It includes as well the factor of obedience, at least in the case of children: "obedience is an essential feature in the character of a child . . ." (85-86). By suitable rewards and punishments we can go some way toward producing firm purpose and obedience in children.

But what can we do to promote the formation of that more specific

---

3. Kant, *Education*, translated by A. Churton (Ann Arbor: University of Michigan Press, 1960), p. 84. Subsequent references to this volume will be made parenthetically in the text.

thing which is *moral* character? Any person with character will have the *form* of the moral life. What can be done to bring it about that that form has *moral content?* One can guess Kant's answer. "We must place before children the duties they have to perform, as far as possible, by examples and rules." By way of examples of right conduct and by way of what Kant calls a *"catechism of right conduct"* (103) we place before children their duties, and we hope that it 'takes' — that their supranatural nature will act, where relevant, on the basis of the maxims embedded in these examples and catechisms.

In addition it is worth placing forcefully before children the ideal of human dignity, emphasizing that only by acting out of duty does one honor dignity, in oneself and others. We must teach children, says Kant, that "man possesses a certain dignity, which ennobles him above all other creatures, and that it is his duty so to act as not to violate in his own person this dignity of mankind" (101). How do we teach them this? Well, punishment, you remember, does not make a person moral. Nonetheless, the right kind of punishment can help not only in the formation of character but also in getting children to see the connection of duty with dignity. We can "do something derogatory to the child's longing to be honored and loved (a longing which is an aid to moral training); we can humiliate the child by treating him coldly and distantly. This longing of children should . . . be cultivated as much as possible. For this kind of punishment is the best, since it is an aid to moral training. . . . If a child tells a lie, a look of contempt is punishment enough, and punishment of a most appropriate kind" (87-88). "The withdrawal of respect is the only fit punishment for lying" (91).

In summary, "Moral culture must be based upon 'maxims,' not upon discipline; the one prevents evil habits, the other trains the mind to think. We must see, then, that the child should accustom himself to act in accordance with 'maxims,' and not from certain ever-changing springs of action. . . . The child should learn to act according to 'maxims,' the reasonableness of which he is able to see for himself" (83). "Everything in education depends upon establishing correct principles, and leading children to understand and accept them" (108).

I have presented Kant's theory of moral education not to plunge you into the world of Kant scholarship but for illustrative purpose: to show that strategies for moral education have to be determined in the light of what we understand the goal of such intervention to be; and that on the goal, we differ. Though the end here does not *determine* the means, particular means are nonetheless *relevant* only to certain ends. Our discussion of Kant has also served, along the way, to raise with clarity some of the deep issues on which we ourselves must reflect.

A Shalom View of Human Flourishing

You and I here are members of the church; as such, we take the Scriptures of the Old and New Testaments as authoritative. What in them is authoritative for us, and how we are to apply that to our contemporary world, are, of course, matters of much dispute. But that they are authoritative is not in dispute; indeed, their being authoritative for us contributes to our very identity as a people. Let us then, in our reflections on moral education, allow ourselves to be instructed by Scripture.

Kant, in the famous opening sentence of the body of his *Fundamental Principles of the Metaphysic of Morals*, said that "nothing can possibly be conceived in the world, or even out of it, which can be called good without qualification, except a *good will*."[4] What Kant meant is that it will always be a good thing that a person have a good will; it is impossible that there be a situation in which it would be better that a person not have a good will. Of nothing else, says Kant, is this true. It is because Kant regards a good will and a good will alone as unqualifiedly good, that he placed the phenomenon of a good will in the center of his reflections on how one should live. He develops a theory as to what it is that makes a will good; and he thereby also answers the question as to what must be done so as to bring about this phenomenon of unqualified goodness.

I submit that the center of the main line of biblical reflection on how one should live is very different. The center is not at all so lean and invulnerable. In the Old Testament prophets and song-writers, and in the New Testament gospel writers, the center of reflection is a certain vision of human well-being, of human flourishing. I am inclined to think that the same vision is operative in the New Testament letters, though there, it must be said, it remains more in the background. *Shalom* is the name that the Old Testament prophets and song-writers gave to the mode of human flourishing that they had in mind. Whereas Kant places on center stage the ideal of the dignity of the transcendent, supranatural, fully autonomous self, these biblical writers place on center stage the ideal of the shalom community. No doubt the full instauration of shalom requires that those who participate in shalom have good wills — though the biblical writers would not agree with Kant as to what makes for goodness of will. But shalom goes radically beyond goodness of will.[5]

4. Kant, *Fundamental Principles of the Metaphysic of Morals*, translated by T. K. Abbott (New York: Liberal Arts Press, 1949), p. 1.
5. In Bernard Williams, *Ethics and the Limits of Philosophy* (Cambridge: Harvard University

I shall assume that all of us here are acquainted with that ideal of human flourishing which the biblical writers call shalom. In particular, I shall assume that all of us here are acquainted with the fact that an indispensable component in shalom is justice: the honoring of every person's rights.[6] It is sometimes said that the recognition of rights, and especially the recognition of natural human rights, begins in the late medieval or early modern periods.[7] That seems to me certainly wrong. There is some plausibility to the claim that *theories* of rights, and more particularly, *theories* of *natural human* rights, first appear then. But the writers of the Old Testament seem to me unmistakably to have worked with the notion of rights. And though there may be some question as to whether they had a clear grasp of the notion of *natural human* rights, as opposed, say, to the rights of Israelis, there can be no doubt whatsoever that the church fathers did. When I am in the presence of an Other, I am in the presence of someone who has legitimate claims on me and others, at least some of these being claims that that Other comes bearing just by virtue of the fact that he or she is human. The shalom community is indeed more than the just community; it is the *ethical* community. And more than that: It is the community whose members exist in harmony with God and nature and find delight in all their relationships. Delight in dwelling in nature, before God, among one's fellows and their works, with oneself, is a prominent part of shalom. But so also, to say it again, is justice. Justice and happiness, though connected in various ways, are nonetheless distinct; shalom requires the presence of both. Just as someone whose rights are honored may nonetheless be intensely unhappy, so too people can be made to feel quite content in situations in which their rights are violated. Neither situation is shalom.

In the prophets and song-writers of the Old Testament one finds highly distinctive views on what is required for justice — on what are the rights of

---

Press, 1985), one finds a sustained attack on the Kantian approach to the question "How should one live?" and a sustained defense of the Aristotelian approach, which centers on well-being rather than goodness of will. Though making clear that he does not entirely accept Aristotle's understanding of well-being, Williams leaves quite undeveloped what he understands well-being to be. It is the *approach* that he wants to recommend; and as will be clear from the text, I am heartily in agreement with that. Unfortunately, Williams repeatedly indicates his conviction that Christian ethics is committed to something different.

6. See Walter Brueggemann, *Living Toward a Vision: Biblical Reflections on Shalom* (Philadelphia: United Church Press, 1976). See also my book entitled *Until Justice and Peace Embrace* (Grand Rapids: Eerdmans, 1983), pp. 69-72.

7. Cf. Alasdair MacIntyre, *After Virtue* (Notre Dame, Ind.: University of Notre Dame Press, 1981), p. 67. For further discussion of this topic, see my essay entitled "Christianity and Social Justice" in *Christian Scholar's Review* 16, no. 3 (March 1987): 211-28.

persons.[8] I do not hold that we must confine our recognition of rights to those recognized by the biblical writers. We too, after all, have moral intuitions and reflective capacities that we ought to put to work. Yet we would do well here too to allow ourselves to be instructed.

What is striking in the Old Testament declarations about justice is the passionate insistence that all the members of the community are entitled to a full and secure place in the life of the community. Hence the clanging repetitive reference to orphans, widows, and sojourners. Over and over when justice is spoken of, that trinity is brought into view. For these were the marginal ones in ancient Israeli society. Justice arrives only when the marginal ones are no longer marginal. Here is just one example from many: The Lord God "executes justice for the fatherless and the widow, and loves the sojourner, giving him food and clothing" (Deut. 10:18). The modern Western liberal notion, that a society is just when each person is free to exercise his or her own will, provided only that no one harms the will of another, is most emphatically not the biblical notion of justice.

Actions Guided by Shalom

So suppose we begin our reflections with this ideal of the shalom community. We must then go on to speak of how one should act with respect to this ideal. Let us here too allow ourselves to be instructed by the biblical writers. While I readily grant the rich variety of what they have to say on the matter, let me suggest that very much of what they say can be put under one or the other of four headings. We are, for one thing, called to engage in the endeavor and struggle to bring about shalom — to introduce one and another dimension of shalom into our human existence. This can be seen as having two quite different dimensions. Some actions are to be seen as themselves part of shalom; they are samples. Others find their validity in their effect of bringing about some phase of shalom; they are instruments. We are called, for example, both to act justly and to struggle against injustice and for justice. Secondly, we are called to pray for shalom, as in the prayer "Thy kingdom come." For we confess that the coming of God's Reign of peace is far from entirely in our own hands; we confess vulnerability and incapacity. The contrast with Kant, great Stoic that he was, is striking: whether a person will attain the ideal

---

8. See my essay entitled "Why Care about Justice?" in *The Evangelical Round Table*, vol. 2: *Evangelicalism: Surviving Its Success*, edited by David A. Fraser (Princeton: Princeton University Press, 1987).

of unalloyed autonomous dignity is entirely within that person's hands. Thirdly, we are invited to savor, to enjoy, to celebrate such traces of shalom as come our way — not just grimly rushing on in joyless dutiful activism. Even in the midst of pain, we enjoy the wine. And lastly, we are invited to mourn the shortfall of shalom in our world. We weep, we cry, in the realization that our Lord has pronounced his blessing on those who mourn. We ache; for we realize that the messianic age in its fullness is not yet here. To act in these ways is to act in the messianic light.

But what, you ask, about *love*? Is this not the first and great commandment, that we should love God above all? And is not the second commandment like it — that we should love our neighbor as ourselves? Yes, indeed. But to love God above all *is* to struggle and pray for the coming of God's Reign of shalom, to savor its presence and mourn its absence. And if we must say, in a word, how those who act in the messianic light will treat their fellows, that word is *love*. In particular, justice flows forth from love: loving one's neighbor requires and includes respecting his or her rights. In Kant, the center of the picture is always me and the moral law — this moral law being the deliverance of my own transcendent self. In the prophets the center of attention is not the moral law but persons — the widow, the alien, and the orphan, the little ones, the voiceless ones, the oppressed ones, the poor ones — the hundredth one, the one left outside. Of course there is law. But the law is grounded in God's love for the little ones.

Cultivating Dispositions to Act Justly

In the light of our discussion up to this point, let me now rephrase the central question to which we must address ourselves: How can we cultivate in students the disposition to work and pray for shalom, savoring its presence and mourning its absence? More specifically, how can we cultivate in them these dispositions with respect to justice? Notice, once again, that I speak of *dispositions*. If it is the coming of shalom that we care about, and more particularly, the doing of justice and the struggling for a just society, then we will not confine our attention to acts of good will but will devote the bulk of our attention to stable traits of character — dispositions of action, desire, and feeling. Of course we shall also cultivate the disposition to deliberate and choose in certain ways in quandary situations.

It would be relevant here to reflect on the obstacles we face in the cultivation of such dispositions. Some of the obstacles are ones present in humanity down through the ages — the "rich young ruler" syndrome, for example. Others are obstacles located in the formation of students peculiar to our own time and place. For obviously students do not come to school unshaped and unformed. They are already disposed to act, desire, and feel in certain ways by virtue of the educative impact of society on them. I think if we scrutinized the character formation of students as they come to us, we would find in them a great deal of the individualism to which Bellah et al. called attention in *Habits of the Heart*. We would also, I think, find a great deal of what I shall call "oblivion to the normative" — a phenomenon that overlaps individualism but is not quite identical with it. An economy of industrial capitalism, such as ours, systematically destroys a society of ethically infused social roles and replaces that with a society of a generalized ethic of contract. Then in turn it acts destructively on an ethic of contract and exerts pressure toward replacing that with a system in which people's deliberations over whether to keep their contracts are conducted in terms of the pleasant and unpleasant consequences to themselves of doing or not doing so. In such a society, ethical discourse is endangered. Discourse about action is more and more tacitly or explicitly couched in terms of what one would feel comfortable doing, or what would be in the interest of one's nation or state. So-called "values clarification" is the pedagogy that fits such a society.[9]

But important — indeed, indispensable — as such an analysis of obstacles would be for a full treatment of our topic, let me here forego that analysis and move on to the question of educational praxis: How, in the light of the wisdom of the ages and the discoveries of contemporary psychology, can we educate students for engaging in that "specific uprising" of which Barth spoke? How can we cultivate in them the disposition to act justly and to struggle against injustice?

A Cognitive Framework: Social Ethic, World-Systems, and Critical Consciousness

We must, in the first place, assist our students in acquiring an adequate cognitive framework for thinking about issues of social justice. Of course our students do not come empty-headed on these matters. They come with some

9. One of the large themes in Alasdair MacIntyre's *After Virtue* is the spread of this "oblivion to the normative." In tracing the causes of this phenomenon, MacIntyre is inclined to give much more credit to the influence of great thinkers than I am. I see it as one of the natural consequences of our economic structure. I also believe, however, that the continuation of industrial capitalism requires a strong ethical base. Thus I see capitalism as destroying what it requires for its continuation.

grasp of the concept of justice and its correlative concepts, infirm as that grasp may be; they come with some inclinations to apply those concepts in certain ways, mistaken though those may be. Furthermore, they typically come with a cognitive framework for interpreting many of the phenomena relevant to social justice, even though they may not themselves interpret those in terms of justice. They may interpret them in terms, say, of freedom. Hence a phase that is pedagogically important in the process of assisting one's students to acquire an adequate cognitive framework for dealing with issues of justice is that of making them aware of their present framework. This point is especially emphasized by Thomas Groome in his *Christian Religious Education*. Groome argues that the cultivation of such self-awareness is best accomplished in group dialogue situations that begin with student judgments as to what should be done in quite specific situations calling for action.[10] I think there is much to be said for this suggestion, though it should not be followed rigidly. But normally one must go beyond the cultivation of self-awareness. Normally one must assist one's students into an amplification and critique of their present cognitive framework for justice.

An adequate framework can be thought of as having three distinct dimensions. It will, for one thing, incorporate a *Christian social ethic*. Such an ethic will, in my judgment, be faithful to, and appropriately grounded in, the story and the torah and the vision of Scripture. In turn, I think we have arrived at a time in Christian history when our exegesis of Scripture must be both ecumenically and globally informed if it is to be responsible. For example, those who are Reformed must listen to how Catholics and Orthodox and Anabaptists interpret Scripture. We who occupy top rungs in the political economy of the world must listen to those who are on the bottom.

A Christian social ethic will have to go beyond biblical exegesis, however. It will even have to go beyond the theological determination of what, in the biblical writers, is authoritative for us today. For it must be an ethic capable of dealing with issues that never arose in New or Old Testament times.[11] I have already made clear that, in my judgment, such an ethic will take *shalom* as one of its basic categories. Partly that is because shalom is the context within which the biblical concern for justice is placed. In addition, the concept of shalom provides us a way of fitting together justice and worship, evangelism and art, piety and rights, and so forth. Unless we do find an ade-

10. Groome, *Christian Religious Education: Sharing Our Story and Vision* (New York: HarperCollins, 1980).

11. I discuss the formation of a Christian social ethic somewhat more amply in "The Bible and Economics: The Hermeneutical Issues" in *Transformation* 4, nos. 3 & 4 (June-Sept./Oct.-Dec. 1987): 11-19.

quate framework for fitting together these various dimensions of the Christian life, we will find ourselves forever impaled on tired but intense controversies that find no resolution: those interested in social action pitted against those interested in liturgy; those interested in personal piety pitted against those interested in art; those interested in evangelism against those interested in theology. Surely these all belong together. They belong together as the content of what the biblical writers call the Kingdom of God. Shalom is simply the content of God's Reign.

A second indispensable dimension of an adequate cognitive framework for dealing with issues of justice is a structural analysis of our present-day social world. Issues of social justice by their very nature involve issues of social structure. I am myself persuaded that this analysis must, from the ground up, be global in character. We must reject the modernization model of our modern social world, which thinks first in terms of separate societies and only later remarks on their interactions, replacing that model with some form or other of a world-systems model.[12] Secondly, we must not shrink from attending to the phenomena of domination and exploitation that result from social structures — domination and exploitation both within areas of the world and among areas. In particular, we must not shrink from attending to such phenomena within our own American society, and in the impact of our area of the world on other areas. We must, in my judgment, reject the notion that the fundamental structural reality of capitalist economies is a free market and that domination and exploitation are purely personal and accidental. That should be seen as heresy, in the strict sense of heresy. If someone in one of our colleges taught theological anthropology by extolling the glories of humanity for twelve and a half weeks and then, at the end of the thirteenth, remarked that "Now, my dear students, before we end this course, let me mention that here and there, now and then, human beings have done what they ought not to have done," we would regard that a heresy. I fail to see why we should regard economists who speak thus any differently. Thirdly, our social analysis should be genuinely *social* analysis; we should resist the tendency of academics to suppose that we have done our work when we have talked about ideas. Social reality is not simply the implementation of big ideas, such as the idea of individualism, the idea of progress, and so on. Social dynamics interact with ideas; there is a circular relation between them. Ideas which arise as the reflection in thought of social dynamics will often slightly alter

12. See Chapter 11 of my book entitled *Until Justice and Peace Embrace*. In addition to the books cited there, see Eric Wolf, *Europe and the People without History* (Berkeley and Los Angeles: University of California Press, 1982).

the dynamics of which they are the reflection; and so forth. In our social analysis we should be neither idealists nor materialists. Lastly, our social analysis should itself be informed by, and faithful to, the Christian gospel. Social analysis is not a religiously neutral practice.[13]

A third dimension in an adequate cognitive framework for dealing with issues of justice consists in the bringing together of the ethic with the analysis. We must apply the general ethic to specific issues. On a Reformed view of things, this will always involve a discriminating Yes and No response to our present societies. Much in our present societies is good; and what is good is to be seen ultimately as divine gift, as grace. But much is also evil, fallen, even idolatrous. What is required, then, is a discerning combination of affirmation and negation. Following Paulo Freire in *Pedagogy of the Oppressed* we may give the title of "critical consciousness" to such a discriminating analysis and appraisal of one's society[14] — assuming that Freire does indeed regard a *truly* critical consciousness as incorporating not only negation but affirmation.

Let me add here that one's attempt to assist one's students in developing a more adequate cognitive framework for dealing with issues of justice is more likely to succeed if one's attempt itself is characterized by justice and mercy. To teach justice, it helps to teach justly.

Ethical Formation: Reasons, Discipline, Models, and Empathy

But now I want to raise what seems to me the most important issue for us to reflect on: Is this enough? If we succeed in leading our students to adopt a more adequate cognitive framework for dealing with issues of justice, is that sufficient for disposing them to act justly and to struggle against injustice? As the last stage in the dialogic process that Groome practices and recommends, he urges the members of the dialogue to *decide* to *choose*, then he breaks off. Is that enough?

Sometimes it probably is. If Freire succeeds in illuminating his oppressed people as to the roots of their oppression, and as to strategies for alleviating their oppression which do not threaten even more unhappiness than the oppression itself, that will probably increase their disposition to engage in emancipatory action. In an obvious way, such illumination taps into what

13. For discussion of this point, see my book entitled *Reason within the Bounds of Religion*, 2d edition (Grand Rapids: Eerdmans, 1984).

14. Freire, *Pedagogy of the Oppressed*, translated by M. G. Ramos (New York: Continuum, 1970).

those people want — taps into their valorized experience. And if Groome's students are ultimately committed to living by the story and vision and torah of the Scriptures, then presenting them with what they come to see as the implications of that commitment will probably increase their disposition to act accordingly.

But notice the cautious *if*'s in what I have said. I myself find Freire and Groome expecting too much of reasoning, and too myopic in their focus on reasoning. There remains too much rationalism in them. Illumination, whether acquired on one's own under the promptings of dialogue, or acquired by receiving it from another, does indeed sometimes dispose us to act differently. But it does not always. And there are other ways of cultivating dispositions than by offering reasons or promptings to the discovery of reasons.

Groome's strategy, scrutinized closely, proves to consist of giving the student, or helping the student to discover, *reasons* for acting a certain way — reasons that go back to his or her deep religious convictions. So too Freire's procedure, scrutinized closely, proves to consist of giving, or helping discussants to discover, *reasons* for taking steps to alleviate their oppression — reasons whose effectiveness inheres in the person's dislike for oppression. But such reasons, though sometimes effective, also have their inadequacies. Though apparently it is characteristic of human beings to prefer consonance between belief and action, sometimes the perceived benefit of continuing to believe as we do and act inconsistently with that is greater than our discomfort over dissonance; so we do what we can to remain in our unstable state of hypocrisy. Or alternatively, when dissonance between belief and action turns up we sometimes change our beliefs rather than our actions.

But let me move on. In addition to offering reasons or assisting in the discovery of reasons, what, according to the wisdom of the ages and contemporary psychology, are some of the great shapers of dispositions to action?

If one expects the consequences or concomitants of acting a certain way to be to one's liking, the chances are greater, other things being equal, that one will act that way; and if one expects the consequences or concomitants of acting a certain way to be not to one's liking, the chances are greater, other things being equal, that one will not act that way. This fundamental fact about human nature makes possible the formative strategy that, for want of a better word, I call *discipline*. We can sometimes, as society or as individuals, attach liked or unliked consequences and concomitants to actions — or at least, produce in people the *belief* that they are attached. We can do things that will lead members of society, young and old, to expect that if they act in a certain way, consequences or concomitants that they find to their liking will ensue — or not to their liking. Probably the word "discipline" connotes, for most of us, *physical* rewards and punishments. But what I am here using the word "discipline" to cover goes well beyond that. Words of praise and words of dis-praise also function as discipline. Of course such words can be spoken in purely cynical, manipulative, fashion. But they need not be: One may praise what one finds praiseworthy. Schools, among other things, are places in which words of encouragement and of chastisement are spoken, words of praise and dis-praise. They contribute, in that way, to the ethical formation of their students.

Discipline regularly evokes skepticism as to its role in truly ethical formation. We heard Kant expressing the skepticism. It is said that if we encourage truth-telling in someone by attaching likeable consequences or concomitants to his or her telling the truth, or unpleasant ones to not telling the truth, then the person will tell or not tell the truth for the sake of those pleasant or unpleasant attachments. What we want, though, is a person who tells the truth because he or she finds truth-telling itself appealing or obligatory.

This negative evaluation of discipline strikes me as reflecting too negative a picture of its workings. May it not be that the outcome of the discipline is that the disciplined person eventually finds something attractive in truth-telling; and may it not be that the person would be less likely to have discovered that without discipline? Typically when children begin music lessons it takes the application of considerable discipline on the part of parents and teachers to get them to practice. But eventually, for at least some students, music-making proves to provide its own intrinsic rewards. Let us also remember that whether or not discipline contributes to the formation of a good will, it is an indispensable component in our struggle for justice. Murder is so horrible a violation of justice that, though of course it would be *best* if everyone loved everyone sufficiently to make it unknown, in our world of defective love it is *better* that the assurance of punishment be attached to murder so as to decrease its incidence than that it not be attached.

The wisdom of the ages and contemporary psychology also teach us that *modeling* is a great shaper of action; under conditions not very well understood, people are disposed to act in certain ways when certain of the people presented to them act in those ways, especially people they love or admire. To develop in students the disposition to act justly and to struggle for justice, it helps for us and our institutions to teach justly, to live justly, and to struggle for justice. It helps to be models.

The psychological literature, to the best of my knowledge, leaves obscure the dynamics operative in modeling. Is there in human beings a tendency to act as certain of those around us act in certain respects? And does this, at least in its more self-aware manifestations, take the form of *liking* to act as those around us act? If so, then modeling works by tapping in to one's valorized experience, as presently constituted. But perhaps there is also another dynamic at work in modeling.

We must not suppose that valorization of experience is fixed and static. In fact it is constantly changing. I have suggested that discipline contributes to some of the changes. The music student of six years old finds no happiness in music-making; that same student six years later does. Something has changed in what that student likes. Perhaps modeling too does not just tap in to some already-present desire to imitate; perhaps modeling in its own way, like discipline in its way, sometimes changes us. Perhaps the model presents to us a way of being that we find attractive. Our imagination was inadequate. Our expectations as to what will prove to our liking are now different. If that is how it sometimes works, and I rather think it does, then models — live models, described models, filmed models — often function in the same way that fictional narratives do. These too sometimes aid our imagination by presenting to us in an attractive light ways of acting that we had either not considered, or considered but found unattractive. Our expectations are different.

Reasoning, disciplining, modeling, be the models actual or fictional — these are ways of cultivating dispositions. Let me suggest one more. It appears that there is in all, or almost all, human beings a dynamic of empathy. There is in us a tendency to empathize with the plight and delight of certain others — to stand in their shoes, in the sense that we feel sorrow over their sorrow and happiness over their happiness. Obviously it is not strong enough in its effects, nor universal enough in its objects, to prevent the most appalling cases of taking satisfaction in causing others to suffer. The Milgram experiments confirm in the laboratory what we know from life: Some people would rather knowingly cause suffering to others than violate orders. But even those who torture with a smile are rarely so empty of empathy as not to feel unhappiness over the unhappiness of anyone other than themselves. Kant, as we have seen, dismisses sympathy and empathy as of no moral significance. In fact I think that empathy is of fundamental importance in ethical formation. The disposition to struggle against some injustice can often be cultivated by evoking in the person empathy for those suffering under the injustice. And in my experience, one of the most effective ways of doing this, in turn, is by presenting to the person the human faces and the human voices of suffering — "the voices of the night."[15] Many have argued that the main fac-

15. I take the phrase from Walter Brueggemann, "Voices of the Night against Justice," in *To Act Justly, Love Tenderly, Walk Humbly* by Walter Brueggemann, Sharon Parks, and Thomas Groome (New York: Paulist Press, 1986), pp. 5-28.

tor causing the revulsion of the American people to the Viet Nam war was the images of suffering on our TV screens. Whether right or wrong, the South African government is persuaded: it has banned all images and recording of violence in the country.

The lesson to be learned by schools is that they must look for ways to confront their students with the faces and voices of suffering — with images and voices of the night. If one is to love another as oneself, it helps to have that other presented in such a way that one suffers over his or her suffering and rejoices over his or her rejoicing.

Empathy is no more all-conquering than any of the other dynamics that can be tapped into so as to cultivate the disposition to justice. We have seen that the impulse to follow orders often overwhelms empathy. So also does *fear*. What prevents Israelis from genuinely hearing the suffering in the voices, and seeing the suffering in the faces, of the Palestinians, and then responding appropriately, is the awful fear of the consequences for their lives if they did genuinely hear and see and respond. So too, what prevents Afrikaners from genuinely hearing the suffering in the voices, and seeing the suffering in the faces, of the blacks in South Africa, and then responding appropriately, is the awful fear of the consequences for their lives if they did respond appropriately. This is a species of the "rich young ruler" syndrome of which I spoke earlier. An important contribution we as teachers can make to the ethical formation of our students is dealing with such fear.

These, as I see it, are some of the great shapers of ethical character: reasoning, disciplining, modeling, offering narratives, expanding the scope of empathy by presenting the faces and voices of suffering, dealing pastorally with fear of the unknown. I suppose I do not have to point out that the implications of taking them seriously are appallingly radical for our teaching, for our living, and for the comportment of our institutions.[16]

16. For a more ample discussion of some of the points I have made here, along with citation of evidence in the psychology literature, see my book entitled *Educating for Responsible Action* (Grand Rapids: Eerdmans, 1980).

It is possible to classify the ways, abstractly considered, in which dispositions to actions can be influenced:

(1) One may contribute to S's believing that some valorized experience, which S formerly did not believe was available to S, now is available (or the converse) — for example, by contributing to S's actually having had that valorized experience (our example of skilled music-making), or by contributing to S's envisaging it (models, narratives).

(2) One may contribute to S's believing, of some experience which was previously available to S, that it has changed its valorization relative to other experiences of S — by, for example, contributing to S's actually experiencing changes in the relative

The Messianic: Beyond Immobility and Inutility

Let me close by calling attention to two responses that characteristically arise in those who are first presented with, or first work at, large issues of social justice and that we, as teachers, must deal with wisely. One response is that of immobility in the face of the immensity of the problems. Help your students to see the worth of taking small steps on a few issues. Encourage them to concentrate on just one or two issues and not try to deal with all. Invite them to see themselves as part of the body of Christ in the world: though the body should be concerned with a broad range of issues, not each and every member need be, or even should be. Encourage them to select one or two issues and get informed about those — that is difficult enough; and encourage them to be content with taking small steps if they see no hope of taking big ones.

Sometimes one does not even see any hope of taking small steps. Remind them that an important dimension of the Christian life is learning to cope. We must learn what to do when there is nothing to do. We in the Western world have lost the skills for coping. We have become so adept at changing things that when we are confronted with what we cannot change we typically become infantile in our behavior: petulant, threatening, aggressive, evasive. Part of living the struggle for justice is learning to cope with the fact that the powers are still alive and active in our world, rebelling against the Lord God and crushing his human children. We in the West naively underestimate evil's power. We have much to learn from the oppressed of the world. Russian Christians have learned to cope; it is worse than naive to suppose that they can and should throw the rascals in Moscow out.

---

valorization of that experience. (One may contribute to S's finding Longfellow's poetry less interesting, or more interesting, than S once found it.)

(3) One may contribute to S's believing, of some experience which was previously available to S, that positively or negatively valorized experiences have been attached to that first experience as concomitant or consequence (discipline).

(4) One may contribute to S's acquiring new beliefs as to what will bring about an experience which S expects to be positively valorized, or avert one which S expects to be negatively valorized.

No one, to the best of my knowledge, has ever explored the workings of different strategies with respect to this taxonomy — for example, how reasoning works, how modeling works, and so forth. In the text above I offer incomplete hints on the matter.

Notice the prominence of *beliefs* in the taxonomy above. Dispositions, I am convinced, are the consequence of stable beliefs as to the valorization of experience coupled with beliefs as to how to attain (or avert) experiences. Dispositions are not autonomic behavior. Neither are they habits one must "break" to eliminate. On the other hand, to see oneself in a *quandary* calling for *deliberation* is to see oneself in a situation which falls outside the scope of one's dispositions.

Another response is that of a despairing sense of "inutility," as Jacques Ellul calls it in "Meditation on Inutility" at the end of *The Politics of God and the Politics of Man*.[17] It is very easy, in one's struggle against injustice, to feel that in all one's endeavors one is getting nowhere — indeed, to feel that things are worse than when one began.

We place our endeavors in the hands of God; for all our action occurs in the context of the prayer "Thy Kingdom come."[18] We live in the hope and even the expectation that God will make something of abiding worth out of what we have done. But what God makes of it may well be something different from what we expect; and it may be something that only our children, or children's children, discern. Christ came in the fullness of time; yet he came in a manner unexpected.

I end where I began. Christians exist under a binding requirement to engage in a specific uprising. The goal and nature of that uprising can be fully understood only from the standpoint of redemption, only in the messianic light. That is true in part, I have come to think, because only in the messianic light do the tears of God over the world's injustice show up. One of the greatest challenges for us today in the Reformed tradition of Christianity is to recover that sacramental consciousness that was so deep in Calvin's thought — the consciousness that as we wind our way through this world we meet God blessing us, chastising us, speaking to us, nourishing us, empowering us, forgiving us. Part of that recovery must involve recovering that bold and haunting theme in Calvin, that as we wind our way through this world and come across injustice, we meet a wounded God. Beneath and behind the injustice of this world are the tears of God. We live in the presence of suffering Love. Were this teaching deeply fixed in our minds and hearts, says Calvin, that to perpetrate injustice is to wound God, we would be much more reluctant than we are to inflict injuries on our fellow human beings, or even to tolerate injuries inflicted.[19]

How can we teach our students to see the wounds of God behind the world's injustice? I do not know. Maybe teaching cannot do it. Maybe only through one's own tears can one see God's tears. Maybe we as teachers must humbly acknowledge our limitations before the mysterious and troubling fact that suffering illuminates.

17. Ellul, *The Politics of God and the Politics of Man*, edited and translated by G. W. Bromiley (Grand Rapids: Eerdmans, 1972).

18. Barth, *The Christian Life*.

19. For a detailed discussion of Calvin's views on this matter, see my essay entitled "The Wounds of God: Calvin's Theology of Social Justice" in *The Reformed Journal* 37, no. 6 (June 1987): 14-22.

Autobiography: The Story of Two Decades of Thinking about Christian Higher Education

After reflecting for a couple of weeks on the style to adopt for my remarks, I decided to take seriously the fact that this is an *informal* gathering. I know indeed that most of you are academics, and that in the course of your induction into academia you learned how to write and speak in the mode of lofty impersonality and how to rampart what you say with footnotes and learned allusions. So did I. But as I envisaged this talk, that tone seemed thoroughly unfitting. So I decided that rather than striving for impersonality I would make this talk entirely personal. I decided to lay out for you in a frankly personal manner some of the lines of thought that have led me, with varying degrees of excitement and reluctance, to move from what I once thought about the ends and means of Christian collegiate education to what I now think.

By the end of my talk you will see that instead of ramparts having been erected and gates battened shut against the assaults of scholarly critics, a pile of building materials has been dumped in front of us. There will be building materials all over the place; they will not have been assembled into a nice, castellated structure. They will not have been assembled into any structure at all. Partly that's because at this point I myself do not know how to put all the pieces together. It is also because we are not assembled here today as a curriculum revision committee which, after all the talk is over, has to make decisions. We are assembled to spark ideas in each other; and I hope that my somewhat unorthodox procedure will succeed in doing that. I realize, of course, that the open-ended character of my discussion will lead some of you, upon returning home this afternoon and being asked by your spouses

---

This speech, originally titled "Reflections on Future Directions for the Christian College," was delivered at Wheaton College in the 1980s.

what took place, to remark, "Oh, nothing at all; just a lot of talk again. Why did God ever inflict philosophers on us?"

On the American scene today there are a large number of significant administrative and technological changes taking place that the wise Christian college will pay attention to and, after appraisal, make appropriate use of. None of us, for example, can ignore computers and their rippling effects in our society; none can ignore the fact that as we in our colleges become more internally diverse, we need more administrators, and administrators of a somewhat different sort than we had in the past; and none of us can ignore the fact that as American business changes from an occupation into something more nearly resembling a profession, we in the Christian colleges will have to teach business differently. But today I want to talk less about those changes in society to which we should be alert and responsive and more about the animating vision that should lure us — while fully acknowledging that at many points this distinction between context and vision is hazy. A friend of mine is fond of saying that if you don't know where you're going, any road will get you there. What I would like to do is talk mainly about where we are going. But to repeat: I propose doing so not *in abstracto* but by briefly narrating to you some of the stages of reflection on my own life's way.

Christian Humanism

I began my thinking about Christian collegiate education in terms of what might be called the Christian humanist model; I did so because, as I now see more clearly than I did then, this was the model embraced by the teachers I most admired in my days as a student at Calvin College.

What do I mean when I speak of the *Christian humanist* model? Well, in the thought of the people whom I have in mind, *liberation* was a prominent theme. They liked to play on the etymology of the word "liberal" in the phrase "liberal arts education." "Liberal," they said, comes from the Latin word *liber,* meaning free. Liberal arts education is meant to free us — free us from all that accompanies the particularities of our local existences: our narrowness of vision, our prejudices, and so on. It does this by introducing us to the great stream of high culture, the best that has been thought and said, a stream with tributaries reaching back into many different places and many different times. The consequence of one's immersion in this transcendent realm of high culture — to change the metaphor from stream to realm — is that a certain mind is formed in one, a mind freed from the particularities of growing up in southwest Minnesota in the 1930s and 1940s of this century, as I did.

My teachers always went on to make clear that their goal for the student was the formation of a *Christian* mind. Thus it was not humanist education in general that they practiced but *Christian* humanist education. They were persuaded that to be human is to exist as part of a spiritual kingdom; it is to exist within a particular community's way of being-in-the-world, a way shaped by its answer to the question "Who God is." Christian liberal arts education was thus understood both as an expression of that spiritual kingdom which is the church of Christ and as induction into that kingdom. There is no such thing, they said, as religiously neutral education. Christian education serves the cause of Christian culture — that is, of a faith in Christ that is incarnated — enfleshed, embodied — in culture.

That, very briefly described, was the model on which I was reared. I found it enrapturing. And what I found enrapturing above all was the way Christ and culture were brought into union rather than tension. Rather than being told that I had to choose between these, I was told that my allegiance to Christ was to be worked out *in* my cultural activities. I was told further that in such endeavor I was not acting as an individual but as a member of a people, the people of God, a people spread out around the globe but spread out also in time, stretching all the way back through the evangelicals and the Reformers and the medievals to the patristics, and from the patristics through the apostles to our Lord, and from our Lord to the prophets and the patriarchs. For a young fellow from a tiny farming village in southwest Minnesota, it was a bright and shiny world I had entered — a world at once holistic in its cultural inclusiveness and committed in its religious dynamic.

Christian Academic Discipline

But it did not take long for me to move away from this to what might be called the *Christian academic-discipline model.* It is clear to me now that it was my induction into the world of American philosophy that changed my mind. It is also clear to me now that the changes were less vast than I supposed at the time. Most of the vision I had been bequeathed I still preserved. But there was one feature of it that I came very much to dislike — namely, its orientation toward the past. I was a young philosopher imbued with the challenge of *doing philosophy;* for three years I had been immersed in stuff "hot off the philosophical press." It seemed to me that in spite of all their talk about serving Christ in culture, and all their talk about developing Christian culture, my former Christian college teachers were not much interested in actually *doing* philosophy or sociology or whatever. Though they were interested in coming to understand the philosophy that *had been* done, and doing that in Christian perspective, they were not much interested in the creative philosophical task. That disturbed me. The Christian humanist model struck me as too much oriented toward the past and not oriented enough toward the future.

So I began to insist that our fundamental calling in the Christian colleges is to develop the various disciplines and to do so in Christian perspective. This would include history; history too is a discipline that must be developed. But I thought it a serious mistake to make history the all-embracing context of the whole curriculum. I continued, however, to embrace the vision of Christian learning — that is, of learning which is expressive of the Christian gospel. The notion that scholarship can be or should be neutral never tempted me. And to the question about the point of inducting our students into Christian learning thus understood, I answered that this was a means to the end of equipping our students to live as Christians in the world.

I came to those conclusions some twenty years ago. Since then, they have been both amplified and undermined by various lines of thought that one and another episode has provoked me into following out. As a consequence, by now it seems to me that the Christian academic-discipline model is no more satisfactory than the Christian humanist model.

I began to be discontent with the ways in which I had been taught to describe the relation between faith and learning. For one thing, I began to think that the words used did not have much content; they remained too abstract. It was said that Christians approach scholarship with a different perspective and that it shapes their scholarship into something different. Perhaps so; but just how does that take place? It was said that Christians approach scholarship with different presuppositions and that those shape their scholarship into something different. Perhaps so, but how does this *shaping* by presuppositions work? I wanted more clarity, and more concreteness of insight, on the connection.

I also began to be uneasy about the unidirectionality of the model. I was persuaded that in some deep and important ways faith does shape scholarship, and that it is right that it do so; I was ready to combat all those who insisted that faith should stay out of scholarship. But I began to ask myself whether it does not also sometimes go the other way round. Does not scholarship sometimes shape faith — and does it not sometimes do so legitimately? This makes us nervous; we feel the ground shifting under our feet. But, for example, nobody in the modern world thinks it is part of Christian fidelity to hold that the sun travels around the earth; we have all become heliocentrists; and it is obvious that what has induced this change in us is developments in the new science. So too, may it not be — this gets closer to the nerve ends — that biblical and archaeological scholarship sometimes legitimately changes our view of the content of the faith?

I felt yet a third source of discomfort with the model of faith and learning that I had been bequeathed. Prominent in that model was the theme that Christian scholarship is *different* scholarship. But is that correct? Do we not tie ourselves into knots when difference is treated as a goal? Is not the project of Christian scholarship simply the project of *faithful* scholarship? And is it not the case that sometimes fidelity will yield disagreement on some topic with one or another of our non-Christian colleagues, and sometimes not?

Learning as Social Practice and Moral Formation

So I began to reflect anew on the connections between faith and learning — always persuaded that there are in fact deep and important connections. Eventually I concluded that to understand the connections we must turn away from the *results* of science — these often conceal the connections — and look instead at the *practice* of science. Once we do this, we see that science is profoundly shaped by cognitive goals and standards that scientists set for themselves. We see further that these goals and standards and the methods embraced for achieving or meeting them change throughout history; and that at almost any time in history, they are contested. For a time in the seventeenth century the majority of scientists thought it was legitimate to hypothesize about nonperceptible entities; then in the eighteenth century the notion caught on that such hypotheses are to be rigorously repudiated. Today we have come around again to the eighteenth-century view. It is true that in some of the disciplines the results appear to us as a monolithic block; one is then baffled as to what faith and commitment could have to do with that. My suggestion was, however, that if one looks into the practice that yielded these results, then one will see that they have been determined by what I called the *control beliefs* of the theorizers, and that these control beliefs, so far from being just obviously right, represent commitments on the part of the theorizers. I suggested that it is especially here that the faith of the Christian is relevant in the practice of science, at the point where a commitment is made as to the *sorts* of theories which are acceptable.

Initially this line of thought had nothing to do with reflections on the curriculum. But shortly I began to wonder whether it did not have curricular implications. If we in the Christian colleges want to show our students how faith gets embodied in life, including the life of the scholar, does this not require focusing less myopically on the results of science and beginning to look at the history of the *practice* of science?

While I was following out this line of thought, I also found myself lured down quite a different path. Being convinced as I was that Christian education is ultimately oriented toward a Christian way of being-in-the-world, I began to reflect that in addition to cultivating *knowledge* in our students, along with *abilities*, we must also cultivate dispositions, inclinations, and propensities. That is, if we are concerned about how our students will act and not just about what they will think and what they can do, then we must cultivate a certain character formation, where "character" is understood not as some purely inner thing but as something that gets manifested in doing. And that led me on immediately to these questions. How do our dispositions to act in certain ways get formed in us? If we are aiming to equip our students to live as Christians in the world, what is the pedagogical strategy for achieving that goal? I decided that rather than speculating on the answer to this question, I should look into contemporary psychology to see what it said on the matter.

This proved to be for me a most illuminating and unsettling line of inquiry. What I studied was what psychologists have been saying about moral education; for, though my own interests were broader than moral, including religious, ecological, and so on, these other modes of character formation have been relatively little discussed by psychologists; most of their attention has been focused on moral education.

What I discovered very soon was that throwing the abstract disciplines at students has almost no effect on their actions. You are not going to change somebody's political behavior just by putting political theory in front of him or her. Thus at once my Christian academic-discipline model was thrown into disarray, as indeed was the Christian humanist model. I had proposed the study of the academic disciplines as the means to the goal of equipping and training our students to live as Christians in the world; now I was made to see that it was an illusion to think that this means would achieve this goal.

What *does* shape a person's moral character? Well, on the basis of my reading of the literature, I concluded that it was mainly three things. Here I shall have to state them briefly and sketchily, thereby running the risk of your not fully seeing their significance. On the other hand, all of them are familiar to you; there are no surprises here.

Discipline is one way of shaping a person's embodied moral character. If you want to shape how people are disposed to act, then it helps to induce in them the expectation of desirable or undesirable consequences of their actions. Naturally, these words "desirable" and "undesirable" cover an enormous range of different phenomena. Secondly, *modeling* is a way of shaping embodied moral character. If you want to shape how people are disposed to act, it helps to present them with loved or admired models who act that way. And thirdly, *casuistry* is a way of shaping embodied moral character. If you want people to act a certain way, it helps to give them reasons for acting that way. Naturally, a reason that works well for one person may not work well for another.

Even at the time I was working on this I never suggested that these three ways exhausted the matter; I suggested only that they were the three dominant ways of shaping embodied character. I now think there is a fourth way which, though mysterious in its workings and scarcely noticed in the literature, is also of tremendous importance. To shape a person's caring about one and another mode of pain and suffering in the world, it helps to present that person with a human face and a human voice in which that pain is present. Of course it does not always work, any more than discipline and modeling and casuistry always work. In my experience, people's fear of the consequences of acting on their sympathy will often prevent its formation. Yet I submit that there is nothing so powerful for energizing concern for the plight of Christians in Russia as to be confronted with a Christian in Russia, and nothing so powerful for energizing concern for the plight of the blacks in South Africa as to be confronted with a black from South Africa.

So there are, I suggest, at least these four phenomena that shape our embodied moral characters: discipline in a broad sense, modeling, casuistry, and face-to-face confrontation with suffering.

Culture, Society, and Justice

If these conclusions are correct, and if we do sincerely want to contribute to shaping how our students will act, then we shall obviously have to engage in some radical rethinking of our pedagogical strategies. I know, of course, that some people hold the view that a teacher should avoid shaping how students will act: put the food in front of them and let them choose. But that response is purely "academic"; discipline and modeling do their work no matter what.

One of the things we shall have to do, as I now see it, is build bridging elements into our curricula, the aim of which is actually to work through with students reasons for acting one way rather than another. Another thing we shall have to do is break down the walls between "town and gown" so that our students can be presented with genuine models; along with this we shall have to reflect on how to counteract the powerful modeling influence of the American media. The question that comes to mind is whether the Christian college can succeed in our non-Christian society. Yet another thing we shall have to do is bring our students into direct contact with the faces and voices of suffering. And throughout all of this we are going to have to reflect on the unnerving fact that we as individuals and as institutions unavoidably have a modeling impact. Indeed, I have come to think that we must put behind us the notion that education occurs by way of what is said in classrooms and that everything else is support for that, and begin to acknowledge that the entire school situation functions educatively; and that what is said in classrooms is only one component within this educative situation — albeit a tremendously important component.

At about the same time that I was following out these lines of thought, I found myself also forced to reconsider how I thought about art. I thank the Lord that I was never raised to believe that art is the enemy. Never in my childhood was it suggested to me that one had to choose between Christ and art. I come from a three-generations-long line of cabinetmakers, and was reared with a veneration for craftsmanship. In addition, my father used to spend his evenings out there on the southwest Minnesota prairies doing drawings; and an aunt of mine saw to it that she never missed the Saturday-afternoon broadcast of the Metropolitan Opera. Once when I asked her why she listened to "that stuff," she replied, unforgettably, "It's my window onto the world."

But then one day some thirteen or fourteen years ago I experienced a sort of secular epiphany in the National Gallery in Washington, D.C. I was sitting in the rotunda on a bench just inside the turnstiles, resting my weary legs, watching the people. Suddenly a most extraordinary phenomenon caught my eye. Mothers and fathers with little children in tow would walk through the turnstiles and then lean down to these squirming, squalling beings and say, "Ssshh, ssshh." And the mothers and fathers would themselves begin to talk in hushed tones. This occurred a few months after my family and I came home from Europe, where we had visited a good many of the great cathedrals; I was struck by the analogue. Art is our modern surrogate for the bones of the martyrs; and the art museum is our modern cathedral. I now know that other people have noticed and commented on the same phenomenon, especially André Malraux.

But having been reared as a Calvinist to see idolatry as an ever-threatening phenomenon, I said to myself, "This can't be right." It was the pursuit of the ramifications of that thought which eventually led me to begin to see art in a different light. Slowly in my study and teaching of aesthetics I began to see that hardly anybody ever talked about the fallenness of art, Christians included. Christians would talk about art in all sorts of elevated ways, as the recovery of a lost order and so forth; but not about the fallenness of art. And here I do not exempt the evangelical Christians who were trying to make a case for art. Most of the time they, too, spoke just as religiously about art as the most secular of Romantics.

What also then began to strike me was the hammerlock that high art has on our thinking about art. All of us here sing hymns, and every writer on art and aesthetics knows about lullabies and advertising art, yet when we speak about art and write about it, such phenomena as these become either invisible or unworthy of attention. I found myself reflecting on the practices and institutions of art in a way wholly analogous to that in which I found myself reflecting on the practices of science. I was led to conclude that works of art, instead of being functionless, are instruments and objects of human action. One of those actions is aesthetic contemplation, and more generally, perceptual contemplation. But this is only one of many functions of art in our human existence.

As you can see, these reflections also were not originally stimulated by reflecting on the appropriate curriculum for the Christian college. But soon I did begin to speculate about the curricular implications. If it is true that what we call high art is only one among many modes or functions of art, tremendously valuable indeed but not alone valuable, is it not important that in our curricula we try to give our students a much broader understanding of art in life than is customary? It became clear to me that the music, art, and literature programs in our colleges function basically to induct students into high art. Might it not be valuable to expand our sights and acquaint our students with the multiplicity of ways in which art has enriched our human existence — and yes, the multiplicity of ways in which it has served as an instrument of oppression, deprivation, and idolatry?

But now things were really beginning to come unstuck. We have all had the experience of suddenly seeing the familiar in a new light, so that it seems we had never before seen it for what it really was. I have told you about one such experience of mine, sitting there in the National Gallery. Let me now tell you about another. I was reading a book by the important American sociologist Talcott Parsons, his *Evolution of Societies*. And there on one of the pages Parsons remarked that one of the salient differences dividing modern societies from traditional societies is that we have a large deposit of culture available to us that did not arise from within our society and that has relatively little direct function in our society.[1] I dare say that this is really pretty obvious;

---

1. See Parsons, *Evolution of Societies*, edited by J. Toby (Englewood Cliffs, N.J.: Prentice-Hall, 1977).

and the passage itself was unremarkable. I considered quoting it for you here, but upon looking it up again, I found it much too bland. Nonetheless, for me it was revelatory. I had been trying for many years to understand the inner core of the notion of liberal arts education, never feeling that I had succeeded in getting hold of it. Suddenly I saw what it was. Liberal arts education, as it has taken shape in the West over the last four or five centuries, is an attempt to induct the student into that enduring, socially transcendent stream of high culture — into the philosophy, the literature, the art, the music, and the science of humanity.

But now at the same time that I felt I finally saw the liberal arts tradition for what it was, I realized that I had to put some large question marks around it. For in having been led to see science and art as fundamentally social practices, I had in effect seen that the stream of high culture into which we try to induct our students is not at all so socially transcendent as we like to think it is. Of course one can, if one wishes, take a painting in hand and look at it appreciatively while remaining pretty much ignorant of the practice that gave it birth. Nonetheless, I had come to think that our understanding of these phenomena of art and science is profoundly impoverished if we rip them out of the social contexts that gave rise to them. And that led me, in turn, to ask whether we in the Christian colleges have perhaps been led to neglect society while focusing on culture. Have we not in good measure neglected trying to give our students an understanding of the dynamics of society? Must our curricula not show a balance here? And if that leads us to become something more than a liberal arts college — not less but more — so be it.

Some of you will realize that in being led to ask this question, I was really beginning to distinguish between what, in a speech some years ago, I called Stage II and Stage III, and to wonder whether we must not move into Stage III.

Those reflections coincided with my coming to see, over the last ten years or so, some of the wounds of the world with a vividness and an intensity that they had never had for me before. I have seen the pain in the faces of black South Africans and, yes, the anxiety in the faces of some Afrikaners. I have heard the pain in the voices of the Palestinians and, yes, the fear in the voices of many Israelis. And in my own life I have experienced painful wounds. With the wounds of humanity before my eyes and in my ears and in my heart, I turned to look back at those models of Christian collegiate education that I had earlier embraced; I found them now sadly deficient. In these curricula, the wounds of humanity are scarcely seen, the cries of humanity scarcely heard. The academic-discipline model reminds us that the cultural mandate requires humanity to develop the potentials of creation by bringing forth science and art. I agree; but I ask: What about our mandate to free the captives? The Christian humanist model stresses that we must be freed from our cultural particularities to participate as Christians in the great cultural conversation of humanity. I do not seriously disagree; but I ask: What about those who are excluded from the conversation? Our traditional models speak scarcely at all of suffering and injustice in the world, and thus scarcely at all of our calling to do mercy and justice. They do not teach for mercy and justice.

World-Systems

These questions began to interact in my mind with yet another line of thought. Looking back, I see clearly that by way of my training in American academia and my reading of American magazines and newspapers, I had adopted a *modernization* understanding of the world. That is to say, I saw the world as a large collection of internally cohering societies that interact with each other. Further, I pictured these as being at various stages of modernization, of advancement, of progress; and I assumed that, for the most part, what hindered the modernization of a given society was some lack within the society itself — lack of natural resources, lack of energy sources, lack of a work ethic, lack of capital, and so forth. In addition, I believed that most of these lacks could be supplied by other societies that were more advanced; and that where these lacks were supplied, those now underdeveloped societies would soon join us at our high stage of development.

Then, in the course of preparing lectures to deliver at the Free University of Amsterdam, lectures that eventually took the form of my book entitled *Until Justice and Peace Embrace,* I decided that I had better look more closely at this modernization theory, which for me had always remained in the background of my thinking. My original intent in bringing it into the foreground was to describe it with more depth. But the more I read and reflected, the more skeptical I became about the theory — until finally I concluded that it was in great measure illusion. Modernization theory is mainly false; sociologist friends of mine tell me that it is on the way to disappearing from the mind-set of our social theorists.

The question that then faced me was whether there was any other theory to put in place of the old discredited one. What I found irresistibly attractive was the so-called world-systems theory, worked out especially by Immanuel Wallerstein.[2] I had better state clearly that by no means do I accept all

2. See Wallerstein, *The Modern World-System* (New York: Academic Press, 1974).

the claims of standard world-systems theorists. But I do find the basic picture compelling. Suppose we say that one group of people share *an economy* with another group of people if between the two there is a significantly integrated division of labor. Then if one looks at the world today, one has to come to the conclusion that most areas of the world are joined together into one single economy with, of course, all sorts of gradations in intensity of integration. However, overlapping this single economy we have a multiplicity of states and a multiplicity of peoples, or nations, with peoples or nations by no means coinciding with states. What the world-systems theorists mean, then, by a world-system is just this phenomenon of a single economy straddling distinct states and/or peoples; it is one of their theses that our world today comprises pretty much just one single world economy.

The classical picture of how economic integration occurs is the free-market picture. Wool growers in England meet with wine growers in Portugal and say, "Let's exchange," whereupon they freely make a trade agreement with each other. The world-systems theorist says that that is not how it usually goes. And in particular, if one traces the growth of our present world-economy from seventeenth-century Europe outward, one sees duress operating at very many points — duress of military arms, duress of monopolies on desired goods, and so forth. The duress — I need hardly mention this, so familiar is it to all of us — was mainly duress by the West on the areas it subjugated, and more recently, duress by the First World on the Third. In the growth of the world economy it was the West that more often than not held the upper hand of power, and the West that more often than not used that power to get the better of the interchange between the two parties. Thus there is a connection between the development of the Netherlands in the seventeenth century and the underdevelopment of Indonesia. Indonesia did not enter the relationship in an impoverished state, or of course the Dutch would never have been interested; it *became* underdeveloped. Underdevelopment is not due solely to internal factors.

Now suppose that this new picture of the world, this world-systems theory, is by and large correct. What implications does that have for the curricula of our colleges? One implication that fairly leaps out is that we must seek to develop an international consciousness in our students. I do not deny that in some respects our education has long been internationalized. Our historians have taught us what it was like to be human in other places and other times. And in all our colleges our students have acquired some feel, no doubt, for the breadth and scope of the church — for its transnational character. But now when I speak of the development of an international consciousness, I mean something more than that. We must try to give our students some sense of the interlocking structure of the modern world, and some sense of the impact of the West, particularly today of the United States, on the rest of the world. I am inclined to think that, for one thing, a good many of our students must in one way or another be involved in the Third World. Traditionally our foreign-study programs have been heavily oriented toward Europe; I think we must begin to try to achieve some balance here. But in addition to having some students on location in the Third World, I think we must do our best to acquaint all our students with the structure of the modern world and its formative dynamics.

Praxis-Oriented Scholarship

Several of the preceding points lead naturally into the next line of reflection. I was reared to think that the primary scholarly task of the college and university was to develop *pure* scholarship — that is, scholarship aimed at no practical end but aimed simply at developing a body of laws that satisfy our cognitive goals and standards, or a body of interpretations of cultural artifacts that satisfy our demands for acceptable interpretations. Of course, I knew very well that scholarship can be applied, and I thought that the scholar along with the rest of us has certain responsibilities for such application; but application did not seem to me the business of the liberal arts college.

I have begun to think, however, that this neat distinction between pure scholarship and applications thereof cannot really be sustained. Or rather, I have come to think that there is a mode of scholarship that comes in between these two. I have come to believe in the tenability and importance of praxis-oriented scholarship.

It is evident to everyone that scholarship is often of use in lifting humanity's burdens of deprivation and oppression. Yet it is not automatically so; there is no reason to believe that pure scholarship will always just happen to have developed what is needed. Thus it is that there arises the need for scholarship that assists one and another form of praxis. Understand me correctly: I am not here arguing that pure scholarship is wrong. But if it is true, for example, that fundamental features of the economic arrangements of humanity are duress and domination, why should some of us not then engage in economic research in order to understand how such domination works, in the hope that we will be able to propose ways to relieve some of it? The educational program of the Christian college will have to be undergirded by a substantial component of praxis-oriented scholarship.

To a person committed to the traditional understanding of the liberal arts college, a good many of the above lines of thought will appear profoundly threatening. But I have so far not even mentioned the curricular development which, for most of our colleges, has been the most effective in moving them away from being pure liberal arts colleges. I have in mind the growth of professional and preprofessional programs. At Calvin College, for example, not only has the business program expanded, both in terms of majors and in terms of size of program; the college has also introduced a major in computer science and a major in communications, and has expanded its engineering program. These developments have caused alarm among a good many of my colleagues in the so-called liberal arts.

I do not deny that there are some threatening aspects to these developments; but I think there are also some exciting challenges. And I think that we must neither become immobilized by the threats nor become fixated on the challenges, but be aware of both.

For one thing, the growth of a business major is not, as some of my colleagues represent it as being, a college's collapse in the face of external pressure. It is in part a thoroughly responsible response to important changes in American business. Where not long ago a young person going into business would regard a high-school education as entirely sufficient, now almost no one holds that view; business has become an intensely knowledge-oriented occupation, as law, medicine, and education have been for centuries. Business has rapidly acquired many of the traditional hallmarks of a profession. The response of our colleges is in good measure a response to that.

Furthermore, business is surely one of the most formative of all occupations in American society — both for good and for ill. No doubt we in our colleges, when introducing professional and preprofessional programs, do all too often respond purely to external and financial pressure. It seems to me that the better way to go is to ask which, from a Christian point of view, are the truly formative professions in American society; it is those, then, on which we should concentrate. I would think that on anyone's list, in addition to education, law, and medicine, would appear business, communications, and politics.

But if we do introduce some professional program in our Christian colleges, then it is imperative that we require all the students engaged in the program to think seriously within a Christian context about the place of that occupation or profession in our society. Here I have more in mind than courses in business ethics, in medical ethics, in legal ethics, and so on. Customarily such courses simply take for granted the goals and practices of the profession and reflect on the puzzles and dilemmas that arise. What is of vastly more importance is that we stand back and, rather than simply taking for granted the shape of that profession in our society, subject it with our students to discriminating analysis. If we really managed to do that for our business majors, then the introduction of a business major in the Christian college would be an enormously important contribution to the cause of our Lord.

Teaching for Shalom

There are still other lines of thought that I have been following out in recent years that I could present to you. For example, we have all become aware — not sufficiently, no doubt, but still somewhat — of the sexism and racism that thrive in our colleges; we must not shirk from the task of working to root them out. But I must bring this discussion to a close. So rather than developing that line of thought, let me conclude by posing a question that I have been mulling over a good deal in recent years, and which by now you also will be asking.

How can all these lines of thought be brought together? What I visualize is a college that teaches for justice without neglecting the arts; a college that engages in praxis-oriented scholarship without denying the worth of pure scholarship; a college that gives its students some sense of the social practices of science and art without neglecting the results of science and the works of art; a college that concerns itself with the multiple nonverbal ways in which it shapes the actions of students without neglecting the importance of classroom learning; a college that presents to us the faces and voices of suffering humanity without neglecting the importance of books; a college that teaches for mercy and justice without neglecting the importance of liturgy and devotions and contemplation; a college that responsibly inducts some students into the formative professions of American life without neglecting the arts and sciences and humanities. What holds all these emphases together? Does this not simply threaten to be a grab bag of good things? How are we to assess priorities? What goal can we set for ourselves that will give all these things their appropriate place?

H. Richard Niebuhr, in his book *The Kingdom of God in America*, draws a contrast between two Christian understandings of salvation: that of the Vision of God and that of the Kingdom (Realm) of God. Here is how he lays out the difference:

> To call the vision man's greatest good is to make contemplation the final end of life; to put the sovereignty of God in the first place is to make obedient activity superior to contemplation. . . . The principle of vision sug-

169

gests that the perfection of the object seen is loved above all else; the principle of the kingdom indicates that the reality and power of the being commanding obedience are primarily regarded. The first term may also be interpreted to mean that the initiative lies with the one who seeks to see while the object is conceived as somehow at rest. . . . The term "Kingdom of God" puts all the emphasis on the divine initiative.[3]

Probably there are no pure examples of either of these two types; probably every Christian thinker lies somewhere on a continuum between these two paradigmatic ways of thinking, with no one located at the extremes. Yet I think there can be little doubt that the move from medieval Christianity to Reformation Christianity involved a profound shift from thinking predominantly of salvation in terms of the Vision of God to thinking of it primarily in terms of the Kingdom of God. I think there can also be little doubt that Roman Catholicism since Vatican II has moved significantly in the same direction. Furthermore, it seems to me that in making these moves the Reformers and the contemporary Catholics have moved from a more Hellenic way of thinking to a more Hebraic way.

As for myself, it is the paradigm of the Kingdom of God that shapes my thought. I think of the goal of Christian higher education as preparation for life and work in the Kingdom of God. But that remains so abstract as to be useless unless we also have an answer to this next question: What is the content of life in the Kingdom? Perhaps we can say that life in the Kingdom of God is a special and unique type of human flourishing. But what type of human flourishing is it, then? Here in recent years I have come to think that we need look no farther than the Bible for at least the basic outline of our answer. The Bible presents us with a picture of the content of the Kingdom. And the word which the biblical writers use to capture that content is *shalom*, or *eirene*. Shalom is the appointed destiny of human existence. Shalom is the biblical version of what constitutes human flourishing.

Justice is the ground floor of shalom. Shalom incorporates responsible action in general: to God, to nature, to our fellows, to ourselves. And beyond that, it incorporates delight; in shalom we find delight in our right relationships. You see, I trust, how art and pure science are both elements in shalom. And as to your and my relation to our appointed destiny of shalom, the biblical witness is clear. We are to pray and struggle for the incursion of shalom into our world, both struggling against injustice and developing the enrich-

3. Niebuhr, *The Kingdom of God in America* (Middleton, Conn.: Wesleyan University Press, 1988), pp. 20-21.

ing potentials of God's creation; and we are to celebrate its presence among us and lament its absence.

I do not see how the Christian college can do anything else than guide its endeavors by this vision of shalom. If God's call to all humanity is to be liberators and developers, celebrators and mourners, then will not the Christian college also have to find its place within this call? It will keep in mind the uniqueness of its calling. A college is a school, and as such, it places disciplined study at the center of its project. But the lure of shalom will direct and energize it. The goal of the Christian college, so I have begun to think, is to promote that mode of human flourishing which is shalom.

Well, there you have it: some nine or ten different lines of thought that I have been following out in recent years that are eminently relevant to the programs and methods of our colleges. I have not tied them all together into a package. My not doing so is not the result of coyness on my part; it is because I really do not yet know in detail what a curriculum and a pedagogy that fit together these various lines of thought would look like. I cannot set out for you a completed model. Perhaps that's a good thing. Perhaps what we in the Christian college movement need at this point in our history is a decade or so of imaginative brainstorming before we try to fit things together.

Can Scholarship and Christian Conviction Mix?
Another Look at the Integration of Faith and Learning

The central assumption of this essay is that the topic of Faith and Learning is not some eternal problem that enters history at the time of its "discovery" and whose relation to history thereafter is only the history of successive answers to the "problem." Learning, I shall argue, is through and through a historical phenomenon — an *ever-changing* historical phenomenon. Christians who wish to be faithful in their scholarship — faithful to their Lord, faithful to their fellow believers, faithful to their fellow human beings, faithful to the earth — never have any other choice than to engage in learning in the particular form in which they find it in their particular time and place. Always trying to alter it, but still always engaging it. I begin then with reflections on learning as we find it today — not with reflections on *the nature* of learning, on *the essence* of science, on *the nature* of theoretical reason, but on learning as we find it. Enormous alterations have taken place in learning, and in our understanding thereof, over the past quarter century. That makes it more imperative that we begin by trying to understand its present form; otherwise we are likely to presuppose some antiquated understanding. For once again: learning is not some timeless essence.

It has been a long time now since my days as a graduate student in philosophy at Harvard; but I remember well the basic thrust of the philosophy of science course I took and of the various public lectures on philosophy of science that I listened to. Teachers and speakers were all engaged in trying to uncover *the logic* of science — or in case the teacher or speaker was one of those who thought that the logic of the social sciences is different from that

---

This essay was originally a speech given at the *Universitas Forum* at Messiah College on May 25, 1993. It was subsequently published in the *Journal of Education and Christian Belief*, and is reprinted here with permission.

of the natural sciences, engaged in trying to uncover *the logics* of science. The thought was that there is some entity called "science" with which we were all acquainted, that this entity has *a logic* or *logics*, that that logic for some reason or other was concealed from us, and that it was the business of the philosopher to uncover that logic — to reveal the hidden. Sometimes it was assumed that science has an *apparent* logic in addition to a *real* logic, and that its apparent logic conceals from us its real logic. We talked in my day about how terribly difficult it was to accomplish this uncovering; philosophy of science is extremely hard work. There was the infamous "problem of the counterfactual" over which we all furrowed our brows. Scientists use counterfactuals all the time; but the logic of the counterfactual is terribly difficult to uncover.

My teachers were assuming, of course, a certain understanding of the relation between philosophy and science — a roughly Kantian understanding. Kant was the first to formulate explicitly the great anxiety of the philosopher in the modern world: Given the growth of the "special sciences," what is left for philosophy to do? Kant's answer was that it remains for the philosopher to explore certain issues of *modality* — certain issues of possibility and necessity. The assumption of my teachers, that it is the province of philosophers to deal with the logic of science, was a descendant of that Kantian view. But beyond operating with a certain understanding of the relation between philosophy and the "special sciences," they were making certain assumptions about the nature of science and its place in the academy and modern culture. It is my judgment that those assumptions have never been better articulated than they were by Max Weber, who set them in the context of his theory of modernization. Let us take a few moments to glance at Weber's theory.

Weber's Theory of Differentiated Spheres

Weber was convinced that the essence of modernization is to be located in two related phenomena. First, in the emergence of *differentiated spheres;* specifically, in the emergence of the differentiated *social spheres* of economy and state, along with household, and in the emergence of the differentiated *cultural spheres* of science, art, law, and ethics. And second, in the ever more pervasive practice of rationalized thought and action within these spheres. The fundamental dynamic of action within our modern, capitalist economies is rationalization, Weber thought, just as the fundamental dynamic of action within our modern, bureaucratic states is rationalization; so too, the fundamental dynamic of thought within modern science is rationalization, oriented as that science is toward prediction, grounded as it is in sensory experience, intertwined as it is with technology.

Not only does the dynamic of rationalization account for what takes place within these differentiated social and cultural spheres; it accounts as well, Weber thought, for the emergence of these differentiated spheres of rationalized thought and action. Weber's argument at this point came in three parts.

Disenchantment of the World

First, Weber regarded it as characteristic of "primitive" religions for the participants in those religions to think of the world as filled with magical and sacred powers — to think of the world as *enchanted*. A condition of the emergence of the differentiated spheres of rationalized thought and action is the disappearance of such a view; modernity presupposes the disenchantment, the *Entzäuberung* (literally, de-magicalizing) of the world. The world for a modern person is an inherently meaningless, indifferent terrain for thought and action.

The displacement of "primitive" religions by the world religions was the first large step along the road to disenchantment. That step, by now far back in the mists of human history, already represented the dynamic of rationalization at work. Religions are attempts to find meaning in human existence; but the meanings proposed by the "primitive" religions always found themselves without a satisfyingly "rational" account of suffering and injustice. The emergence of the world religions was the beginning, though only the beginning, of the process of disenchantment; the process has continued to work itself out within these religions, the dynamic still being rationalization in response to questions of theodicy.

Though Weber apparently believed that the dynamic of rationalization, operating within each world religion as a sort of "internal logic," would eventually lead each of them to adopt a *fully* disenchanted view of the world, he clearly regarded the dynamic as operating most powerfully in religions exhibiting that particular configuration of attitudes and convictions that one finds in Judaism, Christianity, and (presumably) Islam.

World religions can be distinguished along three dimensions. Some, the theocentric, sharply separate the divine from the world; others, the cosmocentric, locate the divine within the world. Some, the world-affirming, see the world as basically good; others, the world-rejecting, see the world as basically bad. And some proclaim the active "ascetic" life as the road to salvation, whereas others proclaim the contemplative "mystical" life as that. Weber speculated that the pressures of rationalization toward a disenchanted view of the world would be felt most powerfully in religions that are theocentric, world-rejecting, and ascetic; he interpreted Judaism and Christianity as exactly such religions. In Judaism and Christianity there was, he thought, a powerful critique of actions performed simply out of habit or affect, and a powerful pressure toward the formation of a generalized ethic of principle — the corollary of which, he thought, is that the world itself is viewed as devoid of meaning, spread out before the agent simply as the objective terrain in and on which action obedient to God is to be performed. Weber regarded the lifestyle of the monks as the finest example in medieval times of this religious type; they were the *virtuosi* of the day. Their lifestyle was the most methodical, that is, the most *rationalized*.

Development of Capitalism

A disenchanted view of the world is not, however, sufficient to account for the emergence of our differentiated spheres of rationalized thought and action; necessary, but not sufficient. Additional changes had to take place, especially in religion, for the emergence to come about. Though he did not entirely neglect the other spheres of culture and society, Weber focused most of his attention at this point on the emergence of our capitalist economy. How, he asked, could our capitalist economy, with its inherently "unbrotherly" modes of operation, have emerged from the cradle of a religion whose ethic, though indeed coupled with an increasingly disenchanted view of the world, was nonetheless an ethic of brotherliness? What convictions were available for legitimating capitalist entrepreneurialism? We all know Weber's answer: it was the English Puritans in particular, and the Calvinists in general, who first exhibited the fully methodical, fully rationalized character-formation of "inner-worldly asceticism" requisite for capitalist entrepreneurship; and they legitimated their actions by replacing the ethic of brotherliness in the economic sphere with "the Protestant ethic," as Weber called it, according to which the believer's entrepreneurship is legitimated by its being the *calling* (*vocatio*) given him or her by God, success therein being a sign of one's belonging to the company of God's elect.

Emergence of Autonomous Internal Logics

And what, thirdly, accounts for the emergence of these *differentiated spheres* themselves? The rationalization characteristic of thought and action within these spheres presupposes that one view the world as disenchanted, and presupposes further, in the economic sphere, at least, that one reject the relevance of an ethic of brotherliness. But what accounts for the emergence of these spheres as such? What I take to be Weber's answer is undeveloped, but interesting. Consider what he says in the following passage from his famous and brilliant essay entitled "Religious Rejections of the World and Their Directions":

> An especially important fraction of all cases of prophetic and redemptory religions have lived not only in an acute but in a permanent state of tension in relation to the world and its borders. The more the religions have been true religions of salvation, the greater has this tension been. The tension has also been the greater, the more rational in principle the ethic has been, and the more it has been oriented to inward sacred values as a means of salvation. Indeed, the further the rationalization and sublimation of the external and internal possession of — in the widest sense — "things worldly," has progressed, the stronger has the tension on the part of religion become. For the rationalization and the conscious sublimation of man's relations to the various spheres of values, external and internal, as well as religious and secular, have then pressed towards making conscious the *internal and lawful autonomy* of the individual spheres; thereby letting them drift into those tensions which remain hidden to the originally naive relation with the external world.[1]

The picture that comes to the surface here is the neo-Kantian picture according to which those "individual spheres," each with its own "internal and lawful autonomy," reside in the very nature of things. What Weber has added to the neo-Kantian picture is the claim that rationalization is the dynamic that brings those spheres to light and sets thought and action within them free from external domination, so that life within each can develop according to the "internal logic" of that sphere.

---

1. Weber, "Religious Rejections of the World and Their Directions," in *From Max Weber: Essays in Sociology,* edited and translated by H. H. Gerth and C. W. Mills (New York: Oxford University Press, 1981), p. 328.

Academic Learning's Self-Image

Weber is here giving expression to a way of thinking that is deep in our modern mentality. Previously art was intertwined with other cultural phenomena; now in the modern world it has been differentiated, and more or less liberated from external demands, so that it can begin to follow its own internal dynamics and come into its own. Previously the economy was intertwined with other social and cultural phenomena; now in the modern world it has been differentiated, and more or less liberated from external demands, so that it too can follow its own internal dynamics and come into its own. And so too science. Previously science was intertwined with other social and cultural phenomena; in the seventeenth century it was finally differentiated, revealed to view, and liberated from external demands, so that it can now follow its own internal "logic." Few if any of my professors would have been able, or indeed willing, to articulate their assumptions with anything like the grand sweep of Weber; nonetheless, I think it was along these lines that they were thinking.

I want to submit to you for your consideration a very different way of thinking of science in particular, and of academic learning in general. But I want to lead up to that by taking note of the fact that my professors were not only working with a picture of science as something that finally, after millennia of fitful preparation, has gained its own differentiated sphere in modern society where, freed from extraneous demands, it has come into its own by following out its own "logic." They were working as well with some prior notion of what that "logic" was. And not only has that been true for philosophers. Characteristic of the modern academy in general has been a certain self-image, a certain understanding, of what it is that the academy is supposed to do.

The past quarter century has witnessed the shattering of that regnant self-image, with the consequence that academia today is very different from what it was twenty-five years ago. Let us try to understand the basic character of these recent developments, beginning with a brief sketch of that once-regnant self-image. And let me make explicit that when I speak of "learning" or "academic learning," I have in mind what the Germans mean by "*Wissenschaft.*"

Generically Human

Perhaps the deepest component in the once-regnant self-image is that reputable learning is a *generically human* enterprise. To put the point pictorially:

Before entering the halls of learning we are to strip off all our particularities, particularities of gender, of race, of nationality, of religion, of social class, of age, and enter purely as human beings. If it turns out that we have failed to strip off some particularity and the others in the hall of learning notice this, they are to order us back into the entry, there to remove the particularity which, unintentionally or not, we kept on. Thus, on the once-regnant understanding of learning, black history, feminist sociology, Muslim political theory, and liberation theology are *bad* history, *bad* sociology, *bad* political theory, *bad* theology. In the practice of learning we are to make use only of such belief-forming dispositions as are shared among all human beings, and we are to accept only the deliverances of such shared human dispositions.

To this general characterization a few qualifications must be added if we are to have a fully accurate picture of this component of the once-regnant self-image of the modern academy. In the first place, if we bring infants into the picture along with those adults whose belief-forming capacities are in one way or another malformed — the color blind, the schizophrenic, and so on — then it is not clear that we will find much at all by way of belief-forming dispositions truly common to all human beings. The response of those who held to the regnant self-image of learning is clear: Only adults are to be allowed into the halls of learning, and, within the halls, malformed adults are to concern themselves exclusively with those parts of learning in which their particular malformation plays no role. Do not let the color blind develop theories of color vision!

But second, we human beings are not autonomic information-processing mechanisms. We always put our belief-forming dispositions to use in certain ways. And we learn those ways. In part we are taught them by others; in part we learn them from our own experience. A fundamental determinant of such learning is what are judged to be more reliable and less reliable ways of using one's indigenous dispositions. For example, each of us learned early in life that in general one can get more reliable beliefs about the size and shape of objects by looking at them from a distance appropriate to their size — close up if they are small, farther off if they are big. Here then is the question: Which learned uses of indigenous capacities are allowable within the halls of learning? Obviously not any learned use whatsoever; not the learned use that consists of reading tea leaves to predict fortunes. On the other hand, obviously more is allowed than those learned uses of indigenous capacities which are engaged in by all normal adults; we allow our scientists to engage in all sorts of sophisticated uses of their indigenous capacities of which non-scientists know nothing. So how do we pick and choose? The fundamental idea is to allow those learned uses whose reliability can be defended by reference solely to the indigenous capacities of normal adults.

In short: fundamental in what has been the regnant self-image of academic learning is the conviction that one is to practice academic learning just *qua* normal adult human being — not *qua* American, not *qua* black, not *qua* Christian, not *qua* female, not *qua* proletarian, not *qua* any particularity whatsoever. We can expect that the results of learning so practiced will eventually gain consensus among all normal adult human beings knowledgeable in the discipline. When learning, *Wissenschaft*, is rightly conducted, pluralism in the academy is an accidental and temporary phenomenon. Particularist learning — learning practiced not *qua* human being but *qua* some particular kind of human being — is misbegotten learning.

Classically Foundationalist

Another fundamental component in the once-regnant self-image of the modern academy is a certain hierarchy of the academic disciplines. The paradigmatic disciplines are the physical sciences and mathematics, with everything else ranged down from there. At the bottom, of course, is theology, though the humanities in general are not much better; the social sciences occupy a position somewhere in between the physical sciences and the humanities. What underlies this hierarchy is a certain notion of *true science* that has its origins in the medieval notion of *scientia* but was then significantly revised by John Locke and his cohorts in the Royal Academy. The thought is that mathematics and the natural sciences have attained the status of true sciences, whereas the other academic disciplines have not yet done so. When their Newtons appear and their revolutions take place, they too will become true sciences. Accordingly, in speaking of the logic of the sciences we are not speaking of something unique in principle to the natural sciences and mathematics; we are speaking of the logic that any academic discipline will exhibit once it attains the status of a true science. As it so happens, that logic is now exhibited only in mathematics and the natural sciences. But that is happenstance; we hope for the day when all the disciplines will have become true sciences exhibiting the "logic" of science. In the meanwhile, we can compose a hierarchy of the disciplines in terms of how far they appear to be from meeting that ideal — call it, *the science ideal*.

On the issue of the "logic of science" there has been somewhat less consensus than on the two matters already mentioned; nonetheless the dominant view has been that true science is foundational in structure — more specifically, *classically* foundationalist. Let me explain. In the first place, we should not think in terms of foundationalism but rather in terms of foundationalisms; there is not some one theory which is foundationalism but rather a whole family of foundationalist theories. Foundationalist theories constitute a certain species of theory as to the conditions under which one or another truth-relevant merit is present in our beliefs — as to when our beliefs are *properly scientific*, or when they constitute *knowledge*, or when they are *warranted*, or when they are *entitled* (justified), and so forth. Every foundationalist theory, in order to specify the conditions under which a belief has one of such merits, begins with a distinction between beliefs that we hold on the basis of other beliefs, and beliefs that we do not hold on the basis of other beliefs but as the consequence of some other belief-forming or belief-sustaining dynamic than that one. Call these, respectively, *mediate* beliefs and *immediate* beliefs. Having made this distinction, every foundationalist then goes on to distinguish the conditions under which a mediate belief possesses the merit in question, from the conditions under which an immediate belief possesses the merit in question. All foundationalists hold that a *mediate* belief possesses the merit in question just in case it is held on the basis of immediate beliefs that properly support it and which themselves possess the merit in question; thus, the image of a *foundation*. Naturally there have been different views as to what constitutes proper support by the foundation, though prominent in the modern world has been the notion that being properly supported by the foundation consists of being probable with respect to the foundation.

As to the conditions under which *immediate* beliefs possess the merit in question, foundationalists differ among each other. But prominent in the Western tradition has been the habit of singling out at this point those immediate beliefs which are *certain*. What makes a foundationalist theory a *classically* foundationalist theory is just the insistence that an immediate belief has the merit in question if and only if it is certain for the person in question. As one would expect, this thesis has given rise to a new set of disputes, viz., disputes over which beliefs are certain for a given person. However, in modern philosophy there has been something of a convergence among classical foundationalists toward the view that a belief is certain for a person just in case the proposition believed is either an incorrigible report of a state of consciousness of that person, or a necessary truth which is self-evident to that person.

One more component of the once-regnant self-image of the modern academy should be mentioned: It has been widely held that it is the business of philosophers to offer a general account of things, with the other disciplines then filling in the specifics, that it is the business of philosophers to construct or display foundations for all the disciplines, and that it is the business of philosophers to uncover the necessary conditions, in human nature, of scientific activity; philosophers are to do all this in a way that is itself generically human, truly scientific, and classically foundationalist in structure.

One might ask how, on this once-regnant self-image, a person's religion is related to his or her practice of learning. Obviously it will not be regarded as an allowable particularity. Some have thought of Christianity and other religions as providing motivation for engaging in learning while yet not entering into the practice itself; that is one option. Others have held that it has nothing at all to do with learning but belongs to some other sphere of human life, possibly to its own unique sphere; Weber himself seems to have thought of it as a remnant of the irrational rather than as a differentiated value-sphere of its own. But also, down from the middle ages through the Enlightenment and on into the modern world, there have been those who have held out the hope of constructing a scientific theism, even, a scientific Christianity: One starts with evidence for God's existence, then reasons to the nature of God, then turns to history for evidence as to the divinity of Christ and the divine origin of Scripture, then concludes that Scripture is infallible, then reasons to the right way of interpreting Scripture, and then believes all that Scripture says, thus interpreted.

This once-regnant self-image of the modern academy, whose major contours I have outlined, has been shattered over the past quarter century. Let me move on to trace briefly how and why that happened.

Shattering the Self-Image

First to go was the conviction that the "logic" of true science is classical foundationalism. The emergence among philosophers of what one might call "meta-epistemology" played an important role in this collapse. It is now clear, looking back, that the most influential epistemology during the first half of our century was resolutely foundationalist in character — *classically* foundationalist. It is true that the pragmatists in America, and Heidegger in Europe, were not foundationalists; but their protests at the time had relatively little impact. More influential than the pragmatists were the positivists; more influential on this point than Heidegger was Husserl. The courses that I took in epistemology as a graduate student were, to my mind, stupefyingly boring. At the time I did not understand why that was; now I do: Classical foundationalism was simply taken for granted, so much so that it was not even identified as such; we just worried over one and another problem within the system. But then, starting about twenty years ago, something happened to make philosophers stand back and survey the general options for the structuring of epistemological theories. Classical foundationalism came to be isolated as one of the options, the option we had all been taking for granted. And when it was held up to view, it seemed to most of us profoundly implausible.

Discrepancies with the Practice of Natural Science

Though these developments in philosophical epistemology clearly did play a role in shattering the reigning ideas about the logic of science, I am myself inclined to think that a different development was more decisive. Starting around twenty-five years ago, a group of people who were trained as scientists, philosophers, and historians — all of those — began to study episodes from the history of modern Western natural science so as to compare the *regnant self-image* of science to the *actual practice* of science; what they over and over bumped up against was reputable, even admirable, episodes from the history of modern Western natural science that simply did not fit the self-image of science as a classically foundationalist enterprise. Thomas Kuhn became the best known of these. In his now-famous book, *The Structure of Scientific Revolutions,* he argued that revolutions in science do not occur because the new theory is discerned to be more probable, on evidence accepted by all parties, than is the old theory, nor — to bring Karl Popper into the picture — because the old theory has been falsified. Instead, something like a conversion takes place. Kuhn himself used religious language at this point.

Three things are worth noting about this development. In the first place, the fact of such discrepancy between self-image and actual practice tells us something important about the workings of natural science. Often the picture presented by those who talk about the workings of science is that there is something called "the scientific method," that scientists learn this method, and that in their work they apply this method. But if that were how things go, there would be no discrepancies between self-image and actual practice, other than failed attempts to apply the method. The new historians did not invite us to look at the fumbles of modern natural science but at its great celebrated achievements; *these* were the episodes that did not fit, so they argued, the regnant self-image, *these* were the episodes that were not implementations of the method. Science does not come about by scientists taking what they have formulated for themselves as *the scientific method* and then applying that.

Secondly, to interpret the historical evidence as showing that much good natural science has not in fact followed what everybody had supposed to be the logic of science, namely, classical foundationalism, required a fascinating alteration of mentality from that characteristic of my teachers. My teachers never denied, in fact they freely conceded, that actual natural science does not appear to be classically foundationalist in structure. But from these appearances they did not conclude that it does not have that structure; instead they concluded that we philosophers have to work hard to show that it really does, and that appearances are deceiving. We know *a priori*, by philosophical reflection, that true science *must have* that structure. The new historians were saying that the appearance is the reality; nothing is hidden. Many admirable episodes of science do not appear to be foundationalist in structure; *and they are not.*

Why this alteration in interpretation, when the protests of Heidegger, of the pragmatists, and of numerous others over many years had had negligible impact? I think it was above all the wealth of historical detail provided by the new historians that produced the alteration. Before the new historians came along, history of science, in courses on the philosophy of science, served basically as a source of examples for illustrating points arrived at *a priori*. The new historians drew their conclusions about the logic of science from their detailed study of its actual practice. They didn't think; they looked!

Trusting the Practice of Science

Perhaps the most important thing to observe about this development, though, is this: when finally one gives up dismissing appearance in favor of some hidden reality and concedes that there really is discrepancy between self-image and actual practice, one can say either "So much the worse for the practice" or "So much the worse for the self-image." For centuries, whenever discrepancy was acknowledged between regnant self-image and actual practice with respect to some segment of academic learning outside the natural sciences, the response had been: "So much the worse for the practice." Now the response was different. No one said: "So much the worse for modern natural science." Everyone said: "So much the worse for the received self-image." That shows, of course, the enormous prestige of natural science in our culture, its position at the top of the hierarchy of the academic disciplines. That very prestige was crucial to the shattering of the self-image. When the paradigmatic disciplines proved not to be sciences, judged by the regnant self-image of science, then something deep had to go. The prestige of the natural sciences was indispensable to bringing it about that it was the self-image that went.

Strictly speaking, all that Kuhn and his cohorts showed was that natural science in the modern world does not have the classically foundationalist structure that it was traditionally assumed to have, nor the falsificationist structure that Karl Popper had proposed as the alternative. They were not discontent with the actual practice of natural science, nor did they question other parts of the regnant self-image of the academy. Nonetheless, their conclusions had the consequence of making many things come unstuck. For suppose that one has had some *a priori* notion of the logic of true science, suppose that one has interpreted the "success" of the modern natural sciences and the relatively high degree of consensus within them as an indication that those disciplines are true sciences exhibiting that logic, and suppose that one has located the other disciplines (in their present form) somewhere lower in the hierarchy for the reason that they do not exhibit that logic. Now suppose that one is forced to surrender that *a priori* notion of the logic of true science because the disciplines that one admires most do not exhibit that logic, and suppose that no alternative suggestion as to "the logic" of true science becomes widely accepted. This is our situation. Then the old hierarchy of the disciplines, present already in the medieval distinction between *scientia* and *dialectic,* has lost even the appearance of any rationale. The conviction that the humanities, the interpretative disciplines, are inferior to the natural sciences is without ground.

I think it is exactly these dynamics that are being played out in the academy today. The passion for hermeneutics is no accident. Literary critics, instead of waiting for the coming of their Newton to revolutionize their discipline into a true science, are declaring their discipline acceptable as it is. The science ideal is losing its grip. And what else could it do but lose its grip when we no longer have any idea as to what is that *logic of true science* which, so it was supposed, the natural sciences exhibit.

Perspectival Learning

But something more important even than the repudiation of the science ideal has been taking place: the conviction that reputable academic learning must be generically human is being repudiated and avowedly *perspectival learning* is flowering. Traditionally the academy in the West has been populated in overwhelming proportions by white Eurocentric bourgeois males. Slowly, as the result of various liberation movements and tendencies in society generally, that has changed, so that now significant numbers of the disenfranchised have been empowered within the academy. About a decade ago their numbers reached a critical mass sufficient to embolden them to say what they had long felt if not thought, or thought if not said; namely, that it is sheer pretense to present the learning of the academy as generically human in character — pretense in the service of power. The learning of the modern Western academy reflects the particularities of those who have peopled it. The reason for its dominance is not that it so successfully renders the truth of the matter as any impartial human being would see it; its dominance has been secured by power.

Here too, as with the point of discrepancy discussed earlier, various options are available to the person who acknowledges discrepancy between image and practice. One can insist on the importance of the image and urge that we do all in our power to *make* the learning of the academy live up to its self-image of being generically human. It is my impression that that was the lesson most people initially drew from Carol Gilligan's charge against Lawrence Kohlberg to the effect that his account of moral development was heavily male-oriented: Gilligan had pointed out where Kohlberg's work was not generically human; now she and he ought to work together to make it so by eliminating the bias. But it is also possible to embrace the other alternative and repudiate the image. Having done that, one could in principle go on to argue for the perpetuation of white Eurocentric bourgeois male learning in the academy; alternatively, one could argue for the right of other particularities to engage in learning from their own perspective. I know of no one who has openly chosen the former of these.

The debate, thus, is among those who embrace the ideal of generically human learning and refuse to concede that the academy, to any significant degree, reflects the particularities of white Eurocentric bourgeois males; those who embrace that ideal and argue or concede that the academy has indeed reflected that particularity; and those who reject that ideal and argue that justice requires that perspectival learning of many forms be allowed to flourish in the academy. I judge that more and more members of the academy are embracing this last option. Partly out of self-defense, I suppose. Were feminists to accept the offer of their male colleagues to work with them, each pointing out the biases of the other, together struggling toward the ideal of generically human learning, they would not only run the clear risk of having their voices muffled but would forego the opportunity to work out their own perspective with depth and scope. And partly because the conviction is now widespread that there can be no such thing as generically human learning; the ideal of such learning is and always has been illusory. The learning of the academy is unavoidably perspectival. So what we are witnessing is something more than the empowerment within the academy of the disenfranchised. We are witnessing such empowerment taking the specific form of an embrace of perspectivalism. The pluralization of the academy is the ineluctable consequence.

Note the following feature of the structure of these developments: Kuhn and his cohorts, after arguing that the actual practice of natural science does not fit the self-image of good science as classically foundationalist in structure, did not go on from there to urge any change in the practice of science. They urged only that we change our image. By contrast: most of those who argued that the actual practice of learning does not fit the self-image of reputable learning as generically human in character, went on to urge that we both discard that part of our self-image of academic learning and that we change that learning itself. Thus it is that this second revolution is vastly more important than the first. The first helped to prepare the way for the second. But the disturbance caused by giving up certain illusions about the logic of natural science was minor compared to the disturbances caused by conceding that learning in general never has been, and cannot be, generically human, and going on from there to embrace particularized perspectival learning and the pluralizing of the academy that flows from that. The past decade has seen the flowering of perspectival scholarship to a truly astonishing degree. Liberation theology, feminist psychology, black history, on and on — where once the very phrases would have grated on our ears, now, however we evaluate the substance, the phrases and the reality have become familiar.

The shattering of the regnant self-image of academic learning, and the profound change in the actual practice of learning that has accompanied this shattering, obviously also require a new understanding of the role of philosophy in the academy. That old worry, which Kant enabled philosophers to suppress for a couple of centuries, has returned: What if anything is left for philosophy to do? On this occasion I will forego commenting on that and instead submit for your consideration what I promised earlier; viz., a quite different way of thinking of the very phenomenon of science and academic learning from that which has shaped our thought in the modern West.

On the neo-Kantian view, academic learning, with modern natural science as its paradigmatic form, is a value sphere that in the very nature of things is distinct from art, from religion, from ethics. Science had a long prehistory, consisting of anticipations among the ancient Greeks, among the medieval Arabs, and so forth, until finally in the early modern world learning was differentiated from other value spheres, liberated from servitude to extraneous demands, and set loose to follow the logic of science.

Parenthetically, it might be asked how, on this view, we are to understand the recent flowering of particularism in the academy. Is this to be seen as regression, the result, perhaps, of political co-optation? Or is science still following its own logic? Or are we, upon noticing that there is little by way of particularism in the natural sciences and mathematics, to conclude that all this flurry of particularism has nothing to do with science but is just one more example of the chaos which periodically erupts in disciplines that have not yet had their Newton?

Academic Learning as Social Practice

I propose that instead of thinking of learning as a value sphere with its own distinct logic that finally gets manifested in the modern world, we think of learning in general and science in particular as a long-enduring *social practice*. The medieval intellectuals were not John the Baptists preparing the way for the coming of science; they were themselves engaging in the practice of science, and in that of learning generally. Let me explain; and in my explanation let me follow, rather closely, Alasdair MacIntyre's explication of the idea of a social practice in his *After Virtue*.

MacIntyre's Idea of a Social Practice

A social practice is an activity of a certain sort — characteristically, an activity that involves the manipulation of material of one sort or another in one way or another. That material will usually reflect technological developments in society. Thus practices interact with technologies. Technologies are themselves embedded in practices; but apart from that, practices require technologies and new technologies suggest new practices.

More specifically, a social practice is an activity that requires learned skills and knowledge. Some things we are born able to do; others, we naturally acquire the ability for doing in the process of maturation. Not so with the skills enabling practices. They must be learned, most of them, anyway. And to a large extent the skills and knowledge requisite are not just picked up on our own but taught us by others, sometimes by modeling, sometimes by explicit verbal instructions. In that way, among others, practices are inherently social.

Furthermore, in the case of a practice the new learner confronts a situation in which the requisite skills and knowledge are in good measure already being exercised by practitioners of the practice. Thus a practice is an ongoing activity into which new members are inducted. Practices have histories; they have traditions. As MacIntyre remarks,

> To enter into a practice is to enter into a relationship not only with its contemporary practitioners, but also with those who have preceded us in the practice, particularly those whose achievements extended the reach of the practice to its present point. It is thus the achievement, and *a fortiori* the authority, of a tradition which I then confront and from which I have to learn.[2]

In that last sentence, MacIntyre alludes to the fact that when an activity is a practice, those who engage in the activity, along with those who teach the activity, will regard some performances of the activity as better than others. There will be standards of excellence operative within the activity whereby some people are judged to farm better than others, whereby some people are judged to figure-skate better than others, and so on. To be inducted into the practice is not just to pick up the skills and knowledge requisite for its performance but also to be taught current standards of excellence for the practice. As MacIntyre puts it,

> A practice involves standards of excellence and obedience to rules. . . . To enter into a practice is to accept the authority of those standards and the inadequacy of my own performance as judged by them. It is to subject my own attitudes, choices, preferences and tastes to the standards which currently and partially define the practice. . . . If, on starting to listen to music, I do not accept my own incapacity to judge correctly, I will never learn to hear, let alone to appreciate Bartok's last quartets.[3]

The learning of the standards of excellence operative within a practice does not usually occur by way of learning formulated criteria of evaluation; the *formulation* of criteria is a difficult and sophisticated task. The learning in question usually occurs by way of modeling and casual hints.

---

2. MacIntyre, *After Virtue* (Notre Dame, Ind.: University of Notre Dame Press, 1981), p. 181.
3. MacIntyre, *After Virtue*, p. 177.

Internal and External Goods of Social Practices

In thinking of the standards of evaluation operative within a practice such as science, or learning, it is of prime importance not to think of those standards as an unshakable monolith. Often there will be critics of the current standards. Often different practitioners will operate with somewhat different standards. And in most practices the standards will have changed over the course of history — sometimes subtly, sometimes dramatically. Such changes will often call forth new knowledge and new skills; and these in turn will often suggest new standards again. Innovations in knowledge, in standards and in skills, nourish each other; among these three there is a circular process of discovery and innovation. Practices alter and expand our human modes and degrees of achieving excellence.

The way we evaluate what goes on in practices is, of course, directly connected to what we find desirable in those practices. Here it is important to distinguish between goods *internal* to activities and goods *external;* and correlatively, between engaging in an activity for external goods, that is, goods that are only contingently attached to that activity and that can in principle be attached to a wide variety of significantly different activities (goods such as fame, profit, and self-satisfaction), and engaging in an activity for *internal* goods, that is, goods that can only be achieved by engaging in this activity or ones closely similar. The internal goods in question may be either *products* of the activity or *experiences* that come our way in the course of engaging in the activity — in the case of farming, for example, they may be either foodstuffs or the pleasurable experience of working the soil.

In the course of the history of a practice, new internal goods may come to light and old ones become unattractive. A fundamental feature of social practices is this plasticity with respect to internal goods and goals, and indeed external. There is no such thing as *the* purpose of farming, of painting, of figure ice-skating — or of science and learning. There may be some abiding goals inherent in these practices; but what is just as important to observe is that the goals as a whole, of those who participate in practices, shift.

It is clear, looking back, that deep alterations in the social practice of science and in the understanding thereof, and more generally, in the social practice of learning and the understanding thereof, took place in the seventeenth and eighteenth centuries; until recently, we have been living in the wake of those alterations. Medieval learning was understood by the high medievals as coming in two main divisions: *dialectics,* the art of extracting from the received texts the rich and highly articulate body of wisdom that they were supposed to contain, and *scientia,* that nobler art of deducing conclusions from propositions evident to some rational being or other. (A full picture of the medieval situation would also have to bring into the picture such "lower sciences" as alchemy.) By the seventeenth century, the idea that the received texts of the West contained a rich, highly articulate, unified body of wisdom, extractable by dialectics, had collapsed; in its place there emerged the hostility to tradition characteristic of the Enlightenment and of the modern academy, and the view that learning in general should be generically human, reflecting neither tradition nor any other particularity. In addition, truly deep alterations took place in the seventeenth century within the natural sciences themselves. Here, for the first time in history, prediction, technological utility, explanation, and high epistemic status were joined together into one body of learning. And alongside this there emerged our modern conviction that natural science and mathematics are the paradigmatic disciplines; they have reached the status of true sciences.

Current Dynamics of Learning as Social Practice

I suggest that we today are living through alterations in the social practice of learning and in our understanding thereof that may well prove as fundamental as those that took place in the seventeenth and eighteenth centuries. The collapse, which I have traced, of the once-regnant self-image of the modern academy, and the emergence of avowedly particularist perspectival learning in diverse forms, make the academy today profoundly different from what it has been for some three hundred years.

Many find these changes alarming. And there are indeed dangers in the situation. It is my own conviction that those who self-consciously engage in particularist perspectival learning must always face in two directions. On the one hand, it is legitimate and even important for them to engage in reflection with the members of their own communities, sharing insights, expanding perspectives, deepening thought. But it is also important that they engage in conversation with those who represent other perspectives, so as both to share insight and submit to correction. The goal is thereby to arrive at a richer, a broader, a more accurate perspective. This, I submit, is what should replace that old but impossible ideal of generically human learning.

It is proving to be the case today that there are a good many members of a good many groups who are interested only in facing in the first of these two directions; and who reject facing in the second — reject transparticularist, cross-perspectival, conversation. Sometimes what motivates that rejection is long-suppressed resentment against the hegemony of Eurocentric bourgeois white males. Sometimes what motivates it is the claim that the perspective of one's group on reality is interwoven with their suffering, that that suffering is like unto no other, and that those who have not experienced that suffering can never understand it. And of course, there is truth in these latter claims.

Either way, the determination now widespread in the academy — never again, one voice — is being played out in such a way as to raise the anxious question whether the academy as a cooperative enterprise can endure. Or is hegemony necessary? Whereas for a long time now it has been the calling of the Christian scholar to emphasize that Christianity offers a distinctive perspective on reality, the time may be coming when it will be at least as important to emphasize our shared humanity and the importance of mutual listening. If what emerges from the overthrow of the hegemony of Eurocentric bourgeois white males is not speaking and listening in dialogue but hard-of-hearing multiple power constellations, then nothing has been gained.

So indeed, some of the developments are worrisome. Nevertheless, I think we should celebrate the shedding of illusions. There never was any sound basis for taking modern natural science as the paradigmatic form of learning; the learning of the academy never was a generically human enterprise; it never was right to grant hegemony to one particularity; natural science never was classically foundationalist in its "logic"; philosophers never did do what the regnant image said they were doing. Does not the recognition of these facts represent an important gain? Or do we need illusion?

Christian Academic Learning as Social Practice

In my judgment, the most important lesson for Christian scholars to learn from the developments I have traced is that they are entitled to engage in the practice of learning *as Christians*. They do not have to try to become The Human Being Itself, or The Scientist Herself, and enter the hall of learning only if they succeed at that. Christians are people who acknowledge Jesus Christ as Lord, for whom the Scriptures are authoritative, and who participate in the liturgy of the church. They are entitled to engage in learning as just that kind of person, with those particularities, from that perspective. For we have learned that the practice of learning is not some generically human enterprise, nor is science some autonomous, self-governing, self-sustaining project. Learning is an eminently concrete social-historical enterprise incorporating goals and standards, intuitions and values, that the participants bring to it and that emerge from their interaction with each other.

Entitled to Practice

We engage in the practice of science in particular and learning in general as concrete beings of diverse convictions and commitments. We do not shed all our ordinary convictions and commitments at the door of the hall of learning and enter nakedly human; nor do we shed them all to put on some white cloak of science. We enter as who we are; and we begin conversing on whatever is the topic in hand. When some disagreement turns up, we deal with that. We do not make sure that we have forestalled it in advance. Often we learn from our disagreements. As I put it already in my little book called *Reason within the Bounds of Religion,* "In weighing a theory one always brings along the whole complex of one's beliefs. One does not strip away all but those beliefs functioning as data relative to the theory being weighed. On the contrary, one remains cloaked in belief — aware of some strands, unaware of most."[4]

Christians should, I say, see themselves as *entitled* to engage in learning as Christians. But unless their Christianity is of a winsomely eccentric sort — Old Order Amish, say — they should expect to encounter a good deal of hostility and resentment. For the hegemony of Eurocentric bourgeois white males is widely perceived as having been undergirded by Christianity.

In saying that one is entitled to engage in the various practices of learning *as a Christian,* I am assuming, of course, that it is relevant to do so — that there really is *a* Christian perspective on many of those matters that academicians deal with. I am assuming what one might call an *interactional* model of the relation between Christianity and learning. Down through the ages thinkers have tried to put faith and learning in separate areas. They have tried to build fences between them so as to keep them separated. Christianity, so it is said, must confine itself to dealing with matters on this side of the fence; learning and science, with matters on that side. But always, before the fence can be erected, Christianity and learning must be disentangled and drastically pruned, so much so that either learning is no longer recognizable as learning or, more often, Christianity no longer recognizable as Christianity. I propose that we throw away the pruning shears and live with the entanglement.

4. Wolterstorff, *Reason within the Bounds of Religion,* 2d edition (Grand Rapids: Eerdmans, 1984), pp. 66-67.

Theory Weighing: The Equilibrium of Data,
Theory, and Control Beliefs

What actually happens when Christians enter the hall of learning and begin conversing? A great many different things happen; we should honor the diversity. Sometimes Christians find that they agree with everyone in the room on the topic of conversation. At other times, they find they disagree. Sometimes the root of their disagreement seems to them to lie in their adherence to Christianity; sometimes, it does not seem to them to lie in that. Either way, they will argue their case and try to bring the others around to their view. They will try to offer reasons that attach to what they already believe, or provide experiences which will alter others' beliefs. They may find they have some allies in this. These allies may be Christians. Then again, they may not be. Christians may in fact find that they have other Christians in opposition. And sometimes, though they don't much disagree with what is said in the conversation, they may find the topic unimportant; then they try to change the topic. Or they may find the discussants assigning far too much importance to science and learning; then they argue against that. And so forth.

The point is that learning pursued by Christians does and should take many forms. Let us be open to all of them. Let us honor the diversity. Let us not try to squeeze them all into a single formula.

These remarks have focused entirely on the "group dynamics" of the situation. What is it what Christian scholars are *aiming* at? Granted that those aims will be advanced in a variety of different group situations. How are we to think of the aims? It was to this question that I addressed myself in the book of mine to which I have already referred, *Reason within the Bounds of Religion*. I tried to speak as generally as possible there, so that my discussion would apply not just to what we normally think of as covered by the English word "science," but to the academic disciplines generally.

In place of the customary practice of working simply with the distinction between data and theory, I recommended that we add to data and theory what I called *control beliefs*. I had the usual thing in mind when I spoke of "data" and "theory." As to control beliefs, I had in mind the fact that always, when engaging in learning, we operate with certain convictions as to the *sorts* of theories that we will find acceptable. Understood thus, control beliefs are of many different sorts. Sometimes they take the form of methodological convictions; a huge dispute raged in the seventeenth and eighteenth centuries over whether hypotheses were acceptable in natural science. Sometimes they take the form of ontological convictions. The picture I offered of theorists was that, insofar as they are engaged in what I called *theory weighing*, they try to find a theory which both fits the data and satisfies the control beliefs. And what I argued then was this:

> The Christian scholar ought to allow the belief-content of his authentic Christian commitment to function as control within his devising and weighing of theories. For he like everyone else ought to seek consistency, wholeness, and integrity in the body of his beliefs and commitments. Since his fundamental commitment to following Christ ought to be decisively ultimate in his life, the rest of his life ought to be brought into harmony with it. As control, the belief-content of his authentic commitment ought to function both negatively and positively. Negatively, the Christian scholar ought to reject certain theories on the ground that they conflict or do not comport well with the belief-content of his authentic commitment. And positively he ought to devise theories which comport as well as possible with, or are at least consistent with, the belief-content of his authentic commitment.[5]

The picture this passage evokes is that of everything going rather smoothly. Not easily, indeed; I mentioned that it might prove extremely difficult to devise those alternative theories. But nonetheless smoothly. Yet I also went on to observe that sometimes the right thing to do in response to developments in some discipline is to revise one's view as to what constitute one's fidelity to God in Jesus Christ; we do, after all, make mistakes on that score. So let me on this occasion say a bit more as to what we are to do in cases of perceived conflict between what we take, or are disposed to take, as data, what we take, or are disposed to take, as theory, and what we take, or are disposed to take, as control beliefs.

The answer is that we are to try to eliminate the conflict and achieve *equilibrium* by making a revision in one of the three — preferring that complex of data, theory, and control beliefs which seems to us to have the most likelihood of being true as a whole. Sometimes to achieve that end we revise or discard the theory; sometimes we alter our convictions about the data; and sometimes we alter our control beliefs.

I find it fascinating that essentially this same paradigm emerged independently at roughly the same time in two other areas of philosophy. In his *Theory of Justice*, John Rawls introduced the notion of *wide reflective equilibrium* to explain the method that he thought appropriate for ethics. The method was carefully elaborated and discussed in a 1979 article by Norman Daniels

5. Wolterstorff, *Reason within the Bounds of Religion*, p. 76.

entitled "Wide Reflective Equilibrium and Theory Acceptance in Ethics." Let me allow Daniels to describe the method in his own words:

> The method of wide reflective equilibrium is an attempt to produce coherence in an ordered triple of sets of beliefs held by a particular person, namely, (a) a set of considered moral judgments, (b) a set of moral principles, and (c) a set of relevant background theories. We begin by collecting the person's initial moral judgments and filter them to include only those of which he is relatively confident and which have been made under conditions conducive to avoiding errors of judgment.... We then propose alternative sets of moral principles that have varying degrees of "fit" with the moral judgments. We do *not* simply settle for the best fit of principles with judgments, however, which would give us only a *narrow* equilibrium. Instead, we advance philosophical arguments intended to bring out the relative strengths and weaknesses of the alternative sets of principles (or competing moral conceptions).... Assume that some particular set of arguments wins and that the moral agent is persuaded that some set of principles is more acceptable than the others.... We can imagine the agent working back and forth, making adjustments to his considered judgments, his moral principles, and his background theories. In this way he arrives at an equilibrium point that consists of the ordered triple (a), (b), (c).[6]

Though a few of the details are different, the structure of Daniels's proposal is obviously the same as that which I proposed.

Essentially the same model is also to be found in Mary Hesse's essay entitled "Models of Theory-Change," included in her 1980 collection, *Revolutions and Reconstructions in the Philosophy of Science,* though first published in 1973. We can think of science, says Hesse, as a "learning device" — as a "learning machine." The machine has a *receptor* whereby it receives empirical input from the environment. It has a *formulator* whereby it describes that input in sentences. It has a *theorizer* whereby it formulates theories designed to fit and explain the data. And it has a *predictor* whereby it draws out empirically observable consequences of the theories.

These are the functions of that learning machine which is science. And now two things about the way in which the machine carries out those functions. First, in its theorizing the machine tries to satisfy certain "coherence

6. Daniels, "Wide Reflective Equilibrium and Theory Acceptance in Ethics," *Journal of Philosophy* 79 (1979): 258-59.

conditions," as Hesse calls them. "For example," she says, "we may be interested in finding universal law-like generalizations within the observation sentences, or our desire for an economic and coherent system of laws and theories may involve more elaborate considerations, such as requirements of symmetry, simplicity, analogy, conformity with certain *a priori* conditions or metaphysical postulates."[7] And secondly, "the machine permits internal feedback loops for the adjustment of theory to observation sentences, as well as the usual external loop which allows comparison of predictive output and empirical input. The internal feedback loops make a direct comparison of the current best theory with the observation sentences."[8]

And what happens if there is what Hesse calls a "mismatch"? Sometimes we conclude that the receptor mechanism was malfunctioning; sometimes we get the formulator mechanism to describe the data differently; sometimes we get the theorizer to yield a different theory. But sometimes, "usually as a last resort," we modify the coherence conditions

> in the light of success and failure of the sequence of best theories in accounting for the available observation sentences, and in making successful predictions. There seem to be a number of examples of this kind of modification in the history of science: abandonment of the postulate of circular motions of the heavenly bodies; rejection of the notion that some theoretical postulates such as Euclidean geometry or universal determinism, can be known *a priori;* adoption and later rejection of the mechanical philosophy as a necessary condition of scientific explanation; the postulate of reducibility of organic processes to physiochemical theories. Such varieties of coherence conditions in fact constitute the main subject matter of philosophical dispute regarding science, and it will now be my contention that the more usual disputes between different accounts of the structure of science are almost vacuous except insofar as they reflect different views about the nature of the coherence conditions.[9]

In summary, what we find in all three of these discussions is a picture of the theoretical enterprise as typically involving something that can be called *data,* something that can be called *theory,* and something that can be called

---

7. Hesse, "Models of Theory-Change," *Revolutions and Reconstructions in the Philosophy of Science* (Bloomington: Indiana University Press, 1980), p. 126.

8. Hesse, "Models of Theory-Change," p. 127.

9. Hesse, "Models of Theory-Change," p. 128.

theory constraints, or *control beliefs.* If the focus of our attention is on the weighing of theory, then what has to be said is that the theorizer tries to find a theory that fits the data and satisfies the constraints. If the focus of our attention is instead on situations in which there is perceived conflict among data, theory, and theory constraints, then what has to be said is that theorizers try to achieve equilibrium by juggling prospective revisions in data, in theory, and in theory constraint, until finally they arrive at a complex that seems to them likely to be true and seems on balance to possess more of what they judge to be the relevant cognitive/doxastic merits than any other alternative that comes to mind.

Christian Learning as Faithful Interaction

On the interactional model that I proposed earlier, Christian faith and the theoretical disciplines are such that we must expect conflict — that is, disequilibrium — to emerge repeatedly. Sometimes the conflict will be the result of some part of learning having been developed under theory constraints alien to Christianity. A friend of mine who works in world religions mentioned to me recently that he finds almost all contemporary anthropology assuming that religion is irrational and epiphenomenal. Sometimes the conflict emerges out of the work of scholars pursuing their work in fidelity to the Christian gospel. But however it arises, we who are committed to engaging in learning in fidelity to our Lord must acknowledge that sometimes the revisions required to bring our faith and our learning into satisfactory equilibrium should go in one direction, and sometimes, in the other direction. Sometimes the best recourse is to revise something in our complex of Christian belief, other times, to revise something in what learning offers us.

The tendency is deep and strong in the modern academy to assume that in cases of conflict between science and religion, religion must give. But why should that be? Suppose that part of what it means to affirm the authority of Scripture is to say that Scripture gives us our best access to certain realms of truth. Then to say that always, in cases of conflict between religion and learning, religion has to give, is to imply that either Scripture does not have such authority or that theorizing somehow never speaks about that realm of truth to which Scripture give us our best access. On what seems to me the best equilibrated view of the matter, neither of these implications is correct. Nevertheless, there are indeed times when one ought to acknowledge that one was mistaken in some aspect of one's Christian belief.

It is extremely important to keep in mind here that within the totality of Christian belief there is a hierarchy of importance: Giving up some elements of the totality would require relatively little alteration in the remainder, giving up others would require a ripple of alterations throughout almost all of the remainder. Some elements are in that way *more deeply ingressed* into the totality than others. If it is alterations in one's Christian belief that seem to be called for so as to achieve or restore equilibrium, one ought to begin with those elements which are least deeply ingressed. And one ought not to conduct one's reflections in lonely isolation but as a member of the Christian community, in prayer.

I am well aware of the fact that such views evoke deep resentment in many secularists and anxiety in many Christians. Let me close by speaking briefly to the latter. Some Christians are made uneasy by the fact that I have proposed no criterion specifying when we ought to achieve equilibrium by changing our learning and when we ought to achieve it by changing our religious convictions. Others fear that if we surrender uni-directionality between Christian faith and academic learning, the acids of history will eat away at fidelity until nothing is left.

This worry deserves full discussion. Here I must content myself with doing no more than setting forth the main point, since I do not have the time for a full discussion. The Christian conviction that there is a Word of God from outside our existence, a Word of command and promise, is fully compatible with acknowledging that we as Christians, along with the rest of humanity, are often mistaken in our religious convictions. It is compatible with the claim that we are sometimes in the presence of evidence so compelling against some element of our religious convictions that we ought to give up that element. The Word of God comes to creatures who are fallen in their religion as well as in the rest of their existence.

Abraham Kuyper on Christian Learning

In this lecture I want to present to you for your serious consideration the model of Christian learning developed and articulated about a century ago by the Dutch theologian, journalist, churchman, and politician, Abraham Kuyper. Though I have presented Kuyper's model on other occasions as well, I have always done so in a rather fragmentary way. On this occasion I want to present the model whole. While long popular in the Reformed segment of Christianity, in recent years Kuyper's model has also gained acceptance among sizeable segments of the evangelical community in North America. It is my impression that in both cases the model has been known only in piece-meal fashion. I want on this occasion to present it in its totality.

My aim in doing so is not to unearth and exhibit an interesting histori-cal artifact; it is, rather, to have the model before us for our "serious consider-ation." My strategy, accordingly, will not be that of historicist exegesis: I will not linger over the precise details of Kuyper's thought and expression, with its ambiguities, inconsistencies, exaggerations, gaps, outdatedness, and so forth. My strategy instead will be what is sometimes called "rational recon-struction." My goal is to uncover and state what Kuyper was trying to get at on the topic of Christian learning, in order to be able to engage him as our discussion partner. For on that topic Kuyper remains, in my view, someone extraordinarily interesting and worthwhile to converse with.

The Regnant Model of Learning

In his presentation of his model, Kuyper was heavily polemical. I judge that our understanding of Kuyper's model and of his motivations for proposing it

---

This lecture was delivered at Wheaton College in the late 1980s.

will be very much aided and enhanced if we know what model it was that he was polemicizing against. In fact it was not an alternative model of *Christian* learning that Kuyper was opposing but a model of learning in general — specifically, that which Kuyper judged to be regnant in the Dutch and, more generally, the European universities. One gets the clear impression from reading Kuyper that in the Dutch situation in which he initially found himself, there was no substantial concern with Christian learning — apart from theology. The situation in North America, in the nineteenth and early twentieth centuries, was different. For sociological reasons it almost had to be. For whereas in the Netherlands the universities were all state universities, the United States was blanketed with hundreds of private colleges and universities that advertised themselves as Christian. It is true that the model of learning regnant in the colleges and universities of North America was basically no different from that regnant in northwest Europe; but here, unlike Europe, Protestants and Catholics alike were forced to reflect on how to employ that learning so that it would become, in a certain way, Christian learning.

Locke's Model of Belief Formation: Rational Foundations

Let me describe this regnant model, doing so in my own way rather than Kuyper's — a way more directly relevant to the American scene. Later in the discussion, Kuyper's way of describing the model will become apparent.

Ever since the classical Greeks, an image that has both expressed and shaped our Western ways of thinking about the academy and its place in human life is the image of leaving the everyday and entering another and higher world of intellectual activity. On what exactly one leaves behind, there have been disagreements, as on what exactly is the nature of that higher world that one enters; but the image of departing from the everyday to enter a superior world of intellectual activity has survived the coming and going of those disagreements. On this occasion, it is the thought which emerged in the Enlightenment that is our main concern. Whereas Kuyper would have taken Kant, or some neo-Kantian, as his paradigm, let me take John Locke. On the issues at stake here, it makes no difference.

In everyday life we regularly make hasty generalizations from experience, regularly allow passion to shape inquiry, regularly think associatively rather than logically, and so forth. The result is that our beliefs as a whole are a mélange. Some are the result of reliable modes of belief formation and practices of inquiry; many are the result of such unreliable modes and practices as those mentioned. So too, in everyday life we regularly believe people purely on their say-so and uncritically think in accord with the dogmas of the traditions into which we have been inducted. These habits, so it is said, are even worse than those mentioned earlier. In generalizing hastily from experience, one at least begins from the facts of one's own experience; in believing people purely on their say-so and in accepting tradition uncritically, one allows other people's beliefs to determine one's own beliefs without ever assuring oneself that their beliefs rest on the facts.

Locke was not so naive as to suppose that by resolute act of will one could empty one's head of beliefs. What he did believe, though, was that one could resolve to make no use in the academy of the beliefs one has acquired in the everyday. Without in any way appealing to them — placing them, as it were, in the cold storage of memory — one could, in the academy, employ just those indigenous, generically human faculties that give one direct awareness of facts: perception, reflection, intellection, and reason. One could, in that way, start over — or, better stated, start from the ground up, from the things themselves. That's what one *ought* to do in the academy: without at any point appealing to the beliefs one already has, one is to start anew from the ground up by employing only those generically human faculties which yield direct awareness of facts. Employing those faculties in that way will yield objectivity in both senses of the word: it will put one in touch with the objects, the facts; and it will free one from the influence of all that is parochial and particular — from all that is not generically human.

Naturally, if one is to work in the academy, one needs to know more than just which faculties are to be employed; one must know how they are to be employed. Here Locke's general rule was that we are to employ them in that manner which constitutes doing our human best for arriving at truth on whatever be the matter under consideration. His own view about what that came to was this: First, unless the proposition under consideration has immediate certitude for one, one is to collect evidence concerning its truth or falsehood, this evidence to consist of an ample and representative body of beliefs each of which is certain for one because its content corresponds to some fact of which one is, or remembers having been, directly aware. That done, one is to calculate the probability of that proposition on that body of evidence. Finally, one is to adopt a level of confidence in the proposition that corresponds to that probability.

And what, you ask, does all this have to do with *Christian* learning? In one respect, nothing. The whole point of the Lockean model is that in the formation of beliefs within the academy, one is to place on the shelf, or in cold storage, the particularity of one's everyday belief-system, resist all temptation to appeal to it, and allow one's beliefs to be formed just *qua* human being.

Not *qua* Christian or *qua* Muslim, not *qua* American or *qua* French, not *qua* male or *qua* female, not *qua* African-American or *qua* Native American, not *qua* gay or *qua* straight — not *qua* any particularity of believer whatsoever, just *qua* sane adult human being. One's particularity as Christian believer is to be as insulated from the formation of beliefs within the academy, as is every other particularity of belief that one has in the everyday.

It is when the issue arises of which topics to explore within the academy that differences among scholars legitimately come into view. Which topics it is obligatory for a given researcher to explore, which important, and which permissible, is a highly situated matter, differing from person to person; little can helpfully be said about it in general. Obviously considerations internal to the academy are relevant to one's decisions; but so too are considerations external to the academy, derived from one's belief and action in the everyday. It is in this way that one's Christian belief may well have a legitimate bearing on one's life in the academy.

Two points must immediately be added, lest the relation to Christian belief of the Lockean model for the academy be seen as more optional and tentative than Locke and his followers thought it to be. Though Locke emphasizes that the issues on which it is obligatory to do the human best by employing his method vary a good deal from person to person, it was also his conviction, shared by many of his Enlightenment cohorts, that on matters of religion and morality, all adult human beings are obligated to do the human best by employing the method. This is the origin of what has come to be called "evidentialism" concerning religious beliefs. Very few religious beliefs are immediately certain for any of us; accordingly, we are obligated either to refrain from such beliefs or to hold them on evidence of the sort specified in the Lockean method.

A second point, especially important for our purposes here, is that if one believes that one does in fact have evidence of the requisite sort for one's Christian beliefs, then one will naturally regard the articulation and presentation of such evidence as not only a legitimate but also an important part of the instructional program of the academy. Thus it was that a common part of the curriculum of North American Protestant colleges throughout the nineteenth century was a senior capstone course, typically taught by the college president, in which evidence for Christian belief was laid out for the students before they commenced their adult lives in the everyday.

The name of Thomas Reid and that of Scottish Common Sense philosophy were often invoked in these courses. It is my own clear impression, however, that the true genius of Reid's thought was entirely obscured. The intellectual ethos of these colleges was Lockean, with a strong tinge of Baconian inductivism. Reid was thought to have decisively answered Hume's challenge to Locke, thus making it intellectually defensible to forget about Hume and return to Locke.

Locke's strategy for putting Christianity on rational foundations — that is, for making Christian belief satisfy his methodological requirements — required first distinguishing natural from revealed religion. One began with natural religion. Though Locke himself offered cosmological arguments for God's existence, the strong preference of nineteenth-century American Protestants was for inductive-design arguments. Either way, once theism had been established, one moved on to revealed religion — specifically, the *Christian* revealed religion. Locke's strategy here was as follows. First one offered evidence for the veracity and reliability of the biblical writers; Locke's own view was that they were infallible. Then one used the miracles reported by the biblical writers as evidence that those who performed those miracles were agents of divine revelation. Finally, by appropriate interpretation of what those agents are reported to have said, one arrived at a grasp of God's revelation. To the best of my knowledge, no one has yet done a careful and comprehensive study of the content of those capstone courses in nineteenth-century Protestant colleges. Everything I know about them, however, confirms my guess that the basic pattern of most of them conformed closely to the pattern Locke had outlined already at the end of the seventeenth century. The obsession with evidentialist apologetics so characteristic of American evangelicalism is to be traced to its Lockean ancestry.

Christian Learning on Locke's Model: American Evangelicalism

Let me highlight four points in concluding our glance at the Lockean model of the academy and how it was understood to be related to Christian belief. In the first place, notice that what could be identified as distinctively *Christian* learning in this scheme was understood as an addendum. The difference between the curriculum, say, of Baylor, a Southern Baptist institution, and that of Texas Tech, a nearby state institution, was located in the presence of the capstone course at Baylor and its absence at Texas Tech, plus the presence at Baylor of the Bible courses which the argumentation presented in the capstone course was seen as legitimating.

Second, it is important to see clearly that the capstone course and the Bible courses which the argumentation of the capstone course was seen as legitimating were not regarded *in their method* as in any way peculiarly Christian. The method was to be the method laid out by Locke, employing nothing but those generically human faculties that yield us awareness of facts. What motivated the presence of these courses in the curriculum was no doubt Christian belief, and appropriately so; but in the conduct of the course one was to place the Christian beliefs one already had in cold storage, never making use of them, and consider the evidence *qua* human being.

Third, the fact that some people did not accept the evidential arguments for Christianity, and that state colleges for that reason typically did not include the capstone course, nor courses in Bible, in their curricula, was regularly interpreted by nineteenth-century Protestants as a failure of obligation on the part of the nonbeliever, motivated by some sort of perversity. If one set aside one's everyday framework of belief and attitude and fulfilled one's obligation to look at the evidences for Christianity with an open mind, thus allowing one's generically human faculties of awareness to do their work, one would emerge a believer. The evidential facts are out there, and all adults share the indigenous faculties yielding awareness of those facts; what accounts for unbelief must then be a perverse defection from the obligation to devote unprejudiced attention to the arguments displaying those facts.

Lastly, it was simply taken for granted that in those areas where properly conducted scholarship did not actually yield Christian belief, it nonetheless always yielded results *compatible* with Christianity. Or to put it the other way round: If academic inquiry at any point yielded results incompatible with Christianity, then at some point in that inquiry the proper method had not been properly employed. One knew in advance that scholarship which yielded results incompatible with Christianity was defective scholarship. Of course it might take considerable time to spot the defect; scholars being what they were, it would usually take even longer to convince the scholar in question of his deficiency. Nonetheless, pluralism in the academy was a sign of deficiency in scholarship.

The rise of evolutionary theory and of higher criticism of the Bible had a devastating effect on those who held this model of learning and this understanding of its relation to Christian belief. That will now come as no surprise. Evolutionary theory offered an explanation of how there could be design *in* nature without there being a designer *of* nature; and higher criticism made the Bible look anything but infallible. Thus both stages of Locke's strategy for rendering Christianity rational — the natural-religion stage and the revealed-religion stage — were subjected to powerful attack. After Darwin and Wellhausen, Christian scholars could no longer content themselves with reciting the old, familiar mantra that Reid had answered Hume. Neither could they content themselves with announcing that perversity was preventing the Darwinians and the Wellhausians from attending with open mind to the evidence for Christian belief and submitting to its force, since, rather than looking the other way, the Darwinians and Wellhausians had directly attacked that supposed evidence. Now one had to show that somewhere, somehow in their attack they were not properly using the proper method; one had to make the case that their scholarship was unacceptable *qua* scholarship, that it was undeserving of a place in the academy. Obviously many people never found that case compellingly made. As a consequence, it came to be widely accepted in many quarters that Christianity is not a rational system of belief and hence should have no role in the academy. Many of those who did not flat-out accept that thesis nonetheless had the nagging worry that just maybe it was true. My guess is that everyone who is a teacher in a Christian college or university has had anxious evangelical students in his or her office wondering whether perhaps it is Christians who are suffering from wishful thinking, rather than Darwinians and Wellhausians who are suffering from incompetence in science and perversity in affect.

Kuyper's Alternative Model of Learning

Kuyper presented his polemic against this regnant model of learning and unfolded his alternative model in two stages. Let me do so as well. Perhaps I should emphasize, before we set out, that the word "science," as it occurs in the English version of Kuyper's writings, is being used as the translation of the Dutch *wetenschap*, synonymous with the German *Wissenschaft*. A closer English translation is probably the word that I have been using all along — namely, "learning."[1]

Kuyper begins by making some comments about the *subject* and the *object* of learning, and then about the relation between the two. Three times over the dominant theme will be that of *organic relationships*.

The Subject Who Learns and the Object of Learning

Suppose we take the content of learning to be the totality of what has come to be known scientifically. Then let us ask this question: Who knows this content? That is, who is the *subject* of learning, thus understood? Obviously

---

1. Almost all my quotations from Kuyper will come from his *Principles of Sacred Theology* (Grand Rapids: Eerdmans, 1954), which is the translation from the Dutch by J. Hendrik de Vries of selections from Kuyper's three-volume *Theological Encyclopedia*. Subsequent references to this volume will be made parenthetically in the text.

there is no human being to whom one can point as the subject, if for no other reason than that "the content of knowledge already known [scientifically] is so immeasurably great, that the most learned and the most richly endowed mind can never know but a very small part of it" (63-64). "The subject of science cannot be this man or that . . ." (63). Better to say that it is "man*kind* at large, or, if you please, *the* human consciousness" (63), since the knowledge of the content is dispersed spatially and temporally across human beings. However, it is not dispersed atomistically — one piece here in this person's consciousness, and another separate piece there in that person's consciousness. For science is a cooperative endeavor of humanity; science is anything but the achievement of individuals acting independently.

The cooperation has an element of mystery about it, however. For science arises and develops without there being any human being who plans how all the contributions will fit together; science develops, one might say, "organically." The intellectual leaders "of our race, without perceiving it and almost unconsciously, go to work according to a plan by which humanity at large advances" (64), without there being any human being who knows the plan. The ultimate agent of humanity's scientific endeavors can be none other than God: "There can be no science for the human consciousness as such without a God to impel man to pursue science, to give it, and to maintain its organic relation" (65).

Something similar needs to be said about the object of science. One could say that the object of science is "*all existing things*, as far as they have discovered their existence to our human consciousness, and will hereafter discover it or leave it to be inferred" (65). But existing things lying "atomistically side by side" do not constitute the object of science. "For the idea of science implies, that from the manifold things I know a *connected* knowledge is born, which would not be possible if there were no relation among the several parts of the object. The necessity of organic inter-relations, which was found to be indispensable in the subject, repeats itself in the object" (65-66). The object of science is nothing else and nothing less than things *in their relationships*.

And now, thirdly, for the relation of science's subject to science's object. "It is not sufficient that the subject of science, i.e., the human consciousness, lives organically in thinking individuals, and that the object, about which thinking man wants to know everything he can, exists organically in its parts; but there must also be an organic relation between this subject and this object" (67). If the objects in their relationships are to enter into the content of our science, humanity must come to be related in certain ways *to those objects and their relations*. We must become "attuned" to them, which presupposes, in turn, an "affinity" of subject of science to object. Specifically, we must become *aware* of those objects and must *comprehend* their relations. What that requires, in the first place, is that those objects affect our bodies — specifically, our sensory organs; secondly, that they enter our consciousness by way of our apprehension and conception of them; and thirdly, that they be taken up into what might be called *our world of thought,* whereby we come to understand the whole world of relations in which those objects stand. "If science means that our human consciousness shall take up into itself what exists as an organic whole, it goes without saying that she makes no progress whatever by the simple presentation of the elements; and that she can achieve her purpose only when, in addition to a fairly complete presentation of the *elements,* she also comes to a fairly complete study of their *relations*" (75).

The Human Sciences

Up to this point Kuyper's eye has been on the natural sciences. When he comes to what in the English translation are called "the spiritual sciences" — by which he means the humanities and social sciences — he makes two important qualifications. In the first place, sensory perception obviously plays a very different role in the spiritual or human sciences from that which it plays in the natural sciences. Second, and more fatefully, in the human sciences, the *subject* of science, namely, human consciousness, along with its products, itself becomes the *object* of science. This carries the implication that subjectivity and objectivity play rather different roles in the human sciences from those they play in the natural sciences.

In everyday life we all operate with a substantial body of assumptions about human beings. This everyday self-understanding cannot be stored and circumvented when one enters the academy and sets about constructing the human sciences; inevitably it plays a role in the construction itself. Empiricism in the human sciences represents an attempt to get around this fact. Kuyper's judgment on empiricism, after a brief discussion, is brisk and dismissive:

> Your own subjective-psychical life is ever shown to be your starting-point [in the human sciences], and empiricism leaves you in the lurch. This is most forcibly illustrated by philosophy in the narrower sense, which, just because it tries logically to interpret, if not the cosmos itself, at least the image received of it by us, ever bears a strongly subjective character, and with its [leaders], least of all, is able to escape this individual stamp. (103-4)

Kuyper recognizes that similar observations can be made about the natural sciences: just as a good many of our everyday beliefs about humanity that we carry with us into the academy unavoidably play a role in our construction of the human sciences, so also a good many of our everyday beliefs about the natural world that we carry with us into the academy unavoidably play a role in our construction of the natural sciences. In fact, just as our everyday beliefs about humanity — about human consciousness, activities, and products — play a role in our development of the human sciences, so also some of those same beliefs play a role in our development of the natural sciences.

Kuyper's full view, then, is that we are dealing here with a matter of degree. What was said above about the human sciences is only somewhat *less* true of the natural sciences. "That a science should be free from the influence of the subjective factor is inconceivable" (169) — that is Kuyper's most fundamental theme in his polemic against the Lockean model and in his construction of an alternative. The theorist is not and cannot become a blotter soaking up the facts of the world; the theorist is always a dynamic, structured self. The dynamics and structure of that self unavoidably contribute to the theorist's arriving at the results at which he does arrive. And that dynamic and structure are never just generically human.

In saying that beliefs we bring with us from the everyday into the academy unavoidably play a role in our development of the sciences, Kuyper is challenging the Lockean model at its very foundation. He is claiming that there is no hope of the academy being or becoming a generically human enterprise. What are his arguments for this radically anti-Enlightenment position?

At this point he lets us down. He does not give us arguments. Instead he contents himself with offering evidence to the effect that the academy *does not in fact* operate according to the model which it espouses; he points to examples which show that though the Lockean model may be regnant in ideology and self-understanding, it certainly is not regnant in practice. The point is important, and by now familiar. Over the past twenty-five years or so we have been taught by feminists that the learning of the modern Western academy is at many points *male* learning, not generically human learning; we have been taught by African-Americans that at many points it is *white* learning, or the learning of *people in power*, not generically human learning; and so forth.

Kuyper's Postmodernism

Kuyper was already making such points more than a century ago — calling attention to the prevalence of the discrepancy, now so familiar, between professed model and actual practice. Kuyper was a postmodernist born out of season. The point, to repeat, is important. But we want to know more than *that* this is the case; we want to know *why* it is the case. It is on this point that Kuyper fails us. So let me try to help him out.

Imagine yourself seeing a table at some distance but believing strongly that you are not seeing a table. Perhaps your reason for believing that you are not seeing it is that you are looking at a highly illusionistic stage-set, and that you were told in advance that what looks like furniture up against the wall is just fool-the-eye painting on the wall. In such a situation, it is highly likely that you would not believe that you were seeing a table — whereas if you had not been told what you were told, your perception of the table would have induced in you the belief that you were seeing a table — plus the belief that there's a table over there.

Computer language provides us with terminology that will serve nicely for a metaphorical description of what is going on in this situation. The formation of perceptual beliefs requires an appropriate form of hard-wiring. But the case before us illustrates that which beliefs get formed and which do not get formed by some sensory experience is a function not just of one's hard-wired perceptual-belief-forming equipment, but also of how one has been programmed. It is a function, for one thing, of one's conceptual programming. In the case under consideration, if you had not possessed the concept of a table, then your perception of the table would not evoke in you the belief that "there's a table over there." But also, and more interestingly, which beliefs get formed and which do not via sensory experience is a function of what might be called one's *doxastic* programming — from the Greek word *doxa*, meaning "belief." It is because you firmly believed you were not seeing a table that your perception of the table did not evoke in you the belief that you were seeing a table, and that "there's a table over there." As I took pains to emphasize in my presentation of the Lockean model, the classic assumption was that the beliefs one already has are deposited in the storehouse of memory, where they inertly await one's taking them out for one purpose or another. It was then insisted that in the academy one should not take one's everyday beliefs out of storage; one should not appeal to them in the construction of science. But scarcely anything could be farther from the truth than that assumption. In good measure the beliefs we already have function as components in our belief-forming programming. The beliefs we already have — plus the concepts we possess, the habits of attention and inattention we have acquired, and so forth — contribute to determining the beliefs we will have. They are not just deposited in the storehouse of memory.

Now if the doxastic programming that we all unavoidably undergo in the everyday could somehow be circumvented or rendered inoperative, at least in the academy, then Locke's model for the academy would still be intact. But one way to understand Kuyper's point is that this cannot be done. I think he is right about this. Contrary to the Lockean hope, it is not possible for us, when working in the academy, to bring it about that our hard-wired capacities for perception, reflection, intellection, and reasoning will function in such a way that the beliefs we already have play no role in determining the beliefs we will come to have. Of course, some of the doxastic programming that plays a role in the academy is acquired within the academy; much of it, though, is brought from life in the everyday into the academy.

All of this would still make no significant difference if, with regard to the issues that arise within the academy, the programming we acquire by life in the everyday was substantially identical from person to person. But that too is most definitely not the case; and because it is not the case, within the academy we find ourselves immersed in disagreements whose origins lie outside the academy. Here is how Kuyper makes this point:

> The subjective character which is inseparable from all spiritual science, in itself would have nothing objectionable in it if . . . the subjectivity of A would merely be a variation of the subjectivity in B. In virtue of the organic affinity between the two, their subjectivity would not be mutually antagonistic, and the sense of one would harmoniously support and confirm the sense of the other. . . . But alas, such is not the case in the domain of science. It is all too often evident, that in this domain the natural harmony of subjective expression is hopelessly broken; and for the feeding of skepticism this want of harmony has no equal. By an investigation of self and of the cosmos you have obtained a well-founded scientific conviction, but when you state it, it meets with no response from those who, in their way, have investigated with equally painstaking efforts; and not only is the unity of science broken, but you are shaken in the assurance of your conviction. For when you spoke your conviction, you did not mean simply to give expression to the insight of your own ego, but to the universal human insight; which, indeed, it ought to be, if it were wholly accurate. But of necessity we must accept this hard reality, and in every theory of knowledge which is not to deceive itself, the fact of sin must henceforth claim a more serious consideration. (106-7)

Human Fallenness

"The fact of sin." We are dealing here with sin, Kuyper believed. I myself think he should have said that we are dealing here with *fallenness*. For not all the glitches in our programming are culpable glitches, nor did Kuyper think they were; not all of them represent sin on our part. Rather, it is human fallenness that we are dealing with — or, to use one of Kuyper's words, "disturbance." If we were not only constituted but also programmed as God meant us to be, there would be no defects in our programming giving rise to disagreements within the academy. In fact, however, we fall short of that divine intent. Of course, even if we did not fall short, even if there were not the disturbance, the fallenness, we would not all just be "uniform repetitions of the self-same model." For that we must be grateful, since only by "the multiform individualization of the members of our race" does science advance (90). Yet "in the absence of a disturbance, this multiformity would have been . . . harmonious"; with "mutual supplementation there would have been no conflict. And there would have been no desire on the part of one individual subject to push other subjects aside, or to transform the object after itself" (90).

So fundamental are these phenomena for our overall interpretation of the nature of learning that it would not be an exaggeration to say that "the entire interpretation of science, applied to the cosmos as it presents itself to us now, and is studied by the subject 'man' as he now exists, is in an absolute sense governed by the question whether or no a disturbance has been brought about by sin either in the object or in the subject of science" (92). Since his own answer to this question is affirmative, Kuyper at this point in his reflections embarks on an extensive discussion of the ways in which our fallenness affects our work in the academy (106-14), structuring his discussion by developing a typology and then offering examples of the various types. The whole discussion is extraordinarily insightful and suggestive. On this occasion I can do no more than give you the flavor of it by citing just three of the types, along with a few examples of each.

Among the most powerful effects of our fallenness on our work in the academy, says Kuyper, "is the influence of the sin-disorganized *relationships of life* — an influence which makes itself especially felt with the pedagogic and the social sciences" (109). For example:

> He who has had his bringing-up in the midst of want and neglect will entertain entirely different views of jural relationships and social regulations from him who from his youth has been bathed in prosperity. Thus, also, your view of civil right would be altogether different if you had

grown up under a despotism, than if you had spent the years of early manhood under the excesses of anarchism. (109)

Another manifestation of our fallenness that influences our work in the academy is our distorted and parochial "personal interests." For example:

An Englishman will look upon the history of the Dutch naval battles with the British fleet very differently from a Netherlandish historian; not because each purposely desires to falsify the truth, but because both are unconsciously governed by national interests. . . . A Roman Catholic has an entirely different idea of the history of the Reformation from a Protestant's, not because he purposely violates the truth, but simply because without his knowing it his church interests lead him away from the right path. (110)

And thirdly, our hatreds — though by the same token, our loves — shape our work in the academy. Where "love, the sympathy of existence," is active,

you understand much better and more accurately than where this sympathy is wanting. A friend of children understands the child and the child life. A lover of animals understands the life of the animal. In order to study nature in its material operations, you must love her. . . . Sin is the opposite of love. . . . Our mind feels itself isolated; the object lies outside of it, and the bond of love is wanting by which to enter into and learn to understand it. . . . What once existed organically exists now consequently as foreign to each other, and this *estrangement* from the object of our knowledge is the greatest obstacle in the way to our knowledge of it. (111)

By no means does it follow from all this, says Kuyper, "that you should skeptically doubt all sciences, but simply that it will not do to omit the fact of sin from your theory of knowledge. This [omission] would not be warranted [even] if sin were only a thelematic conception and therefore purely ethic; how much less [is it warranted given that] sin modifies so largely all those data with which you have to deal in the intellectual domain and in the building-up of your *science*. Ignorance wrought by sin is the most difficult obstacle in the way of all true science" (113-14).

Humanity's Learning: Struggling for the Truth

One more point remains to be made here. If Kuyper is right, then obviously the Lockean model has to be given up. We do not and cannot, when we enter the academy, function simply as generic human beings. For, to say it again, the beliefs we have acquired in the everyday, some of them true, many of them false, are not just deposited in the storehouse of memory; they are components in the programming that is part of the belief-forming self which enters the academy. That belief-forming self consists not just of its hard-wiring but of its doxastic programming as well. So the question arises: Must we just resign ourselves to the perpetuation in the academy of disagreements rooted in our lives in the everyday?

Kuyper's answer is: Not at all. The ideal remains before us of a science that is not this person's science and that person's science but *humanity's* science. The road to that ideal is not the road sketched out by Locke, however — everyone using nothing but one's own hard-wiring to form beliefs that are certain because they simply record the facts of which one is directly aware. The road toward that ideal is dialogue, each listening to the other in the course of trying to show the others where they have gone wrong. As Kuyper puts it,

> In the domain of the sciences experience shows that, after much resistance and trial, the man of stronger and purer thought prevails at length over the men of weaker and less pure thought, convinces them, and compels them to think as he thinks, or at least to yield to the result of his thinking. Many convictions are now the common property of the universal human consciousness, which once were only entertained by individual thinkers. (151)

A fascinating feature of this passage is its inadvertent recognition of the role of power in the academy. But let that pass, so that we can take note of the warning that Kuyper immediately adds to the point just made. Yes, in the academy we do sometimes convince the others of their errors; and when we do not convince, we sometimes subdue. But let us not exaggerate the possibilities here; the ideal of a consensus, and certainly the ideal of a rationally achieved consensus, remains forever unachieved. One of the fundamental reasons is that what drives scientists is not just the desire, focused on the objects, to discover the objects in their relationships; what typically drives them is also a certain desire focused on those of their colleagues who disagree with them — namely, the desire to attack their views as false and to defend their own as true. In this desire to oppose the false and defend the true, we once again touch on sin and fallenness. For had there been no disturbance, there would have been no such thing as "defending the truth" against its "opponents"; only the pointing out of mistakes. Kuyper says,

> It is because of sin that where two scientific people arrive at directly opposite results, each will see the truth in his or her own result, and falsehood in the result of the opponent, and both will deem it their duty to fight in the defense of what seems to them the truth, and to struggle against what seems to them the lie. If this concerns a mere point of detail, it has no further results; but if this antithesis assumes a more universal and radical character, school will form itself against school, system against system, worldview against worldview, and two entirely different and mutually exclusive representations of the object, each in organic relation, will come at length to dominate whole series of subjects. From both sides it is said: "Truth is with us, and falsehood with you." And the notion that science can settle this dispute is of course entirely vain, for we speak of two all-embracing representations of the object, both of which have been obtained as the result of very serious scientific study. (117-18)

Thus "the unity of science is gone. The one [person] cannot be forced [by argument] to accept what the other holds as truth, and what according to his view he has found to be truth" (119). And to suppose that there is some sort of "absolute science," available to us human beings, that would settle such issues "is nothing but a criminal self-deception" (118). "There is no . . . objective certainty to compel universal homage which can bring about a unity of settled result" (116).

Kuyper's Model of Christian Learning

In my opening comments I said that my project in this talk was to present to you for your serious consideration Kuyper's model of Christian learning. I have not yet said a word about Kuyper's understanding of Christian learning. That is because I have been following Kuyper himself in presenting his thought in two stages. First he speaks of learning in general; then, in the context of his model of learning in general, he offers his model of Christian learning. We are ready to enter that second stage.

Kuyper's model of learning in general was highly provocative and eccentric at the time he worked it out. Today its basic tenets are widely accepted as more or less standard postmodernism — with the important exception that the majority of postmodernists are not inclined to see sin and fallenness as underlying the pluralism and dissent so characteristic of the academy. Lust for power, yes; sin and fallenness, no. The fate of Kuyper's model of Christian learning has been very different. It has lost none of its power to startle and provoke over the one hundred years separating us from him.

Normalists and Abnormalists

Kuyper launches this part of his argument not from an analysis of the role of subjectivity in the sciences but from theological considerations. Among all the differences in conviction and commitment among human beings, there is one that does not have its root in psychological dynamics — one that "does not find its origin within the circle of our human consciousness, but *outside* of it" (52). So, at least, the Christian religion claims.

> For it speaks of a regeneration *(palingenesis)*, of a "being begotten anew" *(anagenesis)*, followed by an enlightening *(photismos)*, which changes man in his very being; and that indeed by a change or transformation which is effected by a supernatural cause. . . . This "regeneration" breaks humanity in two, and repeals the unity of the human consciousness. If this fact of "being begotten anew," coming in from without, establishes a radical change in *the being* of man, be it only potentially, and *if* this change exercises at the same time an influence upon his *consciousness,* then as far as it has or has not undergone this transformation, there is an abyss in the universal human consciousness across which no bridge can be laid. (152)

Let me articulate just a bit the thought that lies behind this passage. Christianity is a soteriological religion; it speaks of salvation. Of the salvation of the entire cosmos, Kuyper insisted;[2] but then, in particular, of human beings. The fact that Christianity is a soteriological religion presupposes that there is, in its judgment, something that we and the cosmos need saving

---

2. Cf. a passage from his *Lectures on Calvinism,* which is the text of his Stone Lectures for 1898-1899 (New York: Fleming H. Revell Co., n.d.): "If everything that is, exists for the sake of God, then it follows that the whole creation must give glory to God. The sun, moon, and stars in the firmament, the birds of the air, the whole of Nature around us, but, above all, man himself, who, priestlike, must consecrate to God the whole of creation, and all life thriving in it. And although sin has deadened a large part of creation to the glory of God, the demand — the ideal, remains unchangeable, that *every* creature must be immersed in the stream of religion, and end by lying as a religious offering on the altar of the Almighty" (61).

from. It presupposes that there is something amiss in our situation. Things are not right as they are; they are not as they ought to be. Things are, in that way, *abnormal*. And the Christian believes that an abnormal remedy is required if we are to be saved from this abnormal situation.

God and God alone can ultimately save us from what we need saving from, save us for what we're meant to be. Christianity teaches that part of God's strategy of salvation is, by the agency of the Holy Spirit, to grant to certain human beings new birth, *palingenesis*. Palingenesis, rather than proceeding "from the sphere of our human life . . . is effected by a power, the origin of which lies outside of our human reach, so that man is passive under it as a tree under grafting" (153-54).

Putting these various points together, Kuyper astutely observes that one of the most fundamental points of division between Christianity and most other systems of belief to be found in the modern world is that Christians are what he calls *Abnormalists,* whereas the adherents of most other systems of belief are *Normalists.* The terminology never caught on; but it is not difficult to see what Kuyper had in mind: "The cosmos, as it exists today, is either in a *normal* or *abnormal* condition. If it is *normal,* then it moves by means of an eternal evolution from its potencies to its ideal. But if the cosmos in its present condition is *abnormal,* then a *disturbance* has taken place in the past, and only a *regenerating* power can warrant it the final attainment of its goal."[3] With this terminology in hand, we can now say, looking back over the points Kuyper made in the first stage of his discussion, that the academy in general exists in an *abnormal* state. There has been a disturbance in human and cosmic affairs, the disturbance of sin and fallenness; and very much of the dissent and pluralism characteristic of the academy are a manifestation of that disturbance. The ideal of a unified science both haunts us and eludes us. The root of John Locke's error is that in formulating his model of learning, he crossed over to the side of the *normalists.*

An Expressionist Model of Christian Learning

But back to *palingenesis.* How are we to understand this new birth, granted by the Spirit, of which the Christian gospel speaks? Is it simply a change in status of the human being before God, leaving no trace in consciousness? Alternatively, is its trace in consciousness limited perhaps to certain inward spiritual feelings, or to will but not thought? If so, then there is no need to mention new birth in our discussion of learning.

3. Kuyper, *Lectures on Calvinism*, p. 174.

Kuyper had no patience with any of these suggestions. Over and over he returns to his conviction that the new birth which is the gift of the Spirit works its way *throughout* one's existence, outward from the spiritual center, which is the sense and reality of living before the face of God in love and adoration. Accordingly,

> A religion confined to feeling or will is . . . unthinkable. . . . The sacred anointing of the priest of creation must reach down to his beard and to the hem of his garment. His whole being, including all his abilities and powers, must be pervaded by the *sensus divinitatis,* and how then could he exclude his rational consciousness — the *logos* which is in him — the light of thought which comes from God Himself to irradiate him? To possess his God for the underground world of his feelings, and in the outworks of the exertion of his will, but not in his inner self, in the very centre of his consciousness, and his thought; . . . all of this [is] the very denying of the Eternal Logos.[4]

From here it is but the shortest step to the conclusion that I had in mind when I said that Kuyper's model of Christian learning has lost none of its power to startle and provoke. Let us have it before us in Kuyper's own words:

4. Kuyper, *Lectures on Calvinism,* p. 62. Cf. this passage from the same volume: "As mere *entities* we share our life with plants and animals. *Unconscious* life we share with the children, and with the sleeping man, and even with the man who has lost his reason. That which distinguishes us, as higher beings, and as wide awake men, is our *full self-consciousness,* and therefore, if religion, as the highest vital function, is to operate also in that highest sphere of self-consciousness, it must follow that soteriological religion, next to the *necessitas* of inward *palingenesis,* demands also the *necessitas* of an assistant light, of revelation to be kindled in our twilight" (70). And speaking of what he regards as the ideal type of Christian — namely, the Calvinist — Kuyper says this:

> The Calvinist is led to submit himself to the conscience, not as to an individual lawgiver which every person carries about in himself, but as to a direct *sensus divinitatis,* through which God Himself stirs up the inner man, and subjects him to His judgment. He does not hold to religion, with its *dogmatics,* as a *separate entity,* and then place his moral life with its ethics as a *second entity* alongside of religion, but he holds to religion, as placing him in the presence of God Himself, Who thereby embues him with His divine will. Love and adoration are, to Calvin, themselves the motives of every spiritual activity, and thus the fear of God is imparted to the whole of life as a reality — into the family, and into society, into science and art, into personal life, and into the political career. A redeemed man who in *all* things and in *all* the choices of life is controlled solely by the most searching and heart-stirring reverence for a God Who is ever present to his consciousness, and Who ever holds him in his eye — thus does the Calvinistic type present itself in history. (*Lectures on Calvinism,* pp. 90-91)

We speak none too emphatically, therefore, when we speak of two kinds of people. Both are human, but one is inwardly different from the other, and consequently feels a different content rising from his consciousness; thus they face the cosmos from different points of view, and are impelled by different impulses. And the fact that there are two kinds of *people* occasions of necessity the fact of two kinds of human *life* and *consciousness* of life, and of two kinds of *science;* for which reason the idea of the *unity of science,* taken in its absolute sense, implies the denial of the fact of palingenesis, and therefore from principle leads to the rejection of the Christian religion. (154)[5]

This would not be true "if the deepest foundations of our knowledge lay outside of us and not in us, or if the palingenesis operated outside of these principles of knowledge in the subject." But neither of these is the case. "Like sin, whose result it potentially destroys, palingenesis causes the subject to be different in his innermost self from what he was before; and . . . this disposition of the subject exercises an immediate influence upon scientific investigation and on scientific conviction" (168).

Christian Learning as a Mode of Privileged Cognitive Access

Is this right: *two kinds of human beings, hence two kinds of learning?* Before deciding, let us do our best to make sure that we do not take Kuyper as saying what he has no intention of saying.

5. Cf. this passage from *Lectures on Calvinism:* "We . . . have to acknowledge *two kinds of human consciousness:* that of the regenerate and the unregenerate; and these two cannot be identical. In the one is found what is lacking in the other. The one is unconscious of a break and clings accordingly to the *normal;* the other has an experience both of a break and of a change, and thus possesses in his consciousness the knowledge of the *abnormal.* If, therefore, it be true that man's own consciousness is his *primum-verum,* and hence must be also the starting-point for every scientist, then the logical conclusion is that it is an impossibility that both should agree, and that every endeavor to make them agree must be doomed to failure. Both, as honest men, will feel duty bound to erect such a scientific edifice for the whole cosmos which is in harmony with the fundamental data, given in their own self-consciousness. . . . The difference between the science of the Normalists and Abnormalists is not founded upon any differing result of investigation, but upon the undeniable difference, which distinguishes the self-consciousness of the one from that of the other" (182-83).

Possible Misreadings of Kuyper

In the first stage of his discussion Kuyper argued, in effect, that because there are *many* kinds of human consciousness, there are *many* kinds of science. That thesis still stands; the new thesis — "two kinds of human beings, hence two kinds of science" — is not to be interpreted as in conflict with it. Furthermore, Christians will be found exhibiting pretty much all of those many forms of consciousness previously noted, and consequently practicing pretty much all of those many forms of science — as will non-Christians. New birth

> does *not* alter the differences of temperament, of personal disposition, of position in life, nor of concomitant circumstance which dominate the investigation. Neither does palingenesis take away the differences born from the distinction of national character and the process of time. Palingenesis may bring it about, that these differences assume another character, that in some forms they do not appear, and that they do appear in other forms unknown outside of it; but in every case with palingenesis also subjective divergence continues to exist in every way. . . . . Friction, fermentation and conflict are the hallmark of every expression of life on higher ground in this present dispensation, and from this the science of the palingenesis also effects no escape. (170-71)

In propounding his "two-two" thesis, Kuyper is contending, in the first place, that Christian consciousness, like the many other modes of consciousness to which he has called attention, has an impact on one's practice of learning; it is relevant to one's work in the academy, and it too cannot be circumvented. Secondly, he is claiming that there is something special about this particular manifestation of the "many-many" thesis. The secularist, or normalist, in Kuyper's terminology, will of course recognize the presence of a Christian consciousness in certain human beings and its absence in others. But the secularist will regard that distinction as having ultimately the same status as, say, the presence of a feminist consciousness in certain people and its absence in others. Any effects that a Christian consciousness might have on the practice of science — and the normalist will not deny such effects — will be viewed by him as just one more illustration of the "many-many" thesis.

But suppose someone locates herself within the Augustinian tradition and holds that there is one type of consciousness that is brought about not by the normal order of things but by the action of the Spirit — specifically, that type of consciousness which recognizes the abnormality of our present condition and is oriented in gratitude around love of God. That type will then inevitably have a special significance for her. It will not be seen as just one among many. Kuyper's claim, let it be said emphatically, is not that the bringing about of this type of consciousness is the only work of the Spirit, nor that the Spirit works only in people of this type. Over and over Kuyper insists that the Spirit works in all humanity to bring about what is good; "common grace," Kuyper calls it.[6] What the Spirit does not effect in all humanity, however, is devotion to God in the context of recognition of the abnormality of our present situation.

An important point to be made is that Kuyper does not regard the "two-two" thesis as implying that whereas the Christian is engaged in genuine science, the non-Christian is not. It cannot be the case that the results produced by both are entirely true, since at a good many points they contradict each other; nonetheless, both are engaged in science.[7]

So too, the two-two thesis does not imply that in cases of scholarly disputes, the Christian is always right and the non-Christian wrong. Far from it: Christian learning is littered with mistake and error.

Neither does the two-two thesis imply that non-Christians are practicing science incompetently. They may be; but then again, they may not be. Christian scholars, confronted with a body of scholarship that they find incompatible with Christian belief, need not try to trace that incompatibility to scholarly incompetence; they have the option of tracing it instead to the fact that its authors are working, in Kuyper's words, with a "non-Christian consciousness." This is why the rise of evolutionary theory and of biblical criti-

---

6. "There is a particular grace which works Salvation, and also a *common grace* by which God, maintaining the life of the world, relaxes the curse which rests upon it, arrests its process of corruption, and thus allows the untrammeled development of our life in which to glorify Himself as Creator" (*Lectures on Calvinism*, pp. 30-31).

7. "What we mean [in speaking of two kinds of science] is that both parts of humanity, that which has been wrought upon by palingenesis and that which lacks it, feel the impulse to investigate the object, and, by doing this in a scientific way, to obtain a scientific systemization of that which exists. The effort and activity of both bear the same character; they are both impelled by the same purpose; both devote their strength to the same kind of labor; and this kind of labor is in each case called the prosecution of science. But however much they may be doing the same thing formally, their activities run in different directions, because they have different starting points. . . . Formally both groups perform scientific labor, and . . . they recognize each other's scientific character, in the same way in which two armies facing each other are mutually able to appreciate military worth. But when they have arrived at their result they cannot conceal the fact that in many respects these results are contrary to each other, and are entirely different; and as far as this is the case, each group naturally contradicts whatever the other group asserts" (*Principles of Sacred Theology*, pp. 155-56).

cism never had the devastating effect on Christian scholars working with the Kuyperian model that it did on Christian scholars working with the Enlightenment model. On the Enlightenment model, radical pluralism in the academy implies incompetence in one party or the other; not so on the Kuyperian model.

Nor does the two-two thesis imply that practitioners of these two kinds of science are incapable of cooperating on any scientific tasks. Here are Kuyper's words: "As scientists we do not simply walk independently side by side, but . . . we remain together in logical fellowship, and together pay our homage to the claim of science as such. . . . However plainly and candidly we may speak thus of a twofold science, . . . we are equally emphatic in our confession, which we do not make in spite of ourselves, but with gladness, that in almost every department there is some task that is common to all" (161).

And lastly, the two-two thesis does not imply that there will be nothing on which Christian and non-Christian agree. Admittedly this is the case in part because working out the implications of Christianity — as of other similarly fundamental positions — within the various fields of learning is arduous and ongoing. A slow process "must ensue," says Kuyper, "before any activity can develop itself from what potentially is given in palingenesis. If palingenesis operated immediately from the centrum of our inner life to the outermost circumference of our being and consciousness, the antithesis between the science which lives by it and that which denies it, would be at once absolute in every subject. But such is not the case" (162). Even apart from that, however, we must expect and be grateful for agreement between Christian and non-Christian on a good many issues — more, Kuyper thought, in the natural than in the human sciences, and more on matters of perception and logical inference than on, say, the appraisal of complex theories (157-60; 168). The non-Christian is not *blind* to reality.

A Mode of Privileged Cognitive Access

Yet — and the "yet" is of prime importance — Kuyper was persuaded that if Christian consciousness is indeed born of the Spirit, then one must expect that somewhere along the line intractable disagreements will turn up between Christian and non-Christian within the sciences. The difference that Christian conviction makes in learning is not confined to addenda: Bible courses and theology courses. At some point in the other disciplines as well "it will be impossible to settle the difference of insight" (160); at some point there will appear "an abyss in the universal human consciousness across which no bridge can be laid" (152). At this point, all that can profitably be done is that each party explain to the other "what it is that compels us . . . to draw our line as we do" (160). The worth of doing this is not to be underestimated. Pointing to the humility, fellowship, and recognition of common ideal that such mutual account-giving both requires and promotes, Kuyper hyperbolically speaks of it as "an infinite gain" (161). Yet even at this point one must expect disagreement; one must expect that the parties will not accept as true each other's accounts of their disagreements. For whereas Christians will ultimately attribute why they see things as they do to the work of the Spirit, normalists will reject that account.[8]

It should come as no surprise now to learn that Kuyper had no use for evidentialist apologetics. He regarded such apologetics as committed to the thesis that even the most fundamental disagreements between Christians and non-Christians are not rationally intractable. Non-Christians, so the apologist assumes or claims, have it in their power to decide to attend with open mind to the arguments displaying the evidence for Christianity; if they do so attend, they will be convinced. In fact, says Kuyper, "apologetics has always failed to reach results, and has weakened rather than strengthened the reasoner" (160). That is so, at bottom, because evidentialist apologetics mistakenly assumes the truth of normalism. It assumes that the re-orientation of one's life toward God can be born of reason.

Enough of clarifications; back to Kuyper's provocative and startling thesis: Two kinds of people, two kinds of learning. In the first stage of his argument, Kuyper, speaking as a postmodernist born out of season, argued that the Lockean model is based on a fundamental misunderstanding of, if not oblivion to, the role of subjectivity in learning. Many of the subjectivities that we bring with us to the academy from life in the everyday cannot be circumvented; they influence our work in the academy. In the second stage of his argument, Kuyper argued that the Christian consciousness is one of

---

8. "It is not strange that so far as they have not come into contact with this fact of palingenesis, thoughtful men should consider the assertion of it an illusion and a piece of fanaticism; and that rather than deal with it as fact, they should apply their powers to prove its inconceivableness. This would not be so, if by some tension of human power the palingenesis proceeded from the sphere of our human life; for then it would seem a thing to be desired, and all nobler efforts would be directed to it. . . . The dilemma is the more perplexing, since he who has been wrought upon by palingenesis can never convince of it him who has not been similarly wrought upon, because an action wrought upon us *from without* the human sphere does not lend itself to analysis by our human consciousness; at least not so far as it concerns the common ground on which men with and without palingenesis can understand each other" (*Principles of Sacred Theology*, pp. 153-54).

those subjectivities, brought into the academy from one's life in the everyday, that shapes one's work in the academy; then, speaking as a Christian, he identified Christian subjectivity as born not of flesh but of the Spirit. The implication, obviously, is that the Christian ought to struggle to expand the influence of this subjectivity on his or her work in the academy rather than struggling to minimize or eliminate its influence. Christian consciousness, though not lifted above our fallenness, is nevertheless not, at its core, a manifestation of our fallenness. It is not even a manifestation of our *normal* mental processes. It is, to say it yet again, a work of the Spirit.

Can this be right: two kinds of people, two kinds of learning? I have said nothing on one crucial point in the argument, partly because Kuyper, rather than developing the point, treats it as more or less obvious. One way to escape Kuyper's conclusion would be to argue that Christian consciousness, and Christian belief in particular, has no bearing on the issues that arise in the academy. If it did have bearing, then the arguments offered concerning the impossibility of circumventing or rendering inoperative one's programming would be to the point. But it does not have bearing.

This way out has repeatedly been explored and proposed in the modern world: Christianity deals with values, so it is said, science with facts; or Christianity deals with the transcendent, science with the immanent. And so forth. On this occasion I do not have time to discuss this attempt at a way out; adequate discussion would require an essay of its own. Suffice it to note that such proposals are always revisionist rather than descriptive in character. Christianity *as it comes* has over and over been intertwined with learning — sometimes creatively so, for one or both parties, sometimes destructively. It is to forestall such intertwinement in the future that the theorist proposes that Christianity be *reduced* in content until intertwinement is no longer capable of occurring. Admittedly, such Christianity is usually not *advertised* as reduced; it is advertised instead as *true* Christianity, as *purified* Christianity — as Christianity *rightly* understood.

I dare say that if one is sufficiently determined and intellectually imaginative, it is possible to come up with a proposal for a Christianity reduced sufficiently to meet the stipulated requirement. I myself doubt that anything short of a Christianity shorn of all claims whatsoever — factual, normative, and evaluative — would fill the bill. And about such a Christianity, I, at least, cannot refrain from asking: Why bother?

So once more. Can this be right: two kinds of people, two kinds of learning? Yes, I think it is. Of course we are dealing with ideal types. Non-Christian learning comes in many sorts; often it is important to distinguish the sorts. Christian learning likewise comes in many sorts; often it is important to distinguish those too. And sometimes the question about whether a body of learning is Christian learning or not has no clear answer. Sometimes that's the case because Christian and non-Christian themes are mingled in the learning at hand. Sometimes that's the case because — praise God — the piece of learning at hand is acceptable to both Christians, or at least some of them, and non-Christians, or at least some of them. So we're dealing more with ideal type than actuality, more with vocation than description.

But, given that understanding, surely Christian belief *is* part of that Christian self which is born of the Spirit. And surely Christian belief *is* relevant to a great many of the fundamental issues that arise within the academy. Accordingly, if one is a Christian who is a scholar, one will find it a matter of both gratitude and duty to discover and articulate that relevance — as indeed one will find it a matter of both gratitude and duty to grow into that body of Christian belief, the mind of Christ, which the Spirit is working within us to bring to birth.

On the model of learning bequeathed us by the Enlightenment, the particularities of subjectivity that we bring with us to the academy are regarded as prejudices; and prejudices, so it is assumed, conceal reality from us. Prejudices prevent us from attaining objectivity. Kuyper, standing in the Augustinian tradition, insisted, on the contrary, that certain particularities of subjectivity, rather than being prejudices that conceal reality from us, are conditions of reality becoming accessible to us. They give us *privileged cognitive access* to certain dimensions of reality. A good many particularities of subjectivity may be of this sort: feminism may be; love for animals on the part of a naturalist may be. The main burden of Kuyper's argument is that Christian belief is of this sort. A Christian mind, born of the Spirit, is a mode of privileged cognitive access to dimensions of the world, humanity, and God.

Allow me to take my peroration from Kuyper:

A [Christian] who seeks God does not for a moment think of limiting himself to theology and contemplation, leaving the other sciences, as of a lower character, in the hands of unbelievers; but on the contrary, looking upon it as his task, to know God in all his works, he is conscious of having been called to fathom with all the energy of his intellect, things *terrestrial* as well as things *celestial;* to open to view both the order of creation and the "common grace" of the God he adores, in nature and its wondrous character, in the production of human industry, in the life of mankind, in sociology, and in the history of the human race. . . .[9]

9. Kuyper, *Lectures on Calvinism,* pp. 164-65.

Formerly we [Christians] showed [the Normalists] the door, and now this sinful assault upon their liberty is by God's righteous judgment avenged by their turning us out into the street, and so it becomes the question, if the courage, the perseverance, the energy, which enabled them to win their suit at last, will be found now in a still higher degree with Christian scholars. May God grant it! You cannot, nay, you even may not think of it, deprive him, whose consciousness differs from yours, of freedom of thought, of speech and of the press. That they from their standpoint pull down everything that is holy in your estimation is unavoidable. Instead of seeking relief for your scientific conscience in downhearted complaints, or in mystic feeling, or in unconfessional work, the energy and the thoroughness of our antagonists must be felt by every Christian scholar as a sharp incentive himself also to go back to *his* own principles in his thinking, to renew all scientific investigation on the lines of these principles, and to glut the press with the burden of his cogent studies. If we console ourselves with the thought that we may without danger leave secular science in the hands of our opponents if we only succeed in saving theology, ours will be the tactics of the ostrich. To confine yourself to the saving of your upper room when the rest of the house is on fire is foolish indeed.[10]

10. Kuyper, *Lectures on Calvinism*, pp. 184-85.

Particularist Perspectives: Bias or Access?

Feminist epistemology, Native American history, gay literary studies, liberation theology, Jewish hermeneutics — we are familiar with all of them, and with a good many other inquiries of the same sort. Until a couple of decades ago all would have been dismissed from the academy as inappropriate, if not disreputable. Today there is a thriving cottage industry in each. In this essay I want to reflect on why it is that in previous times particularist learning of these sorts would have been dismissed from the academy, and on the significance of the fact that it is no longer dismissed.

The Propriety of Particularist Perspectives

Let me unceremoniously reject the bland interpretation. There have always been controversies in academia — Aristotelians versus Platonists, Occamists versus Thomists, Newtonians versus Cartesians, Reidians versus Humeans, Hegelians versus Kantians, behaviorists versus hermeneutic psychologists. The bland interpretation of the significance of feminist epistemology, Native American history, gay literary studies, liberation theology, and Jewish hermeneutics is that they are more of the same.

No practitioner of these latter approaches would accept this interpretation; none would accept the interpretation that the relation to the academy at large of his or her approach is that it is just one more example of an intra-academy controversy. All would see their approach as challenging the very

This essay was first published as a book chapter titled "Suffering, Power, and Privileged Cognitive Access: The Revenge of the Particular," in *Christianity and Culture in the Crossfire*, edited by David A. Hoekema and Bobby Fong (Grand Rapids: Eerdmans, 1997), pp. 79-94. It is reprinted here with permission.

basis of the traditional academy. I think they are right about this. The controversy of the Aristotelians with the Platonists was over various philosophical issues; feminist epistemology, by contrast, is not a position on a debated issue within the field of epistemology. It's not comparable to a coherentist theory of justified belief, a representationalist theory of perception, or any other such position within the field. Better to think of it as a *perspective on* the field of epistemology — a way of thinking about the field, a way of approaching the issues within the field. Further, the perspective in question is a way of looking at many fields, not just epistemology, and is identified not by naming someone who happens to have developed it, but by specifying those for whom this comprehensive perspective on things is a significant part of their own narrative identity. To set out to develop a feminist perspective on epistemology is not to set out to articulate a certain position on one of the contested issues within epistemology but to set out to discover how the field as a whole looks when this aspect of one's narrative identity is allowed to function as perspective.

Far and away the most common interpretation nowadays of the rise of particularist perspectival learning is the following. Historically, white, Western, middle-class, heterosexual males have enjoyed hegemony in the academy. A crucial element in the strategy they have employed for securing their hegemony has been presenting themselves as having thrown off all particularist perspectives so as to engage in scholarship simply as generic human beings. Theirs is a view on the world from nowhere in particular by The Human Being Itself. In fact, however, they have conducted their scholarship within the perspective characteristic of their identity — that of white, Western, middle-class, heterosexual males. Equity demands that their hegemonic grip on the academy be broken and that the academy be opened up to the representatives of any particular perspective who have something interesting to say.

This, I say, is nowadays the most common interpretation. And almost always the context for the interpretation is an eager embrace of metaphysical antirealism. There is no ready-made world; things exist and propositions are true only relative to a particular conceptual scheme. The decision as to which scheme to adopt can in the last resort be made only by reference to which best serves one's interests. We differ in our interests. Accordingly, the academy at bottom is a vast constellation of interests contesting for power.

I think we are all indebted to those who have espoused this interpretation of what transpires in the academy. They have had their eye on something real and important. Those who have traditionally undertaken to speak on behalf of the academy have presented the academy otherwise; but it is in fact a locus of struggles for power in the service of interests. The response of Christians in particular should be: "So what's new? Exactly what I would have expected!" The academy is like all other social institutions in that it participates in the fallenness of our human existence rather than transcending it.

But to say that those who espouse this interpretation have their eye on something real and important is by no means to say that the interpretation they have offered of what they have discerned is correct and worthy of acceptance. It should, in my judgment, be rejected. Though not without insight, it is nonetheless glibly vulgar Marxism; and its antirealism I regard as untenable. It's true that in the academy's rejection of such particularist perspectives as feminism and liberationism, its own interests are at work. But to suppose that that is the whole of the matter — that it's all nothing more than self-interested power exercised with false consciousness — is appallingly imperceptive.

The Academy's Grand Project: Objective Knowing

What has also been at work all these years in the academy is the grip on our imagination, from the classical Greeks on into the contemporary world, of what I shall call The Grand Project. The academy, until very recently, has always rejected anything like feminist epistemology, Native American history, gay literary studies, liberation theology, and Jewish hermeneutics. "Anything like," I say. For it has also rejected learning conducted from the particularist perspective of white, Western, heterosexual males belonging to the power structure of society. That is to say: though in practice it has no doubt engaged in such learning, *officially* it has rejected it. The Grand Project to which the academy has for millennia been committed — in profession though often not in practice — is incompatible with all particularist perspectival learning. Those who engage in particularist perspectival learning within the academy are right to see themselves as challenging the very basis of the traditional academy, rather than merely espousing a position on some of the issues under debate within the traditional academy. But what they are challenging is not just the hegemony and false consciousness of a certain party within the academy; they are challenging the visionary project that for millennia has inspired the academy. The false consciousness presupposes that ideal; if that project had no grip on our imagination, the attempt to justify what one was doing — be it made in false consciousness or not — by pleading that one was engaging in that project, would fall on bewildered ears.

Begin by noticing that from Plato onwards the standard imagery for what one does when entering the academy and engaging in *Wissenschaft* is that of *turning away* from the everyday. It would be possible to think of what transpires in the academy as an extension and intensification of what transpires in the everyday. In fact the dominant image has always been that of departure. One leaves the everyday behind so as to go into another land.

Take a line, says Plato in the sixth book of the *Republic,* and divide it into two (unequal) segments. Let one segment represent the perceptible; the other, the intelligible. Then divide each of these segments in turn. Of that initial segment which represents the perceptible, let one part represent the appearances of perceptible things; the other, the perceptible things themselves. And of that initial segment that represents the intelligible, let one part represent things knowable only by inference from things known, perhaps with the assistance of perceptible illustrations; let the other part represent things knowable immediately and without the assistance of illustrations. We can then pair off modes of intellectual activity with these different parts of the line and what they represent. There will be imagining *(eikasia)* and believing *(pistis)* corresponding to the two parts of the first segment, these together constituting opinion *(doxa)*; and there will be thinking *(dianoia)* and knowing *(episteme)* corresponding to the two parts of the second segment.

Plato's instruction, *Take a divided line and let its parts represent,* opens with language that is nonevaluative. He does not say, "Let the *lower* part of the line represent. . . ." He says simply, "Take a line divided into two unequal parts, one to represent. . . ." But anyone who has read this far in the *Republic* knows Plato's assessment of *doxa* and *episteme.* And by the time we are instructed to pair off mental states or actions with the parts of the line and what they symbolize, the evaluation has become fully explicit: "take, as corresponding to the four sections, these four states of mind: *intelligence* for the highest, *thinking* for the second, *belief* for the third, and for the last *imagining.* These you may arrange as the terms in a proportion, assigning to each a degree of clearness and certainty corresponding to the measure in which their objects possess truth and reality."[1]

Episteme is highest; *doxa,* in its two forms, is lowest. For *episteme* occurs when we are in touch with what is fully real: with the realm of the necessary, eternal, immutable. Plato postulated the presence in us human beings of a faculty that puts us in touch with necessity: the faculty of reason. In the *Timaeus* he argued that apprehension of the contingent can never be certain; only apprehension of the necessary can be that. *Episteme* is certain, *doxa* uncertain. For Plato the "moral" was clear: the ideal activity is the activity of

---

1. Plato, *Republic,* translated by F. M. Cornford (Oxford: Oxford University Press, 1945), p. 511.

theoria, contemplation of the realm of the eternal and necessary, retaining only so much of *doxa* as is unavoidable. The academy is the institutional locus for that activity of *theoria.*

Whitehead once remarked that Western philosophy is a series of footnotes to Plato. On no point is that more true that on the point at hand. Let me mention a few of the footnotes. By the time we get to the medieval Aristotelianism represented by Aquinas, the practices Plato recommended for the exercise of *theoria* had been crystallized into the project of *scientia.* In *scientia* we start from what is or has been evident — preferably self-evident — to some rational being or other, and we proceed to draw inferences, preferably by deduction. *Scientia* proper consists of the conclusions arrived at; it is the superstructure erected on the foundation of what is or was evident. As to *doxa,* however, Aquinas' conclusion was that Plato's response was too monolithic, too lacking in nuance. Very much of *doxa* we must indeed leave behind when we enter the academy. But not all. We do not leave behind the texts that have been handed down to us. We discard a few as irredeemably heretical. But for the rest, we employ strategies of interpretation so as to extract from them the articulate wisdom that as a totality they contain. The result is still *doxa,* not *scientia.* But it is a higher form of *doxa* from that which we find in the everyday. It is true that *scientia* is nobler than the wisdom which emerges from the dialectical interpretation of the textual tradition. But discarding such wisdom would be an irreplaceable loss. To which must be added that there is no better preparation for engaging in *scientia* than just exactly such dialectics.

Descartes, to leap some four hundred years, sided more with Plato in this debate than with the medieval Aristotelians. He had no disagreement with the medievals in their ideal of *scientia;* in fact he devoted his entire career to breathing new life into that ideal. But he disagreed firmly with them on their estimation of the worth of the textual tradition. Close all the books, said Descartes. No doubt there is some truth contained therein. But everybody agrees that the ideal of the academy is the project of *scientia;* and rather than dialectical interpretation of the textual tradition being the best preparation for the practice of *scientia,* it is very nearly the worst. The practice of *scientia* requires that one be clear, at the beginning, as to what is evident to one — what is certain for one. The reading of books, rather than clarifying one's mind on this matter, introduces all sorts of *praejudicia.* It makes us *think* things are certain for us when they are not. Practice instead the Therapy of Doubt.

John Locke and his Royal Society cohorts in the seventeenth century composed yet a different set of footnotes. Though the traditional concept of *scientia* was still to be found in Locke's conceptual arsenal, and though Locke was as convinced as were his predecessors of the nobility of the project, he no longer thought it came to much. Mathematics was a *scientia*, perhaps moral theory could eventually take the form of a *scientia;* but that was about it. Yet the image of departing from the everyday as one entered the academy was as present in Locke as in anyone. Obviously it was not *doxa* that one departed from; as Locke saw it, to depart from *doxa* would be to leave the academy almost entirely depopulated. So far, then, Locke was in agreement with the medieval Aristotelians. But most emphatically he did not think that the academy should supplement its meager exercise of *scientia* with the interpretation of texts. Locke followed Descartes in insisting on the closing of the books. In entering the academy one leaves behind the everyday ways of arriving at *doxa* so as to employ a new and better way of arriving at *doxa* — the *best* way, the *optimal* practice. It goes like this: when the issue arises of whether or not to believe some proposition, one assembles a satisfactory body of evidence consisting of beliefs of which one is certain because the corresponding facts are evident to one; then one calculates the probability of the proposition on that evidence; and finally one believes or disbelieves with a firmness proportioned to that probability. The result will usually still be *doxa.* But it will be *doxa* firmly grounded, as the *doxa* of the everyday is not.

It would be easy to continue in this vein, citing more such footnotes; but let me halt, since the point is now clear. From Plato on into the contemporary world, entering the academy is described as departing from the everyday so as to engage in something better. On what exactly constitutes that "better," there have been disagreements, as there have been on what exactly one is leaving behind. But the image of *departure* is pervasive — departure from the everyday for something not just different but better.

Thus far I have emphasized the different ways in which other and better were understood. But we must not allow the differences to obscure a fundamental continuity; for my purposes on this occasion, the continuity is more important than the differences. From Plato onwards, what transpires in the academy is seen as better than the everyday because it is *more objective* and *better grounded.* We nowadays are mightily impressed with the expansion of knowledge that the academy affords us. I daresay that most people, if asked to reflect on why that is so, would say that it has something to do with the fact that the practices of the academy yield more objectivity and better groundedness than those in ordinary life.

Objectivity is a Janus-faced concept. On the one side, it denotes being genuinely in touch with the object, with what is objectively there, with what is out there. On the other side, it means being impartial, not reflecting one or another particular perspective on what is out there but approaching it simply as a perceptive human being. These two sides of the concept are connected;

231

otherwise they would not be two sides of one concept but two concepts. The connection is the assumption that to get genuinely in touch with the object, or to do so in a more reliable way, one must eliminate the particularity of one's perspective. The assumption is that particularity represents bias, prejudice, obstruction. And the better groundedness of what transpires in the academy is understood as connected with its greater objectivity. Removing one's biases and genuinely and reliably getting in touch with the object is what yields groundedness.

To understand this with any depth at all we will have to dip our toes into a bit of epistemology. The dominant picture that comes to mind when reading epistemology in the contemporary analytic tradition, and its antecedents in modern philosophy, is that of a solitary person sitting in a chair passively receiving such sensory stimulation as comes his way, taking note of the beliefs which that stimulation forms in him, recalling certain events from his past, observing what is going on in his mind, and drawing inferences. It is the epistemology of a *reactor,* of someone who receives stimulation and then goes off on his own interior course of thought. It is the epistemology of a *solitary* reactor; for almost no attention is paid to other persons — to the role of testimony in our lives, for example. And it is the epistemology of an *immobile* solitary reactor. Paraplegic epistemology. The body enters the picture only so far as sensation requires a body. And even that requirement is treated as a contingency; witness the popularity of thought-experiments in which all that is left of the body is the brain.

Generic Cognitive Practices: Foundationalism

Now compare. To be sure of the color of the sweater I am considering buying I take it out from under the blue fluorescent light in the back of the shop to the front where there is daylight. To make sure that the signature on the painting is not a forgery I fetch a magnifying glass and look closely at the brushwork. To find out the location of The Gambia I dig out my atlas and scrutinize the map of Africa. To understand what caused the conflict in the family I get the wife's and children's side of the story as well as the husband's. I find Anton Webern's music fascinating but baffling; so I enroll in a course on classical music of the twentieth century in the hope of learning how to listen to it. In short, I employ ways of finding out things, and better ways of finding out thing on matters about which I already have views; and ways of gaining awareness of things, and ways of gaining more discriminating awareness of things of which I am already aware. I employ what might be called belief-practices and awareness-practices. We all do. And when we do, we move around bodily in the world and interact with our fellow human beings — all the while intentionally acting upon our environment, including our technological environment, and not just reacting to it. Traditional epistemology — if the characterization I gave is anywhere near correct — has massively neglected to reflect on the belief-practices and awareness-practices in which we all engage.

Neglected such reflection in favor of what? In favor of reflecting, first, on our cognitive *constitution*. What is the *nature* of perception? Does it consist of having mental representations of external objects or do we have direct awareness of objects? What is the *nature* of memory? Those are the sorts of questions asked. And in favor, secondly, of reflecting on the *nature* of knowledge — not on how we go about acquiring knowledge but on its very nature. It is my own conviction that the sterility and stalemates of epistemology are in good measure due to its myopic focus on our cognitive constitution at the expense of reflecting on the practices in which that constitution is employed. But I am not going to argue that case here; here it is enough to be aware of both constitution and practices.

In turn, we must learn to think of our cognitive constitution in a much more nuanced way than is customary. I can best make the point I want to make here by using a certain aspect of the workings of computers as a model for thinking about the doxastic side of our lives. We as human beings are all dispositionally hard-wired in such a way that, upon such-and-such things happening to us, we become aware of such-and-such entities; and upon becoming aware of such-and-such entities, we believe thus-and-so. In addition, we are all dispositionally hard-wired in such a way that upon such-and-such things happening to us, we acquire new awareness-dispositions and new belief-dispositions.

But in addition to being hard-wired in this way, each of us is also programmed in a certain way. And whereas the hard-wiring is remarkably similar from person to person, the way we are programmed differs wildly from person to person — and indeed from time to time within a given person's life. Depending on how one is programmed, a given input will or will not yield a certain awareness, and a certain awareness will or will not yield a certain belief.

How do we acquire our cognitive programming? We acquire it by way of the outputs of our already programmed constitution becoming components of our new program. Which beliefs will be formed in us by a given input is almost never a function just of the input to our dispositional nature coupled with the concepts we possess and our attentiveness at the moment. Almost always, beliefs we already have function as elements of our programming; and those beliefs were the output of earlier operations of our programmed constitution. In that way, we function *inside* our system of beliefs. Inside our constitution too. Inside our doxastically programmed constitution. We use beliefs to form beliefs, and then we use those latter to form yet others. Lest there be misunderstanding, let me add that much of our programming is not so much personal as social. We also operate inside a tradition.

And now for a sad but crucial point: many of the beliefs that function as elements of our programming are false, with the consequence that our personal programs at many points do not enable access to reality but obstruct it. Running throughout all our personal programmings are glitches consisting of false beliefs functioning to obstruct the formation of true beliefs — and other such glitches as habits of inattention. Though of course nobody's program is just one big glitch!

To return to The Grand Project of the academy: nobody who has thought about the matter has ever supposed that in the academy one just stares at the truth. All have supposed that to enter the academy is to be inducted into certain practices of awareness and belief — certain ways of conducting one's cognitive constitution. Nobody in the past ever put it quite that way; but surely that is what Plato had in mind when he spoke of the philosopher's employment of dialectics, what Aquinas and Descartes had in mind when they spoke of *scientia*, what Locke had in mind when he outlined his optimal practice. One leaves behind the everyday practices for the new and epistemically superior practices — leaves them behind for one's work in the academy, not for one's life in general. And secondly — this is crucial — inside the academy one lays aside or circumvents the particularity of one's everyday programming and develops a new and fresh program for the matters at hand, free of all those glitches present in our everyday programmings.

How could one ever do that? How could one circumvent the programming one already has? Supposedly by allowing the cognitive constitution that one shares with all human beings — that one possesses just *qua* human being — to put one in touch with the relevant facts. "To the things themselves," as Locke put it. One lets one's perceptual capacities put one in touch with external objects. One lets one's reason put one in touch with necessary truths. One lets one's consciousness put one in touch with one's own mental life. And then, by the exercise of reason, one makes valid inferences. In all those at whom we looked — Plato, Aquinas, Descartes, Locke — one finds this picture of beginning with direct awareness of facts and then proceeding by good inference from there. Of starting from that foundation and building the house right this time, as one does not and cannot start from that foundation and build the house right in everyday life. Foundationalism is fundamental to The Grand Project. Particularities will of course emerge. The trained art historian learns things by looking at paintings under a magnifying glass that I now could not learn in that way; he has been suitably programmed, I have not. But these particularized programmings are to be ones that emerge within the academy, in the course of starting from the foundation by using our generic constitution. Instead of obstructing access to reality, such grounded particularities enable access.

Christian Learning: A Particular Privileged Cognitive Access

Something like that is The Grand Project which has inspired the academy of the West. And once we see that that was the project, it's obvious why such particularities as feminism and liberationism — along with masculinism and Occidentalism and all the others — have been rejected out of hand. These are particularities which are *brought to* the academy from the everyday rather than emerging within the academy from the superior practices of the academy employed by persons functioning *qua* generic human beings. They have not been developed from the ground up. And though of course they will exhibit some bit of insight here and there — nobody is totally out of touch with reality — overall they represent bias and prejudice, obstructing rather than enabling access to reality.

The Grand Project has come under relentless attack in recent years from many directions. I myself think it is pure illusion to suppose that upon entering the academy we can circumvent the programming we have acquired in everyday life and begin afresh by employing our hard-wired, unprogrammed cognitive constitution to gain awareness of certain facts. Locke himself, in a fascinating passage in the penultimate chapter of his *Essay Concerning Human Understanding*, admitted as such, without ever quite realizing that he had done so. The admission occurs in his discussion of why people sometimes go wrong in their employment of the practice he recommends — why they sometimes make "wrong estimates of probabilities," as he puts it. One illustration that he offers is this: the doctrine of transubstantiation, so Locke says, is necessarily false, self-evidently so. Yet a person reared in Catholicism from youth up will not emerge believing it false, no matter how intently he stares at the doctrine. Instead he will sort through all his other beliefs and eliminate those that seem to him incompatible with the doctrine.

Here is another example, this time in Locke's own words. It is especially relevant to those of us who are teachers:

> Would it not be an insufferable thing for a learned professor, and that which his scarlet would blush at, to have his authority of forty years standing, wrought out of hard rock Greek and Latin, with no small expense of time and candle, and confirmed by general tradition, and a reverend beard, in an instant overturned by an upstart novelist [i.e., deviser of novelties]? Can any one expect that he should be made to confess, that what he taught his scholars thirty years ago, was all error and mistake; and that he sold them hard words and ignorance at a very dear rate?[2]

You see the point. The person reared in Catholicism has been programmed in such a way that grasping the doctrine of transubstantiation does not produce in him what Locke thinks is the right outcome — the belief that the doctrine is necessarily false. And the old professor has been programmed in such a way that when presented with the novel theory of a young scholar which contradicts his own, he fails to see any plausibility in it whatsoever.

The point is general. The image of departing from the everyday and entering the special and better is profoundly misleading. We cannot, upon entering the academy, manage to use just our generic cognitive constitution on the topics of concern to the academician. Whether we like it or not, the particular programming we acquire during our life in the everyday functions as we work within the academy. Dichotomizing is not possible. Indeed, without such programming we could not even operate in the academy. The programming we acquired during our life in the everyday contributes to determining our response not just to the facts with which we deal in ordinary life but to the facts with which we deal in the academy. What transpires in the academy is not an alternative to everyday life but an intensification and extrapolation of that.

The point could be elaborated. But since it is familiar — though not, indeed, in quite the form I have presented it in — I propose to move on to the topic that brings us around to our opening. The particularities of programming — that is, of particular habits of awareness, of particular concepts, of particular beliefs — that we bring with us from everyday life to the academy have traditionally been regarded as biases and prejudices obstructing our access to reality. That has been the ground for turning away all particularist perspectival learning at the doorway of the academy. The prevalent current argument for allowing them entrance, on the other hand, is starkly political; it assumes that no one ever has any awareness of reality and argues on that

---

2. Locke, *An Essay Concerning Human Understanding*, iv.xx.11, edited by Peter H. Nidditch (Oxford: Clarendon Press, 1975), p. 714.

ground that it would be unjustly discriminatory to exclude any perspective, except perhaps those whose representatives have nothing interesting to say. If we are all prisoners in our own houses of interpretation, what justification could there be for preferring one prison to another?

I want to present for your consideration an approach very different from either of these. May it not be that certain of the perspectives that belong to our narrative identities give us access to realms of reality that would otherwise be extremely difficult to come by? May it not be that some of them constitute in that way privileged cognitive access? It is true that justice requires admitting forthrightly perspectival learning into the academy. But may it not be that there is another reason as well, one that pertains more directly to what the academy is all about? May it not be that we can expect to learn something from the working out of a feminist perspective on epistemology, something that it is most unlikely the rest of us would ever learn on our own? May it not be that we can expect to learn something from the working out of a liberation perspective on theology, something that it is most unlikely the rest of us would ever learn on our own? And so forth.

"May it not be?" I have asked. That is only to pose a possibility. What about actuality? I do not know what to offer here other than personal testimony. I have in fact found it illuminating to read some of the writings of those whose narrative identity comprises belonging to the underside of society and who look at the Bible and Christian theology from that particularist perspective. I have in fact found it illuminating to read some of the writings of those whose narrative identity comprises being women and who look at the literature of the Western tradition from that particular perspective. I have in fact found it illuminating to read some of the writings of those whose narrative identity comprises being victims of Western imperialism and who look at history from that perspective. And so on. I do not dispute that much of what has been written from one and another such perspective has been silly — though I am not myself of the view that silliness had to await entrance into the academy until twenty years ago or so when particularist perspectival learning forced its way in. Neither do I dispute that much of what goes into particularist perspectives functions to obscure rather than illuminate. All I insist on is that there is more to it than that. Narrative identities also afford privileged cognitive access. Privileged cognitive access to facts of concern to the academy. Our narrative identities lead us to notice things and believe things that otherwise would almost certainly go unnoticed and unbelieved.

Important implications for the ethos of the academy follow from this way of regarding the emergence of perspectivalism. The academy must be a place where genuine dialogue takes place among the representatives of different perspectives. By genuine dialogue I mean: dialogue characterized by willingness to speak and willingness to listen. The hope of all together beginning from a foundation of facts discerned by the employment of our generic constitution, unprogrammed by any particularities, is a hopeless hope. But if the dying of that hope results in nothing more than a multiplicity of perspectival ghettos within the academy, then woe are we. I have argued that the deep significance for the academy of perspectival learning is that it is characteristic of our narrative identities — of some, not all — to give us privileged cognitive access to certain aspects of reality. The academy should be a place where insights of that sort are elicited into consciousness, then articulated and developed. But the ultimate point of such intraperspectival endeavors is that what is discerned and learned be shared with those of us whose narrative identity is different — so that all together we can arrive at a richer and more accurate understanding. Agreement is an asymptotic goal of the academy rather than a secured beginning. But that presupposes that the representatives of each particular perspective are willing both to share their insights with those outside and willing to listen to their critique.

It has already become clear that such an ethos will neither be easily come by nor easily sustained when achieved. One thing that undermines it is *the nursing of resentment*. Now that the hegemony of the purportedly universal has been lifted and particularisms of many sorts have found their voice in society and academy, one is startled to learn how deep resentment goes — women against men, people of color against whites, the rest of the world against Islam, Islam against Christianity, atheists against religion, gays against straights, Ukrainians against Russians. The list goes on and on. Genuine dialogue is impossible in the presence of nursed resentment. That must first be taken care of. There has to be forgiveness. But let me add that for the *unrepentant* victimizer to ask forgiveness from the victim is immoral manipulation.

Even more destructive of the ethos needed for genuine dialogue is *claiming the privilege of silence on the ground of suffering*. Nowadays one hears one group or another insisting that its identity has been shaped by its suffering, that its suffering has been like unto no other, that those who have not experienced its suffering can never understand it, and that consequently dialogue is impossible. For whereas dialogue aims at agreement, its prerequisite is understanding. So what's the point of talking to the other? We will talk to ourselves; there dialogue is possible. This, I say, is what one hears. And there is deep truth in it. Suffering does isolate. Yet it is possible to go beyond nursing one's suffering to owning it redemptively — at which point one no longer claims it as entitlement to the privilege of silence but offers it as strange gift to the other.

"Forgiveness," "repentance," "suffering owned redemptively." I have deliberately chosen words with Christian connotations. What is needed, if the academy is to survive in the face of injury and suffering, are those fundamental acts of the soul taught us by Christ for walking in his Way: forgiveness, and the redemptive owning of suffering, and repentance on the part of those who need the forgiveness for causing the suffering. And beyond those acts of the soul, what is needed, if the academy is to survive amidst the revenge of the particular, is the embrace of the conviction, fundamental to Christianity, Judaism, and Islam alike, that there is more to human beings than the merely particular. There is a shared nature. Split, indeed, into fallen on the one hand and created and destined on the other. About our fallen nature it is often true that we seek to gain power over others while eluding their attempt to gain power over us. But about our created and destined nature something quite different has to be said; in this aspect of our nature we image God, and by virtue of this aspect of our nature we are entitled to the attitudes and actions that acknowledge the presence within us of an inalienable and inviolable dignity.

I have been hinting in these last paragraphs that to be a Christian is to have a narrative identity that incorporates a perspective on reality which enables, rather than inhibits, discernment of dimensions of reality. Enables, for example, discernment of the role of forgiveness in life, and of redemptively owned suffering, and of repentance; enables discernment of a human nature split into fallen on the one hand and created and destined on the other, with the latter possessing an ineradicable dignity calling for respect. But this only begins to detail the discernment enabled by possessing the narrative identity of being a Christian. The academy as a whole must also provide a place for that perspectival learning which is Christian learning — provided that those who practice it not only articulate their own perspective but honor the other by taking the risk of engaging in genuine dialogue.

My argument has been that to understand what is going on in the academy today we must take note of more than just the play of power in the service of interest. We must discern the loosening of the grip on our imaginations of The Grand Project which has inspired the academy for some twenty-five hundred years. I myself believe that the grip of that project on our imagination *should* be loosened, and that it should be loosened for a number of reasons. The reason I have chosen to develop on this occasion is that certain of our narrative identities enable, rather than obstruct, access to dimensions of reality. They constitute positions of privileged cognitive access.

In closing, let me come clear and admit that the way of looking at the academy and academic learning for which I have argued does not go against the *entire* Western tradition. That tradition is not quite as monolithic as I have presented it as being. At bottom what I have argued for is an Augustinian way of looking at the matter. Augustine believed that only if one departs from the condition of generic humanity and adopts that highly particular stance which consists of loving God above all else can one genuinely understand the fundamental structure of reality. Misplaced love and hostility hinder knowledge; loving the truly lovable enables knowledge. I believe he was profoundly right about that. Christian learning, so I believe, sides with Augustine against The Grand Project.

Academic Freedom in Religiously Based Colleges and Universities

My topic is academic freedom in religiously based colleges and universities. Before I get to what I want to say on the matter, I must make some comments about what it is that we are talking about. *Religiously based colleges and universities:* that's not a difficult concept to understand. But what is *academic freedom?*

Infringement versus Qualification

Let's begin with something that academic freedom is not. Academic freedom, though it definitely has something to do with freedom of speech, is not the same as that civil liberty which we call "freedom of speech." One way to see the difference is the following: over the past fifty years or so, the U.S. Supreme Court has moved in the direction of saying that the right to free speech guaranteed by our Bill of Rights implies that governmental regulation of speech must be, among other things, content-neutral. In their regulation of speech, governmental entities may attend to the *effects* of speech but not to the *content.* That distinction is useless when it comes to academic freedom. Academic institutions necessarily judge the *competence* of what present and prospective faculty members say and write; and to make such judgments they have no choice but to attend to content.

That is not, however, the fundamental difference between the civil liberty of free speech, on the one hand, and academic freedom on the other; the fundamental difference lies in the fact that the civil liberty of free speech comes into the picture when we are talking about the polity of society,

---

This conference paper, originally entitled "Ivory Tower or Holy Mountain: Academic Freedom and Faith," was presented at Baylor University in March 2000.

whereas academic freedom, as the phrase itself suggests, comes into the picture when we are talking about the academy. Truck drivers in a liberal democratic society enjoy the civil liberty of free speech; they neither enjoy nor lack academic freedom — for the simple reason that they are not members of the academy.

Infringing on Academic Freedom

So what, then, is academic freedom? Perhaps it is easiest to see what it is by considering what constitutes an infringement on it. And let me content myself with saying what's true of paradigmatic cases of such infringement; I will not here attempt the analytic philosopher's "thing" of formulating necessary and sufficient conditions! Infringing on a person's academic freedom consists of impairing or threatening to impair a person's academic position or standing in some way or other: firing her or threatening to fire, refusing to promote her or threatening to refuse, preventing her from serving on important committees or threatening to prevent her from so serving, rejecting her candidacy for some post or threatening to do so, and so forth.

Many such impairments or threats thereof do not constitute infringements on a person's academic freedom. What has to be added is something about the *grounds* for the actual or threatened impairment. Infringement on academic freedom typically happens when the actual or threatened impairment occurs on account of the person's *position* on some issue, or on account of her *publicizing* her position. The issue may or may not be an issue within the person's academic field; it is all-too-usual for the threat to be issued on account of the person's position on some political or religious issue.

The fact that the academy has to make judgments of competence requires that we say more than just this, however. If the university refuses to promote some young philosophy professor because of the scholarly incompetence of the positions she holds, then, though it would be impairing that person's academic standing on account of certain of her positions, such impairment would not constitute infringement on her academic freedom. For such infringement to occur, the impairment of the person's academic standing would have to be based on some aspect of the positions she holds other than their scholarly competence or incompetence. It would have to be based on what I shall call the *ideological content* of the position.

The distinction between disapproving of the ideological content of what a person said and judging it incompetent is, of course, fraught with difficulty in application. Not that the distinction can never be confidently drawn; certainly it can be. We have all been embarrassed by what we recognized to be incompetent formulations of positions we agreed with, and disconcerted by what we acknowledged to be extremely competent formulations of positions we heartily disagreed with. Nonetheless, those who talk as if the several academic guilds — the guild of historians, the guild of philosophers, and so on — have arrived at ideologically neutral criteria of competence, and suggest that it is easy to distinguish the employment of these from ideological discrimination, seem to me to be living in a fantasyland.

Let me now join together the two components to which I have called attention: to infringe on a person's academic freedom is to impair or threaten to impair that person's position or standing in the academy on account of the ideological content of the position he or she holds or publicizes on some issue. Let me say once again that I mean this as a description of paradigmatic cases of such infringement, not as a formulation of necessary and sufficient conditions. A full account of what constitutes academic freedom would also have to take account of those cases in which a person's academic standing is impaired or threatened on account of behavior, other than speech, which is neither forbidden by law nor injurious to the academic enterprise.

Qualifying Academic Freedom

A related point is important to mention: the civil liberty of free speech is not absolute. The formulation in the U.S. Bill of Rights is absolute; but if one looks at the law that emerges from judicial decisions having to do with free speech, it is clear that it is a qualified liberty. The present American law concerning free speech is not that stark, unqualified statement in the Bill of Rights but the totality of judicial decisions on the matter as it exists at this moment. It is tempting for philosophers to try their hand at composing a general formulation of the qualifications; I myself regard this as an endeavor that has no chance of succeeding, and hence a temptation to be resisted. Philosophers are no more capable than anybody else of anticipating the sorts of cases that will confront our courts. And in any case, judges do not have in mind some highly qualified universal generalization which they then simply apply to the facts of the free-speech cases before them. The law itself emerges from the decisions.

The same sort of thing is true for academic freedom; it is no more absolute than is the civil liberty of free speech. What is to serve as guideline for the practice of the academy is not that stark formulation which I offered above but that formulation as duly qualified.

How should we describe those cases in which the court declares that it is acceptable for the government to impose some restriction on a person's speech? Should we say that in those cases the court declares that it is acceptable for the government to *infringe* on free speech? That falls strange on the ear; it belongs to the connotation of the word "infringe" that infringing on someone's right is a bad thing to do. Better to borrow the term actually used in the Bill of Rights and say that the court declares that it is acceptable for the government to *abridge* the right in such cases — except that what the Bill of Rights actually says is that Congress shall make no law "abridging the freedom of speech." So better yet to say that the court's decisions function to *qualify* the freedom.

I shall speak of academic freedom in the same way. Though it is never a good thing to *infringe* on academic freedom, every educational institution does and should attach *qualifications* to that freedom. The issue will always be which qualifications are appropriate.

Contexts for Academic Freedom

Let me move on now to present a number of considerations — eight of them — that seem to me necessary or useful to bear in mind in our thinking about academic freedom. Some of these considerations will be aspects of the social context in which the issue of academic freedom arises for you and me; others will be matters of semi-philosophical background.

In the first place, the issue of academic freedom arises for you and me within the context of a modernized society in which there has been substantial differentiation of distinct spheres of social and cultural life. I am alluding here to Max Weber's theory of modernization; let me say just a word about it.

Weber was convinced that the essence of modernization is to be located in two related phenomena. It consists, in the first place, in the emergence of *differentiated spheres* of activity — specifically, in the emergence of the differentiated *social* spheres of economy, state, and household, and in the emergence of the differentiated *cultural* spheres of academic learning (*Wissenschaft*), art, law, and ethics. The picture that underlay Weber's thought at this point was the picture (common among neo-Kantian philosophers of his day) according to which individual spheres of activity, each with its own dynamics, reside in the very nature of things, albeit hidden and concealed throughout most of history. Learning is intertwined with monastic life, art is intertwined with the life of the church, and so forth, until, in the early modern period, art comes into its own, science comes into its own, the economy comes into its own, and the like. The phrase that I am using here, "comes into its own," is in fact commonly used by intellectual historians in their description of what happened in the field of the arts in the eighteenth century. What Weber added to this standard neo-Kantian picture was the claim that it is the dynamic of rationalization which, after disenchanting the world and confining the ethic of brotherliness to the realm of the private, brings these spheres to the light of day by differentiating them from each other and securing the relative independence of action within them from outside influence.

The other main aspect of Weber's theory of modernization was his account of what transpires within these various social and cultural spheres once they have been differentiated from each other and activity within them freed from outside influence. Activity within the spheres, so Weber thought, becomes autonomous; it begins to follow its own internal logic. Any outside influence is a distortion of that logic. Weber thought that these internal logics are all manifestations of *rationalization*. Thus in his theory rationalization plays the double modernizing function of accounting for the emergence of these differentiated spheres and accounting for what happens within these spheres once they have been differentiated and action within them allowed to become independent and autonomous. Weber famously argued, for example, that the fundamental dynamic of action within our modern differentiated economies is the rationalization typified by the mentality of "the bottom line"; he somewhat less famously argued that the fundamental dynamic of thought within modern science is the rationalization manifested by the orientation of that thought toward prediction, the grounding of that thought in sensory experience, and the entwinement of that thought with technology.

Whether or not Weber was right in his claim that rationalization is what accounts for the differentiation of spheres is something we need not settle for our purposes here. What's relevant is rather the basic claim that modernized societies — of which ours is certainly one — are characterized by such differentiation. For it is only in such societies that the issue of academic freedom, in anything like the form it takes for us, can arise. Indeed, it is my impression — based on no historical research whatsoever — that our phrase "academic freedom" had its origin in the German word *Lehrfreiheit;* and that *Lehrfreiheit* became a battle cry in late-eighteenth-century Germany when the state, abetted by the church, tried to impose religious requirements on the universities even though the universities were well on the way toward becoming institutionally distinct from both church and state. Weber's other claim — that, spurred on by rationalization, life within the differentiated spheres follows its own inherent laws unless distorted by outside influence

— is not something we will be able to set to the side; I will be coming back to it later.

Second, the issue of academic freedom arises for you and me within the context of a religiously pluralistic society with a liberal democratic polity. The liberal democratic form of polity emerged in the West as a solution to the problem of social order posed when the citizens of a single state embrace a diversity of incompatible comprehensive perspectives on God and the good — some of these comprehensive perspectives being religious, some not. The problem posed is obvious: How can citizens enjoy equal justice at the hands of the state in a peaceful and enduring society if they do not share a comprehensive perspective on God and the good? For the purposes of our discussion here, it will be important to keep in mind both the religious pluralism of American society and the fact that we enjoy a liberal democratic form of polity. Two features of such a polity are worth emphasizing. A liberal polity is one that accords to its citizens such civil liberties as freedom of conscience, freedom to exercise one's religion, freedom of speech, and freedom of assembly. And a liberal polity is one that refrains from indoctrinating its citizens into any comprehensive religious or philosophical perspective; in that way it treats impartially all the comprehensive perspectives to be found in the society.

Third, the issue of academic freedom arises for you and me within the context of a society that exhibits extraordinary scope and vitality in its civil dimension. It is not easy to describe with rigor what constitutes civil society; for our purposes here we will not go wrong if we think of it as all those institutions, organizations, and social formations that lie between the state, on the one side, and the family on the other. What's characteristic of totalitarian regimes is that, in order to curb all significant anti-regime impulses, they push civil society back to the margins by massively expanding the scope of the state: business, banking, manufacturing, and farming all become state-owned; educators become state functionaries, as do clergy in extreme cases. American civil society is obviously subject to a good deal of governmental regulation — this being the ground of much grumbling by those on the political right; nonetheless, it is extraordinary how many of our institutions and organizations do not in any way belong to the government, and extraordinary how few of us are government employees. Beyond that, what's extraordinary is the vitality of our civil society — a ferment of new initiatives and new organizations of every imaginable sort.

Fourth, the issue of academic freedom arises for you and me within the context of an educational system that, as a whole, is radically decentralized, full of voluntary organizations and voluntary activity, and highly competitive. The extent to which this is true first became clear to me when, in the 1980s, I taught for five years at the Free University of Amsterdam. In the Netherlands there is a Minister of Education who sits in the Hague and is responsible for regulating the entire system of Dutch education, from top to bottom; almost all education is fully funded by the state, and most faculty members of the universities are officially employees of the state. When I pointed out to my Dutch colleagues that in the United States there is no similar post of federal Minister of Education, that even within most *states* there is no similar Minister of Education, that a great deal of higher education is private, and that even the state colleges and universities depend heavily on private philanthropy, they found it impossible to imagine how such a system could work; it sounded to them like a recipe for chaos. My response was not that there is no chaos in the system; that would have been disingenuous. My response was rather that it did not seem to me that the chaos produced by the Dutch educational bureaucracy was substantially less than that which bubbled up from the bottom in the United States. Be that as it may, however; academic freedom necessarily takes a rather different form in the decentralized and competitive American educational system from that which it takes in the centralized systems one finds in Europe.

Fifth, it is important for us to recognize and keep in mind that the religion of a great many people in our society is what can best be called "holistic." No doubt the religion of some people is no more than a *sector* of their lives — perhaps for them a very important sector, but a sector nonetheless, having little to do with the rest of their lives: little to do with their politics, little to do with their economic activity, little to do with their recreation, little to do with their moral code. Surely the differentiated character of modern society and culture, to which Weber called attention, contributes to the tendency of some to confine their religion to a sector. But there are plenty of other people for whom their religion is anything but a sector; it decisively shapes their political and economic activity, how they rear their families, what they believe about the origins of life, about medicine, about the dynamics of the self, about the nature of justice and the benefits of freedom, and so forth. John Rawls, in his book *Political Liberalism*, includes religions among what he calls "comprehensive perspectives." For many people — not all — that is exactly what their religion is: a comprehensive perspective. Though seldom will it be *only* a "perspective"; almost always a person's religion will also, for example, incorporate practices of worship and devotion.

Sixth, it is important for us to recognize and keep in mind that over the past twenty-five years or so there has been an upheaval in the regnant understanding of the academic enterprise. I think that on this occasion I can forego analyzing that upheaval. Let me simply call to your attention one of the most important and striking outcomes: the academy today is full of forthrightly particularist perspectival learning, learning that makes no pretension of describing the view from nowhere. I have in mind such projects as African-American history, feminist epistemology, and liberation theology. When I was in graduate school in the mid-1950s, there were no such projects; had anyone proposed any such project, their proposal would have been dismissed out of hand as hopelessly and unacceptably biased.

A seventh thing to keep in mind is that ideas matter to people. Different ideas matter to different people; but for everybody there are some ideas that matter to them. We all invest ourselves in the world; and part of that investment is our investment in the fate of certain ideas. A consequence of such investment is that the fate of ideas, or their apparent fate, stirs up our emotions. We get angry, discouraged, or disturbed when the ideas we treasure seem threatened; we feel jubilant when the ideas we treasure appear to be flourishing.

This is all obvious: people care about ideas. I mention it only because I find it endemic among academics to act as if it is not true. More precisely: academics want members of the public to feel jubilant over their thoughts, but they do not want the public to get angry about their thoughts. If anybody ever gets angry, they feel aggrieved, hurt, injured. The assumption seems to be that nobody has a right to get angry with what an academic says. Academics want to be allowed to say and write whatever they wish with only positive consequences. Of academics alone should courage never be required.

My response is: Grow up! Stop being adolescent. People do care about ideas. We had better expect that people will sometimes get angry with what we say.

Eighth, and last: let us keep before us why it is important for society to allow its scholars the duly qualified freedom to work out their thoughts as they see fit. There is, for one thing, a pragmatic reason. How enormously impoverished, in multiple ways, humanity would be if there had been no such freedom. How impoverished are those societies in which such freedom is absent.

A reason of quite a different sort seems to me even more important. Over and over the abridgement of academic freedom constitutes a profound violation of the person; and in this world of ours, there is nothing of greater worth than persons, and correspondingly, no greater evil than the violation of persons. The violation of a person is the desecration of one of the images of God. Galileo's personhood was violated by the behavior of the Inquisition; that's what was evil about that behavior. Granted, his personhood might have been violated even more deeply than it was if he had been tortured, for example. But examples of that supreme violation of personhood — torture — are also not hard to come by. What I have found most appalling about many of the cases I have known of the infringement on duly qualified academic freedom is that a person was violated. The loss of that person's contribution may have meant that the flourishing of humanity was somewhat diminished; much worse was the fact that an icon of the Holy One had been desecrated.

Religiously Qualified Academic Freedom

After saying a few words concerning what we are talking about when we talk about academic freedom, I have offered eight points of social and semi-philosophical context to keep in mind. Let me now close with some comments about the issue itself: academic freedom at religiously based colleges and universities.

Maintaining Pluralism in Civil Society

The institutions we are talking about all belong to the private sector of American society — to what earlier I called "civil society"; and they are multitudinous. The total number of students enrolled in such institutions is considerably less than the total of those enrolled in the state institutions plus the private secularized institutions; nonetheless, there are hundreds of religiously affiliated institutions of higher education in this country. Their existence in such numbers is a prime manifestation of that extraordinary vitality of American civil society which I mentioned earlier. In no other country in the world is there anything like it.

Thus, on the one hand, there is this extraordinary vitality and variety of education in the private sector, and on the other hand, ours is a liberal democratic society, and in such a society the state is to refrain from inducting its citizens into any comprehensive perspective on God and the good. A consequence of these facts is that in this country there is nothing academics are free to teach in the public educational sector that they are not free to teach somewhere in the private educational sector, whereas the converse is not true: there are many things academics are free to teach somewhere in the private educational sector that they are not free to teach in the public sector. There is, in this respect, a great deal more academic freedom in the private sector of the American educational system than there is in the public sector. In discussions on academic freedom, it is a point seldom made; yet it is indisputably true. In the private sector one can explore and espouse religiously grounded lines of thought that one would not be allowed to explore and espouse in the public sector. The memory is fresh in my mind of a case that arose recently in my own university — Yale — which, though not public, nonetheless sees itself as secular, or better perhaps, pluralist: a candidate for a post in religious studies was rejected because, so it was said by some, her lecture was too confessional.

It would be a tragedy of massive proportions if the extraordinary scope of academic freedom in the private sector of American education were in any way infringed upon — if it were in any way abridged and restricted. Persons like the candidate I just mentioned would be left without a teaching post unless they "shaped up." Some writers tend to think through the contours of duly qualified academic freedom for state and secular private educational institutions, and then to argue, or simply assume, that those same contours ought to hold for all educational institutions. But imposing those contours would not only violate the personhood of many of those who teach in these private institutions, many of whom believe with all their heart that they are called to live out in the academy their religious convictions, rather than confining those convictions to the sectors of the familial and the ecclesiastical. It would in addition impoverish our society as a whole by seriously diminishing the rich diversity of learning that the American educational system now produces.

Appropriate Religiously Qualified Academic Freedom

But if it is indisputably true that the private sector of American education, including then the religiously based institutions, offers freedom to a much wider variety of academics than does the public sector, why is it so commonly thought that religiously affiliated institutions uniquely threaten academic freedom? Why devote a conference to the topic of academic freedom at religiously affiliated institutions of higher education?

The answer to that question is clear. I do think it is important to compare, as I just did, the entire private sector of higher education in America with the entire public sector on the matter of academic freedom. But one has to supplement that comparison of total sectors with talk about particular institutions; it is, after all, not sectors but institutions which hire professors, instruct students, and are governed by administrators. At most religiously based colleges and universities, a professor's position and standing in the institution depends in some way or other on the ideological content of what he or she says or publicizes on certain issues. And to a good many writers on the subject, that fact in and of itself constitutes an unacceptable infringement on academic freedom. It will appear that way especially if one focuses all one's attention on just one aspect of what goes on at state universities, neglecting the rest — namely, if one focuses on the fact that state institutions do not officially have religious requirements for membership on their faculties, and neglects the fact that those same state universities have severe restrictions on what a professor may and may not teach with respect to religion.

Earlier I made the point that just as it is *legally qualified* free speech that governs our lives as citizens, rather than the unqualified affirmation of free speech that the U.S. Bill of Rights speaks of, so also it is what I have called *duly qualified* academic freedom that we have to deal with in our institutions. So the question is not whether it is acceptable for religiously based colleges and universities to attach qualifications to academic freedom. All educational institutions attach qualifications to academic freedom; none allows professors to teach whatever they wish. The question is whether attaching religious qualifications to academic freedom in religiously based colleges and universities is inherently inappropriate; and if not inherently inappropriate, whether the form such qualifications sometimes take makes them nonetheless in fact inappropriate.

Ever since the founding of Harvard College it has been characteristic of American civil society for groups of people with shared religious convictions to get together to found colleges that reflect their religion: a faculty is assembled, students are enrolled, and a supporting constituency is developed. The religion in question is almost always to some extent holistic; those whose religion is confined to the distinct sectors of the familial and the ecclesiastical are much less inclined to found colleges than those whose religion is not thus confined. Colleges in the private sector also get formed for other than religious reasons: St. John's, for example, was formed out of a secular vision of education as grounded in the Great Books. But far and away the most common foundations have been religious foundations.

Almost invariably, when such a college gets founded, religious qualifications are attached to the academic freedom of the faculty. I see no reason whatsoever for supposing that such qualifications are inherently wrong. I dare say we can agree that it is perfectly okay, in the context of American society, for a group of people to get together to form a "Great Books" college — even though such a college will perforce not welcome those who think that an educational program based on the Great Books is a pack of nonsense. So why would it be wrong for a group of people to get together to form a college grounded on one or another form of religion — even though such a college will perforce not welcome those who think that that species of religion is a pack of nonsense? Might the thought be the Weberian idea that *Wissenschaft* must now follow its own internal dynamics, so that any influence from the side of religion is now intellectually irresponsible? This point might have had some plausibility before that upheaval in our understanding of learning occurred, of which I spoke earlier; now, after the upheaval, it seems to me to have no plausibility whatsoever.

I have argued for a double negative: it is *not* inherently *in*-appropriate for a college or university to attach religious qualifications to the academic freedom of its faculty. Just as important, if not more so, is this positive point: it would be a violation of the very idea of a liberal democratic society if there were a movement to prevent or restrict the formation of religiously affiliated colleges and universities. To prevent or restrict their formation would be a violation of freedom of religion, a violation of freedom of speech, and a violation of freedom of assembly. It is universally characteristic of *totalitarian* regimes to try to prevent all private initiatives in education.

But though religious qualifications on academic freedom are not inherently unacceptable in the American system, what must at once be added is that when we get down to the details — as we must — what we find is that religiously based colleges and universities do often illicitly infringe on academic freedom. No doubt about it. Whether they more often illicitly infringe on academic freedom than do state and secular private institutions, I do not know. Those who have taught at state institutions, and at secular private ones, would have to have their heads in the sand to not be aware of the extent to which ideological considerations, as distinct from considerations of competence, enter into hiring, promoting, and firing. But be that as it may; duly qualified academic freedom is often egregiously infringed upon in religiously based institutions. The infringements occur when the religious qualifications are applied unjustly: for example, when they are never fully stated or not stated clearly in advance, when their application is arbitrary and irregular, or when there is no recourse available to the victim.

Over the years I have acquired a rather broad acquaintance with the religiously based colleges and universities of America; in the course of that experience I have learned that the history of these colleges and universities is littered with stories of unjust — often grossly unjust — infringements on academic freedom. These stories constitute a shameful blotch on the reputation of these institutions; the stories call into question the sincerity of those who profess high religious ideals for these institutions. I will defend the right of these colleges and universities to attach religious qualifications to academic freedom within their institutions. But I must and will add that all too often they violate the personhood of their faculty members in the way they apply these qualifications. In violating a person one perpetrates the greatest evil that one can perpetrate: one violates one of God's icons. To which I must add that often the person violated is a brother or sister in the faith of those who perpetrate the violation.

My own view, then, is that the best service the American Association of University Professors can render to this teeming multitude of American institutions of higher education is to draw up model codes of procedure for the handling of cases of academic freedom. For almost always it is in the procedure, not in the qualifications as such, that the injustice lies. Where there is no rule of law but only the command of persons, where secrecy and arbitrariness reign, where one never knows when and why the axe will fall, there justice weeps.

Christian Learning In and For a Pluralist Society

Is Christian Learning a Contradiction? A Story

It happened on a summer evening in Vancouver. I had just given a speech that I titled "Does Truth Still Matter in the Postmodern University?" My analysis and reflections were an example of what I regard as Christian learning. I had expected a tiny audience. Who wants to listen to a lecture about the problems of the postmodern university on a beautiful summer evening in Vancouver! But there was a standing-room-only crowd. The questions afterward were intense and probing; the applause lengthy, and to my biased ear, enthusiastic. When I finally got away, I felt both exhilarated and exhausted. So I suggested to Claire, my wife, that we go somewhere for a drink. As I was standing at the bar ordering a beer for each of us, a beautiful, middle-aged woman, heavily decorated and richly dressed, came up, said that she had been at the lecture, and asked whether she could talk with me about it. I warmly invited her to join us, in the expectation — let me be candid — that she wanted to tell me how wonderful the lecture had been.

She began by telling her story. She had spent her entire adult life wandering about from religion to religion until, just a few years ago, she had hit on Christianity; in this she had finally found peace. The complexities of life that had haunted her all her years had found resolution in the simple truth of the gospel of Jesus Christ.

And what she wanted to tell me now was that she had found my lecture revolting, repulsive. Words failed her. The gospel was simple. I had made it complex. It doesn't *have to be* complex.

A wet towel had been slapped into my self-satisfied face! I took a long

---

This is a conference paper given at Baylor University in the 1990s.

slow drink to regain composure. "I agree," I said. "I agree that it doesn't have to be complex. But the gospel is rich. I was exploring some of its riches."

"But it doesn't *have* to be complex," she replied. "Why do people like you always think you have to make it complicated?"

"I agree with you," I said again, "it doesn't have to be complex."

"Why do you make it so complicated then? It's simple. The gospel is simple. It doesn't have to be complex."

"I already told you that I agree it doesn't have to be complex. But the gospel is not just simple; it's also rich. It's both simple and rich. And God has invited us to explore the richness."

"But it doesn't *have* to be complex."

"I didn't *say* it had to be complex. I don't *believe* it has to be complex. But. . . ."

"Why do you make it complex then? It doesn't have to be complicated."

"Look. I didn't say it had to be complex and complicated. Why don't you listen to what I said? I didn't *say* it had to be complex. I said it *didn't* have to be. I don't *believe* it has to be complex and complicated. But. . . ."

"Why do you make it so complicated then? It doesn't have to be complicated."

Then I lost my cool. I plunked my beer down, stood up, said to Claire, "Let's go," said to the woman opposite, "I'm sorry; I'm not going to talk with you anymore, you won't even pay me the respect of listening to what I say, you just keep repeating yourself," and took about two paces. Whereupon I felt terribly guilty, spun around, came back, embraced the woman — clumsily, since she was still sitting at the table — blurted out, "I embrace you as a fellow member of Christ, but I'm not going to talk with you anymore," and strode off into the darkness without a backward glance, stunned wife in tow.

It really did happen, in a bar in Vancouver. I, believing deeply in the cause of Christian learning, having spent my entire mature life in its practice and having just presented an example of my results to appreciative applause, got into an intense argument with a fellow Christian who with stubborn passion brushed aside my life's work and evening's accomplishment by insisting that learning corrupts the gospel of Christ by making the simple complicated. Christian learning is a contradiction in terms.

Christian Learning: Shaped by One's Christian Cultural Formation

Now that my temper has cooled and I've had a chance to collect my thoughts, what's my case? Best to begin with a comment on what I mean by Christian learning. The topic could be developed at considerable length; on this occasion I'll be very brief. I take it that to be a Christian is, for one thing, to acknowledge God as creator of the universe, as having dwelt among us in Jesus Christ, and as working within us in the person of the Spirit; and then to place one's faith in God as thus acknowledged. I take it that to be a Christian is, secondly, to participate in the life of the church and to make one's membership therein part of one's narrative identity — part of who one is. And I take it that to be a Christian is, thirdly, to accept the Christian scriptures as canonical. Faith of a specific sort, interwoven with identification with a specific community, interwoven with acceptance of specific scriptures as canonical — I take those things to single out Christians from other human beings. Other things as well; Christians carry the mark of baptism. But at least those three things.

To engage in Christian learning, then, is to allow that faith, that communal identification, and those scriptures, to shape one's learning. To allow them to shape one's judgments as to what is legitimate to investigate: for example, one's judgment as to whether it is legitimate to engage in research on aborted embryos. To allow them to shape one's judgments as to what is important to investigate: for example, one's judgment as to whether it is important to find out why the disparity between rich and poor in the United States has been increasing over recent decades. To allow them to shape one's convictions as to the conditions that a theory on a certain matter must satisfy if it is to be acceptable: for example, one's convictions as to whether a theory of jurisprudence is acceptable if it works entirely in terms of maximization of utility and not at all in terms of justice and rights. To allow them to shape how one treats one's fellow scholars: for example, one's willingness or unwillingness to speak abusively of men, or of women, of whites, or of blacks, of conservatives, or of liberals. To allow them to shape how one thinks about faith and church and scripture themselves. And so forth, on and on. To allow the metaphors of the psalmist, St. Paul's fruits of the Spirit, the parables told by Jesus, the narrative of Christ's resurrection, the pathos for the social outsiders preached and exemplified by the prophets, the prayers of the Eucharist, the philosophy of Augustine and Aquinas, the theology of Bonaventure and Barth, the hymns of Wesley, the paintings of Dürer and Rouault, the poetry of Milton and T. S. Eliot — to allow all of these, each in its own way, to shape one's learning, after one has oneself been formed by them. That, I say, is Christian learning. Put just a bit differently: Christian learning is faithful learning. Learning faithful to faith in the triune God, learning faithful to the Christian community and its tradition, learning faithful to the Christian scriptures.

In addition to that, it's the learning whereby one is formed by Christian faith, by the Christian community and its tradition, and by the Christian scriptures. Let me develop just a bit this point about Christian formation and the role of learning therein. Anthropologists in our century have powerfully made the point that, unlike other animals, the biological component in the make-up of us human beings is woefully insufficient for our flourishing — insufficient even for our continuing existence. If we are to survive and flourish we have to be cultured — or better, *encultured*. Our difference from other animals is not indeed total in this regard; some of them are also not hard-wired with feeding and mating habits, for example, but have to learn them from their seniors. But in the case of us human beings, our cultural programming is vast as compared to our biological hard-wiring. There must be some hard-wiring or we could not even get going in acquiring that programming which consists of our enculturation. Some writers nowadays talk as if everything about us is culture, nothing is nature; I am at a loss to explain how anyone who has given the matter even a moment's thought could think that. If there is no hard-wiring inside your computer case, then, no matter what program you try to install, nothing will happen. Yet compared to even the highest of the non-human animals, a human being's cultural programming is much more important relative to his hard-wiring in explaining why he thinks and acts, feels and imagines, as he does.

But there is no human culture in general — no human culture *allgemein*. There are only human *cultures*. The enculturation undergone by a member of the Benin tribe in West Africa in the seventeenth century was profoundly different from that which you and I have undergone. Thus it is that there is such a thing as *Christian* culture — or more precisely for my purposes here, Christian *en*-culturation. Always a person's Christian enculturation will intersect and interact with other modes of cultural formation: with twentieth-century American modes, twelfth-century Byzantine modes, and so forth. But if to be a Christian is to exhibit a specific sort of faith, to identify with a specific community, and to accept specific scriptures as canonical, then, perforce, whatever else may go into being a Christian, being a Christian will incorporate a certain identifiable cultural formation. And for the acquisition of that formation, education is indispensable. Not necessarily academic learning; but certainly education.

What we have so far then is this: Christian learning is learning *shaped* by one's Christian cultural formation, and learning that is the *medium* of one's Christian formation.

Christian Learning: A Medium for Shalom

The woman in the Vancouver bar will have spotted an opening in what I just said. I said that to be a Christian is, among other things, to be enculturated in a certain way. And I said that while Christian enculturation requires education, it does not require academic learning. Many are the devoted Christians who never brush up against academic learning. There's the opening. Stay away from it, she says. Learning isn't necessary. Those complexities which are the life-blood of academics — Jesus was ignorant of them.

On a number of occasions in my speaking and writing I have referred to what Brian Gerrish, theologian at the University of Chicago, singles out as a central theme in the theology of John Calvin. Let me put it in my own words: *To be human is to be that place in creation where God's goodness finds its answer in gratitude.* I see Christian learning as fundamentally an act of gratitude to God. The Greek word for gratitude, or thanksgiving, is *eucharistia.* Christian learning is a eucharistic act. "Oh the depth of the riches and wisdom and knowledge of God!" exclaims St. Paul. "To God be the glory forever" (Rom. 11:33, 36). One of the eucharistic acts of the Christian community — by no means its only such act, and then not of each and every member of the community but of the community as a whole — one of the eucharistic acts of the Christian community is the scholarly exploration of that richness. Out of a spirit of deep gratitude to engage in philosophy, literary criticism, sociology, or whatever, doing so *as* Christian, that is, as someone formed by Christian culture — while also allowing what one learns to correct one's Christian culture where that proves necessary. For of course that culture is itself far from perfect.

At the same time that Christian learning is a eucharistic act, it is what one might call an *eirenic* act. *Eirene* is the Greek word for peace; in the New Testament it serves as the Greek equivalent to the Hebrew word *shalom,* which in the Old Testament is probably better translated as "flourishing" than as "peace." Shalom is human flourishing, in all dimensions. My suggestion is that Christian learning contributes to our human flourishing, and that it is, in that way, an eirenic act on the part of the community at the same time that it is a eucharistic act. In the modern world one thinks immediately here of the technological benefits of learning: learning enables us to alter nature, society, and self in such a way as to enhance our flourishing — as well, let us not overlook, in such a way as to impair our flourishing! But what impresses me, a philosopher, just as much about us human beings as that we use systematically acquired knowledge to *alter* reality, is that we use such knowledge to *interpret* reality and to *answer our questions.* Indigenous to our humanity is that we do and must *interpret* reality, and do and must *ask and wonder* about reality. Indeed, so deep in our nature is this hermeneutic/interrogative component that often our inability to interpret what is happening, and our inability to answer our questions, plunges us into the pit of terror or despair. Misinterpretation and ignorance matter. Christian learning contributes to our shalom by interpreting reality and answering our questions.

What, then, about the learning that functions as the *medium* of one's cultural formation as a Christian? Is there any good reason for undergoing the long and arduous discipline required for reading the poetry of T. S. Eliot and of John Donne, for understanding the philosophy of Augustine and of Aquinas, for grasping the theology of the patristics, for looking at the paintings of Duccio and Giotto?

Well, these are my people, and yours as well — clay-footed as well as golden-tongued though they be. Americans are also your people and mine; and to be an American is likewise to be a member of a community with a cultural tradition. How impoverished our lives as Americans would be if there were no scholars among us keeping alive the memory of the tradition and helping to hand it on — helping to induct new members into the American tradition. So too for the Christian community and its tradition. How impoverished our lives as Christians would become if we all foreswore the learning that helps to keep alive and hand on that tradition which consists of the eucharistic and eirenic cultural activities of our forefathers and foremothers in the faith. And not only how culturally impoverished our own lives would become; how dishonoring of those forefathers and foremothers. I know, of course, that in America especially there is the impulse among Christians to forget the work of the hands and hearts and minds of those who have preceded us in the faith and, with New Testament in hand, to think and act as if the church began here this morning. To me this seems profoundly dishonoring of our forebears in the faith. That's not an argument, I realize. It's more like a shudder.

Christian Learning: A Public Voice for Justice

What remains to consider is what business Christian learning has in a pluralistic society. Up to this point I have not said a word about that. I have talked about becoming enculturated into the Christian community and tradition; I have talked about the learning which is the medium of that enculturation and about the learning which is shaped by that enculturation; and I have asked what reasons there are for the community to engage in such learning.

But I have done all this without taking note of the pluralistic society within which such learning, in contemporary America, takes place.

Social pluralism comes in several different forms, most of them richly exemplified in contemporary America. There is, for one thing, what one might call *institutional pluralism*. In a totalitarian society, those at the head of the society have authority to command anything of anybody; such institutions as there are in such a society gain what rights and authority they have by delegation from those who are at the head. I do not suppose that, understood in this way, there has ever been a *fully* totalitarian society; there have, though, been societies which have come rather close, including some in our own day. In any case, the United States exhibits luxuriant institutional pluralism. I would guess, in fact, that contemporary American society is as institutionally pluralistic as any society ever has been. To mention just one point: Europeans regularly find the pluralism of American education almost beyond comprehension. We do not have any Minister of Education handing down directives to all the schools in our society.

A second form of social pluralism is *ethnic pluralism*. This occurs when, within a given society, there is a diversity of *peoples* with which the members of the society identify themselves. The former Soviet Union was a better example of such pluralism than is the United States; since, though the citizenry of the United States derive from a large number of different *ethnoi*, America has been extraordinarily successful in bringing it about that after just a few generations, people no longer identify themselves as Italians, Dutch, German, or whatever, but as Americans. In the Soviet Union, by contrast, there seems to have been almost no melting down of distinct ethnic identifications.

Third, what is typical of most if not all modernized societies — and of a fair number of empires going back into antiquity — is *religious* pluralism. Or somewhat more generally, what one might call *directional* pluralism: a pluralism of embodied visions of God and the good. When Europeans first set foot on the North American continent there was no religious pluralism among them whatsoever: everybody was a dissenting Protestant. Gradually the diversity has increased, until the United States today also represents luxuriant directional pluralism: adherents of virtually all extant religions are to be found here, along with adherents of a variety of different forms of secularism.

It is this last form of pluralism on which I have my eye here: directional pluralism. The question for consideration is this: What business does Christian learning have in a society characterized by this form of pluralism? What business does it have in a directionally pluralistic society? The answer at bottom seems to me simple: beyond what I have already suggested, the business of Christian learning in our pluralistic society is to give content to the Christian voice in that dialogue which ought to be taking place in the public square of American society.

Not so long ago, most Christians would have given a different answer. America has been dominantly shaped by the liberal vision of society, according to which public life, in a society that incorporates diverse visions of God and the good, should be grounded on and legitimated by principles that are neutral as among all those diverse visions. It should be grounded on and legitimated by, so it was traditionally held, the deliverances of human reason. Traditionally those deliverances were thought to include not only basic human morality but also the rudiments of theism; since theism, so it was held, could be rationally defended on the basis of evidence. What was excluded from the public sphere was so-called "sectarian" religion. Sectarian religion belongs to the private sphere; what belongs in the public sphere is such theism and morality as can be delivered by the reason that we share alike as normal adult human beings. Recall those famous words from the founding of our nation: "We hold these truths to be self-evident." Throughout the nineteenth century and for roughly the first half of the twentieth, many if not most Christian colleges and universities saw it as an important part of their contribution to the public good to articulate for their students the rational case for the truth of theism and of basic human values.

I tell you nothing you do not already know when I tell you that this vision no longer carries conviction. We all feel in our bones that we are not only undergoing a revolution in our understanding of the academy but a revolution in our understanding of how to live together in a religiously pluralist society. Our Civil War tested severely the conviction that we Americans all agree on a set of moral and religious principles thick enough to orient and legitimate our public life together; if I read my history correctly, however, it did not destroy that conviction. The destruction occurred later, perhaps during the last twenty-five years or so. Today there are hardly any believers any more. Hardly anybody any longer believes that the thick body of principles we once all shared were the deliverances of reason; they were the remnants of our Christian tradition. There are today a fair number of Americans who would like to reinstall the religious and moral principles of that once-upon-a-time common faith as the principles used by all of us for legitimating and orienting our public life; some are very noisy about it. Among their strategies is the attempt to get the public schools once again to inculcate those principles. But they too are under no illusion that we Americans do in fact still have a common faith of which those principles are the content.

So what to do in this new situation? What else, than for our various communities to engage in civil discourse in the public square, presenting to each other their diverse visions of a just, peaceful, and prosperous society, listening to each other, submitting to correction, and working out ad hoc agreements that satisfy the procedures and conditions specified by our Constitution and our common law? In that conversation in the public square there must be a Christian voice, by which I mean a voice that speaks not just for the welfare of Christians — though I do not downplay the importance of that — but a voice that speaks the healing word of the Christian gospel for all: a healing word about the collapse of our families, about our preoccupation with drugs and sex and violence, about the incivility of our public discourse, about our growing indifference if not hostility to the rest of the world, about our idolization of wealth. If that Christian voice in the public square is to have any profundity, if it is to be an informed voice addressing in depth and with imagination the issues of the day, not just a shrill and strident voice, if it is to have integrity and wholeness, it will require Christian learning. Indeed, though without Christian learning there may be *Christians* speaking in the public square, there will not be a Christian *voice*. The Christians speaking will be speaking in someone else's voice, expressing some alternative vision of God and the good. What they say will come from somewhere, not from nowhere; somebody will provide them with the thoughts they express about poverty and wealth, business and entertainment, poetry and philosophy, crime and freedom. And behind those thoughts — be assured — there will lie a great deal of learning. But if the learning follows the beat of a different drummer, the voice will not be a Christian voice.

Some in the square will want to talk only about the interests of their own group; others will want to talk only about utility maximization. The Christian will insist on speaking of justice. When he does so, he will have in mind primarily the inclusive justice proclaimed by the Bible and articulated by the Christian tradition — justice for the widows, the orphans, the impoverished, the aliens. He will show how justice thus understood applies to contemporary society. And he will do his best to evoke in his fellow conversationalists the desire for such justice — doing so with a mixture of realism and idealism: the realism of recognizing that it is not unlikely that he will fail in his attempt to evoke that desire, the idealism of believing that sometimes he will succeed. If there is to be that voice on behalf of biblical justice, there must be Christian learning. I give this as just one example of what the Christian voice will be saying in the discussion that takes place in the public square of polity and academy.

I admit that it is quite possible the discussion will never take place. The void caused by the decay of the conviction that our public life in academy and polity can and should be grounded on a thick body of principles neutral as among all religions is now being filled by angry abusive talk and naked struggles for power. It may be that things will remain this way. It may be that we Americans will never again engage, to any significant degree, in civil public dialogue as representatives of different visions of God and the good. If so, today is the beginning of our end. But if the dialogue does take place, authentically Christian learning will prove indispensable for a Christian voice in that dialogue. Without that learning, the words of Christians may be shrill and loud; but the voice will be that of someone else. The healing word and persuasive power implicit in the Christian message will never be heard or experienced. Let me add that not only will Christian learning be necessary, but Christian virtues as well — especially the virtue of honoring the image of God in the other by conversing with her and not just shouting at her, by honoring her claim to shalom, and by forever drawing the line at those things that may never under any circumstance be done to her or any other creature who images God.

Embracing Our Long Disputes

I rest my case. Would the woman in the Vancouver bar concede? I rather doubt it. Which leads me to mention one more thing that goes into being a Christian. To be a Christian is not only to embrace the consensus of the community but to own the disputes of the community. What she and I were so passionately arguing about on that summer evening has been a topic of dispute in the Christian community for almost two millennia. The dispute characterizes the community. To be a Christian is to care about the progress of that dispute and its outcome.

But I will never know. I was in no mood to ask her for her business card.

Should the Work of Our Hands Have
Standing in the Christian College?

I propose on this occasion reversing the customary order of academic lectures by leading off with my conclusion. Such dramatic tension as there may be will have to come from not knowing how I'm going to get to where I'm going rather than from not knowing where I am going. But first, a true story.

A Philosophical Consultation

It was about twenty years ago now that I received a call from the personnel manager of the Herman Miller Corporation, asking whether I would be willing to come to their head offices in Zeeland, Michigan, to spend a day as a consultant. I can assure you, in case you have ever wondered, that philosophers are not often asked to serve as consultants. It is, admittedly, not entirely unheard of. A few years back an unemployed philosopher in Amsterdam opened a philosophical consulting service on the premise that many of the problems people experience in modern life are best addressed not by psychological, vocational, or pastoral counseling, but by philosophical counseling. They have logical problems, ontological problems, axiological problems, epistemological problems, and so forth. I understand that he has been a considerable success. But that's the Dutch for you! All in all, it is a rare experience for a philosopher to be asked to serve as counselor or consultant — especially rare to be asked to serve as a consultant to a business enterprise.

I accepted, partly because I was intrigued and partly — let me be candid

---

This essay was originally a book chapter in *Keeping Faith: Embracing the Tensions in Christian Higher Education,* edited by Ronald A. Wells (Grand Rapids: Eerdmans, 1996), pp. 133-51. It is reprinted here with permission.

— because the fee offered made me understand instantly why those who can consult do consult. It turned out that there were five of us consultants from around the country: a journalist, a lawyer, a physician employed by NASA, a free-lance furniture designer, and myself, a philosopher. We met with five or six of the head people at Herman Miller, including Max De Pree, who was then CEO of the company. Max led off the discussion by saying that twice a year he and some of his chief executives took a day out from their regular work to stand back and reflect with a small group of people on what they were doing at Herman Miller. It had been their experience, he said, that a reflective retreat of this sort was important for keeping the big picture in mind. Max said that he had written down ten questions for our discussion. He did not care in what order we discussed them, nor even whether we actually got around to all ten of them. But these ten were on his mind. We, the consultants, were not to concern ourselves with how our discussion might be useful to the company; we were to let the discussion flow. The people from the company would decide what to do with what was said.

Let me mention three of the questions that De Pree posed to us; they will give the flavor of the whole. What is the purpose of business? he asked. Some of his young executives were saying that the purpose of business is to make money. He himself did not believe that; but he would like us to discuss it. Second, is there a moral imperative to good design? Ever since the thirties, Herman Miller had been committed to good and innovative furniture design. Should that commitment to good design continue, on the ground that good design is a moral imperative, or is good design a dispensable option? And third, is growth compatible with intimacy? The company had always striven for intimacy among its employees. Its rapid growth in recent years, and the pressure of its stockholders for even more growth, was forcing it to ask whether growth is compatible with intimacy.

The breadth and depth of the questions took me completely aback. I, as a philosopher, had expected to be like a fish out of water for a day. This was not only water, but *my* water. These were philosophical qustions. I have no memory of what I said. I cannot believe that it proved of much use to Herman Miller, since the issues Max posed were not ones that I had then thought much about. But I remember enjoying the day enormously. I think back to it often. In a number of ways it proved a watershed for me — for example, in my thinking about Christian higher education.

Let me explain. Notice what took place on that day. We were not asked to advise Herman Miller on one or another technological or bureaucratic problem facing it. Nor were we asked to help Herman Miller think through some moral quandary in which it found itself. Truth is, we were not asked to think very specifically about Herman Miller at all; Herman Miller was more illustration than topic. We were asked to stand back and think about one of the major social formations in contemporary society, namely business. We were asked to reflect on the purpose of business and on the imperatives that hold for it. In a word, we were asked to engage in normative reflection on business. Our reflection was meant to aid the normative discrimination of those who operated Herman Miller — to aid them in discriminating between what they ought to say Yes to and what they ought to say No to.

Beyond Liberal Arts: Social Formation

Now for my proposal. The Christian college and university should, among other things, be a place where the Christian community does its thinking about the major social formations of contemporary society — its normative and strategic thinking. It would be acceptable to call the thinking in question *critical thinking*. The Christian college and university, among other things, should be a place where the Christian community does its critical thinking about the major social formations of contemporary society — provided that critical thinking is not understood as just negative thinking, and provided that it is understood as going beyond mere evaluation. For the thinking I propose about our contemporary social formations will be neither purely negative nor purely positive. It will neither laud business to the skies nor condemn it to Sheol; it will neither praise American politics unstintingly nor criticize it unrelievedly. It will exhibit and cultivate normative discrimination. And it will go on to ask how what is good can be preserved and what is wrong, changed. In saying this, I understand myself to be expressing the classic Calvinist attitude toward social formations and institutions: the Christian pronounces not just a Yes on such formations nor just a No, but a discriminating Yes and No. Critical appreciation, appreciative criticism. That done, the Christian then struggles to act redemptively.

In being a place where the Christian community does its normative and strategic thinking about the major social formations of our society, the Christian college that I envisage will be more than just a liberal arts college. Lest you draw the wrong conclusions, let me go on to say that it will be at least that. It will be a place where students are introduced to that great stream of culture which flows down to us from other times and other places, and it will be a place where students are introduced to the results and inducted into the practices of the academic disciplines.

There are features of the tradition of liberal arts education which make the person imbued with the Reformed ethos of Christianity uneasy with that tradition, however. The Reformed Christian will feel uneasy with the pretensions to neutrality so characteristic of the tradition; likewise she will feel uneasy with the elitism so characteristic of the tradition — with its claims to superiority. On many other occasions I have developed the first point; on this occasion let me develop the second.

In liberal arts education one cultivates the mind — using "mind" here in a sense close to that of the German word *Geist*. And from Plato to Aristotle onward the conviction has never lacked for enthusiastic supporters that the fundamental reason for engaging in the liberal arts, when and where that is possible, is that the life of the mind is the highest form of life available to a human being. Those who emphasized engaging in the academic disciplines have typically said that contemplative thinking is the noblest of all human activities. Those who emphasized induction into high culture have typically said that to expand the scope of one's enculturation by appropriating the culture of those distant in time and space is to become more fully human.[1] Either way, the life of the mind is the highest form of human life.

Plato and Aristotle differed in their assessment of civic life, this to be distinguished both from the life of the mind and from ordinary life. Plato saw in the life of the citizen nothing but instrumental worth; Aristotle saw it as having inherent worth. Though inferior to the life of the mind it is, said Aristotle, an indispensable component in the good life as a whole. In their assessment of ordinary life, however, Plato and Aristotle were in full agreement: its worth is purely instrumental. Neither the life of the mind nor the life of the citizen is possible without ordinary life. But a life that consists entirely of ordinary life, a life that includes no life of the mind and no civic life, is not a good life. And a society in which everybody's life consists entirely of ordinary life is not even a true state, or polis, says Aristotle. For "the end of the state is not mere life; it is, rather, a good quality of life. [If mere life were the end], there might be a state of slaves, or even a state of animals; but in the world as we know it any such state is impossible, because slaves and ani-

---

1. Cf. Michael Oakeshott, *Voice of Liberal Learning* (New Haven: Yale University Press, 1989), p. 71: "Education is not learning to do this or that more proficiently; it is acquiring in some measure an understanding of a human condition in which the 'fact of life' is continuously illuminated by a 'quality of life.' It is learning how to be at once an autonomous and civilized subscriber to a human life." And p. 79: In liberal education we do not "attribute an extrinsic 'purpose' to the engagement in which [students] acquire a human character; 'being human' here is recognized not as a means to an end (i.e. living with other human beings), but as a condition for which it is meaningless to ask for a justification in respect of human beings. What else should they be?"

mals do not share in true felicity and free choice."[2] They do not "contemplate the order of things," they do not "deliberate about moral excellence," they do not "deliberate together about the common good, and decide how to shape and apply the laws."[3] Charles Taylor, in his book *Sources of the Self,* nicely summarizes the tradition in these words:

> The influential ideas of ethical hierarchy exalted the lives of contemplation and participation. We can see a manifestation of the first in the notion that philosophers should not busy themselves with the mere manipulation of things, and hence with the crafts. This was one source of resistance to the new experimental science which Bacon advocated. Scholarly humanism was imbued with this hierarchical notion, which was also linked to a distinction between the true sciences, which admitted of demonstration, and lower forms of knowledge, which could only hope to attain to the "probable," in the sense the words had then, e.g., the forms of knowledge practised by alchemists, astrologers, miners, and some physicians.
>
> We see the second idea returning in early modern times with the various doctrines of civic humanism, first in Italy and later in Northern Europe. Life as a mere householder is inferior to one which also involves participation as a citizen. There is a kind of freedom citizens enjoy which others are deprived of.[4]

The Protestant Reformation, and in particular, the Calvinist branch thereof, represents a radical rejection of this scale of values in which the life of the mind is elevated over that of the citizen, in which both modes of life are elevated over ordinary life, and in which the work of our hands is regarded as having no more than instrumental value. Let me briefly develop this point with the aid of the chapter in Taylor's book that he calls "'God Loveth Adverbs'" — in my judgment easily the best chapter in the book.

Taylor explains ordinary life as "those aspects of human life concerned with production and reproduction, that is, labour, the making of the things needed for life, and our life as sexual beings, including marriage and the family."[5] It was these, he remarks, that Aristotle classified as life when he invidi-

2. Aristotle, *Politics,* translated by Ernest Barker (Oxford: Oxford University Press, 1946), III, ix, 5, 1280a.

3. Quoted phrases are taken from Charles Taylor, *Sources of the Self: The Making of Modern Identity* (Cambridge: Harvard University Press, 1989), pp. 211-12.

4. Taylor, *Sources of the Self,* p. 212.

5. Taylor, *Sources of the Self,* p. 211.

ously contrasted life with the good life. And it was these that the Reformers, for the first time in the history of the West, bestowed with inherent and not just instrumental worth — provided they were done to the glory of God and the good of the human community.

> What was previously stigmatized as lower is now exalted as the standard, and the previously higher is convicted of presumption and vanity. . . . This involved a revaluation of professions as well. The lowly artisan and artificer turn out to have contributed more to the advance of science than the leisured philosopher. And indeed, an inherent bent toward social levelling is implicit in the affirmation of ordinary life. The centre of the good life lies now in something which everyone can have a part in, rather than in ranges of activity which only a leisured few can do justice to.[6]

This affirmation of holy worldliness was most vigorously expressed in the writings of the English Puritans. Let me cite some representative passages. John Dod says,

> Whatsoever our callings be, we serve the Lord Christ in them. . . . Though your worke be base, yet it is not a base thing to serve such a master in it. They are the most worthy servants, whatsoever their imploiment bee, that do with most conscionable, and dutifull hearts and minds, serve the Lord, where hee hath placed them, in those works, which hee hath allotted unto them.[7]

William Perkins makes the same point in these words:

> Now if we compare worke to worke, there is a difference betwixt washing of dishes, and preaching of the word of God: but as touching to please God none at all. . . . As the Scriptures call him carnall which is not renewed by the spirit and borne again in Christs flesh and all his workes likewise . . . whatsoever he doth, though they seem spirituall and after the law of God never so much. So contrariwise he is spirituall which is renewed in Christ, and all his workes which spring from faith seeme they

6. Taylor, *Sources of the Self,* pp. 213-14.
7. Quoted in Taylor, *Sources of the Self,* p. 223. Taylor in turn is quoting from Charles H. George and Katherine George, *The Protestant Mind of the English Reformation: 1570-1640* (Princeton: Princeton University Press, 1961).

never so grosse . . . yea deedes of matrimonie are pure and spirituall . . . and whatsoever is done within the lawes of God though it be wrought by the body, as the wipings of shoes and such like, howsoever grosse they appears outwardly, yet are they sanctified.[8]

And here is how Joseph Hall makes the point:

The homeliest service that we doe in an honest calling, though it be but to plow, or digge, if done in obedience, and conscience of God's Commandment, is crowned with an ample reward; whereas the best workes for their kinde (preaching, praying, offering Evangelicall sacrifices) if without respect of God's injunction and glory, are loaded with curses. God loveth adverbs; and cares not how good, but how well.[9]

Thomas Aquinas, in explaining his claim that "the liberal arts excel the mechanical arts," had said that the mechanical arts are "works done by the body, which arts are, in a fashion, servile, inasmuch as the body is in servile subjection to the soul, [whereas] man, as regards his soul, is free (*liber*)" (*Summa Theologiae* I'II, q. 3, obj. 3 & ad. 3). Here, by contrast, is a passage from the Puritan Thomas Adams:

Every one thinkes himselfe Gods sonne: then heare this voyce, Goe my sonne. You have all your vineyards to goe to. Magistrates Goe to the bench to execute judgement and justice. Ministers Goe to the Temple, to preach, to pray, to doe the workes of Evangelists. People Goe to your callings, that you may eate the labours of your owne hands: Eye to thy seeing, eare to thy hearing, foote to thy walking, hand to thy working . . . every man to his profession, according to that station, wherein God hath disposed us. . . . The Incitation gives way to the Injunction, worke.[10]

---

8. Quoted in Taylor, *Sources of the Self*, p. 224. Compare this passage from Perkins: "Now the works of every calling, when they are performed in an holy manner, are done in faith and obedience, and serve notably for Gods glory, be the calling never so base. . . . The meanenesse of the calling, doth not abase the goodnesse of the worke: for God looketh not at the excellence of the worke, but at the heart of the worker. And the action of a sheepheard in keeping sheep, performed as I have said, in his kind, is as good a worke before God, as is the action of a judge, in giving sentence or of a Magistrate in ruling, or a Minister in preaching." Quoted in George and George, *The Protestant Mind of the English Reformation*, p. 138.

9. Quoted in Taylor, *Sources of the Self*, p. 224.

10. Quoted in George and George, *The Protestant Mind of the English Reformation*, pp. 131-32.

If these passages express the consensus of the tradition — and surely they do — then whatever be the justification that a college in the Reformed tradition of Christianity offers for engaging in the liberal arts, that justification will abjure any suggestion that the life of the mind is nobler than the work of our hands. Conversely, such a college will neither dismiss proposals for educational programs beyond the liberal arts by arguing that such programs are inherently inferior, nor admit such judgments and then, on the ground of their supposed inferiority, treat them as second-class citizens within the college. A college in the Reformed tradition of Christianity will not look down on the work of our hands.

Obviously no college can be all things to all people; all should avoid even trying. If one does not dismiss educational programs that go beyond the liberal arts on the ground that they are one and all inherently inferior, how then does one choose among them? How does one discriminate?

Beyond Developing Christian Minds: The Work of Our Hands

It is endemic in those engaged in the liberal arts to interpret the appearance of anything beyond the liberal arts in their college as the consequence of the college administration in craven fashion caving in to outside pressures. I do not doubt that college administrators do exhibit a good deal of craven caving in — though I have never been able to bring myself to believe that they have even a near-monopoly on this human failing. Nevertheless, I do agree with the assumption of the critics that it is not an appropriate principle of selection, for adding programs beyond the liberal arts, to do so when and as one's constituency demands it or one's survival requires it.

What then is an appropriate principle? I suggest that the decision should always be made on the basis of the following two considerations: how important are the goals of the proposed program, and does the program utilize one's strengths as a college with liberal arts at its core? Let me say a word about both the importance and the propriety of the expansion of the college's program that I am proposing. First, though, a word about the sort of expansion that I have in mind.

I propose that the Christian college become a place where the Christian community does its normative and strategic thinking about (some of) the major social formations of our society, such as business, church, politics, media, medicine, education, law, and art and architecture. Students should be inducted into such thinking. But what I envisage goes beyond the teaching of students. The college should be a place where those already engaged as leaders in those social formations come apart for a while to do such thinking together — joined by some of the faculty who, though not leaders in those formations, are affected by, and informed about, them.

Why do I think such normative and strategic thinking important? Let me give two reasons. One is a theological reason characteristic of the Reformed tradition; the other is a reason based on analysis of the dynamics of contemporary society.

As I suggested earlier, it has been typical of the Reformed tradition of Christianity to regard not only persons as religiously fallen and sinful but social institutions as well; and to regard the Christian as called to work redemptively for the healing of these institutions. It is this combination of convictions that accounts for that reformist and revolutionary impulse of the Calvinist tradition that Michael Walzer explored in his book, *The Revolution of the Saints*. In contrast to the conviction of so many Christians in America, the Reformed Christian has never believed that America is a Christian nation and that, accordingly, our social institutions and formations, though blemished here and there, are fundamentally in accord with God's will. But neither has she agreed with those Christians who hold that our social institutions and formations are fundamentally corrupt and that the duty of the Christian is to withdraw. Normative discrimination is what she has always regarded as the appropriate stance, coupled with the attempt, once the discrimination has been made, to change what is wrong when that proves possible, to keep discontent alive when change proves not possible, and always to be grateful for what is good. In short, to act redemptively. While praying the prayer, "Thy kingdom come," to join God's cause of struggling against all that resists and falls short of God's will and longing for creation, thus to acknowledge the rightful, and ultimately effective, rule of Jesus Christ over every square inch of creation.

One serves God and humanity in one's daily occupation; that was ringingly affirmed in those passages I quoted from the Puritans. But one does not serve God and humanity by going into business and then just playing the received role of businessman, nor by going into medicine and then just playing the received role of physician, nor by going into the academy and then just playing the received role of the academic. For those received roles are religiously fallen — not fallen through and through, but nonetheless fallen. To serve God faithfully and to serve humanity effectively, one has to critique the received role and do what one can to alter the script. There is a great deal of discussion nowadays about medical ethics, legal ethics, business ethics, and so forth. While often participating in these discussions, the Reformed Christian will also want to bracket most of them. For most of them take for granted the present social formations of medicine, law, and business, and then worry about the ethical quandaries that arise for those who act within those formations. The Reformed Christian will want to step back, as Max De Pree did, to ask what is the purpose of business.

My reason of social analysis, for regarding as important such normative and strategic reflection as I am proposing, goes as follows. I think it is true, historically, that the fundamental principles that legitimated and oriented action within the major social institutions and formations here in America were heavily influenced by Christianity. It was always much too simplistic and undiscriminating to say that they just were Christian principles — and that we were, in that way, a Christian country. There were always influences at work in shaping those principles that were alien to Christianity. But Christianity was an important influence; of that there can be no doubt. That is less and less the case, however — for two reasons, as I see it. For one thing, America is now much more religiously diverse than it was at its founding. At its founding, Protestant Christianity enjoyed near hegemony; that is now a thing of the past. But second, the intelligentsia of American society are now much more indifferent and hostile to institutional religion, and especially to institutional Christianity, than is the society at large. And the intelligentsia play a role out of all proportion to their numbers in shaping our major social formations — they especially play a role out of all proportion to their numbers in setting the course of media, education, and the arts.

It follows that an educated and self-consciously Christian voice in the shaping of these social formations is becoming more and more necessary. I judge that the social discontent so evident among many Christians in American society is due to their intuitive realization that the received principles shaping our major social formations are no longer satisfactory to the Christian. There has been a slippage, and that slippage is now widely perceived. Unless there are educated Christian voices and hands within these formations, that slippage will continue.

Those of us who have been defenders of Christian liberal arts education have of course never believed that what we teach our students is good only for the life of the mind. We have neither thought nor said that only for academics is it of benefit to their professional lives, and that only for their leisure time is it of benefit to those who work with their hands. We have believed, and told all who would listen, that it is of benefit to the physician in her work, to the businessman in his work, to the clergyman in his work, to the lawyer in her work, and so forth. But it has also been characteristic of us to leave in vapors of vagueness what exactly that benefit might be and how exactly it is produced. Every now and then we invite back to campus some graduate who has become successful in politics or whatever to testify, at commencement or convocation, about the relevance of his liberal arts education to his present work. But such talks, in my experience, are rather more productive of heat than light — and of smoke than heat! I do not myself doubt that there really is benefit of the sort claimed — though I would prefer not being asked to pinpoint it!

A presupposition of my case today is that we can do much better, in developing the normative and strategic reflection I am calling for, than just induct people into the academic disciplines or the tradition of high culture and then send them out on their own. The normative and strategic issues I have in mind are thick and complex; witness the complexity of what is happening today in American politics! They require sustained thought. A program of liberal arts education is not aimed at providing that sustained thought; it is aimed at something else. And while the liberal education of those immersed in leadership positions in our major social formations certainly does give them some of the fundamental equipment necessary for engaging in that sustained thought, they do not have the time actually to engage in it while on the job. You will all have sensed how extraordinary was the policy of the Herman Miller Corporation, of having a reflective retreat of its top executives twice a year. But one day twice a year, though certainly better than nothing, does not take one far. I myself judge that what has led to the sprouting of think tanks all over New York City, Washington, D.C., and the Bay Area, is the felt need for sustained normative and strategic thought about our major social formations, especially that of politics. Those think tanks suffer, in my judgment, from their isolation from the liberal arts. And very few are devoted to developing a Christian voice.

In short, normative and strategic Christian reflection on our major social institutions is an obligation of the Christian community and a need of our society. I judge that there is no better place to cultivate such reflection than in the Christian liberal arts college.

I envisage the day when reflective Christians active in the major social formations of our society look to the Christian colleges of the land as a place where they can get together on a regular basis and in the context of worship, Bible study, and recollection of the Christian tradition, engage in normative and strategic reflection on the issues of direction and orientation that confront them. It will be a place where they can safely express their nagging doubts and haunting guilt. It will be a place where they can practice the realization that disagreement is not always evil and consensus not always all: a place where they can learn the Christian ethos of disagreement in which one honors a person in the midst of disagreeing with her, sometimes even honors her *by* disagreeing with her. A place where they can be expanded in their thinking by engagement of the Christian tradition, and where they can learn to own the disagreements of that tradition along with its consensus. There will be short-term conferences, longer-term symposia, and study centers. Expectations will be modest but genuine. Realistic idealism will be the mood. Rarely will participants talk of "transforming" American society; they will be content to make a difference. Sometimes not even that will be possible; then they will work to keep discontent alive. For we live in the expectant hope that God will some day take those differences and that discontent and effect the transformation. Fidelity to the God revealed in Jesus Christ, celebration of the glimpses of what is good, and lament for the suffering and waywardness of the world, will be what moves the participants. The liberal arts faculty of the college will be intimately involved. And students who look forward to working in one or another of these social formations will see their future before them, just as I saw mine before me when I was witness to the thought and work of my professors. They will be inducted into that company of reflective, committed, perplexed, fallible, worshipping men and women who are struggling to think with Christian minds, feel with Christian hearts, and work with Christian hands, within the social formations of contemporary America.

> Let the favor of the Lord our God be upon us,
>   and prosper for us the work of our hands —
> O prosper the work of our hands!

> (Psalm 90:17)

275

What Is the Reformed Perspective on Christian Higher Education?

I have been asked to characterize the Reformed pespective on Christian higher education, in contrast to the Catholic, the Lutheran, and so forth. The word "Reformed," used as an adjectival modifier in such phrases as "Reformed perspective," "Reformed tradition," and "Reformed Christianity," is not common in this country. It's been my experience that to use the adjective without explanation is to produce puzzlement in many audiences. Does it have something to do with prisons? Or perhaps with homes for wayward youth?

"The" Reformed Tradition

Let me begin then with an explanation. So-called "magisterial" Protestantism of the sixteenth century came in two main forms. One was the Lutheran; the other was that which sprang forth, more or less independently of the Lutheran reform, from various of the Swiss cities, especially Geneva and Zurich. The tradition of Protestant Christianity which traces itself to these latter origins is the one that I and others have in mind when we speak of "the Reformed tradition." In Scotland and England the churches who traced themselves to the Swiss reform came to be known as "Presbyterian"; on the continent they were invariably known as "Reformed."

Though the dominant reformer within the tradition of reform originating in the Swiss cities was, of course, John Calvin, the Reformed tradition must not be thought of as just "Calvinistic." Calvin's influence was massive; but it did not, by any means, overwhelm all other influences. When it came

---

This essay appeared previously as "Christian Education in Reformed Perspective" in *Lutheran Education* 134, no. 3 (Jan./Feb. 1999): 129-40. It is reprinted here with permission.

to certain aspects of the liturgy of the Reformed churches, for example, Zwingli was more influential than Calvin.

A prominent feature of the Reformed tradition, as manifested around the globe over these intervening centuries, is its radical decentralization. There is a World Alliance of Reformed Churches; it happens to be the largest international Protestant body. But the locus of authority in Reformed Christianity has always been the local congregation. In American Congregationalism such "decentralization" has taken the form of resistance to the delegation of any significant authority at all to larger denominational structures; in my own denomination, the Christian Reformed Church, congregations have delegated a fair amount of authority to the central denomination. But whatever the differences among Reformed denominations in this regard, the situation, as my words suggest, is that whatever authority the central denominational body may possess has been *delegated* to it by the congregations. And incidentally, it is indeed *congregations* that are the basic ecclesiastical unit in Reformed Christianity, not individuals.

The relevance for my purposes, in this essay, of this point about the decentralized character of Reformed Christianity, is that not only is there no such thing as *the* Reformed view of Christian higher education: there is not even any such thing as *the official* Reformed view. One can pick out certain dominant themes and emphases; that is what I will try to do. But for almost any of these, one could find significant figures within the tradition who would not accept those themes and emphases.

Shortly I will explain how I propose to cope, in this essay, with this messy diversity. But before I get to that, let me articulate a theme which — I will be so bold as to claim — is dominant within all branches of the tradition. Virtually any person who thinks about higher education in a self-consciously Reformed way will do so within the framework of a certain general view about the relation of the Christian to society and culture. Specifically, it is typical of those in the Reformed tradition to think about society and culture in terms of what I shall call "Three Cities." I mean here to allude to Augustine's "Two Cities." The Reformed tradition is deeply Augustinian. Yet one will not understand that tradition unless one sees it as having significantly modified Augustine's pattern of thought, so that the basic pattern is not that of two cities but three.

Augustine's two cities were the city of God and the city of the world — *civitas dei* and *civitas mundi*. Or as he sometimes called them, speaking metaphorically, Jerusalem and Babylon. These cities, these communities, these solidarities, are defined by two loves. "Two loves have created these two cities," says Augustine, "namely, self-love to the extent of despising God, the earthly city; love of God to the extent of despising one's self, the heavenly city. The former glories in itself, the latter in God. For the former seeks the glory of men, while to the latter, God . . . is the greatest glory. . . . The former, dominated by the lust of sovereignty, boasts of its princes or of the nations which it may bring under subjection; in the latter, men serve one another in charity — the rulers by their counsel, the subjects by their obedience."[1]

I spent my undergraduate days as a student in a college within the Reformed tradition — specifically, at Calvin College, sponsored by the Christian Reformed Church, a denomination within the tradition of Dutch Reformed Christianity. One of my charismatic teachers was William Harry Jellema. Jellema very much saw himself as an Augustinian; he tirelessly presented to us students the Augustinian theme of two cities. It is now clear to me, however, that Jellema — along with virtually everybody else in the Reformed tradition — had departed from Augustine on a significant point. He would have been extremely reluctant to concede that he had departed from his beloved Augustine. But he had. For Jellema thought in terms of *three* cities, or communities, or solidarities, not two. The city of God and the city of the world, indeed; but also the city of our common humanity — call it, the *civitas gentium*. The Reformed tradition is a three-city tradition. A good many of the discussions and disputes within the tradition have been over how those three cities are related to each other.

I submit that much closer to the thought of the Reformed tradition than the passage from Augustine that I quoted is this passage from the "Letter to Diognetus," coming to us from apostolic times:

> The distinction between Christians and other men is neither in country nor language nor customs. For they do not dwell in cities in some place of their own, nor do they use any strange variety of dialect, nor practice an extraordinary kind of life. . . . Yet, while living in Greek and barbarian cities, according as each obtained his lot, and following the local customs, both in clothing and food and in the rest of life, they show forth the wonderful and confessedly strange character of the constitution of their own citizenship. They dwell in their own fatherlands, but as if sojourners in them; they share all things as citizens, and suffer all things as if strangers. Every foreign country is their fatherland, and every fatherland is as if a foreign country.[2]

1. Augustine, *City of God*, edited and translated by R. W. Dyson (Cambridge: Cambridge University Press, 1998), XIV, 28.

2. "Letter to Diognetus," in *The Apostolic Fathers*, edited and translated by K. Lake, Loeb Classical Library (Cambridge: Harvard University Press, 1976).

The citizens of the *civitas dei* participate along with the citizens of the *civitas mundi* in the structures, solidarities, and practices of the city they share, the *civitas genus.*

I mentioned above that I would shortly be proposing a way of coping, for the purposes of our discussion, with the decentralized character of Reformed Christianity. A looming figure in the Dutch Reformed Church around the turn of the last century was Abraham Kuyper. Kuyper was master of astonishingly many trades: theologian, journalist, politician, Prime Minister, platform speaker, founder of institutions, university professor. What I shall do is present to you the basic outlines of the Kuyperian perspective on Christian higher education. That was the perspective which dominantly shaped, and continues to shape, Calvin College. More relevantly, when people in our country speak nowadays about "the Reformed perspective on Christian higher education," what they usually have in mind is the Kuyperian perspective. How it has come about that the Kuyperian perspective is now generally viewed as *the* Reformed perspective is a question I will leave to historians to tackle. It will become evident, without my making a point of it, that Kuyper was very much a "three cities" thinker.

Kuyper's thoughts about education — in this regard he very much fits my description of the tradition as a whole — were set within the context of his thoughts about society and culture generally. In fact, those thoughts constitute the core of his thought as a whole; Kuyper was what would nowadays be called a "public theologian."

Let me summarize, in a more or less formulaic way, the core of Kuyper's thought about society and culture. Christians, he said, are called to speak with a Christian voice, and to act out of Christian conviction, within the structures, solidarities, and practices of our common humanity. So as to nourish and sustain such speaking and acting, Christians need their own institutional base. In speaking with a Christian voice and acting out of Christian conviction within the structures, solidarities, and practices of our common humanity, Christians will find themselves in one and another sort of tension and conflict with those who speak with different convictions within those shared structures, solidarities, and practices.

A comment or two about these formulaic statements is in order. Speaking with a Christian voice and acting out of Christian conviction is not confined to churchly affairs, leaving one to speak with some other sort of convictions when engaged in the affairs of everyday life; but neither is it something that one only does in structures, solidarities, and practices unique to Christians. It is something one does within *our common human* structures, solidarities, and practices. It is within our shared state and economy, within our shared practice of scholarship, and so forth, that one is called to speak with a Christian voice and to act out of Christian conviction. If this is to happen, a distinct institutional base is required. The Christian college and university is part of such an institutional base.

Theological Themes Shaping a Reformed Vision

Let me bring to the surface six theological themes that constitute the background to this vision of Christian existence. Most of these themes will be characteristic of the Reformed tradition in general, not just of Kuyper.

A Good Creation

First of all, there is a strong emphasis within the Reformed tradition in general, and within its Kuyperian version in particular, on God the Creator. God created a world which God pronounced good — good, in particular, for human beings. God's intent was that we would flourish, that we would find our *shalom*, in this world. And in spite of the incursions of evil into this created order, God has not abandoned the creation; on the contrary, Christ's resurrection is the vindication of the created order.

Kuyper works out the "non-abandonment" of the creation order in two ways. For one thing, in his doctrine of providence. Part of God's providence is to work within humanity so that, in spite of the incursions of evil into the created order, God's creational purposes will still, to some extent, be achieved. Thus there is, says Kuyper, not only God's redemptive grace but God's common grace. In this regard Kuyper echoes, in his own way, the tradition of Clement of Alexandria — a tradition that also comes to the fore in a famous and influential passage from Calvin's *Institutes*. Perhaps it is worth having part of that passage before us:

> Whenever we come upon these matters in secular writers, let that admirable light of truth shining in them teach us that the mind of man, though fallen and perverted from its wholeness, is nevertheless clothed and ornamented with God's excellent gifts. If we regard the Spirit of God as the sole fountain of truth, we shall neither reject the truth itself, nor despise it wherever it shall appear, unless we wish to dishonor the Spirit of God. For by holding the gifts of the Spirit in slight esteem, we condemn and reproach the Spirit himself. What then? Shall we deny that the

truth shone upon the ancient jurists who established civic order and discipline with such great equity? Shall we say that the philosophers were blind in their fine observation and artful description of nature? Shall we say that those men were devoid of understanding who conceived the art of disputation and taught us to speak reasonably? Shall we say that they are insane who developed medicine, devoting their labor to our benefit? What shall we say of all the mathematical sciences? Shall we consider them the ravings of madmen? No, we cannot read the writings of the ancients on these subjects without great admiration. We marvel at them because we are compelled to recognize how pre-eminent they are. But shall we count anything praiseworthy or noble without recognizing at the same time that it comes from God? Let us be ashamed of such ingratitude, into which not even the pagan poets fell, for they confessed that the gods had invented philosophy, laws, and all useful arts. Those men whom Scripture calls "natural men" were, indeed, sharp and penetrating in their investigation of inferior things. Let us, accordingly, learn by their example how many gifts the Lord left to human nature even after it was despoiled of its true good.[3]

One discerns here in Calvin a deep sacramental consciousness — and what goes with that, the call for a eucharistic response.

It was Kuyper's conviction, however, that God's non-abandonment of the creation is not only to be seen in what might be called maintenance; it is even more to be seen in *progress*. God works not merely to maintain the created order but to move history toward a consummation. Common grace goes beyond providential maintenance. It is best to let Kuyper speak for himself on this point:

We must emphatically state that the interval of centuries that have passed since the fall is not a blank space in the plan of God. The ages lying behind us, by God's decree, must have a purpose and goal, and that purpose can be understood only if we understand that the ongoing development of humanity is *contained in the plan of God*. It follows that the history of our race resulting from this development is not from Satan nor from man *but from God* and that all those who reject and fail to appreciate this development deny the work of God in history. Scripture speaks of the "consummation of the ages" [Matt. 13:39-40], a term that does not mean

3. Calvin, *Institutes of the Christian Religion,* translated by Ford Lewis Battles (Philadelphia: Westminster Press, 1960), II, ii, 15.

the centuries will terminate at some point but that they are directed toward a final goal and that everything contained in those centuries is
linked to that final goal.[4]

The Holistic Nature of Sin, Redemption, and Faith

A second theological theme that pervades the Reformed tradition generally,
and is prominent in Kuyper, is that of the holistic effects of evil and sin. Admittedly it sounds odd to speak of the "holistic" effects of evil and sin. What I
mean is that it is characteristic of the Reformed tradition to resist all attempts
to draw lines between some area of human existence where sin and evil have
an effect and some area where they do not. The intuitive impulse of the Reformed person is to see sin and its effects as leaping over all such boundaries.
To the medieval thinkers who suggested that sin affects our will but not our
reason, the Reformed person says that, No, it affects our reason as well. To
the Romantics who assume that it affects our technology but not our art, the
Reformed person says that, No, it affects our art as well. And so forth.

Humanity is thus, to use a classic Calvinistic phrase, "totally depraved."
The phrase, in the sense it has in contemporary English, is thoroughly misleading. We speak sometimes of some exceedingly bad person as "depraved."
And we might call someone who is as thoroughly depraved as anybody can
be, *totally* depraved. But in their use of the phrase, Calvinists have not meant
that everybody is as depraved as anybody can be; they have not even meant
that everybody is depraved, in the current sense of that word. That is clear,
for example, from the passage I quoted from Calvin; it's obvious that he does
not think of all the ancient writers as depraved persons. What is meant by the
phrase "totally depraved" is the point I just made: our fallenness is manifested
in all dimensions of our human existence. The incursions of evil are to be discerned throughout our existence — in the *totality* of our existence.

Third, corresponding to this holistic understanding of evil and sin
there is, in the Reformed tradition generally, and certainly in Kuyper, a holistic understanding of the scope of Christ's redemption. The Reformed tradition, and especially the Kuyperian version thereof, resonates deeply to the
hymn to the cosmic Christ that we find in the first chapter of St. Paul's letter
to the Colossians. Let me again allow Kuyper to make the point in his own
words:

4. Quoted in *Abraham Kuyper: A Centennial Reader*, edited by James Bratt (Grand Rapids:
Eerdmans, 1998).

You cannot see grace in all its riches if you do not perceive how its tiny roots and fibers everywhere penetrate into the joints and cracks of the life of nature. And you cannot validate that connectedness if, with respect to grace, you first look at the salvation of your soul and not primarily on the *Christ of God.* For that reason Scripture continually points out that the *Savior* of the world is also the *Creator* of the world, indeed that he could become its Savior only *because* he already was its *Creator.*[5]

Fourth, corresponding to the holistic understanding of evil and sin is also a holistic understanding of faith — and of the "new birth" that characterizes the Christian. Faith is not an addendum to our existence, a virtue, one among others. The faith to which we are called is the fundamental orientation and energizer of our lives. Authentic faith transforms us; it leads us to sell all that we have and follow the Lord. The person of faith has been born anew. The thought is not that everything in the life of the believer is different. The thought is rather that no dimension of life is closed off to the transforming power of the Spirit. Yet faith — this reflects the preceding point — is only one component in God's program of redemption. The scope of divine redemption is not just the saving of lost souls but the renewing of life as a whole, and beyond that, the renewing of all creation.

God's Sovereignty over All of Life

Fifth, deep in the Reformed tradition is also the conviction that the Scriptures are a guide not just to salvation but to our walk in the world — to the *fundamental character* of our walk. They are a *comprehensive* guide. They provide us with what has often in the tradition been called "a world and life view." This theme, of the comprehensiveness of the biblical message for our walk in the world, matches, of course, the holistic view of sin, redemption, and faith.

And last, Reformed theology, especially in Kuyper's hands, is through and through political theology. By this I mean that it speaks pervasively of the sovereignty and rule of God and of Christ. "The doctrine of common grace," says Kuyper,

proceeds directly from the Sovereignty of the Lord which is ever the root conviction of all Reformed thinking. If God is sovereign, then his Lordship *must* remain over *all* life and cannot be closed up within church walls

5. Quoted in *Abraham Kuyper: A Centennial Reader*, p. 173.

or Christian circles. The extra-Christian world has not been given over to Satan or to fallen humanity or to chance. God's Sovereignty is great and all-ruling also in unbaptized realms, and therefore neither Christ's work in the world nor that of God's child can be pulled back out of life. If his God works in the world, then there he must put his hand to the plow so that there too the Name of the Lord is glorified.[6]

And to cite the sentence that is probably better known than any other in Kuyper, "No single piece of our mental world is to be hermetically sealed off from the rest, and there is not a square inch in the whole domain of our human existence over which Christ, who is Sovereign over *all*, does not cry: 'Mine!'"[7]

Critical Discernment

One upshot of these various theological themes is that the Reformed tradition characteristically, though not, indeed, uniquely, exhibits a certain dialectic of affirmation, negation, and redemptive activity. On the reality within which we find ourselves, physically, culturally, and socially alike, and on the reality which we ourselves are, the Reformed person pronounces a differentiated Yes and No: a firm Yes to God's creation as such and to God's providential activity, but a differentiated Yes and No to the way in which the potentials of creation have been realized in culture, society, and self. What is called for is not just approbation and not just critique but *critical discernment*. Having engaged in critical discernment, the Reformed person then goes forth to act out of the conviction that we are called by God to promote what is good and oppose what is bad and evil.

Christian Higher Education in the Reformed Tradition

Let me now bring my discussion to its conclusion by highlighting five of the most prominent features of Christian higher education as understood and practiced in the Reformed tradition. I will not be calling attention to the ways in which these characteristics reflect the theological themes that I have cited above, since that will be for the most part obvious.

6. Quoted in *Abraham Kuyper: A Centennial Reader*, p. 166.
7. Quoted in *Abraham Kuyper: A Centennial Reader*, p. 488.

First, within this tradition of Christianity, deep honor and respect are paid to learning. Different persons within the tradition will no doubt articulate the grounds for this respect in somewhat different ways. But within any institution of higher education in the Reformed tradition there will be this deep respect for learning. Learning is a gift of God to humanity that we are to receive and practice with gratitude.

Secondly, especially within the Kuyperian version of the Reformed tradition, learning in general, and Christian learning in particular, is understood as a *perspectival* enterprise. Learning is not a generically human enterprise; it is not an enterprise that we can and should enter by first stripping off all our contingent particularities and then engage in as generic human beings. We neither can nor should strip those off. Learning is unavoidably shaped by our contingent particularities: also by our affects, our loyalties, our prior convictions. At the heart of the Kuyperian tradition in Christian higher education is explicit rejection of the Enlightenment dream of a learning that is neutral as among all our diverse human perspectives on God and the good.

Kuyper's way of developing this version of learning as ineradicably perspectival was to emphasize the nature and role of the "subject" in the academic enterprise. The agent of learning, so Kuyper argued, is never some generically human self, stocked with inherent capacities for perception, reason, and so forth, from which all contingent particularities of affect, conviction, loyalty, gender, and so forth have been stripped off, but is always a self shaped by such particularities. Let me give you the flavor of the argument by quoting a passage or two. In one passage Kuyper observes, "He who has had his bringing-up in the midst of want and neglect will entertain entirely different views of jural relationships and social regulations from him who from his youth has been bathed in prosperity. Thus, also, your view of civil right would be altogether different if you had grown up under a despotism, than if you had spent the years of early manhood under the excesses of anarchism."[8] And in another passage he notes, "An Englishman will look upon the history of the Dutch naval battles with the British fleet very differently from a Netherlandish historian; not because each purposely desires to falsify the truth, but because both are unconsciously governed by national interests."[9]

Perhaps it is necessary to add an explanatory note. Kuyper's insistence on the perspectival character of learning makes him sound like a postmodernist born out of season. But unlike our present-day postmodern-

8. Kuyper, *Principles of Sacred Theology* (Grand Rapids: Eerdmans, 1954), p. 109.
9. Kuyper, *Principles of Sacred Theology*, p. 110.

ists, Kuyper's perspectival understanding of learning was always combined with a vigorous insistence on metaphysical realism. His perspectivalism is epistemological, not ontological. There's a ready-made world, independent of your and my ways of conceptualizing, created by God, awaiting our attempts at discovery. While by and large agreeing with the postmoderns on epistemological matters, Kuyper disagrees with them on their anti-realist ontology. By contrast, while by and large agreeing with the Catholic natural law tradition on its realist ontology, Kuyper disagrees with its epistemological confidence concerning the ability of us human beings to arrive at consensus concerning the reality that confronts us.

One consequence of the fact that Kuyperians have always understood learning as ultimately perspectival in character is that they were never as devastated by developments in biblical criticism and by the rise of evolutionary theory as were scholars in the American evangelical tradition. If one regards competent scholarship as an objective, neutral, and impartial enterprise, as American evangelicals of the nineteenth century generally did, then the very competence of biblical criticism and evolutionary theory argues for its acceptance.

Third, the Reformed tradition generally, and the Kuyperian tradition in particular, has insisted that Christian learning, understood as a perspectival enterprise, is to be conducted *within* our common human practice of scholarship, not in some corner by itself. In turn, it has understood such scholarship as not only in service of humanity but, more particularly, in service of the Christian voice and of Christian conviction within the structures, solidarities, and practices of our common humanity. How well higher education in the Reformed tradition has managed to combine these two emphases — we are to speak and act *within* the structure of our common humanity but *with* a distinct Christian voice — is a good question. But that has been the goal.

Fourth, what you will also typically find in colleges and universities of the Reformed tradition is an honoring of the whole long tradition of Christian learning and culture. Admittedly the insistent "presentism" of American evangelical Christianity affects also those colleges that locate themselves within the Reformed tradition. However, in my own education at Calvin College, for example, it was just as important that we absorb the thought of the church fathers and the medievals as that of the Reformation and of modernity.

Christian learning is learning *shaped* by Scripture and the entire Christian tradition; if such learning is to be practiced, it must be nourished by learning that *explores* Scripture and the Christian tradition. Christian learning is learning in which one allows the metaphors of the psalmist, the parables told by Jesus, the narrative of Christ's resurrection, the pathos for the social outsiders preached and exemplified by the prophets, the prayers of the Eucharist, the philosophy of Scotus and Ockham, the theology of Barth and Brunner, the hymns of Isaac Watts, the etchings of Rembrandt — in which one allows all of these and more, each in its own way, to shape one's learning, after one has oneself been formed and nourished by them. It is learning shaped by Scripture and the Christian tradition and also the learning whereby one is thus shaped.

Lastly — and this is suggested by the preceding point — within any college in the Reformed tradition there will be an emphasis on Scripture and theology. Scripture is the fundamental source for one's speaking with a Christian voice and acting out of Christian conviction. And theology is disciplined reflection, in the light of Scripture, on God and God's relation to the world and humanity. Without such disciplined reflection one cannot build a community capable of speaking with a Christian voice and acting out of Christian conviction within the structure, solidarities, and practices of our common humanity. In particular, without knowledge of Scripture and theology one cannot build an academic community that speaks with a Christian voice and acts out of Christian conviction.

Call to Boldness: A Response to Fides et Ratio

The issuance of the papal encyclical *Fides et Ratio* is an extraordinary event. That a subtle philosophical discourse should be issued by the head of a vast ecclesiastical bureaucracy! We must all behold with awe and astonishment this achievement of the Church of Rome. Those of us who are not members will find a good dose of envy mixed in with our awe and astonishment!

"Both/And": Use Reason and Exercise Faith

Pervading the entire document is the *both/and* style of rhetoric, as in, "*both* faith *and* reason." In our time and place we are not much drawn to this rhetorical style. We prefer the disjunctive over the conjunctive. The conjunctive style smacks to us of indecision; give us the confrontational, attention-getting bite of *either/or*. But *Fides et Ratio* is by no means indecisive. Its *both/and* is full of bite.

With one single discourse, *Fides et Ratio* addresses two quite different sorts of intellectual ills in contemporary society: on the one hand, the scepticisms of immanentism, on the other, the suspicions of fideism. *Both/and.*

On the one hand, there are those who, in the words of the encyclical, "distrust ... the human being's great capacity for knowledge." They "rest content with partial and provisional truths, no longer seeking to ask radical questions about the meaning and ultimate foundation of human, personal and social existence" (§5). They have "lost the capacity to lift [their] gaze to the heights, not daring to rise to the truth of being. Abandoning the investi-

---

This essay first appeared in *Books and Culture* 5, no. 4 (July/August 1999). It is reprinted here with permission.

gation of being, modern philosophical research has concentrated instead upon human knowing. Rather than make use of the human capacity to know the truth, modern philosophy has preferred to accentuate the ways in which this capacity is limited and conditioned" (§5). We are, it is said, "at the end of metaphysics." In thus speaking, philosophy has "forgotten that men and women are always called to direct their steps towards a truth which transcends them" (§5).

That is one of the intellectual ills to which the encyclical is addressed: the scepticisms of immanentism. On the other hand, there are the suspicions of fideism. The *fideist* is one who, again in the words of the encyclical, "fails to recognize the importance of rational knowledge and philosophical discourse for the understanding of faith, indeed, for the very possibility of belief in God" (§55). Among the manifestations that the encyclical cites of the scepticisms of fideism are biblicism in scriptural interpretation, and disdain for philosophy and speculative theology (§55).

The Pope addresses both these intellectual illnesses at once by offering a discourse, informed and subtle, on faith and reason, *fides et ratio*. That discourse grounds, in turn, a vigorous and visionary call to boldness. To the immanentist the Pope says: do not be content with exploring the subjective and the anthropological; inquire boldly into what lies beyond the self. To the fideist the Pope says: do not be content with "mere faith"; appropriate boldly the riches of the philosophical tradition so as both to deepen our understanding of the faith and to exercise "critical discernment" on the intellectual endeavors of humanity generally. *Fides et Ratio*, to say it again, is a vigorous and visionary call to boldness — boldness in the use of reason and boldness in the exercise of faith. Once again: *both/and*.

I am a philosopher who stands in the Reformed tradition of Christianity — that tradition which traces its roots to the reformation that originated in the Swiss cities and was shaped, above all, by John Calvin. When I read the Pope's discourse on faith and reason, I read it with the eyes and mind of such a person. Calvinists have been known to say some rather bracing things about Catholic modes of thought in general, and about popes in particular! Could it be that those disputes are on the way to disappearing? For I find myself in almost complete agreement with what the Pope says about the relation of faith and reason. I would want to debate with him some of the things he says about the history of philosophy: I think, for example, that there is rather less core consensus than he seems to think there is. And I have some hesitations on a few peripheral matters: what he says about the authoritative status of tradition, for example, and some of what he says about the role of Mary. But what he says on the topic of faith and reason seems to me both true and needing to be said. Such convergence between these two traditions, though disappointing to the agonistic spirit implanted in all of us by life in a competitive society, is a wonderful thing for anyone formed by the spirit of the gospel.

Let me move on to state what it is that I am agreeing with — that is, what I understand the Pope to be saying. And let me begin by offering you what I regard as the key for unlocking the interpretation of the whole discussion — the hermeneutic key. I suggest that if one is to understand what the Pope is saying, one must constantly keep in mind the distinction between *properly functioning* human reason, and human reason as it *actually functions* in its fallen state. When the Pope is speaking of the former, he can sound exceedingly confident and optimistic concerning the powers of reason; when he is speaking of the latter, he can sound eminently realistic, and on occasion, even judgmental. If one fails to take note of the always implicit distinction between properly functioning human reason and actually functioning fallen reason, one will think he is contradicting himself — wanting things both ways. But not so.

Faith Seeking Understanding: Critical Discernment

We in the Reformed tradition have thought that our brothers and sisters in the Catholic tradition speak too little of the actuality of fallen reason, too much of the ideality of properly functioning reason; those in the Catholic tradition have thought exactly the opposite of us — that we Calvinists major in fallenness and minor in proper functioning. Whatever the accuracy of those historical judgments, the Pope, in *Fides et Ratio,* splits the difference. "At the deepest level," says the Pope, "the autonomy which philosophy enjoys is rooted in the fact that reason is by its nature oriented to truth and is equipped moreover with the means necessary to arrive at truth" (§49). But then, after a few intervening paragraphs, comes this reminder: "it is necessary to keep in mind" that the "formulations" actually offered by philosophy "are shaped by history and produced by human reason wounded and weakened by sin" (§51). "Reason wounded and weakened by sin" — no Calvinist could ask for more! "Reason oriented by its nature to truth and equipped to arrive" — no Catholic could ask for more than that. Indeed, in one brief extraordinary paragraph of just two sentences, the Pope puts both themes together: "It was part of the original plan of the creation that reason should without difficulty reach beyond the sensory data to the origin of all things: the Creator. But because of the disobedience by which man and woman chose to set themselves

in full and absolute autonomy in relation to the (
this ready access to God the Creator diminished"
continue to be disagreements on the details of rea
erly functioning, and on the extent to which the wo
tioning.

Using as my hermeneutic key this distinction
tioning and actual fallen functioning, let me now brie
cyclical's pattern of thought. A central component in   ut the
human being from the rest of God's earthly creatures is t _.. tne human being
is *"the one who seeks the truth"* (§28). Truth comes of course in many forms, and
as the answer to many questions. What especially impels the search for truth
that we find exhibited in philosophy and the sciences is the innate human impulse "to ask why things are as they are" (§3), and the impulse to discover the
meaning of life (§26). These impulses impel us beyond partial and fragmentary truths toward "universal and absolute truth" (§27). People, says the Pope,
"seek an absolute which might give to all their searching a meaning and an
answer — something ultimate, which might serve as the ground of all things.
In other words, they seek a final explanation, a supreme value, which refers to
nothing beyond itself and which puts an end to all questioning" (§27). "It is
unthinkable," he adds, "that a search so deeply rooted in human nature
would be completely vain and useless" (§29). On the other hand, there are
distinct limits to the powers of human reason, even when functioning properly. Though reason can "discover the Creator" (§8), it can do relatively little
by way of discovering the nature and deeds of the Creator.

And now for the role of faith: "Underlying all the Church's thinking is
the awareness that she is the bearer of a message which has its origin in God
himself" (§7). This message is revelation, the loving acceptance of which is
faith. This revelation comes not as the repudiation of reason, but as its perfection. For just as the goal and attainment of reason is truth, so too, the content of revelation, and hence of faith, is truth — truth about God, truth also
about God's dealings with humankind and the world. This truth of revelation
"perfects all that the human mind can know of the meaning of life" and of the
explanations of things (§7). Accordingly, reason accepts it gladly — even
though it comes to reason as gift rather than achievement.

It must not be supposed that reason simply stands passive before this
gift. The long tradition of *fides quaerens intellectum*, faith seeking understanding,
testifies otherwise. Faith enables reason to exercise its powers within realms
to which it would otherwise have no access whatsoever; we are able now to reflect, for example, on the Trinity. In the words of the encyclical, faith serves "to
lead the search for truth to new depths, enabling the mind in its autonomous

...on to penetrate within the mystery by use of reason's own methods, ...ich it is rightly jealous" (§13). Mystery of course remains, and will always ...emain; God is not to be grasped. Yet, though revelation appears within our existence as something gratuitous, it not only "seeks acceptance as an expression of love" but also "itself stirs thought" (§15).

This, so far, is about reason when functioning properly and about its relation, when thus functioning, to revelation and faith. Now for reason in its fallen actual functioning — "weakened and wounded" reason, as the Pope calls it. Weakened and wounded reason ever and again fails to achieve what it could achieve; it fails, for example, "to recognize God as Creator of all, . . . not because [it lacks] the means to do so, because . . . sinfulness [places] an impediment in the way" (§19). And worse than failing to achieve what it could achieve, it takes "wrong turns" (§49), these wrong turns often bringing its results into conflict with revealed truth.

As a consequence, revelation and faith stand to the results of unaided reason not just as supplement, stimulus, and aid to further endeavor; they also stand to those results as *corrective* and *guide*. Accordingly, it becomes the Church's duty, mainly through her philosophers, though also through her theologians and bishops, "to indicate the elements in a philosophical system which are incompatible with her own faith." Thereby the Church fulfills "a humble but tenacious ministry of service which every philosopher should appreciate, a service in favour of recta ratio, or of reason reflecting rightly upon what is true" (§50).

What this presupposes is *critical discernment* on the part of the philosophers, the theologians, the bishops, and indeed, all the members of the Church. The Church must speak neither a blanket "Yes" nor a blanket "No" to the results of philosophical endeavor; she must speak always and only a critically discerning *both* "Yes" *and* "No." This theme of critical discernment first gets sounded about a third of the way through the encyclical, when the Pope is discussing the attitude toward Greek philosophy of those two great, and customarily opposed, fathers of the Church, Clement and Tertullian. Once sounded, the need for critical discernment remains one of the dominant themes for the remainder of the encyclical.

A presupposition of this insistence on the need for critical discernment is worth bringing to the fore. A common strategy in the modern world has been to construe revelation in such a way that it could not possibly come into conflict with philosophy, nor with any of the other disciplines. The Pope will have nothing of this — rightly so, in my judgment. The concern of both reason and revelation is with truth. And given the impulsive character of those fundamental questions of meaning and explanation that drive reason on its journey, and given the expansive character of revelation, what we must expect, when reason becomes weakened and wounded, is that conflicts will arise between revelation, on the one hand, and academic learning, on the other. Hence the need for critical discernment.

Fides et Ratio is an extraordinarily rich and dialectically subtle encyclical. I have tried to communicate some of its dialectic subtlety by laying out what I interpret as its central argument — an argument with which, as I have already noted, I am in full agreement. Its richness cannot be communicated in any summary.

Emboldening Theologians and Philosophers

Let me close with some brief comments on the significance of the encyclical. As with most encyclicals, *Fides et Ratio* is an intervention — an intervention, in this case, into two developments within the Christian community, and in society more generally — one of them, a development within theology, the other, a development within philosophy.

To my mind there can be no doubt whatsoever that the Pope has put his finger on the fundamental ill from which theology has been suffering in recent years. All too often in recent years theology has been in headlong flight from metaphysics — that is, from a willingness to speak about God in particular and reality in general. Sometimes this flight takes the form of repudiating philosophy in general. About twenty-five years ago it often took the form of embracing phenomenological or linguistic philosophy. In recent years it regularly takes the form of embracing one and another sort of deconstructionist philosophy. Whichever form it takes, traditional philosophy is treated either with suspicion or disregard; and the theologians of the tradition are either ignored, or reinterpreted as deconstructionists, phenomenologists, or whatever, born out of season.

Into this miasma of metaphysical pusillanimity the Pope issues a ringing call for boldness on the part of the Church's theologians: have the boldness to acknowledge that revelation, whatever else it may be, is a revelation of truth — truth about what transcends us, but also truth about what surrounds us. Revelation is not just "God-talk" but talk *about* God — *true* talk.

Fides et Ratio is also an intervention into philosophy. And there can be no doubt that the Pope has also put his finger on at least one of the ills from which philosophy has been suffering in recent years. One of the reasons theology has become so metaphysically pusillanimous is that philosophy has become that. What has characterized large stretches of philosophy in the twentieth century is that reality has receded ever farther away, to the point where some have asked, What's the point of speaking about reality at all? Many philosophers and their devotees have understandably drawn the conclusion that truth and goodness, if they are not simply to be discarded, will have to be relativized.

To this, the Pope's response is not that the Church repudiate philosophy, which is what so many among my fellow Protestants would say, but that the philosophers of the Church have the boldness to develop what he explicitly calls "Christian philosophy" — that is, "philosophical speculation conceived [and practiced] in dynamic union with faith" (§76).

How surprising and ironic that roughly two centuries after Voltaire and his cohorts mocked the Church as the bastion of irrationality, the Church, in the person of the Pope, should be the one to put in a good word for reason, and for faith as reason's ally. Surprising, ironic, and gratifying! It's my own deep hope, speaking now both as philosopher and as Reformed Protestant, that the Pope's call for boldness will embolden theologians and philosophers to do exactly what he is calling for. In doing so, they will both respect the extraordinary dignity of human reason, and honor the love displayed by God in revealing to us dimensions of truth that would otherwise forever have eluded us, or left us in wavering indecision.

Afterword

Some scholars and teachers think about academic learning the way they were taught to think about it, or the way everyone around them is thinking about it. It will be evident to the reader of the preceding addresses, covering some twenty-five years, that I have not been one of those. Evidently there was some burr under my saddle prompting me to depart from the familiar.

Actually there were three burrs; that became clear to me when I went through the collection as a whole. One thing the reader will observe taking place is a struggle to identify and articulate a comprehensive goal for Christian collegiate education. Or more precisely: the earliest of these talks and essays were written around the time that the struggle was ending; I had identified what I regarded as an appropriate and comprehensive goal. What the reader will observe taking place is the attempt to unravel the full implications of that goal. Does the goal justify and perhaps even require disinterested learning? Praxis-oriented learning? Learning that requires the use of our "hands"? Does it require teaching for justice?

It is clear to me in retrospect that those college teachers of mine who most influenced me embraced what in these essays I call the *Christian humanist* model of Christian higher education. Their goal was to induct their students, from a Christian perspective, into our heritage of high culture. At the time I was enrapt. The theological defense that some gave to this approach was what they called "the cultural mandate." In the story of creation, as we have it in the first chapter of Genesis, we read that God, after having created human beings, "blessed them" and said, "Be fruitful and multiply, and fill the earth and subdue it; and have dominion over the fish of the sea and over the birds of the air and over every living thing that moves upon the earth." It may seem a stretch to hear in these words a divine mandate to compose poetry, build cathedrals, write theology, and all of that; but that's how it was interpreted. I should add that my most influential teacher, William Harry Jellema, was dismissive of this argument. I do not know whether he too heard in those words a cultural mandate; but what he said is that culture should be seen as a fulfillment of our created nature and not as the response to some obligation laid upon us. I myself have come to think that there is no mandate there at all; God is *blessing* humankind. The sense of the words is, *May you* be fruitful and multiply. . . .

My graduate education in philosophy at Harvard loosened the grip that the Christian humanist model had on me. The talk there was all about *doing* philosophy, not about *studying* it; we were being trained to *be* philosophers. When I returned to my alma mater, Calvin College, after this immersion in activism, the Christian humanist model felt much too passive to me, much too backward-looking; without at all wanting to repudiate history, I wanted a model that would overall be forward-looking. I found that in what I now call the *Christian academic-discipline* model: the goal of Christian collegiate education is, within Christian perspective, to introduce the student to the results, and to induct the student into the practices, of the academic disciplines. That was the model that I articulated and defended in the report of a curriculum revision committee at Calvin College that I headed in the 1960s, a report published as *Christian Liberal Arts Education*.

Were it not for two unsettling experiences, I might have lived happily with that model. Nowhere in these talks and essays do I mention those experiences; let me do so now. In September 1976 I was sent by my college to a conference at the University of Potchefstroom in South Africa. It was an epiphany. I knew about apartheid, and knew that it was wrong; but it was for me a purely intellectual sort of knowledge. In Potchefstroom I was plunged into the most heated arguments I had ever known: the Dutch were furious with the Afrikaners, the blacks were not so much furious as in deep pain, the elderly Afrikaners were on the defensive, and a few young ones were doing their best to distance themselves from what they knew was deeply wrong. After the conference, late at night, I walked the streets of Pretoria with one of the blacks; he poured out his soul. I felt that I had been issued a call from God to speak up for these people suffering under oppression.

Then in the late spring of 1978 I received an invitation to a conference on Palestinian human rights to be held on the west side of Chicago. I have never known why I was invited, and it has never been clear to me why I decided to attend; but I did. The Palestinians there, mostly Christian, poured out their guts in rhetoric too hot for most Americans to handle. It was another epiphany; again I had been confronted with the call of God to speak up for these suffering people, without ever forgetting the Israelis' deep fear that on the horizon somewhere lies another holocaust.

296

I suppose that some would have said that, important as struggling for the alleviation of injustice may be, college education just deals with something else; they would have remained firm in their conviction that collegiate education is for enabling us to engage our heritage of high culture, or for enabling us to appropriate the results of the academic disciplines and engage in their practices. That was not possible for me; the Reformed tradition, with its insistence on the worth of all of life, had sunk its roots too deep within me. I saw no way around the conclusion that Christian collegiate education, whatever else it does, must teach for justice.

The cultural mandate, assuming there is one, was useless; it speaks of development, not of liberation. Engaging our heritage of high culture is just something else than struggling for justice, as is appropriating the results of the academic disciplines and engaging in their practices. I needed something new that would fit it all together. I found what I was looking for in one of the pivotal concepts in the psalms and the prophetic literature of the Old Testament: the concept of *shalom*. *Shalom* is customarily translated as "peace." A much better translation, to my mind, is "flourishing." Shalom is a particular understanding of what constitutes human flourishing. Human flourishing requires justice; but justice is only the ground floor of what makes for a flourishing life. What you see going on in these addresses is a kaleidoscopic look at the various ways in which a Christian collegiate education can and should serve to promote human flourishing.

A second burr came attached to the first. How does one teach for justice? I knew how to teach students to engage philosophical texts and to think philosophically for themselves — or so I thought. But how does one teach for justice? That is, how does one not just teach *about* justice but teach one's students to pursue justice and to struggle against injustice? I found myself plunged into reflecting on how one shapes dispositions — virtues, if you will. My struggle to answer that question weaves in and out of these addresses. Some of what I say on the matter is a summary of my conclusions in *Educating for Responsible Action;* some is a correction of, and a supplement to, what I say there.

There was a third burr. My teachers had set before me a vision of Christian learning — not theological learning, not neutral learning capped with a touch of Christianity, not apologetic learning, but learning that emerges from faith seeking understanding, *fides quaerens intellectum*. In my own field of philosophy I saw such learning in Augustine, in Anselm, in Aquinas, even, I now think, in a somewhat eccentric way in John Locke. But how to explain such an understanding of learning in twentieth-century America so that it did not seem just bad learning, biased learning? That was the challenge. To meet the challenge, I felt that I had to understand the alternative in order to find the precise point at which to initiate the debate. What you see in these addresses are my repeated attempts to locate the fundamental point of disagreement between those who find the idea of Christian learning offensive and those of us who have devoted our lives to it; and then, within Christian learning, to locate the precise point of connection between faith and learning.

In the earliest addresses I suggest that the academy of the modern world has been Cartesian in its devotion to consensus; later I suggest that Locke has been the crucial figure. Finally, at the end, I suggest that ever since Plato the academy has been inspired by what I call "The Grand Project," and that the tenability of The Grand Project is the fundamental issue. I can understand that some readers may find it all just a bit neurotic.

My earliest attempt at locating the precise point of connection between faith and learning came in my small 1976 book entitled *Reason within the Bounds of Religion*. What occurs in these addresses is an amplification and further explanation of what I said there, plus the exploration of alternative accounts of the connection.

When I was just well under way in my attempt to articulate the project of Christian learning and to defend it by identifying the fundamental flaw in the regnant understanding which said that Christian learning is untenable, fundamental changes began occurring within that self-understanding of the contemporary academy. It is my conviction that the changes I and my generation have lived through are as radical as any that the academy in the West has ever undergone. My attempt to understand those changes, and to show how the project of Christian learning stands with respect to them, becomes more and more prominent as these addresses come closer to the present. In retrospect, how dull things would have been had the dominant self-understanding of the academy that I bumped up against in my graduate-school days never changed!

In the earliest of the addresses in this collection, the one that comes first, I lay out an agenda of sorts for reflection on Christian collegiate education. It turns out that I have never gotten around to several of the items on the agenda. Everything in this collection originated as an invited address. In those few that have been published, evidence of this origin has been almost entirely rubbed out; but that's how they all began. I have never been asked to speak about the place of worship in the Christian college; I have never been asked to speak about an appropriate distribution of authority and responsibility. And so forth. Had I been asked, I might have accepted the challenge. Or had something in one of those areas been a burr under my saddle, I might have *created* the opportunity to speak about it. But that did not happen. So this is not a comprehensive discourse on Christian collegiate education. It is no more than the record of one person's wrestling with the issues that arose as he attempted to understand and defend the project of Christian learning in which he was engaged — and to deal with the issues that confronted him in such a way that he had no choice but to answer the call.

After teaching for thirty years at Calvin College, I have now taught for thirteen years at Yale University. My old habits have continued in this new situation. I have been thinking about the place of religion in the modern secular university. Or in the case of my own university, Yale, better to call it a *pluralist* university; Yale is not a secular university. Some of my preliminary thoughts, pertaining especially to theology at Yale, can be found in a pair of lectures, "What New Haven and Grand Rapids Have to Say to Each Other."[1] In the not-too-distant future I hope to publish a small book entitled *Religion in the University,* in which I discuss the issues in greater generality.

In conclusion, let me warmly thank Clarence Joldersma and Gloria Stronks for doing the work of collecting, organizing, and editing these addresses — and for suggesting the idea of the collection. The thought had never occurred to me.

---

1. These have been reprinted in *Seeking Understanding: The Stob Lectures, 1986-1998* (Grand Rapids: Eerdmans, 2001).

Bibliography

Adorno, Theodor. *Minima Moralia: Reflections from Damaged Life.* Translated by
    E. F. N. Jephcott. London: Verso, 1978.
Alston, William P. "Christian Experience and Christian Belief." In *Faith and Ratio-
    nality,* edited by Alvin Plantinga and Nicholas Wolterstorff, 103-39. Notre
    Dame, Ind.: University of Notre Dame Press, 1983.
Aristotle. *Politics.* Translated by Ernest Barker. Oxford: Oxford University Press,
    1946.
Augustine. *City of God.* Edited and translated by R. W. Dyson. Cambridge: Cam-
    bridge University Press, 1998.
Barth, Karl. *The Christian Life.* Translated by G. W. Bromiley. Grand Rapids:
    Eerdmans, 1981.
Bellah, Robert N., and Richard Madsen, William M. Sullivan, Ann Swidler, and
    Steven M. Tipton. *Habits of the Heart.* Berkeley and Los Angeles: University
    of California Press, 1985.
Berger, Peter. *Facing Up to Modernity.* New York: Basic Books, 1977.
Bernstein, Richard. *Beyond Objectivism and Relativism.* Philadelphia: University of
    Pennsylvania Press, 1983.
Bratt, James, editor. *Abraham Kuyper: A Centennial Reader.* Grand Rapids:
    Eerdmans, 1998.
Brueggemann, Walter. *Living Toward a Vision: Biblical Reflections on Shalom.* Phila-
    delphia: United Church Press, 1976.
————. "Voices of the Night against Justice." In *To Act Justly, Love Tenderly, Walk
    Humbly,* by Walter Brueggemann, Sharon Parks, and Thomas Groome, 5-
    28. New York: Paulist Press, 1986.
Calvin, John. *Institutes of the Christian Religion.* Translated by Ford Lewis Battles.
    Philadelphia: Westminster Press, 1960.
Daniels, Norman. "Wide Reflective Equilibrium and Theory Acceptance in Eth-
    ics." *Journal of Philosophy* 79 (1979): 256-82.

Dooyeweerd, Herman. *Roots of Western Culture.* Translated by J. Kraay and edited by Mark Vander Vennen and Bernard Zylstra. Toronto: Wedge Publishing Foundation, 1979.

Drenth, P. J. D. *Scholae aut Vitae.* Amsterdam: Vrije Universiteit Uitgeverij, 1987.

Ellul, Jacques. *The Politics of God and the Politics of Man.* Edited and translated by G. W. Bromiley. Grand Rapids: Eerdmans, 1972.

Evans, C. Stephen. "Must Psychoanalysis Embrace Determinism?" *Psychoanalysis and Contemporary Thought* 7 (1984): 339-75.

————. *Preserving the Person.* Downers Grove, Ill.: InterVarsity Press, 1977.

Feyerabend, Paul. *Against Method.* London: Verso, 1975.

Foley, Richard. *The Theory of Epistemic Rationality.* Cambridge: Harvard University Press, 1987.

Freire, Paulo. *Pedagogy of the Oppressed.* Translated by M. G. Ramos. New York: Continuum, 1970.

George, Charles H., and Katherine George. *The Protestant Mind of the English Reformation: 1570-1640.* Princeton: Princeton University Press, 1961.

Gilligan, Carol. *In a Different Voice: Psychological Theory and Women's Development.* Cambridge: Harvard University Press, 1982.

Goldmann, Lucien. *The Philosophy of the Enlightenment.* Translated by H. Maas. Cambridge: MIT Press, 1973.

Groome, Thomas. *Christian Religious Education: Sharing Our Story and Vision.* New York: HarperCollins, 1980.

Habermas, Jürgen. *The Philosophical Discourse of Modernity.* Translated by F. G. Lawrence. Cambridge: Polity Press, 1987.

Hacking, Ian. *The Emergence of Probability.* Cambridge: Cambridge University Press, 1975.

Hatch, Nathan O. "Evangelical Colleges and the Challenge of Christian Thinking." In *Making Higher Education Christian: The History and Mission of Evangelical Colleges in America,* edited by Joel A. Carpenter and Kenneth W. Shipps, 155-71. Grand Rapids: Eerdmans, 1987.

Hesse, Mary. *Revolutions and Reconstructions in the Philosophy of Science.* Bloomington: Indiana University Press, 1980.

Jellema, Harry. *The Curriculum in a Liberal-Arts College.* Grand Rapids: Calvin College, n.d.

————. *God-Centered Living.* Grand Rapids: Baker, 1951.

Kant, Immanuel. *Education.* Translated by A. Churton. Ann Arbor: University of Michigan Press, 1960.

————. *Fundamental Principles of the Metaphysic of Morals.* Translated by T. K. Abbott. New York: Liberal Arts Press, 1949.

Kuhn, Thomas S. *The Structure of Scientific Revolutions.* Chicago: University of Chicago Press, 1962.

Kuyper, Abraham. *Lectures on Calvinism: Stone Lectures, 1898-1899.* New York: Fleming H. Revell Co., n.d. Reprint, Grand Rapids: Eerdmans, 1994.

————. *Principles of Sacred Theology.* Translated by J. Hendrik De Vries. Grand Rapids: Eerdmans, 1954.

Lakatos, Imre. *The Methodology of Scientific Research Programmes.* Edited by J. Worrall and G. Currie. Cambridge: Cambridge University Press, 1978.

Laudan, Larry. *Science and Values: The Aims of Science and Their Role in Scientific Debate.* Berkeley and Los Angeles: University of California Press, 1984.

"Letter to Diognetus." In *The Apostolic Fathers,* edited and translated by K. Lake. Loeb Classical Library. Cambridge: Harvard University Press, 1976.

Locke, John. *An Essay Concerning Human Understanding.* Edited by Peter H. Nidditch. Oxford: Clarendon Press, 1975.

Lyotard, Jean-François. *The Postmodern Condition: A Report on Knowledge.* Translated by G. Bennington and B. Massumi. Minneapolis: University of Minnesota Press, 1984.

MacIntyre, Alasdair. *After Virtue.* Notre Dame, Ind.: University of Notre Dame Press, 1981.

Niebuhr, H. Richard. *The Kingdom of God in America.* Chicago: Willett, Clark & Co., 1937. New edition, Middleton, Conn.: Wesleyan University Press, 1988.

Oakeshott, Michael. "Education: The Engagement and Its Frustration." In *Education and the Development of Reason,* edited by R. F. Dearden, P. H. Hirst, and R. S. Peters, 19-59. London: Routledge & Kegan Paul, 1972.

————. *Voice of Liberal Learning: Michael Oakeshott on Education.* Edited by T. Fuller. New Haven: Yale University Press, 1989.

Parsons, Talcott. *Evolution of Societies.* Edited by J. Toby. Englewood Cliffs, N.J.: Prentice-Hall, 1977.

Plantinga, Alvin. "Reason and Belief in God." In *Faith and Rationality,* edited by Alvin Plantinga and Nicholas Wolterstorff, 16-93. Notre Dame, Ind.: University of Notre Dame Press, 1983.

Plato. *Republic.* Translated by F. M. Cornford. Oxford: Oxford University Press, 1945.

Popper, Karl. *Conjectures and Refutations.* London: Routledge & Kegan Paul, 1963.

Rawls, John. *Theory of Justice.* Cambridge: Harvard University Press, 1971.

Reid, Thomas. *Inquiry into the Human Mind on the Principles of Common Sense.* Edited by D. R. Brookes. Edinburgh: Edinburgh University Press, 1997.

Schaeffer, Francis. *Art and the Bible.* Downers Grove, Ill.: InterVarsity Press, 1973.

Shapiro, Barbara J. *Probability and Certainty in Seventeenth-Century England.* Princeton: Princeton University Press, 1983.

Skinner, B. F. *Beyond Freedom and Dignity.* New York: Bantam Books, 1971.

Taylor, Charles. *Hegel.* Cambridge: Cambridge University Press, 1975.

———. *Hegel and Modern Society.* Cambridge: Cambridge University Press, 1979.

———. *Sources of the Self: The Making of Modern Identity.* Cambridge: Harvard University Press, 1989.

Van Inwagen, Peter. *An Essay on Free Will.* New York: Oxford University Press, 1983.

Van Leeuwen, Henry G. *The Problem of Certainty in English Thought: 1630-1690.* The Hague, The Netherlands: Martinus Nijhoff, 1963.

Van Reijen, Willem. *De Onvoltooide Rede.* Kampen, The Netherlands: Kok, 1987.

Wallerstein, Immanuel. *The Capitalist World-Economy.* Cambridge: Cambridge University Press, 1979.

———. *The Modern World-System.* New York: Academic Press, 1974.

Walzer, Michael. *Interpretation and Social Criticism.* Cambridge: Harvard University Press, 1987.

Weber, Max. "Religious Rejections of the World and Their Directions." In *From Max Weber: Essays in Sociology,* translated and edited by H. H. Gerth and C. W. Mills, 323-63. New York: Oxford University Press, 1981.

Williams, Bernard. *Ethics and the Limits of Philosophy.* Cambridge: Harvard University Press, 1985.

Wolf, Eric. *Europe and the People without History.* Berkeley and Los Angeles: University of California Press, 1982.

Wolters, Albert. *Creation Regained.* Grand Rapids: Eerdmans, 1985.

Wolterstorff, Nicholas. "Are Concept-Users World-Makers?" In *Philosophical Perspectives,* volume I: *Metaphysics,* edited by James E. Tomberlin, 233-68. Atascadero, Calif.: Ridgeview Publishing, 1987.

———. *Art in Action.* Grand Rapids: Eerdmans, 1980.

———. "The Bible and Economics: The Hermeneutical Issues." *Transformation* 4, nos. 3 and 4 (June-Sept./Oct.-Dec. 1987): 11-19.

———. "Christianity and Social Justice." *Christian Scholar's Review* 16, no. 3 (March 1987): 211-28.

———. *Divine Discourse.* Cambridge: Cambridge University Press, 1995.

———. *Educating for Responsible Action.* Grand Rapids: Eerdmans, 1980.

———. *John Locke and the Ethics of Belief.* Cambridge: Cambridge University Press, 1996.

———. *Keeping Faith: Talks for New Faculty.* Grand Rapids: Calvin College, 1989.

———. *Lament for a Son.* Grand Rapids: Eerdmans, 1987.

———. "The Migration of the Theistic Arguments: From Natural Theology to Evidentialist Apologetics." In *Rationality, Religious Belief, and Moral Commit-*

ment, edited by R. Audi and W. J. Wainwright, 38-81. Ithaca, N.Y.: Cornell University Press, 1986.

————. "On Christian Learning." In *Stained Glass: Worldviews and Social Science,* edited by Paul Marshall, Sander Griffioen, and Richard Mouw, 56-80. Lanham, Md.: University Press of America, 1989.

————. *On Universals.* Chicago: University of Chicago Press, 1970.

————. "Public Theology or Christian Learning?" In *A Passion for God's Reign,* edited by Miroslav Volf, 65-87. Grand Rapids: Eerdmans, 1998.

————. *Reason within the Bounds of Religion.* Grand Rapids: Eerdmans, 1976; 2d edition, 1984.

————. *Thomas Reid and the Story of Epistemology.* Cambridge: Cambridge University Press, 2001.

————. *Until Justice and Peace Embrace.* Grand Rapids: Eerdmans, 1983.

————. "What New Haven and Grand Rapids Have to Say to Each Other." In *Seeking Understanding: The Stob Lectures, 1986-1998,* 251-93. Grand Rapids: Eerdmans, 2001.

————. "Why Care about Justice?" In *The Evangelical Round Table,* volume 2: *Evangelicalism: Surviving Its Success,* edited by David A. Fraser. Princeton: Princeton University Press, 1987.

————. *Works and Worlds of Art.* Oxford: Oxford University Press, 1980.

————. "The Wounds of God: Calvin's Theology of Social Justice." *The Reformed Journal* 37, no. 6 (June 1987): 14-22.

Index

Skinner, B. F., 39, 40, 45, 48, 49, 56, 59
social practice, and internal goods, 189; norms, 118; standards of, 188; and traditions, 188
social roles, 90, 92; ascriptivism, 90; choice, 92; ethically infused, 145
society, 31, 34, 35, 99, 100; civil, 94, 246, 249, 251; consensus, 93; global world, 94; as liberal democratic, 249, 252; loyalty, 93; neglect of, 164; public discussion, 93
Society of Christian Philosophers, 31
South Africa, 152, 161; Afrikaners, 152, 164; South Africans, 164
Soviet Union, 32, 131
St. Paul, 258
subjectivity: Christian, 223; as privileged cognitive access, 224
subjunctive conditionals, 56
suffering, 33, 138, 151, 152, 154, 161, 239; confrontation with, 161; empathy, 99, 133, 151, 152; faces and voices of, 133, 152, 162; humanity, 169; Palestinians, 32; of the world, 165; wounds, 22, 88, 164

Taylor, Charles, 80, 268
teaching, 6, 20, 22, 24, 25, 63, 82, 100, 102, 152, 250, 271, 295, 299; aesthetics, 162; behaviorism, 8; character formation, 160; contemplation, 169; coping, 99; devotions, 169; and discipline, 99, 149, 151, 160; dispositions to action, 149, 160; disposition to justice, 152; and giving reasons, 161; of humanity, 133; John Calvin, 154; for justice, 150, 169; justice and mercy, 148; liturgy, 169; about the media, 161; modeling, 82, 99, 150, 151, 160; offering narratives, 152; pedagogy, 8, 145; radical conversion, 99; reasoning, 99; reasons for action, 149; self-realization, 8; social analysis, 147; social ethic, 146; social structures, 147; and suffering, 154

theory, 194; metaphors, 115; simplicity, 115; theory-laden, 115, 127
theory weighing, 192, 193

United Nations, 131

van Leeuwen, Harry G., 114
van Reijen, Willem, 109
Viet Nam war, 152

Wallerstein, Immanuel, 165
Walzer, Michael, 131
Watts, Isaac, 287
Weber, Max, 72, 92, 94, 113, 173, 176, 177; and modern society, 247; on modernization, 121, 173, 244; monks, 175; neo-Kantian, 176; and rationalization, 174, 245; rationalization of action, 92; and religion, 181; and spheres, 176
Wellhausen, Julius, 204
Williams, Bernard, 141
Wissenschaft, 21, 103, 123, 177, 179, 205, 244; dynamics of, 252
Wittgenstein, Ludwig, 47
Wolters, Albert, 74
Wolterstorff, Nicholas, 40, 76, 142, 148, 192
world, 45, 74, 174; as disenchanted, 121, 174, 176, 245; as enchanted, 174; in need of reformation, 32; religions of, 174
World Alliance of Reformed Churches, 277
World Court, 131
world-systems, 147, 166; exploitation, 147; Third World, 167; underdevelopment, 166
world-systems theory, 95, 98, 121, 145, 165; periphery, 96; core, 120; world economy, 95
worldview, 17, 34, 74, 214, 283; beliefs, 74; ground-motive, 75; as mind, 16, 74

Zwingli, Ulrich, 277